The Collected Works
of
St. Teresa of Avila

VOLUME THREE

The Collected Works
of
St. Teresa of Avila

VOLUME THREE

The Book of Her Foundations
Minor Works
The Constitutions—On Making the Visitation
A Satirical Critique—Response to a Spiritual Challenge—Poetry

Translated by
Kieran Kavanaugh, O.C.D.
and
Otilio Rodriguez, O.C.D.

ICS Publications
Institute of Carmelite Studies
Washington, D.C.
1985

ICS Publications
2131 Lincoln Road, N.E.
Washington, D.C. 20002

Typesetting by Carmel of Indianapolis

Library of Congress Cataloging in Publication Data

Teresa, of Avila, Saint, 1515-1582.
The collected works of St. Teresa of Avila.
Includes bibliographical references and indexes.
Contents: v. 1. The book of her life.
Spiritual testimonies. Soliloquies—v. 2.
The way of perfection. Meditations on the song
of songs. The interior castle—v. 3. The book
of her foundations. Minor works.
1. Catholic Church—Collected works.
2. Theology—Collected works—16th century.
BX890.T353   1976   248   75-31305
ISBN 0-9600876-2-1 (v. 1)

CONTENTS

THE BOOK OF HER FOUNDATIONS

MINOR WORKS

THE CONSTITUTIONS

ON MAKING THE VISITATION

Contents

NOTES

The Book of Her Foundations

THE BOOK OF HER FOUNDATIONS

INTRODUCTION

ST. TERESA WROTE her extraordinary story *The Book of Her Life*[1] under obligation to her confessors and spiritual directors hopeful that they would come to understand and enlighten her about the path along which the Lord was leading her. Interwoven in her account were the simple biographical data of everyday experience and the exceptional data of the intense inner life that resulted when God began to pour out His mystical graces on her. As she delved into her past, her narration grew into something more than plain history and became a witnessing to the realities of the interior life and their transforming power. The story of Teresa's life evolved into a story of God's mercy.

Teresa's story, however, did not end there. Hardly knowing where to turn with the burning love that resulted from her raptures in God, she became obsessed with desires to serve "His Majesty," as she referred to her Lord. Her first brave attempts to do something about these desires are told dramatically in five of the final chapters of her *Life*.

Although the foundation of the new community of St. Joseph's brought much happiness to Teresa, love's desires were not entirely appeased. In *The Way of Perfection*[2] the foundress told about the pain she felt over the troubles of the Church in Europe. Now in her *Foundations* she tells that she was further tormented when the Franciscan missionary Alonzo Maldonado came to St. Joseph's. Recently returned from Mexico, he brought to the monastery grille his tale of the millions who had never heard of Jesus Christ. In Teresa's mind there could be no

3

worse fate. Moreover, she thought that the greatest service one
could render the Lord was to bring souls to Him. This woman,
who as a child ran away from home to become a martyr in the
land of the Moors, now thought not so much of martyrdom as of
bringing others to Christ. "When we read in the lives of the
saints that they converted souls, I feel much greater devotion,
tenderness, and envy than over all the martyrdoms they suffered" (1,7).[3] Wrestling with these afflictions of love and complaining to her Lord of her powerlessness to convert her desires
into deeds, she suddenly heard the Lord speak to her: "Wait a
little, daughter, and you will see great things" (1,8).

In 1567, the prior general of the Carmelites, Giovanni Baptista
Rossi, whom Teresa in Castilian fashion called Rubeo, made his
visitation of the Carmelite houses in Spain. Eagerly, but with
some fearful apprehensions, the new foundress arranged to meet
with him so that she could explain what she had done and manifest her compelling desires.

In reality the meeting turned out to be a happy one for both
Teresa and her prior general. Delighted with the spirituality of
this enthusiastic nun and the contemplative manner of living
that she had established within the context of Carmel, Rubeo
not only approved but asked for more. He wanted Teresa to
found other similar monasteries and provided her with the official letters she would need for the endeavor. Much consoled,
Teresa felt nonetheless helpless despite her official papers:
"Here I was, a poor discalced nun, without help from anywhere
— only from the Lord — weighed down with patent letters and
good desires" (3,6). But with those desires, which could not be
put aside, and with help "only from the Lord," this poor discalced
nun went on to found personally fourteen more Carmels in addition to St. Joseph's in Avila; two other foundations she
directed at a distance. In all, at the time of her death, seventeen
of her little Carmels for women had been founded: Medina del
Campo (1567); Malagón and Valladolid (1568); Toledo and
Pastrana (1569); Salamanca (1570); Alba de Tormes (1571);
Segovia (1574); Beas and Seville (1575); Caravaca (1576); Villanueva de la Jara and Palencia (1580); Soria (1581); Granada
and Burgos (1582). She also instituted her way of life among the

friars and played an active role in both the initial recruitment and the foundations themselves at Duruelo (1568) and Pastrana (1569).

Origin and Composition

On August 25, 1573, while staying in Salamanca to assist her nuns there in the irksome task of finding a suitable house to buy, Teresa began composing the story of her foundations (Prol. 3). The idea for this new book seems to have derived from the Jesuit Jerónimo Ripalda, formerly skeptical of Teresa but now her friend and confessor. Having read her *Life* and its account of the first foundation, Ripalda urged the foundress to enlarge her story and write as well the history of the seven monasteries she had founded since the completion of her first book; she could tell, too, about the first monasteries of her friars. Insisting that "it would be of service to our Lord," an irresistable argument for Teresa, Ripalda may, on the other hand, only have been encouraging his spiritual daughter to follow a grace the Lord had previously given her. In February, 1570, the Lord had appeared to her pressing her to make as many foundations as she could and also to write about them.[4]

Teresa's reluctance to follow the Lord's urgings that she write about her foundations could have been due to her fear that others might then think they were her own accomplishments, an idea she disavows. The work was God's work. In addition, she dreaded taking up the task because of the lack of quiet time for writing. Tangled business matters, endless correspondence, persistent bad health, certainly none of these contributed any spark of enthusiasm for the project. In the end, only the thought of obedience to her confessor provided her with the strength needed to begin.

The first free moments she found came during the period from the end of August, 1573, until March, 1574, while she was living in Salamanca before leaving to make the foundation in Segovia. Not knowing how many chapters she wrote during these months, we can at least surmise that she wrote no more than nine. What she tells us is only that she set the work aside because of duties. But the contents of chapter 10, the story of Doña Casilda de Padilla's vocation, could not have been written until later. Although chapters 10 through 12 seem to have been written in Valladolid—Teresa speaks of not being "here" (11, 3) at the time of Casilda's escape from her family to the cloister— nothing certain can be stated about where or when the remaining chapters were composed. Once Teresa completed chapter 19, her responsibility of obedience to Father Ripalda was fulfilled. She had neither the time nor the convenience for writing more.

Father Gracián entered the scene next and firmly insisted that Madre Teresa finish her story. Her pleas and objections about how tired the work made her were met only with further encouragement and the advice to write just in snatches and to do the best she could (27, 22).

In July, 1576, Lorenzo de Cepeda, Teresa's brother, received a letter from his sister, now a foundress, asking him to send her a box and some documents and also paper containing details surrounding the foundation in Alba.[5] The Father Visitator, she says, "has ordered me to finish the *Foundations*." In a letter to Gracián, October 5, 1576, she announces that she is going to begin writing the rest of the story. Chapters 20-27 were written not so much in snatches but probably rapidly within a month. Judging by the colophon appearing at the end of chapter 27, Teresa definitely thought she was now, November 14, 1576, done with the annoying task. The stormy opposition that her work as foundress was undergoing did not allow her to envision any further foundations about which she would be obliged to write.

But after the storm, between 1580 and her death in 1582, she added five more, in all of which she personally took part with the exception of Granada. Four more chapters had to be written. Although the story of her experiences in each of these final foundations could have been written immediately after each had been made, more probably she finished this whole last section while in Burgos. Perhaps, too, the needed urgings came from Gracián, if not by his words at least by his presence. In the closing lengthy chapter which recounts the foundation of

Burgos, with its interminable troubles, Teresa's handwriting clearly demonstrates her state of exhaustion.

The General Content

The Jesuit Ripalda's desire was that just as Teresa had recorded in *The Book of Her Life* the events, sometimes fiery, surrounding the foundation of St. Joseph's in Avila so too she should record the many events surrounding her other foundations. And this is the main thrust of Teresa's new book. First and foremost, the work is a narrative of the happenings involved in each foundation. The chronological order in which houses were founded provides the general course along which the narrative runs.

But the narration of facts is not the Mother Foundress's sole interest. Once having compared herself to a parrot that knows only how to repeat what it has heard,[6] she confesses her tendency to be ever repeating what she has to say about prayer. In this work, too, encouraged by Ripalda, she expands her account so as to turn again to the theme of prayer and related topics.

Chapters 4 through 8 constitute the longest interruption to the history of the foundations itself. In them, after having declared in a matter-of-fact way that most of the nuns in the houses she had founded were experiencing perfect contemplation (a statement perplexing enough to Gracián to make him tamper with the autograph) and that each house had one or more familiar with raptures, visions, and revelations (4, 8),[7] she gives some pertinent counsels to prioresses flowing from her own observation of what had been happening spiritually in her monasteries. These counsels deal with: the need, at times, out of obedience or charity, to set aside contemplation for the sake of the active works of service (ch. 5); a delightful absorption lasting for hours that is nonetheless deceptive and that stems from bodily weakness caused by austerities (ch. 6); melancholy, the general term used at the time for emotional and mental illnesses (ch. 7); a safe method of procedure in the experience of visions and revelations (ch. 8). Accompanying the counsels on these topics are case histories that Teresa had come to know first-hand or had heard from others.

Further on in her work, she gives some counsels to prioresses on the need for discretion in government and in the practices of mortification (18, 6-13). And scattered throughout her account are the shorter instructions and motherly exhortations concerning the spiritual life to which the narrative gives rise. Examples of these would be her exhortations about fidelity to the way of life she established, or her instructions about not refusing sincere applicants who lack the funds for a dowry through no fault of their own (27, 11-12; 29, 32-33).

All in all, there is reason to believe that Madre Teresa found it much less tedious to give counsels about the spiritual life than to go into the various historical details of her foundations. At one point, when treating of the spiritual life, she firmly declares that "even though writing about such a matter may be a tiresome thing to do, it doesn't tire me" (6, 8).

Over and above these important and insightful digressions from her story, she introduces here and there throughout her work many biographical sketches and anecdotes, some of them quite lengthy. These are told for the sake of edification and show some of the traits of early hagiography, the kind Teresa was accustomed to reading. Among her sketches we find stories of a girl's vocation or descriptions of a nun's exemplary life. We meet Doña Casilda de Padilla (10, 8-ch. 11), Beatriz de la Encarnación (ch. 12), Catalina Sandoval y Godínez (22, 4-24), Beatriz de la Madre de Dios (26, 2-15), and some nuns from the community in Toledo (16, 1-4). In another vein, we read the account of Teresa Layz who brought the nuns to Alba de Tormes (20, 2-14) and the long, bewildering story of Catalina de Cardona who brought the friars to a cave near Villanueva de la Jara (28, 21-36).

The friars, too, are represented in portraits of Ambrosio Mariano (17, 7-15) and Jerónimo Gracián (ch. 23), and in shorter sketches of Antonio de Heredia (3, 16), St. John of the Cross (3, 17), and Nicolás Doria (30, 5).

If many of the carefully described details of the stories puzzle the twentieth-century reader, one might remember that Teresa's own life story is most remarkable and extraordinary. At the same time, however, the author wanted to be sure of her facts. Some of them she herself was disinclined to believe. Of Catalina de Sandoval's illnesses she checked out what she heard: "Had I not been informed by the doctor and those who were in the house, or by other persons . . . it would not have been unusual for me to think that some of this was exaggerated" (22, 23). In telling about the incredible fasts of Catalina de Cardona, she suddenly feels she must assure her reader: "This fact is very certain, for even the friars who are there testify to it" (28, 27). The abuse suffered by Beatriz de la Madre de Dios so shocked Teresa that she confesses she can find no rational explanation for it (26, 9).

Many other characters about whom Teresa makes brief comments enter the drama at their proper times. She takes particular care to mention benefactors, and not merely for the sake of edification but also that her nuns will remember to pray for them. After speaking of the prior of the Carthusian monastery near Seville, she states that she mentions him so that the nuns will remember him in their prayers, and she adds: "it is right that you pray for him and for all those, living and dead, who have helped us" (25, 9).

Two principal concerns about her story weigh on Teresa's mind, and she manifests them at the outset: she must be completely truthful, and the glory and praise must go to God (Prol. 3). Regarding the latter, a fear pervades her book that a reader might think the accomplishments were hers. Whether she succeeds in including every important historical fact and excluding the unimportant does not worry her. Her concern is that God be praised for His works. At one point in the midst of her account, she seems suddenly taken with fear that someone might attribute the successes of her work to herself or someone else. In her mind, "only His Majesty could have raised the work to what it now is" (13, 7).

Indeed, the protagonist in her work is God. Like the contemporary discoverers of new worlds, she also discovers, she enthusiastically searches out and beholds God's efficacious action lying beneath, yet always transcending, the historical facts; further, she learns that He is deeply involved and committed to the historical process even in its minutest details.

Teresa, herself a lover of solitude, now entered more visibly, so to speak, this historical process. Her strength to do so derived from the thought that Jesus Christ out of obedience came from the bosom of the Father to become our slave. The troubles she would get caught up in would be occasions, she reflected, for showing her where virtue was wanting. "How could it be known whether a man were valiant if he were not seen in battle?" (5, 15). And besides, who more than she knew that the true lover loves the Beloved always and everywhere? Then there is her further important teaching for all who must live the active life that "it is not the length of time spent in prayer that benefits one; when the time is spent as well in good works, it is a great help in preparing the soul for the enkindling of love" (5, 17).

The Mother Foundress with her classic determination, her *muy determinada determinación*, embraced the new work God had given her. She quickly made friends wherever she thought she might find help for God's service. She had to decide which cities and towns presented the best opportunities for her foundations and which sites would offer the most advantages. She had to raise money, look for property and houses to rent or buy, and recruit nuns who could endure with all the needed virtues the inevitable problems accompanying her new monasteries, nuns whom she could trust to carry on in her spirit once she went on to another foundation. She had to learn flawless tact in dealing with bishops and others in authority. She had to become an expert in sifting through the legal complexities that surrounded contracts; sometimes the negotiations continued for months and even years. Always careful to avoid whatever might instigate a lawsuit, she was at times, to her dismay, drawn right into one. She was forced to become both an expert in the intricacies of money management and an attentive organizer and planner. She had to search out furnishings for her new foundations and look after the involved travel preparations. In a word, she was thrown into the world of people, money, and property, and all the unwelcome conflicts these are liable to bring forth, especially when individual or collective egos are threatened and in need of being shored up and defended.

To find God in all things, in troublesome clashes as well as in the hermitage—or, in her proverbial statement, even "among the pots and pans" (5, 8)—this was the art she was forced to master; and in finding Him she found the One who could do what she could not. "A useless woman as helpless as I well understood that she couldn't do anything" (2, 3).

After the prior general had given her his encouragement and all the needed permissions, she was left with a keen sense of helplessness, with no way of accomplishing her good desires. But the Lord who gave her the good desires also made it possible for her later to exclaim: "O greatness of God! How You manifest Your power in giving courage to an ant!" (2, 7).

This power of God showed itself as well in the lives of her daughters. After describing the exceptionally mortified and virtuous life and death of Beatriz de la Encarnación, she reminds us that these stories of nuns living in her houses are told so that "we may all praise the Lord who in this way lets His magnificent riches show forth in us weak, little women" (12, 10).

Another character playing a major role in her story and sharing center stage is the adversary, the devil, relentlessly plotting and struggling to spoil the Lord's work. In Teresa's *Life* readers see him trying to impede her wary soul through the bad influences of the surrounding society, through inner cunning, deceptive suggestions, false visions, and even bodily attacks. Now in the *Foundations* the devil appears as the agent and inspirer of the adverse happenings that obstruct the establishment of her new communities of both nuns and friars. At the outset, chronicling the first foundation in this book, that of Medina del Campo, Teresa voices this theme in meeting her first bothersome setback, when the Augustinian friars threatened a lawsuit against the nuns if they tried to rent the available house: "When You, Lord, want to give courage, how little do all contradictions matter! Rather, it seems I am encouraged by them, thinking that since the devil is beginning to be disturbed the Lord will be served in that monastery" (3, 4).[8] In addition, the devil seeks to deceive Teresa's nuns, using as his tools melancholy, disturbing thoughts, and false visions. Some he may tempt at the hour of their death, but the Lord promises through special favor to protect Teresa's nuns at this time (16, 4).

Though angels are hardly mentioned, devils are everywhere. They even follow one into the desert, appearing as huge vicious dogs or as snakes (28, 27). But the devil seemingly keeps busier in some environments. The city of Seville, because of its climate, its riches, and its opulent lifestyle provided an appropriate setting for the demon's work. "I have heard it said that the devils have greater leeway there to tempt souls, for God must grant it to them. They certainly afflicted me there, for I never felt more pusillanimous or cowardly" (25, 1). When the house into which the nuns had just moved almost went up in flames, Teresa blamed the devil who felt "so angry at seeing another house of God . . . that he wanted somehow to get revenge" (25, 14).

The disagreements within the order that put an end for a while to her foundations might have arisen, Teresa conjectures, because the devil was displeased that so many houses were being founded where our Lord was being served. In fact, the devil was so cunning that had it not been for the king everything would have collapsed (27, 20; 29, 31).

At times the Mother Foundress herself became the victim. The devil would confuse her when she was trying to make a decision, or make her feel great repugnance toward going ahead with her work (28, 14; 31, 4). In sum, the devil set snares and stirred up unrest and opposition (29, 9; 31, 14, 22, 31).

The spiritual tradition deeply rooted among the people, particularly from the middle ages to the seventeenth century, told how the devil might act anywhere in the world, among any persons, at any hour of the day or night, but always and only with the permission of God, as St. Gregory affirmed in his commentary on Job. One could happen upon nests of devils in shadowy places and dens. Even some liturgical formulas reflect these sentiments.

In her writings Teresa mirrors these popular notions. But she does not embrace any and every popular idea. She never suggests, for example, resorting to the use of superstitious practices to ward off the devil. One preventive was the burning of bad-smelling aromatics like sulphur, St.-John's-Wort, or galbanum, with the hope of making the devil change direction or chasing him away. Her methods were prayer, "the place where the Lord gives light to understand truths" (10, 13),[9] and the practice of Christian virtues like charity, humility, and obedience. In addition she made diligent inquiry from confessors, learned men, and others so as to discern what might be for God's greater service.[10] Once the latter became clear, she threw herself into the task with determination despite feelings of fear and doubt; "God wants no more than our determination so that he may do everything Himself" (28, 19). Then the devil can do no more than what the Lord allows for the sake of a greater good as in the case of the foundation in Burgos: "But, O Lord, how obvious it is that You are powerful, for the very scheme the devil used to prevent it, You used to do something better" (31, 31).[11]

What might one think of such unsparing talk of the devil? Is there here nothing more than a popular personification of the forces of evil? The difficulty lies in discerning what precisely comes from the human realm and what from that suprahuman realm of "principalities and powers."[12] Though Teresa speaks popularly about the devil, the essential point she makes is by no means incidental to her story nor is it merely an outdated element of sixteenth-century thought. The essential point is that through Jesus Christ she feels liberated, free of worries about all interference coming from either human or demonic powers, and in her efforts to serve Jesus she discovers that in the end He is always victorious, never fails those who seek to serve Him (18, 1; 27, 11, 20). Her work is His not hers. "Therefore, it is often made clear that it is not I who do anything in these foundations, but the work is His who is all powerful in everything" (29, 5).[13]

As for the style of this book, it is that of the Mother Foundress speaking to her daughters; not so much writing in the way she speaks, but speaking by means of writing. In her *Constitutions*, she gives some counsels about recreation and, apparently trying to compensate for a lack of diversion in their life, reminds her nuns that God will give some the grace to entertain others.[14] Teresa herself undoubtedly belonged to this group of entertainers. Surely the nuns enjoyed listening to her stories, the array of characters, great and small, the ever-present thicket of troubles, the drama with its transcendental dimensions in which His Majesty, finally, comes out always the victor. When we read this book, we are as it were invited to a community recreation period in which Teresa entertains. The nuns who knew their Mother Foundress always agreed in their testimony with Ana de Jesús (Jimena) who declared that in reading the works of Madre Teresa she felt she was listening to the Madre speak.[15]

Partly because of our remoteness from sixteenth-century Spain, partly because of Teresa's story itself, at least as strange as fiction if not stranger, much of the drama or deep and practical spirituality that lies beneath the surface of the lines or within an environment so removed from our own could go unperceived without some historical and cultural background in addition to the information supplied in the notes. But providing such background calls for an expansion of this introduction which at the same time presents the danger of making it too lengthy. The reader uninterested in this background may prefer to skip over to the final section dealing with the autograph. In any case, some of the information presented here can serve as introductory material also for the other Teresian writings contained in this volume as well as for those included in the first two volumes. In like manner, the introductions of the first two volumes contain information that can also contribute to the understanding of this work.

The Order of Carmel

A paragraph from a sermon preached in a church at Avignon, France, in 1342 expresses well the thinking that was still common in Teresa's time and explains many of her references to the order of Carmel:

"You are wondering why I refer to the Carmelites as the special and ancient order of our Lady but if you were to know the reasons, you would wonder no more. Trustworthy histories of Elijah and Elisha tell us how these two often dwelt on Mount Carmel, three leagues distant from Nazareth, the city of our Lady. And saintly men continued to live there in solitude, until the time of our Saviour. At that time, the hermits were converted by the preaching of the apostles. On one side of the mountain, they built a Church or oratory in honor of the Holy Virgin, in a spot which, they had been told, she often frequented in her life, with her maiden companions. For this reason, they were the first among all religious orders to be called children of the Blessed Mary of Mount Carmel. From the early days of the Church, they worked with alacrity to preach the Gospel and in later times they were given a rule of life by John, Patriarch of Jerusalem, based on that of St. Paulinus and St. Basil. Thus, quite justly, this Order enjoys the honor of being the oldest of them all."[16]

Not included in this little summary was the legend behind the nuns, which went so far as to say that the wife of Elijah founded a similar institute for women. Later, after Teresa's times, the order of Carmel, without a critical sense of history or a definite founder, got caught up in the challenge to prove its age-old traditions. The signal that sounded the beginning of a literary battle lasting thirty years was the assertion, in 1668, by the Jesuit Daniel Papenbroch, a well known Bollandist scholar, that the Carmelite order was founded in 1155 A.D. by St. Berthold who was identified with the white-haired monk from Calabria mentioned by Phocas. So harsh, unrelenting, and disedifying did the battle become that in 1698 the Holy See imposed silence on both parties. Later, in 1725, when the Carmelite order triumphantly installed in St. Peter's in Rome its celebrated statue of Elijah as the order's founder, its apologists considered themselves the winners.

What can be affirmed historically is that there was a school of prophets on Carmel, that the prophet Elijah undoubtedly had an impressive impact on the hermits and monks of the early Church, and that Christian hermits resided on Mt. Carmel from a very early date.[17]

Carmelites from the fourteenth to the seventeenth century thought that *The Institution of the First Monks* was the rule given to their forefathers around the year 400 by John, the 44th Patriarch of Jerusalem. These monks, it was supposed, dutifully followed this rule until receiving the formula of life or rule written by Albert of Jerusalem in the thirteenth century. Yet even though it is now commonly recognized that the *Institution* in its present form cannot be dated much earlier than the fourteenth century and was not originally written in Greek, the language of its alleged author, the text did give Carmelites their manual par excellence of spirituality.

The unknown author of this work describes the way toward "prophetic perfection" and the purpose of the religious eremitical life. By means of an allegoric commentary on the biblical account of the prophet Elijah, he explains, in eight chapters, the eremitical-contemplative ideal, which lies in the attainment of a two-fold end: first, to offer God a heart holy and pure of all stain of actual sin (through one's own efforts assisted by grace); second, to taste at times, by divine gift, God's sweetness in the depths of one's heart and to experience in one's soul the power of His divine presence. God promised this latter to Elijah through the words: "You shall drink from this brook."[18]

The order's devotion to our Lady grew stronger through another tradition that in 1251, a time of hardship for Carmelites, she appeared to the prior general, Simon Stock, to encourage him and give him the scapular as a pledge of her protection. The oldest written account of this vision comes 150 years after the alleged event, a gap considered too wide for certainty especially in light of the medieval fondness for clothing a spiritual or theological belief in a story. What is more, it now appears certain that the prior general from 1247-1256 was not Simon Stock but a certain Godfrey, whose name appears as prior general on recently discovered legal documents.

Teresa found inspiration in all these cherished Carmelite traditions of her time and speaks about the life of our holy fathers of the past, the antiquity of the order, the order as being our Lady's order, and the habit as being our Lady's habit.

She tells us that prior to his decision to enter the Carmelites Padre Gracián used to pass his recreation hours pouring over accounts about the antiquity and greatness of the Carmelite order (23, 3). One wonders if the writing of history in those times might also have been a form of recreation. Not until the nineteenth century did historians begin to stress the necessity of establishing facts through meticulous research and discriminating criticism. Parenthetically, it is worth affirming that for

Teresa writing the history of her foundations was a burden and she took great pains to avoid giving any false information. "In this work that is being written for the praise of our Lord, any untruthfulness would cause me great scrupulosity. I believe that such a thing would involve not only a waste of time but deception concerning the works of God" (Prol. 3). But as for dates, she warns, we must be somewhat suspicious and think in terms of more or less (25, 4). Teresa, in the end, sums up the story of Gracián's vocation in characteristic fashion: "And this glorious Virgin was the reason he received her habit and became so fond of the order" (23, 4).

The actual date of the formal beginning of the Carmelite order or the real circumstances that brought the hermits together near the fountain of Elijah on Mount Carmel may never be uncovered. Nonetheless, sometime around 1210, a definite community had formed there and decided to petition Albert, Patriarch of Jerusalem, who resided at Acre, to give them a formula of life. In its initial stage, the simple rule written by Albert was destined for hermits and given limited approval by Pope Honorius III in 1226. The hermits became known as the hermit brothers of St. Mary of Mount Carmel, and they kept a little church there dedicated to our Lady. Excavations carried out in 1958 have uncovered the ruins of the church and the nearby cells of the hermits.

Owing to the precarious position of Christians in the Holy Land from 1229 onward, the hermits decided to make foundations in the West. To organize these foundations on a sound basis, a chapter was summoned at Aylesford, England, in 1247. A decision with far-reaching consequences was made at this chapter to petition the pope for changes in the rule. By the papal bull *Quae honorem*, September 4, 1247, the Rule of St. Albert was mitigated and became canonically a rule having the same status as those of the other religious rules already approved, a necessity at that time because the Fourth Lateran Council (1215) had forbidden new rules.[19] This, then, was the version of the rule that Teresa thought was the primitive rule. It allowed the Carmelites to live according to the new forms of Religious life that came into vogue with the institution of the mendicant orders. Though the alterations made in the text of St. Albert's rule were slight, the results were extensive: houses were founded in cities and towns; the cenobitical form of life was developed, and external apostolates were gradually introduced.

In 1432, the Carmelites petitioned the Holy See for further changes, claiming that in some respects the rule was too strict and impeded the advancement of the order. By the bull *Romani pontificis*, dated February 15, 1432, Pope Eugene IV authorized the Carmelites to eat meat three days a week and to walk about at certain times in their churches, cloisters, and grounds, thus not having to remain continually in their cells. These concessions amounted to a last stage in the process whereby the Carmelites became mendicants and are what Teresa refers to when speaking of the mitigated rule. Though never written into the rule, they seem to have had an unhappy negative effect on the order since by some they were viewed as a symbol of betrayal, a relinquishment of the contemplative ideal.

Up to the fifteenth century the order had no monasteries of nuns, nor had it felt concern about this. With nunneries would go responsibilities: the bothersome care of construction and repair of buildings, the safeguards against fire and theft, the service of the church attached to the monastery, and spiritual assistance to the nuns. Blessed John Soreth was the prior general who in the fifteenth century took the feared step and introduced the sisterhood into the life of Carmel by obtaining the papal bull *Cum nulla*, 1452, which bestowed authorization for receiving women into the Carmelite order as nuns.

Soreth, however, never traveled to Spain. The development of communities of Carmelite women there took place apart from his intervention, with the result that the nature of the life of a Carmelite nun in Spain varied from place to place. At first a *beaterio*, a community of devout women affiliated with the order of Carmel and wearing a habit, the Incarnation at Avila was founded in 1479. In 1515, the year of Teresa's birth, the Sisters moved into a much larger edifice they had built outside the walls of Avila. With this move they also introduced a form of religious life. Though large and spacious, the new building was anything but luxurious. Only a bare tile roof covered the church, and the makeshift roofing in the choir let the snow in winter fall through onto the breviaries, and the sun in the summer shine through so as to provide light enough for reading even with the shutters closed.

The immediate increase in the number of nuns soon turned the building into a busy world with unfortunate economic effects. The poverty became so alarming that the nuns had only bread to eat and the construction of the monastery and church were by necessity left unfinished. Despite its meager means, the community became a refuge for ladies from the nobility. They entered sometimes to save face in society rather than out of a desire to live the religious life. These ladies, with the title of *Doña* and with their dowries, were each given a special suite of rooms with their own kitchens, and they were permitted to keep in their company maids and lay relatives and friends. Even children and young girls were allowed to live in the monastery, some girls receiving the habit as early as age twelve. Much bustling about, socializing, and distraction were the result. With their special privileges, the *Doñas* became a source of injustices, class distinctions, and jealousies. It should not be forgotten that Teresa herself at the Incarnation bore the title *Doña*, lived in a suite of rooms, and at times shared them with her relatives.

From the prior general Rubeo's visit to the Incarnation in 1567, we learn that there were one hundred forty-four nuns with the black veil (in solemn profession), that there was only enough food to feed the community for a third of the year, that the monastery was in debt, that the maximum number of nuns sustainable would be sixty, and that the unfinished church was about ready to collapse. Forced by hunger, the nuns had to go out for help to friends and relatives and get permission to keep their own money. At one time between 1560–1565 more than fifty nuns were living outside in the homes of relatives and benefactors. Parlor visits were encouraged as a help toward cultivating benefactors and receiving alms.

From Rubeo's visitation we also gather information about some of the human problems besetting the nuns. There was disagreement over confessors, some nuns wanting only friars from the order, others desiring a wider choice; some objected to preaching by Jesuits since these religious priests would sometimes discuss the nuns' private and "insignificant questions" from the pulpit; others suggested that the Carmelite friars prepare themselves better by reading some spiritual books; a sour complaint was made that the local prior was a disgrace to the whole order.[20]

The many obstacles to a life of recollection and prayer made little headway, though, in wearing down a large, vigorous group of devoted and excellent nuns within the community. Teresa, in her *Life*, extols the many nuns at the Incarnation "who are so good and serve the Lord so authentically that He cannot keep from favoring them."[21] Often showing her esteem for the Incarnation, she left it with a certain reluctance when beginning her new foundation. In fact, she later recruited as many as thirty-four nuns from the Incarnation for her new houses. Out of this number, twenty-two nuns remained; the others, usually for reasons of health, returned to their former monastery. When complaints were made that she was robbing the Incarnation of all their good nuns, Teresa replied that there were still more than forty nuns there who would be capable of founding a religious order.

In chapter 21 of her *Foundations*, Teresa relates how she herself after making the foundations in Salamanca and Alba de Tormes was appointed prioress of the Incarnation. This appointment was made in 1571 by the Dominican apostolic commissary, Pedro Fernández, who hoped that she could bring about some reforms and find some remedy for the community's economic troubles. She called on her new, discalced friar John of the Cross to come as confessor and spiritual director to assist her. In Fernández's view, the step taken was a highly successful one; the community at the Incarnation under the guidance of these two leaders experienced a complete spiritual renewal and was liberated from a number of its problems.

Reform in Spain

In fourteenth and fifteenth century Spain the word "reform" came to symbolize undefined longings for change within the ecclesiastical structure and for more spiritual solutions to problems.

The religious and secular clergy had accumulated large properties and enjoyed exemption from taxes levied by the Crown. Benefices by which the clergy, including religious, received their livelihood, were the source of much abuse and ever recurring disputes. Owing to the total upheaval produced by the Black Plague within the life of the monasteries, members were forced to relinquish the common life and the observance of their rules and constitutions. The practice of buying endowed offices, privileges, and academic degrees did not take long to follow once income and personal possessions were allowed. When groups formed to renounce these dubious privileges and customs and return to the authentic or "primitive" spirit of their founders, they were given the name "observants," in contradistinction to "conventuals" who represented the former groups. Strong communities of observants arose among the Benedictines, Cistercians, Franciscans, Augustinians, and Dominicans. On account of their exemplary reforms, academic as well as moral, these observants quickly gained the veneration of the people.

When in 1474 the Catholic Monarchs, Ferdinand and Isabella, initiated their reform movement, that reform already had a history in this return to the observance. The Monarchs seized on this movement and in adopting it sought to convert conventuals into observants. The spirituality of the observants put emphasis on austerity, the ascetical practice of silence, and on recollection both interior and exterior.

Among the Franciscan observants was the austere Francisco Jiménez de Cisneros whom the queen had taken for her confessor. After Alexander VI, in 1491, had authorized the Catholic Monarchs to take over the reform of the religious orders, Cisneros saw his opportunity and launched into the reform work with unflagging vigor, continuing in the same vein after his appointment to the see of Toledo in 1495. In the face of dogged opposition, he began with his own Franciscan order, imposing a strict observance of the rule. Some thousand Franciscans refusing to yield moved to Africa. Cisneros's reform then spread to the Dominicans, Benedictines, and Jeronimites, finally broadening its reach to include the secular clergy and laity as well.

Throughout the reign of the Emperor Charles V, 1516-1556,

the effort to maintain governmental control of the reform continued, and the movement was assured at least of support if not of new initiatives.

With Philip II, king of Spain from 1556-1598, the process of Spanish reform underwent intense change. Terrified at the thought of heresy entering Spain, Philip's actions show that in his heart he considered religion too serious a matter to be left to anyone else, including the pope, but himself. He aimed to make of the Spanish monarchy a strong fortress against whose walls the heresies seizing hold of Europe would pound to no effect. The inquisition, set up by the Catholic Monarchs to promote a common faith, was turned more or less into a department of state.

Everything that came from Rome met with an attitude of reserve. Neither the king nor the royal court could manage to believe in the seriousness of the proposals for reform decreed by the Council of Trent. Insisting on his right to scrutinize papal bulls and, if necessary, to forbid their publication in his dominions, the king delayed publication of the decrees of the Council of Trent for two years. Nor were they published without a proviso guaranteeing the crown's continuing influence in ecclesiastical jurisdiction and episcopal appointments.

The conciliar fathers had themselves set about a program of reform that could serve for the whole Church. But the measures they worked out needed the support of Rome for their efficacy. Spain, with little confidence in what Rome could achieve, took matters into its own hands. A council was established in the court of Madrid to oversee the reform of religious orders according to Spanish ideas. What were considered in Spain as inviolable privileges of the crown were considered in Rome as acts of rebellion and unwarranted disrespect of papal rights. Ironically, the monarch least esteemed in the Vatican during some pontificates was the king of Spain, known by the title "the Catholic king." Teresa herself reflects the popular opinion, referring to him as "our Catholic king"; nor does she even flinch from calling him "our holy king" (28, 6; 29, 30-31).

Failing in several attempts to gain briefs from Rome enabling him to carry out a reform of religious orders more demanding than that required by the Council of Trent, Philip II finally won out with a new pope who had been his candidate. In 1566 and 1567 with the briefs *Maxime cuperemus* and *Superioribus mensibus*, Pius V gave his nod to the suppression of the conventual communities and the introduction of observant life. In the interval between the time of the first foundation in Avila, about which Teresa wrote in her *Life* and in which she shows the influence of previous Spanish reform movements, and the other foundations described in this book, the authorities in Spain began to apply the work of the Council of Trent with the added measures imposed by the royal power. Within this new, more complicated turn of events Madre Teresa set off on her colorful, adventurous journeys through Spain.[22]

The Teresian Communities

"Whoever has not begun the practice of prayer, I beg for the love of the Lord not to go without so great a good."[23] Even before the founding of St. Joseph's, Teresa's convictions of prayer's transforming powers had grown so strong that others could not resist feeling drawn to her. Experiencing their own inner urgings toward a life of deeper prayer, they approached Doña Teresa obliging her to turn her rooms at the Incarnation into a meeting place for spiritual conversation. María Ocampo, a relative of Teresa's one day half in jest spoke of a possible reform in which they would return to a style of life more closely eremitical, the kind their holy forefathers on Mount Carmel had embraced. The discalced Franciscans, under the guidance of Fray Peter of Alcántara, provided an example.[24] These discalced religious comprised groups who sought to go a step further than the observants and live eremitically in austerity and recollection. They made themselves externally recognizable through their coarse wool habits and their bare feet.

As the half jest turned into an idea worth pursuing Teresa's first consideration, paradoxically, concerned money. Such a venture would need an assured income, enough to allow the community to live without anxieties. The Council of Trent, as a matter of fact, was at the same time legislating that religious communities, with the exception of the Franciscans, should have an income, one that would be in proportion to the number of religious. After further information from María de Jesús about the rule of St. Albert and encouragement from Peter of Alcántara, Teresa changed her opinion about money and resolved to found her house in poverty, that is without a fixed income, with trust in God's providence.[25] When she changed over to the new discalced mode of life in 1562, Teresa dropped her title and changed her name from Doña Teresa de Ahumada to Teresa of Jesus, the name by which she was known thereafter. Not until this century, it seems, did some outside Spain begin to call her Teresa of Avila.[26]

When the prior general Rubeo was making his formal visitations in Spain, he visited the new little community of "contemplative" Carmelites, a term he preferred to "discalced," and despite Teresa's fears went away most impressed. He urged his daughter to found more monasteries providing her with all the necessary permissions. Later, he showed his support by going so far as to tell her to make as many foundations as she had hairs on her head (27, 20).

In a letter to her brother Lorenzo, December 21, 1561, Teresa summed up her idea as she initially envisioned it: "To found a monastery where there will be only fifteen nuns and no possibility for any increase in numbers. They will practise a very strict enclosure and thus never go out or be seen without veils covering their faces. Their lives will be founded on prayer and mortification."

In the compact towns and cities of her day, people lived close together, finding their recreation in carefree, informal talk and their sources of news in the busy streets. The enclosure, or cloister, served as the means to which women felt forced to turn if they wanted to escape from the bustle and dedicate their lives to solitude and recollection.

St. Clare's rule contains the classic features of the cloister which were confirmed by Innocent IV (1247) and Urban IV (1264) and decreed by Boniface VIII (1298). Nuns were never to leave the cloister except in cases of serious illness, and outsiders were never to enter the cloister, so that the nuns could "thus be kept hidden from the gaze of the world and be able to serve God with greater surrender and freedom."[27] Many complained about these norms as being too rigorous, and soon pretexts were invented for abandoning them and establishing private laws to suit the needs of each community.

The practice of enclosure at the Incarnation was not a rigorous one, and Teresa often went outside the monastery. Not until August 21, 1564, when the nuncio Alexander Cribelli exempted her from the observance of the Incarnation was she free to practice enclosure in its rigorous form. In this same period, the Council of Trent dealt with the restoration of the cloister as a tool for reform. But only in 1566 did its decrees become known in Spain. In that same year through the constitution *Circa pastoralis* Pius V imposed rigorous cloister on all religious women including those living in *beaterios* who had never even promised it. When, understandably, requests began pouring into Rome for dispensations from cloister, Pius V resolutely launched, in 1570, the constitution *Decori* reaffirming the previous legislation and abolishing every contrary law or custom, restricting the causes for leaving the enclosure to "a serious fire, leprosy, or an epidemic." In 1572, the next pope, Gregory XIII, with the constitution *Deo sacris* defined the boundaries of the cloister and ordained that the doors leading into the monastery church should be boarded up, forbidding the nuns to go out to close the outside doors of the church. Teresa doesn't seem to have become aware of these laws of Gregory XIII, stricter than her own, before 1581. She then began urging their observance.

Teresa's own enthusiasm for cloister rested on her determination to provide a contemplative environment for her nuns through the authorized means that seemed safest in those times. After all the bothersome complications that marked her many attempts to establish the foundation in Burgos, Teresa writes of the happiness of the nuns when able finally to set up enclosure: "No one but those who experience it will believe the joy that is felt in these foundations once we are enclosed where no secular persons can enter, for however much we love them it is not enough to take away this great consolation in finding ourselves alone" (31, 46). She goes on to point out that the cloister is for her nuns what water is for fish since these contemplative nuns grow so accustomed to living in the clear-flowing streams of their Spouse.

The architecture of the times manifests a fondness for protective constructions, and sometimes took extravagant forms. From the reign of the Catholic Monarchs the social life of Spain began to stabilize, and people started building houses, palaces, and monuments. Architects foreign and national were in abundant supply. Commercial contracts with foreign countries brought, in their wake, new influences. The flamboyant Flemish Gothic style and the new Italian humanistic style were fused with the Jewish, Islamic, and Christian traditions of medieval Castile. The characteristically Spanish architecture that emerged became known as "plateresque" because of its lavish ornamentation suggesting silver plate. It was a rich and extravagant style requiring rich and extravagant patrons. In her *Way of Perfection* Teresa warns the nuns against extravagance in their buildings.[28] In this book of her *Foundations*, she wittily observes that if the building is not elaborately designed the nuns will be spared the necessity of having to go around admiring the walls (14, 5).

From other perspectives, the architecture of the times showed a special bent toward large brick or stone walls, black grilles, strong and simple in shape, and small windows protected by iron bars. The manorial doors were decorated with forged or gilded spikes and with beautifully shaped, pleasant-sounding knockers. Above the lintels were family shields carved in stone.

The classic monasteries reflected these latter traits and sometimes the former extravagant ones as well. The monastery of the Incarnation, like a little fortress, crowned its high walls with a battlement. Granite buttresses, monolithic lintels, and pointed spikes protruding from the doors, all made an impression of might and impregnability. The small windows, too, were guarded by thick iron grates covered with sharp points.

Teresa's monasteries, in humbler style, followed the same form: doors adorned with spikes, small windows protected by heavy bars, and the ritual latticework. The grilles in the parlors were thick and covered with large blunted spikes of iron, an aggressive warning as though some treasure were being defended. More often than not Teresa's nuns had to learn to make do with what they could find or afford. Her foundations were sometimes made in neighboring houses joined together, which she adapted into an acceptable monastery. Her nuns today still continue in some of the same houses, living the contemplative life she established in them. If elaborate or expensive architecture elicited a frown from Teresa as far as her ideals were concerned, a beautiful view and a garden with trees and flowers were all-important to her.[29] The garden, as well, served as a place for hermitages. In St. Joseph's in Avila as many as ten hermitages were put up in the garden while Teresa was living there.

But if elaborate architecture was frowned on by Teresa, the size of her monasteries had to depend on the number of inhabitants. The monastery in Malagón, endowed by Doña Luisa de la Cerda, is the only building Teresa was able to design according to her own wishes and have constructed completely new; otherwise, adaptation of what already existed was the rule. When the nuns were able to move into this new monastery, in 1579, even though it was still unfinished, they rejoiced along with Teresa because of the ample living space, in contrast with the crowded quarters in which they had been living.[30]

The use of veils by women to cover their faces is a custom almost as old as humanity. The veiling of women in certain parts of the ancient Near East, for example, is manifested in the Middle-Assyrian law Code, in which a harlot or female slave may not veil her face, but all other women must veil themselves when appearing in public. The custom of women veiling their faces in public was common in Palestine in the first Christian century, but St. Paul found it difficult to enforce in some other places.[31] Christianity, in fact, inherited the practice from three civilizations, Jewish, Greek, and Roman. Veiling objects or persons consecrated to the divinities was extended to other forms of consecration, such as baptism, marriage, and the consecration of virgins. The custom for women to be veiled gradually fell into disuse in the West but was preserved in the East and among Moslems. Nonetheless, the use of the veil was still current in sixteenth century Spain, especially where there was Moorish influence.

In one of its religious uses the veil became the sign of the consecrated woman. In Teresa's time it caused no surprise or annoyance to see nuns with their faces veiled; this was often done by other women as well when they ventured into the streets. There were, in addition, a number of kinds of veils, each with a different meaning. Suarez speaks of some of these: the white veil, a sign of testing that was worn by novices though also by lay Sisters; the veil of full consecration that was received at age twenty-five; the veil for ordination to the stage of deaconess, at age forty, by which one was enabled to read the Gospel and its respective homily during the recitation of the Divine Office; and the veil of recompense that was bestowed on superiors when they reached seventy-five.[32]

Along with her esteem for the enclosure as a means toward solitude and of avoiding the lax, distracting atmosphere of other monasteries, Teresa esteemed the veil. Her nuns did not appear in public without having their faces veiled, for wherever they went they attracted the curious. Writing of the foundation in Soria, for example, she shows her feelings on the matter: "We were anxious to get inside because of the large number of people. The world is so fond of novelty that were it not for the veils we wear over our faces, these crowds would be a great trial. But with these veils, we can put up with them" (30, 8).

According to an established custom going back to the Rule of St. Clare, the grilles in the parlors, too, were covered with a veil or curtain. In a new foundation, even before an enclosure was established, Teresa would begin to observe in makeshift fashion the laws about the grille, as in Burgos: "Through a window with a grate covered by a veil, I spoke with those who came to visit me" (31, 20).

In visits with parents and family members, or in similar cases, the veil was seen as unnecessary and not required by Teresa. She herself, when asked, would lift the veil for friends. After Teresa's death, Nicolás Doria made stricter rules about the use of the veil.

As foundress, the Madre discovered that fewer nuns meant greater harmony and quiet. Her ideal remained that of a small group of good friends gathered in the Lord to live totally for Him through a contemplative life of prayer useful for His Church. In her *Way of Perfection*, she outlined the spirituality she envisioned for this little group. At the beginning, the number of nuns Teresa had in mind was thirteen, a symbol of Christ and His twelve apostles.[33] When she was obliged to return to the Incarnation as prioress, she felt the contrast between the quiet of her little communities and the commotion among the 130 nuns of the Incarnation.[34] In her last years, Madre Teresa increased the limit to twenty in those houses with a fixed income; in those founded in poverty, she set the limit at thirteen or fourteen choir Sisters. With the foundation in Malagón, she began to allow for lay Sisters, but for no more than three. When in the beginning she had set the number at thirteen, she had in mind nuns healthy and young enough to share in the work. As nuns grew older and some became sick, requiring much care and time from others, adaptations had to be made in the numbers.[35]

In addition to what can be said of the above points summed up in the letter to Don Lorenzo, it must also be stated that the new manner of living Madre Teresa originated for her Carmelite nuns went far beyond a mere reform, or reaction, which would have consisted in the extirpation of abuses and the restoration of regular observance. Inspired by the deepest Gospel spirit, she created, within the framework of Carmelite cenobitical life, a somewhat eremitical mode of living. In addition she illuminated this contemplative mode of life with fresh insight into its meaning and placed emphasis on the apostolic and ecclesial dimensions of prayer, on its relation to all those concerns for the service of Christ that lay so close to her heart. She indeed introduced something new within the Church, the life of prayer as a service.

Austerity in the Reform Movements

Rigorous, at times incredible, types of austerity marked some of the reform movements in the Spain of Teresa's time. In her *Life* she gives a classic description of the harsh penitential practices of St. Peter of Alcántara.[36] Now, in this work of her *Foundations*, she devotes more space than she did for the ascetic Franciscan friar to the extraordinary ascetical feats of a woman, Doña Catalina de Cardona (28, 19–37). According to popular notions of the time, high perfection required rigorous austerity. In a religious world crying for reform, such displays of self-mastery attracted the favor of the people. When they learned of the extreme penances of Doña Catalina in her dark cave near La Roda, the people set out in large numbers to see her. The crowds became so great that she had to be held high so that all could see her and receive her blessing.

Austerity even made its way into the court of Philip II. It was, in fact, the austerity of Teresa's friars that helped win for them the favor of the king. He once defended them to the nuncio Sega pointing out that he found it suspect for the nuncio to be opposing people who profess such rigorous austerity and perfection.

In houses of prayer (of recollection or eremitical life) that arose among Franciscans, Augustinians, Dominicans, and Jeronimites and from which the discalced movements sprang, further steps were taken than in those of the observance to assure that the hours dedicated to what was called mental prayer would be many and the austerities conspicuous. External signs of this austere life were the bare feet and the habits of coarse wool. Teresa's nuns may have gone barefoot at first, but they soon began to wear *alpargatas*, a poor type of sandal made from hemp. Her friars continued going barefoot and only gradually turned to *alpargatas*, first allowing them for the sickly.

The eremitical houses, however, did not look on preaching as a ministry incompatible with eremitism; indeed, they saw it as a part of eremitical living. The theory went that the greater the austerity the more fruitful the preaching.[37]

In its relationship to prayer and recollection, austerity was looked on as an aid. By quieting the activity of the exterior senses a person enabled a kind of sixth sense to make ready for action. In this sixth sense were grouped the spiritual powers capable of grasping realities lying beyond matter and particularly the reality of God who is pure Spirit. Osuna taught that "closing the corporeal and exterior senses would open the soul's interior ones."[38]

Sharing in the common esteem for the life of austerity and penance, Teresa wrote enthusiastically about Peter of Alcántara and Catalina de Cardona. Paradoxically, though, she could not help feeling a certain skepticism about these extremes. While she was once thinking about the life of Catalina de Cardona and feeling regret that her confessors did not allow her to do more, the Lord told her that she was walking on a good and safe path. "Do you see all the penance she does? I value your obedience more."[39] In this spirit, when speaking of the penances and disciplines performed by Catalina Sandoval y Godínez, Teresa, in an incidental but revealing way, points out that they were so many because the girl had no one to guide her (22, 11).

In her celebrated visit to her friars in Duruelo to examine first hand the manner of life they had established, Teresa was in general highly impressed. However, there were some doubts that gnawed at her and they concerned the unsparing penitential practices. She begged the friars for moderation fearing that the whole work could be ruined through excess (12, 12). Later, when Gracián was in fact a novice at Pastrana he was strongly tempted to leave because of the extreme practices to which the novices were subjected by a young emotionally disturbed friar who unwisely had been put in charge of them. On this occasion Teresa wrote for advice to her learned Dominican counselor, Domingo Báñez, and subsequently made arrangements for Fray John of the Cross to go to Pastrana and put some moderation into the novitiate life there (23, 9).

The Madre herself was asked by Doña Leonor de Mascareñas and the ecclesiastical superiors to go to the monastery in Alcalá founded by María de Jesús and try to help the nuns there to moderate the austerities that were beginning to cause illnesses in the community. In her *Life*, Teresa refers to María de Jesús as a "woman who practices much penance and prayer." This was the woman who had walked to Rome barefoot in order to obtain the permissions she needed to found the monastery of her desires, and it was she who first informed Teresa about poverty as prescribed in the rule.[40] But Teresa met with little success in getting the twenty young Sisters to make any changes in their life. Rigidly set in their penitential patterns, they shut out Teresa's gentler ways. María de Jesús continued to go barefoot, winter as well as summer, and to perform her other severe austerities until the day of her death. When one of these nuns was later asked why the community had never kept any souvenirs of Teresa, she matter-of-factly explained that at the time Teresa came there, they found nothing different about her and that raptures in their community were something common. Finally, the Dominican Báñez, after a couple of months, advised Teresa to go on with her own foundations and not waste her time trying to change them.

The Mother Foundress had observed in her own communities that when physical strength is weakened through austerities a kind of delightful absorption may so overpower a nun that she will allow it to possess her for long hours and even days, not wanting to part with such delight. Teresa carefully demonstrates in this work on her foundations how such absorption differs from rapture which is short-lived and extraordinarily beneficial in its effects. On the other hand, the long periods of time spent in the above mentioned absorptions, she warns, are a waste; if austerities have caused the weakness, they must be reduced (ch. 6).

While pleading with her prioresses to practice discretion in government Madre Teresa begs them not to lay the burden of added austerities on her daughters; no prioress must think that because she is eager and able to embrace new austerities others in the community are also. What is important for Teresa is that the nun does not fail in the more essential matters of the rule, with these a nun has plenty to do (18, 6-11).

If by today's measure the austerities of the lifestyle Teresa established might appear extreme, in her day they were often considered insufficient. In the Madre's view the balanced life of prayer, work, and solitude, arrived at through the nuns' experience, set down and approved in her constitutions, along with the spirituality expounded in *The Way of Perfection*, provided all that was necessary for reaching the goal of the spiritual life. This goal consists in conformity with the will of God and with all that is therein implied; for such conformity, harsh austerities are no more necessary than raptures. It is in the *Foundations* that we find Teresa's often quoted passage regarding perfection: "The highest perfection obviously does not consist in interior delights or in great raptures or in visions or in the spirit of prophecy but in having our will so much in conformity with God's will that there is nothing we know He wills that we do not want with all our desire, and in accepting the bitter as happily as we do the delightful when we know that His Majesty desires it" (5, 10).

The method the Council of Trent adopted for promoting the reform of religious orders consisted in fostering the observance of the rules and constitutions. As a preventive against laxity, such a method was highly regarded by Teresa; but she also looked on the observance as a preventive against excessive austerities. The adaptability manifested in the virtues of obedience and humility impressed her much more as means of spiritual growth than did harshness. She puts visitators on the alert against allowing prioresses to add further burdens.[41]

In her love for obedience and in the examples she provides, the Mother Foundress sometimes gives the impression that in this matter, anyway, she encourages extremes, or even apparent foolishness, somewhat in the style of what one reads in the desert fathers. On the other hand, her enthusiasm for obedience is put in perspective when she issues warnings against indiscretion and offers a practical norm easy to grasp: "Anything that would be a mortal sin when not ordered by the superior would still be one if the superior orders it" (18, 11). She urges her nuns to consult with learned men about how to advance with discretion. In fact, she relates how learned men had to be called in to restrain the nuns and explain to them the matters in which they were obliged to obey (19, 1; 16, 3).

When Teresa met Padre Gracián for the first time, she at once understood that he was the man who could promote this same balance among the friars, "because some think one way, and others another" (23, 12). In his first visitation of the friars, "he arranged everything with such moderation and harmony that it indeed seemed that he was helped by the Divine Majesty and that our Lady had chosen him to help her order" (23, 13).

Desiring that her friars be good contemplatives, Teresa also wanted them to be good spiritual directors and preachers and that there be learned men among them. In the reform movements of eremitism, there was opposition at times toward learn-

ing and university degrees. When Teresa consulted learned
men about the founding of St. Joseph's in Avila without a fixed
income, Peter of Alcántara chided her in a letter for consulting
theologians in matters concerned with spiritual perfection.[42]
Nonetheless, Teresa's unequivocal policy throughout her life was
to consult learned men. So often forced by circumstances to make
vital decisions about equally alluring courses of action, she felt
sore need of light and assistance in her process of discernment.
"Never in any business related to these foundations, nor in anything that happened relative to them, did I do anything or would
I have done anything . . . that I understood to go contrary to the
will of God in even one point, and this too, when I thought that in
order to succeed I would have to cover up my intentions" (27, 15).
She then shows her practical wisdom: "I proceeded according to
what my confessors advised me, for since I have been working on
these foundations, they have always been very learned men and
great servants of God, as you know" (27, 15). From the Dominicans and the Jesuits came these main advisors.[43]

In her hopes for learned men among her own friars, Teresa
feared that too much stress on austerity would discourage desirable vocations among university students. And in recognition
of her ideal, the friars did in a short time set up houses in the
university cities of Alcalá and Baeza so that the young members
could pursue their studies.[44]

After the death of Teresa, when Nicolás Doria came into
power, he expanded the nuns' constitutions and placed severe
restrictions on the ministry of the friars. Those seeking to con-
serve the Mother Foundress's spirit, such as John of the Cross
and Gracián, fell into disfavor. Beset with the fear that Madre
Teresa's spirit would be snuffed out, Gracián put up resistance
and in turn was expelled from the order. Gracián's appeals to the
king went unheard because the king looked kindly on Doria's
strong convictions about observance and austerity. Among the
nuns, María de San José and Ana de Jesús, Teresa's intimates,
also underwent punishment within the order (deposition from
office, imprisonment, and a kind of exile) for seeking to save
what their Mother Foundress had established.[45]

Gracián insists in his own written story of the foundations of the friars that Teresa was foundress of both friars and nuns.[46] Doria repudiated this claim and was subsequently followed by others who insisted that Antonio de Jesús founded the first monastery of friars and that its first austere spirit was happily restored by Doria. All in all, it was too much for these tough austere men to admit that they had been founded by a woman. The pervasive thinking went that since men are stronger than women they can practice more austerities; thus the nuns could only share in the perfection of the friars.

The World

The term "world" appears frequently enough in Teresa's writings, but always in a pejorative sense as an irreconcilable enemy of the spiritual person. With this term, then, Teresa refers to only a part of the reality nowadays comprised in the world. Without hesitation she proclaims openly the essential goodness of things and how they show forth the splendor of the Creator. And one of her major themes is the beauty and astounding capacity of the human person made in the image and likeness of God.

When using the expression "world," Teresa is limiting her reference to that sum of realities that opposes or impedes God's work. To her eyes the world appears almost as a real person against whom God struggles for dominion over the soul. Like a liar, trying to deceive Christians and separate them from God, the world robs them of peace and inner serenity of soul. Teresa, in her writings, instinctively speaks to the world and chides it for its deceit. She is inclined to measure spirituality in terms of distance from it: "Blessed the young man and blessed the young girl who have merited so much from God that at the age in which people are usually overpowered by the world, they trampled on it" (10, 12).

From honor and money flows the sap that keeps the world alive. In sixteenth-century Castile honor was the very soul of social behavior. Money, also, played such a pivotal role and was

so much tied up with honor that the two realities could be reduced simply to honor.

In the Teresian writings, the word "honor" bears different
shades of meaning. Mainly, it speaks of prestige, of all that raises
one above another. The important thing was not that persons
try to live up to the renown attributed to them or to what digni-
fied them in the sight of others; the important thing was that
others say these things and believe them whether they existed in
reality or not. With these snobbish concerns the Spaniard became a slave to others, fearful of what they might say.

Since honor was essentially an attribute of nobility, an exceptionally high value was placed on birth and rank. At the top
of the ladder came the grandees, a group drawn from the oldest
families of Castile and Aragon. One of their special distinctions
was the privilege of keeping their heads covered in the presence
of the king. Immediately below them came other titled aristocrats, the *titulos*, who were the dukes, marquises, and counts.
The lesser aristocracy, whose members distinguished themselves
with the title "Don" were called either *caballeros* (knights or
gentlemen) or *hidalgos*. Their status gave them exemption from
taxation. Among these aristocrats, some were rich and others
extremely poor; some came from ancient families, while others
were recently ennobled bourgeois.

The social and practical advantages attached to the possession of *hidalguia* made it an object of universal desire; heraldry,
emblazoned everywhere, became the indispensable key to all the
subtleties of status. Vast amounts of time and effort went into the
construction, or fabrication, of genealogical tables that would
prove the existence of aristocratic ancestors. Despite the emphasis on ancestry, though, from 1520 on privileges of *hidalguia*
were put up for sale as a means of enhancing a dwindling royal
treasury. Wealth then enabled rich mercantile families to ally
themselves with families of respectable aristocratic lineage.

With so much value placed on birth and rank, the ordinary
members of society sought compensation, and they found it in
the doctrine of *limpieza de sangre* (purity of blood). They reasoned
that it was preferable to be born of humble but pure Christian
parentage than to be a *caballero* of "suspicious" background,

Moorish or Jewish. Pure ancestry provided for those in the lower ranks of society what noble ancestry did for those in the higher ranks. Honor was achieved by proving the purity of one's ancestry.

In worldliness, Teresa beheld the eager quest for prestige and possessions. "What friendship there would be among all if there were no self-interest about honor and money! I think this absence of self-interest would solve all problems."[47] The quest for prestige and money puts one in opposition to God's work. Inherent in such a quest lies a deceptive centering on earth, on passing joys, on the superficial and limited, on that which comes to an end. These things offer nothing in exchange for the sublime gifts of God's friendship. But the fundamental problem of the world, understood in this sense, is ignorance of revelation, of the word of God. "All the harm that comes to the world comes from its not knowing the truths of Scripture in clarity and truth."[48]

All-important to noble families was an heir to their properties. Chapter 10 in these *Foundations* gives a striking example of the situation. If some daughters were forced to enter convents for the sake of avoiding family disgrace, others for the sake of preserving or adding to family prestige were prevented from entering. The son and the daughters of Doña María de Acuña, sister of the count of Buendía and widow of the governor of Castile, met with strong opposition in the family when they decided to renounce their inheritance and enter religious life. The lively story of the twelve-year-old Doña Casilda de Padilla's escape from a family-arranged marriage into the cloister leaves a reader nowadays half amazed and half amused. Teresa shares with us her resulting reflections from the incident. "It is a great pity the world is now so unfortunate and blind that it seems to parents their honor lies in not letting the dung of this world's goods be forgotten and in not remembering that sooner or later these things will come to an end." Then, enlarging on the matter, she goes on to lament, "Such parents want to sustain their own vanities at a cost to their children, and very boldly take from God souls that He wants for Himself" (10, 9).[49]

Another mark of honor or prestige, which became an enviable

means to social acceptance, was a chapel for burial. In Toledo, in one instance, Teresa found herself in a sticky tangle when members of the nobility asked for the chapel after she had already promised it to the Ramírez family, who were merchants and probably *conversos*, converted Jews. It is in the context of dealing with this issue that she makes her classic statement: "I have always esteemed virtue more than lineage" (15, 15). Teresa, in fact, received so many opinions from everybody about what to do that she did not know how to proceed and began to waver. The Lord Himself intervened and gave the light she needed in a manner that He often used in enlightening her. By means of a locution He insisted that lineage and social status mattered not at all in the judgments of God. He severely reprimanded Teresa telling her that "concerns of this sort were not for those who had already despised the world" (15, 16).

As for the Mother Foundress's own dealings with money, she first thought, as mentioned, of founding her monasteries with a fixed income that would derive from interest on investments made by the founding benefactor in state, municipal, or private enterprises. The nuns, then, would be free of worries about their basic needs. Madre Teresa's personal love of poverty is obvious from the *Life* in which she says "for a long time I had been desiring that it would be possible for me to go begging for love of God and not have a house or anything." But such lofty ideals could not be imposed on others: "I feared that if the Lord didn't give others these desires their lives would be unhappy."[50] In the end, Teresa opted for a mode of action contrary to what learned men had advised her and followed instead, with the encouragement of St. Peter of Alcántara, the growing urge coming from within to found her monastery in poverty, without a fixed and secure income. With entire dependence on God, she placed her first house under His providence. As things turned out, her companions also came to know the special joy that can accompany poverty. The harsh experience of poverty they underwent in rich Toledo was a communal one and became "the cause of a sweet contemplation" (15, 14). From that time Teresa's desires to be poor increased. "And I felt freedom in having so little esteem for temporal goods, for lack of these goods brings an increase of interior good. Certainly, such a lack carries in its wake another kind of fullness and tranquility" (15, 15).

Madre Teresa's ideals about poverty, in fact, caused her much more difficulty in obtaining permission to make foundations. In addition, as her desires for poverty increased, her need to deal with money also seems to have increased. She wrote to her brother Lorenzo: "So now that I have come to abhor money and business matters, the Lord wills that I deal with nothing else, which is no small cross."[51]

A problem for Teresa's ideal of poverty, however, lurked in the small towns. In them, it was simply impossible to survive without a fixed income. The Madre first resisted Doña Luisa de la Cerda's request for a monastery in the little town of Malagón. Determined to get her way, Doña Luisa found some allies among the theologians and especially in one of Teresa's confessors, Domingo Báñez. Concerning her resistance to a foundation in Alba de Tormes with a fixed income, Teresa was again challenged by Báñez. As a matter of fact, he actually scolded Teresa, as she explains: "He reprimanded me and told me that since the Council had given permission it would not be right to forego the foundation because of a need for an income" (20, 1). Báñez went on arguing that whether or not a monastery had an income made little difference with regard to the holiness of the nuns. In succumbing to the Dominican's arguments, Teresa did so only under the condition that those foundations made with a fixed income be an exception justified by the economic situation of the place where the monastery was to be located. She could never bring herself to the idea of founding monasteries with a fixed income in cities where there was wealth.

When she was called upon to found in small towns, that is, with an income, she was carefully exacting about the endowment so that no economic problems for the nuns would surface in the future. For example, with respect to the foundation in Alba de Tormes, she writes: "We underwent much difficulty in trying to come to an agreement. For in the case of monasteries founded with an income, my goal always was that they have enough to keep the nuns from dependence on relatives, or on anyone, and that food and clothing and everything necessary be given to them in the house, and that the sick be very well cared for" (20, 13). Happy to trust in God, she never worried about those monasteries founded in poverty, but the ones that were dependent on a fixed income for support presented her with a different picture. She figured that if the established income were too small, the monastery would be doomed. In the end, seven of the monasteries were founded with an income: Malagón, Pastrana, Alba de Tormes, Beas, Caravaca, Villanueva de la Jara, and Soria.

To live off investments was the dream of every powerful Castilian of Teresa's day. Money in land, in urban real estate, or in the most active elements of the royal estate proved to be the safest investment. Work was not respected as a source of wealth. It was counter to the current of the times and contrary to the practice in other monasteries, then, that the Mother Foundress wanted her communities to survive with the help of income gained through work, in addition to that coming from donations.

The kind of work recommended by Madre Teresa was the peaceful, uncomplicated labor of spinning, without the pressure of deadlines. But women's work, especially, was poorly paid, and a perusal of account books shows that the income derived from the nuns' work amounted to little when compared to the donations. The latter became the real means of support for the communities. In any case, though the usual donations and the income from labor took care of the nuns' daily needs, additional income was needed to cover the cost of other eventualities such as improvements on a house, erecting new ones, or paying off debts. In these latter instances, generous benefactors usually came forward.

In her *Foundations*, Teresa makes a point of mentioning benefactors by name so that "the nuns living now, and those who are to come after, remember them in their prayers" (31, 29). It was her experience that the Lord always provided for them in their needs by awakening some to come to their aid. "When it is known that a monastery is founded in poverty, there is nothing to fear because everyone helps. But when people think it has an income, to be without one is dangerous and the monastery will be left temporarily without means" (31, 48).

Dowries made up another important contribution to the community's financial needs. According to the practice of the times, a woman entering religious life was required to bring a dowry. The inequality of status in Teresa's former monastery, the Incarnation, was rooted in the difference in dowries. As a consequence, Teresa shows a certain scorn of dowries. She exhorts her nuns never to refuse to accept any applicants because of their lack of money for a dowry. "On the contrary," she says, "I had fear about those with wealth, but the poor filled and enlarged my spirit with a happiness so great I wept for joy" (27, 13).

Though the contribution of a dowry was encouraged, Teresa's trust in the Lord allowed for much flexibility. After her death, in the chapter of Valladolid, 1587, the friars established a fixed rate of five hundred ducats for the dowry. María de San José lamented the law, saying it was foreign to her Holy Mother's spirit.

During the dramatic years of her activity, Madre Teresa faced countless legal actions and financial worries. Never slackening in her efforts, she offered advice on scores of proceedings and profitable investments, averting hardships here, encouraging intercommunity assistance there. She was forced to immerse herself in oceans of red tape, study intricately complex contracts, whose clauses had to be read and reread in every detail. Buying a house required shrewdness. We get a picture of the latter when the Madre was looking for houses to buy in Palencia. "Finally, I went to see them and also those of Our Lady of the Street, although not with the intention of buying these latter but only so that the owner of the others would not think that we had no other choice" (29, 15).

Holiness did not prohibit the Mother Foundress from rejoicing over a bargain. In a letter to Ambrosio Mariano, she shares her joy that the house they bought in Seville for six thousand ducats was worth more than twenty thousand.[52] In writing of the trouble-ridden Burgos foundation, she praises the diligence and intelligence of her good friend Doctor Aguiar who by insisting on secrecy was able to buy a house at a price that in the minds of many "was no less than a miracle" (31, 39). In their experience of poverty in Toledo at the outset, the nuns had only three or four ducats to their name. Teresa shows her pleasure when with the help of Alonso Alvarez they were able to buy an attractive house, "one of the nicest in Toledo," for twelve thousand ducats (15, 6, 17).

The community account books in Medina del Campo offer an idea of income and expenditures. The income for the month of August in 1571 was 5,171 maravedis, the disbursements amounted to 17,003 maravedis. In September the income was 12,780 maravedis and the disbursements amounted to 10,719 maravedis. The surplus for the month of September came from an extraordinary donation by the merchant Juan de Medina who surprised the community with the sum of twenty ducats. The expenditures went mainly for food: bread, eggs, oil, fruit, fish, rice, and greens. An extraordinary expense could unbalance the budget. These would include things like the cost of a trip for superiors, the Mother Foundress's own journeys, sending messengers, repairs on the roof or on the wall.

As for the value of the ducat and maravedi, the two sums of money most often mentioned by Teresa, they might best be measured by what could be purchased with them. The ducat was the most common gold coin and was worth 375 maravedis. Using the year 1560 as a point of reference, a liter of oil cost 43 maravedis, a dozen of eggs 35 maravedis, and a kilo of bread about 6 maravedis. In all these matters with regard to money Teresa's persistent conviction was that God will never "fail those who serve Him, if they live as moderately as we do," in communities where "the nuns are so few and help themselves through the labor of their hands" (18, 1).[53] An astounding testimony to the validity of her conviction is the fact that all of her seventeen foundations are still in existence today, four centuries later; some of the communities are living in the same houses in which the foundations were made.

On Making a Foundation

In making a foundation, Teresa developed her own method of procedure in which she adapted to circumstances. In foundations made in poverty, before starting off on the journey, she endeavored to rent a house that would serve as a temporary dwelling until a house, or houses, suitable for a monastery could be bought. In foundations made with an income, the nuns first lived in the quarters of the founding benefactress until adaptations in the house destined to be the monastery were made.

Teresa arrived at this method through painful experience, as in Valladolid where the first property turned out to be unhealthy and too far from the city. There was another important factor that obliged her to begin by renting. Teresa puts it bluntly: "I didn't have a cent to buy one with" (21, 2). In her boundless trust, she believed that once they were established in a rented house, the Lord would provide. Her subsequent experiences gave support to her belief: "For the Lord Himself, as seen in the other foundations, chooses in each place someone to help Him" (29, 8).

After the embarrassing muddle in Medina del Campo, her first foundation away from Avila, she concluded that it was best to take with her at the start as few nuns as possible. The Mother Foundress and her few nuns would then be accompanied by a chaplain and other helpers, such as Padre Julián de Avila and Antonio Gaytán. They also brought along some basic furnishings; straw, for example, "which was the first thing I provided for the founding of the house, because in having straw we would have a bed" (19, 4).

Moreover, she arranged the daily journeys so that the little group would reach its destination in the secret of night. These nighttime entries proved most advantageous. Mainly, they enabled Teresa and her companions to prepare a room, a place that she often euphemistically refers to as a church, where Mass could be said immediately the following morning so as to make the foundation official. By thus making the foundation secretly and by surprising the townspeople with a *fait accompli*, she was able to preclude opposition, especially the usual opposition from other begrudging religious orders.

Often, then, the nuns spent the first night working hurriedly instead of giving themselves some much needed rest after their tiring travels. Throughout the story of the foundations, it is obvious that Teresa entered wholeheartedly into this and other work and seems to have relished it. "When there was question of work to be done I enjoyed being the first" (19, 6). Some of her humorous accounts in this respect have become classic.

Once the foundation was established in this precarious way, the Mother Foundress had to enter the arena of house searching. Sometimes she met with no trouble, as when in Valladolid she had the help of a friend and benefactress as influential as María de Mendoza, the widow of the brilliant and skillful Francisco de los Cobos, under whose gentle guidance the government of Spain had run smoothly for some twenty years in the absence of Charles V. At other times, wealthy people, or friends, were no help; in Toledo the poor student Andrada found in a short while what Teresa's wealthy friends could not. The search for a house in Salamanca lasted three years. When it finally seemed that all had been arranged, the owner turned up so enraged that at the time of Teresa's writing on the matter the sale of the house had not yet been finalized, so many were the complications he created.

Opposition to Madre Teresa's buying a house sometimes came in the form of lawsuits. In Segovia the nuns were beset with lawsuits from the Franciscans, the Mercedarians, and the cathedral chapter. The cathedral chapter feared losing out on an annuity, and the religious orders feared competition for the charity of the people of Segovia. The only means the nuns found of extricating themselves in this latter instance was money. "Explained in this way," Teresa remarks, "it all seems like nothing; but going through it was something else" (21, 8-10).

In Seville, the Franciscan friars so contested Teresa's buying a house near them that when the nuns moved in they did so fearfully at night, and "every shadow they saw seemed to be a friar." In Teresa's reflections she moves from her own experience of human weakness to relief in the thought that her fears came in the cause of good. "O Jesus! How many fears I have suffered before taking possession of these foundations! I reflect on the fact that if one can feel so much fear in doing something good for the service of God, what must be the fear of those who do evil" (25, 7-8). Also, as a kind of compensation for the opposition of other religious orders, the Madre makes a point of mentioning the ever present assistance of the Dominicans and the Jesuits.

Sometimes, the owner raised the price when he saw that the Mother Foundress was interested. In Palencia the proprietor asked a high price when quite sure that the nuns would buy; when he was certain, he raised it another three hundred ducats. But his little trick backfired, for it enabled Teresa to decide on another house that had captured her interest and which the Lord, through a locution, requested her to buy.

It ought to be mentioned, parenthetically, that in many practical matters Teresa experienced extraordinary help from the Lord through locutions. She continued to receive them up to the end of her life. Her custom with regard to them, though, was to consult a confessor about the locution, always determined to follow his advice even if it went contrary to the locution (29, 21; 31, 4).[54] A powerful example of this determination is the instance in which though our Lord told her to make a foundation in Madrid, she went to Seville instead at Gracián's orders. She believed she had more certitude of doing God's will by obeying her superior than by obeying her locution.[55]

Returning to the matter of buying a house, in Burgos an outcry arose not because Teresa got a house but because she got one at such a low price. This she was able to do through the astute dealings of her friend Doctor Aguiar, after which the people disgustedly moaned that the priest appointed to sell the house had practically given it away.

Troubles worsened when the opposition came from diocesan administrators. In two cases, archbishops opposed her. In Seville, the archbishop, after having promised much, refused just as much once the nuns had arrived. Teresa came close to returning to Castile without making the foundation. Only after the archbishop's personal visit with Teresa did he begin to support the nuns. More painful and disturbing was the conduct of the archbishop of Burgos. Strangely and inexplicably, he would think of a new requirement as soon as a previous one was met. "The archbishop always said that he desired this foundation more than anyone. And I believe it because he is such a good Christian that he wouldn't speak anything but the truth; but in

his deeds it didn't appear that he desired this since he demanded things that seemed impossible for us to comply with"
(30, 31).

In measuring the difficulties she experienced in each foundation, the Mother Foundress concludes that St. Joseph's in Avila
was the hardest, followed by Seville (26, 2). Had she made the
assessment again after her last in Burgos, she would surely have
included it in the category of the most difficult. Nonetheless,
every one of her foundations, with the exception of Soria, which
got off on the right foot from the first moment, amounted to a
physical, psychological, and spiritual trial for the foundress.
"The Lord desired that no foundation be made without some
trial in one way or another" (24, 15).

In a time when churches were being destroyed and the Blessed
Sacrament taken away, a strong motivation for Teresa was the
consolation she felt in seeing another church where the Blessed
Sacrament could be reserved. "For although we often do not
take note, it ought to be a great consolation for us that Jesus
Christ, true God and true man, is present in the most Blessed
Sacrament in many places" (18, 5).[56] In Madre Teresa's mind
the people in a town were actually receiving a precious favor
from God when one of her foundations was made. The thought
that there might be too many monasteries never bothered her.
She firmly held that where there are many monasteries God
brings about great blessings and that he has the power to sustain
many as well as few (29, 27; 31, 13).

In her best-informed attempts, however, she had many con-
flicting opinions to weigh. "O Jesus!" she complains, "what a
trial it is to have to contend with many opinions." As for negative advice, "where there is need one takes poorly any advice
that doesn't provide some help" (21, 9; 19, 8). When immersed
in controversy and doubt, her one desire was always to do the
will of God. She declares that in all the business matters and
everything else related to her foundations she never did or would
have done anything contrary to the will of God, which did not
remove the necessity of frequently choosing secrecy as the best
mode of procedure. "If we begin discussing opinions, the devil
disturbs everything." But in her mind there is never any ques-

tion of having no faults. "Perhaps I am mistaken and have done many things wrong without realizing it; and the imperfections are countless" (27, 15; 19, 8). In telling her story, she tempers her account of those who opposed her and tries to excuse them. As for those who shared as benefactors and helpers in her work for the Lord, she is untiring in expressing her gratitude to them.

If taking possession of a foundation had to be done secretly, the time came later for the public inauguration, an act usually surrounded by festive solemnity. It was the moment for reserving the Blessed Sacrament in a definitive way and for rejoicing in God's triumph over the devil; it was a moment of victory for the nuns, definitely able now to live in solitude with God.

The Mother Foundress never cared to leave a new foundation until the major obstacles were surmounted, the nuns' basic needs were provided for, and everything was in order. She resisted pressures from the princess of Eboli who insisted that she come to Pastrana when things were not yet completely settled in Toledo. In reference to a superior's order that she leave Salamanca to become prioress at the Incarnation, she writes: "I never would, or did, leave any monastery until it was in fit condition, had a spirit of recollection, and was adapted according to my wishes" (19, 6).

To her new foundations, Teresa of Jesus never failed to carry images of Christ and His saints. These sacred images fell in line with her own devotion and were for her a magnificent means of awakening love. One of her joys in life was to adorn her churches and hermitages with statues and paintings of gospel scenes. In Toledo with only three or four ducats to her name, she bought two straw mattresses and a woolen blanket; the rest of the money was spent on two paintings of Christ in His sufferings (15, 6). These paintings have been preserved to this day at the nuns' monastery in Toledo. Similarly, in the other foundations she made, there still exist various statues or paintings that Teresa brought with her or venerated devoutly; in some instances she hired artists to paint scenes on certain subjects. The well known *Cristo de los Lindos Ojos,* in a hermitage at St. Joseph's in Avila, was painted in accord with a vision of Christ that Teresa had received. For the Mother Foundress these images were like portraits of the persons she loved.

Teresa's mysticism was never snobbish. Even after her rich spiritual life had grown to full flower and she was experiencing profound enlightenment from within, she esteemed these simple means to love. In fact, her mystical life, we might say, bestowed on these means a new power, and in turn she received more from them. The mystic understands experientially the divine realities and will often sense a stronger need to give outward expression to this understanding.

Travel

The Carmelite chapter held in Piacenza, Italy, in 1575 attempted to confine the expansion of its discalced friars in Spain and maintain control. At the same time, it made a decision that was not to be published but communicated to Madre Teresa by her provincial, Angel de Salazar. For reasons that will be explained later, Teresa was ordered by the chapter to stay in one Castilian monastery and not leave it. She interpreted the command as a form of imprisonment, a conclusion she came to because "there is no nun who for necessary matters pertaining to the good of the order cannot be ordered by the provincial to go from one place to another" (27, 20). The irony of the situation, not so unusual, was that Teresa now received blame for doing what she had been asked to do.

However, in addition to the troubles springing up within the order on account of the Madre's friars, the thinking in the Church after the Council of Trent had changed. Pius V in his interpretation of the directives of the Council had imposed strict cloister on all nuns. The nuncio Ormaneto, although very friendly toward Teresa, began to get qualms about the Mother Foundress's travels throughout Spain. In letters to Gracián, he confided that he was not wholly pleased with her exits from the monastery and requested some kind of gentle solution that would not sadden "this good and holy Mother."

He misjudged "this good and holy Mother." She was not saddened by the order given her from the chapter in Piacenza not to leave her monastery; she was overjoyed. It was precisely what she had been longing for: to end her days in quiet.

Travel for Teresa, with her bad health, had often been a veritable torment. In those days, even with good health, there was nothing very pleasurable about traveling. In her story, she ordinarily avoids detailed descriptions of the hardships involved in her journeys, but undoubtedly the Mother Foundress felt aversion toward them. In a passing remark she explains: "I am not recording in these foundations the great hardships endured in the traveling: the cold, the heat, the snow. . .; sometimes getting lost, at other times, being very sick and having a fever" (18, 4; 27, 17). Pointing out that she could have mentioned many bad incidents that occurred on the journeys, Teresa does go into some specifics when writing of the trip to Seville. Here the reader learns both what the travelers suffered from the scorching heat and what Teresa in addition endured from her sorry health. As for the latter, she laments: "What a thing sickness is! When we're healthy, it's easy to put up with all kinds of inconveniences" (24, 8). In this journey, too, the celebrated crossing of the Guadalquivir took place. In recounting the trip to Burgos, she again describes more about the traveling conditions. This time, in addition to her fever and a throat so sore that she couldn't eat, the travelers were chilled to the bone by the cold and the heavy rains. The wagons were forever getting stuck in the mud, and at one point all came near to being killed when crossing a flooded bridge.

A number of times on their journeys, they all got lost. Once, the guides, not really knowing the way, misguided Teresa's little group along routes not made for wagons causing the wagons to tip over. Finally, when the guides had got so completely lost that they did not know where to turn next, they excused themselves saying that they had other things to do now and that it was time for them to leave. The danger of getting lost increased, of course, after dark. The nuns' frequent chaplain for these journeys, Julián de Avila, tells in his biography of Teresa how once on a trip to Salamanca the mule carrying the money got lost after dark.[57] One time, Teresa herself got lost from the group.

"And, oh! The inns!", Teresa exclaims. They could be totally without comfort, overcrowded, dirty, and swarming with vermin. The clientele were often rowdy, perverse, and foul-mouthed; sometimes the friars and nuns were made sport of. Nor could anyone ever be certain that an inn would have food to provide for hungry travelers. On the way to Seville, Teresa and her companions stopped at the inn of Albino hoping to soothe their intense thirst and satisfy their hunger, only to find that the inn was out of water and that the sole remaining food was some salty sardines. In a later letter, Teresa writes from Seville: "It's hot, but that's easier to endure than the inn at Albino." Once, in trying to think of something terrible to compare hell to, she opts for a bad inn.[58]

The means of travel used by Teresa and her companions included, with the exception of the litter, all those used in Spain at the time: donkey, mule, horse, covered wagon, coach and carriage. The one preferred and usually used by her was the covered wagon; it kept the nuns hidden from the curiosity of the people. When necessary, she made no fuss and used the coach, a more fashionable and luxurious form of travel favored by the wealthy. It could be drawn by either horses or mules. This was a means offered to Teresa when the business matter or foundation bore some relation to the aristocracy. The coaches she had use of at various times included, for example, those belonging to the Mendozas, the family of the bishop of Avila, to Doña Luisa de la Cerda, founding benefactress of Malagón, to the princess of Eboli, for the foundation in Pastrana, and to the people of Villanueva de la Jara, who sent a coach to bring the Mother Foundress from Malagón. By far the best journey of all turned out to be the one to Soria for which Teresa had three coaches at her disposal, provided by Doña Beatriz de Beamonte and the bishops of Osma and Palencia. Although the coach could be ideal for short journeys on level and dry terrain, on a winter journey in snow and heavy rain, it could become an added burden. Such was the case in the miserable trip to Burgos in the month of January. For the last, and especially unpleasant, journey of her life, to Alba de Tormes, while she was already suffering from her final illness, Teresa was given the most luxurious vehicle she had known, the carriage of the duchess of Alba; but her health had gone beyond the state in which anything like that could be enjoyed.

Madre Teresa also learned what it was to travel by donkey in the middle of December, which she had to do so as to carry out some orders from a superior. A few other times she also traveled by donkey. But, ordinarily, when not journeying by wagon or coach, she rode the mule and was exposed to the heat of the sun or the cold winds of winter. Her visit to Duruelo in the midst of August was made by mule. Gracián, in fact, has left word of Madre Teresa's skill in handling a mule. What he did not leave on record but which we know from other sources is that he himself was not unused to being thrown from his mule. Teresa once jokingly suggested that they tie him to the saddle.

A pervading spirit marked all of Teresa's journeys: she was traveling for an ideal. Creating her own style of travel, she moved through Spain making foundations. What she in reality did was transfer the community life of Carmel into the covered wagon, joining to this life inside the wagon a system of good relationships with the group of helping companions outside of it. Inside, the group had their prioress, their schedule of prayer, a water clock, a tiny bell, their breviaries, holy water, a crucifix and some statues of our Lady, St. Joseph, or the Infant Jesus. Outside, the small group included the wagon drivers and perhaps a nobleman or a merchant or some other friend ready to lend a helping hand when needed; finally, there was the chaplain who would celebrate Mass in whatever little church they might happen upon along the way.

Inside, the Sisters had their times for laughing and joking—they were joyful solitaries—and writing and singing verses so as to help pass the long days; they also recited the Hours of the breviary and observed periods of silence. Outside, the men had to be sure they were taking the right roads, keep the mules in line, sometimes hire a barge to cross a river, or settle for damages, or retrace a road taken by mistake. The clergy and friars among them tried to maintain peace.

The muleteers were usually charmed and inspired by the Mother Foundress who was so solicitous for everyone's needs. But now and again they reverted to their old selves and resisted her pious reflections. Once after a full-day's journey in heavy rains, with no protection and unable to find a place of lodging after miles and miles of journey, the group reached an inn at nightfall only to find that there was nothing for lighting the lamps and no food. In addition, the roof was so full of leaks that the water came in everywhere even on top of the beds. Teresa, in an attempt to lift everyone's spirits, exclaimed: "Come now, take heart, these are days very meritorious for gaining heaven." The mule driver, soaked to the skin and unimpressed, responded: "I could have also gained heaven by staying home."

On approaching an inn, Madre Teresa would send someone ahead to order food and to reserve rooms. One of the rooms had to be sufficiently large to permit the nuns to stay together, and all their needs were to be placed there. On leaving the wagon, the nuns lowered their veils; once in their room, they closed the door, and a portress was appointed. In those inns where the nuns were unable to have a room for themselves, blankets were brought in and hung up so as to allow them their privacy.[59]

Illnesses

From her youth until the moment of her death, Teresa was assailed by bodily illnesses; sickness was one of the great battles of her life. Keenly observant, she has written of these illnesses with impressive objectivity, precise description, and great simplicity. When in her early twenties, already a professed nun in the monastery of the Incarnation, Doña Teresa de Ahumada began to suffer from a febrile illness, which was later seriously aggravated by some dubious methods of cure used by a quack in Becedas. Convulsions and a coma of four-days' duration followed; only slowly did she afterward recover. A critical analysis of the illness from Teresa's description and the testimony of eyewitnesses makes it possible to conclude now that the most probable cause was brucellosis, with complications of meningoencephalitis and neuritis.[60] This illness can come to an end spontaneously without leaving any serious neurological problems; nonetheless, Teresa's physical well-being was affected negatively. Her bad health, though, never interfered substantially with her capacity for intellectual and organizational work or for full spiritual growth.

Undoubtedly, the countless trials and consequent stress that

Teresa had to endure in her mystical life and her life of service as foundress must have taken their toll and contributed to her illnesses. Her own awareness of this possibility seems clear enough in some words of comfort she wrote to María de San José who was at the time in the midst of certain unpleasant troubles in Seville: "I was sorry to hear of the heart touble you have, which is very painful. But I'm not surprised, for your trials have been terrible and you are very much alone. Though the Lord has granted us the favor of giving you the virtue and courage to bear these trials, you cannot help feeling their physical effects."[61]

A further difficulty in the Mother Foundress's case, exacerbating an already delicate condition, was the penchant to take lightly any need for rest and care. It is somewhat surprising to us that the doctor had to tell her that her head would be in a better condition if she did not stay up until two in the morning writing letters and also warn her never to write after midnight.[62]

If her trials could affect her physical state, her bodily illnesses, by the same token, could affect her psyche. She confesses: "Often I complain to our Lord about how much the poor soul shares in the illness of the body. It seems the soul can do nothing but abide by the laws of the body and all its needs and changes" (29, 2).

To add to her infirmities, on Christmas eve in 1577, Teresa fell down the stairs at St. Joseph's in Avila and broke her arm. Since it did not set properly, a well known but unlicensed practitioner from Medina del Campo performed an osteoclasis. In thus breaking her bone again so as to correct the deformity, a most painful procedure, he not only failed to remedy the matter but made things worse. Teresa's arm was left maimed and useless; for the rest of her life she needed help, even for simple tasks such as dressing and undressing.

If Madre Teresa shied away from caring for herself, her own experience of bodily infirmities and spiritual trials heightened her capacity to feel compassion for other suffering people. In a letter to Gracián, speaking of how a soul can have no better sustenance than trials, she also makes it clear that this conviction does not remove the pain of seeing others suffer. "I mean there must be a whole world of difference between suffering oneself and seeing one's neighbor suffer."[63] Thus, she orders that the sick, especially, should be cared for with fullness of love, concern for their comfort, and compassion. Healthy nuns should be ready to deprive themselves rather than allow the sick to go without some deeds of kindness.

One wonders at times how much awareness of mental and bodily hygiene was present in the ascetical practices of sixteenth-century spirituality. With regard to her nuns, Teresa does show a decided concern for monastic hygiene. She wants her foundations to be made in healthy surroundings, requires good health in those entering her communities, and values it in the prioress, or at least in the subprioress if the prioress is sickly. She recommends more than six hours of sleep for her nuns. Insisting on cleanliness, she demands it particularly in the care of the sick.[64]

Teresa's writings abound with comments on a variety of illnesses: tertian and quartan fevers, heart ailments, tuberculosis, vomitings of blood, headaches, lightheadedness, stomach-aches, breast cancer, chills, colds, the plague, inflammation of the liver, gout, sciatica, typhus, tumors, side-aches, shoulder-aches, palsy, stone, rheumatism, toothaches, skin rashes, and more. She agilely and correctly employs the contemporary medical terminology.

She also demonstrates a good familiarity with the therapeutics of her day. The different remedies about which she speaks and gives advice have their basis in the sixteenth-century pharmacopoeia: orange-flower water, sarsaparilla, nuts, coriander, rhubarb, dog rose, lavender, and so on. In a doctor's written account from those times we get a glimpse of the use of these remedies: "Coriander is good but not too good. Rhubarb is used as a eupeptic, purgative, and against worms. Dog rose because of its richness in tannic acid is employed as an astringent and against diarrhea; lavender is applied in cases of rheumatism and on bruises, taken in tincture as a stimulant, and used as a disinfectant in fumigating." If what she wrote in letters and elsewhere about the symptoms, remedies, and treatment for illnesses presupposes close observation and well informed capabilities, Teresa never tried to practice medicine on her own account but always showed a respect for the science of medicine and for doctors. She would often point out that a doctor prescribed a particular remedy for her or give the advice to talk a matter over with the doctor. She was careful, as well, to distinguish between light ailments and something serious. Fever gave the warning sign for concern.[65]

In her detailed account of the incredible illnesses of Doña Catalina de Sandoval y Godínez, Teresa manifests the importance she places on getting the facts straight. Despite all her own experiences with illness, she was so astounded by the many things told to her of Doña Catalina's bodily sufferings that she inquired herself of the doctor so as to check the facts. In speaking of these illnesses of Doña Catalina, Teresa lists as well some of the healing methods of the times: bloodletting, cupping, cauterization, and pouring salt on wounds. Some of these remedies were extremely painful (22, 14–19).

As for mental and emotional illnesses, the Mother Foundress uses the term "melancholy" for the whole gamut of them. Chapter seven of the *Foundations* amounts to a little treatise on melancholy. The reader is amazed at the sharpness of its observations and the extent of its understanding of the human psyche; this from one who had not even the most elemental training or reading knowledge from books on medicine. Attributed to one of the four bodily humors, melancholy (black bile in excess) was in those times considered the cause of mental and emotional dysfunction. Teresa's little treatise on melancholy is a kind of precursor of later Spanish works on the subject. Even Andrés Velázquez's *Libro de la Melancolia*, published in Seville in 1585, comes after Teresa's death.

In this chapter Madre Teresa warns prioresses that however much they may strive to exclude from their communities any applicants who suffer from melancholy, "it is subtle and feigns death when it needs to, and thus we do not recognize it until the matter cannot be remedied" (7, 1). In admitting that one person afflicted with melancholy can be enough to disrupt the quiet of an entire community, she alerts prioresses to the contrivances that this humor uses to get its own way. One must search out and understand these contrivances in order to govern the afflicted in such a way that no harm is done to the other nuns.

The remedy Teresa proposes for those seriously afflicted still has its validity: the condition should be cared for as a major illness; the sick nun should be isolated; she should be treated with

much love, but made to understand that she cannot return to
the community as long as she thinks she will be free to do whatever she wants; on allowing her to return, an all-important
remedy will be to keep her occupied with duties so that she will
not have the opportunity to be imagining things; sometimes the
humor can be reduced by means of medicine. Teresa's sugges-
tion that such a nun not eat fish shows an awareness of the importance of diet. At the time, people probably thought that fish
was less nourishing than meat.

The Inquisition

The intermingling of Christians, Jews, and Moors in Spain
created complex religious and racial problems and prompted the
organization of a tribunal whose solution was the imposition of
Christian orthodoxy. In a land where heterodox views existed in
large number and where new heresies to the north might easily
enter and take root, the Spanish Inquisition would not brook
even the slightest diversion from the most rigid orthodoxy. Any
small deviation, it was feared, would open the way to outright
heresies. To be investigated by the Inquisition was a serious and
dangerous business, to say nothing of all the gossip and loss of
one's honor it would occasion. In her *Life*, Teresa laughed to
herself over these anxieties about being accused to the Inquisition and declared that if she had something to fear with regard
to her faith, she would go herself to seek out the Inquisitors.[66]
The opportunity for her to demonstrate such fearlessness came
when she resided in Seville, where she was accused to the Inquisition (27, 20).

Shortly after the foundation in Seville was made, the first
novices entered. Among them was a forty-year-old widowed beata
with a reputation for sanctity and already canonized by the people.
Her name was María del Corro. However, her age and her own
brand of spirituality made adaptation to the Teresian Carmelite life a demanding chore, and she had to seek dispensation
from one thing after another. Moreover, in Carmel she no longer

received the praise for her holiness on which she had become dependent. Finally, forced to admit to herself her failure, she clandestinely left the cloister telling no one of her intentions. But on discovering that many who had previously considered her a saint now ridiculed her for her inability to live in the monastery, she looked for a way to compensate. With the help of her confessor, who took her side, she denounced Madre Teresa and Isabel de San Jerónimo before the tribunal of the Inquisition asserting that they bore much in common with the *Alumbrados* and that they poked fun at the Inquisition. The news spread quickly through the city, and Gracián began to receive blame for bringing these discalced nuns to Seville. The Mother Foundress spent days under threat of being transferred to the Inquisition, and she was advised to make a general confession of her whole life. Gracián testifies that one day, while on his way to the nuns, he unexpectedly saw outside the monastery many horses and mules and recognized at once that they belonged to the Inquisitors and their ministers who were inside. When he did get to speak to Teresa, he found her to be exuberantly happy at the prospect of having to suffer some affront.[67] Teresa herself wrote: "For these calumnies not only failed to make me sad but gave me so great an accidental joy that I could not restrain myself" (27, 20). She goes on to say that she is not surprised about David going before the ark singing and dancing, for it is what she felt like doing at the time. But Gracián did not feel like singing and dancing. He was in anguish over the whole matter. He could not erase from his memory the fact that it was he who had ordered Teresa to come to Seville and had done so contrary to the locutions and inner light she had received from the Lord in prayer which informed her that it would be better for her to make a foundation in Madrid.

Whether Teresa was obliged to leave the cloister to testify before the tribunal is uncertain. However, at this time, she did write the accounts of her spiritual life for Rodrigo Alvarez, a Jesuit consultant to the Inquisition.[68] In the end, Teresa was acquitted of the charges, having impressed the tribunal with the humility and wisdom of her responses and the spiritual quality of her account written for Alvarez. María del Corro, though, did

manage to touch a sore spot in the community when she accused
Isabel de San Jerónimo along with Teresa. Isabel was a sufferer
from melancholy who would hardly have been the community's
choice to present before the Inquisitors.

Conflict Among The Friars

Blessed John Soreth, when prior general of the Carmelite
order (1451-1471), sought to promote the life of observance and
to remove all the abuses characteristic of conventual friars in
the fifteenth century. He particularly concerned himself with
practices that had gained acceptance but which were out of
keeping with poverty. With these practices, friars were allowed
to have unlimited funds throughout their lifetime and to possess
objects not consumed by use so that they could even bequeath
these latter to other Carmelites or communities. This crumbling
of the practice of poverty gave rise to a double standard of living,
one for the well-to-do friars and one for the needy. But Spain remained isolated from the rest of the order, and consequently the
zealous reform efforts of John Soreth, who had never set foot on
the Iberian peninsula, bore no results there. Neither did any
reform movements rise spontaneously among Carmelites in
Spain despite the general interest in the betterment of religious
orders on the part of the Crown.

During Nicholas Audet's term as prior general (1524-1562),
the Carmelites again turned seriously to reform. The matters
for reform concerned again the practice of poverty, but also the
following: education, to correct ignorance among the brethren
and to prevent the inept and unlearned from ascending the
pulpit; Divine Office, in that every house with at least six priests
was obliged to celebrate the day and night Office in choir; and
laws dealing with residence outside the monastery and exits
from the house. But Audet's efforts to bring about reform in
Spain occasioned an exodus of friars. In Castile, over half the
personnel of the province abandoned the order, leaving that
province with few houses and a scarcity in numbers. In Andalusia, all the reform efforts simply failed.

Following Audet in the leadership role of prior general came John Baptist Rossi, Teresa's esteemed Rubeo. He continued the reforming effort but within the framework of existing obligations. When he came to Spain for his visitation in 1566, the province of Castile, reformed under Audet, consisted of nine monasteries and a little more than a hundred friars.

In chapter two of her *Foundations*, Teresa writes glowingly of Rubeo, who with much kindness consoled and encouraged her. One matter, however, about which the prior general showed reluctance had to do with the foundation of some houses for friars who would live in a style similar to Teresa's nuns. When the Madre wrote to him again after his departure, making her request once more, Rubeo acceded. In a letter from Barcelona, August 10, 1567, he gave his permission, insisting that these foundations be referred to as houses or monasteries of contemplative Carmelites. These friars were also to help their neighbor when the occasion arose and were to observe the "old constitutions" (Soreth's, revised by Audet and Rubeo himself). They were to be subject to the provincial, and only two houses were to be allowed. Not having succeeded in his attempts to reform the Andalusians, Rubeo shows a certain fear of possible problems in the tone of his letter. "It is not our intention to give occasion to hellish quarrels," he says, "but to promote the perfection of Carmelite religious life." The contemplative Carmelites must live united to the obedience of the province of Castile, and "if at any time any friar under pretext of living in greater perfection should seek to separate himself from the province by the favor of princes and with briefs and other concessions of Rome, we pronounce and declare them men moved and tempted by the evil spirit, authors of seditions, quarrels, contentions, and ambitions to the deceit and loss of their souls."[69] As an apostolic commissary at the time, Rubeo was empowered to use a formula employed by the Holy See in its own documents. Unfortunately, many of the things Rubeo feared actually took place.

If Teresa proved capable of preserving homogeneity and coherence among the foundations of nuns through her inspirational leadership, she did not achieve this among the friars. After her idyllic account in chapter fourteen of the *Foundations* about the life lived by the first little community of friars in Duruelo, she makes the significant remark that they paid no attention to her when she made some observations concerning their austerities.

Duruelo was so isolated that growth came slowly. Teresa was delighted, then, when she met Ambrosio Mariano who provided her with the opportunity for making a second foundation of friars, this one in Pastrana. Growth in numbers came more quickly in Pastrana, but some of the new members happened to be friars from Andalusia who had got into trouble with the prior general in his attempts to bring about reform there. In fact, Andalusia soon became the source of nothing but trouble for the Mother Foundress's ideal. When the prior general heard about some of the new admissions, he wrote in a letter August 8, 1570: "We have heard that things have been happening that could give rise to dissent and quarrels." He requires members of the provinces of Spain and Portugal to have his written permission before seeking admission to "our contemplative Carmelites, or discalced as they are popularly called." He then goes on to forbid the contemplative Carmelites to receive those members of the Andalusian province who had been punished by him or had been rebellious and contumacious in their obligation of obedience to him. He forbids this "lest the whole flock of contemplatives be corrupted by them."[70]

At the very time that Rubeo had been in Spain on his mission of reform, Philip II was engaged in plans for his own reform of the religious orders, the Carmelites among them. This comes as no surprise when it is pointed out that according to Philip's information the cause for the success of Lutheranism in the north of Europe could be attributed to laxity among the friars.[71]

With the brief *Maxime cuperemus* obtained from Pius V on December 2, 1566, the king, in a first move, instructed bishops to carry out visitations of religious orders. These visitations were to be done through delegates who in turn were to be accompanied by serious religious appointed by the provincial of the respective religious order. But as for Carmelites, Trinitarians, and Mercedarians (orders that were considered to be lacking in the number of observants who would be able to assist the bishops in carrying out the reform of the conventuals), another brief, *Superioribus mensibus,* April 16, 1567, instructed that two Dominicans were to accompany the bishop's delegate.

This action of the king ignored the privilege of religious exemption, held by these orders, and also the decree of the Council of Trent that entrusted reform to the religious superiors. Moreover, the Carmelites in the general chapter of 1564 had pronounced themselves to be observants and denounced conventualism. Rubeo made a report to the Holy See, both giving an account of his visitation in Spain and asking that the king's visitation be revoked. But in the meantime, Philip's first steps toward reform failed. The situation, in fact, worsened when Philip decided to dispense with the assistance of the Dominicans and leave everything in the hands of diocesan clergy and laymen. The Carmelites in Andalusia who had been expelled or removed from office by Rubeo managed to find favor with the new visitators, were reinstated, and were absolved from excommunication. Learning of this, Rubeo indignantly pointed out that the excommunication he had imposed was reserved by Pope Callistus III to the Holy See.

Perhaps because of the complaints of the superiors general, Pius V decided to remove the visitation from the hands of the bishops. Formally revoking the brief *Superioribus mensibus,* on January 13, 1570, the pope turned to another solution and put the work of reform into the hands of the generals, each being responsible for his own order. He made a careful exception, however, regarding the Carmelites, Trinitarians, and Mercedarians, entrusting their reform to Dominican friars who would remain in their offices as apostolic commissaries for four years. At the end of the four years, the mandate would be extended if necessary.

Pedro Fernández and Francisco Vargas, two Dominican friars, were named visitators of the Carmelites, the former of those in Castile, the latter, of those in Andalusia. They received powers to move religious from house to house and province to province, to assist superiors in their offices, and to depute other superiors from among either the Dominicans or the Carmelites. They were entitled to perform all acts necessary for the visitation, correction, and reform of both head and members of all houses of friars and nuns.

Rubeo responded anxiously by dispatching twenty commissaries to defend the rights of the Carmelite order in Spain. These commissaries were given instructions not to allow directives contrary to the order's legislation for reform or to permit any infringement on the order's privileges granted by the Holy See. Much of the controversy that arose between Teresa's friars and those of the observance grew out of the various interpretations that the authorities in question gave to the powers granted them by the Holy See.

The Dominican Fernández tactfully and diplomatically carried out his responsibilities within the normal legislative channels of the Carmelite order. It was he who ordered Teresa in 1571, after his visitation of the Incarnation in Avila, to interrupt her work as foundress and return to her original monastery as prioress (19, 6-7; 21, 1). Teresa received instructions to do all she could to improve the material and spiritual welfare of that house.

She accepted only reluctantly,[72] and the nuns of the Incarnation protested vehemently at first. But Madre Teresa knew how to win their favor and soon managed to solve some of the hopeless problems of poverty. For assistance in her efforts to improve the spiritual life of the nuns, Teresa appealed to Fernández for Fray John of the Cross, then rector at the new Carmelite college in Alcalá, that he might serve as confessor for the nuns. Fray John stayed on as confessor at the Incarnation until his sad capture and imprisonment in 1577. At the Incarnation, the two saints acted as powerful spiritual catalysts enabling Fernández to write to the duchess of Alba as early as 1573 that though in the monastery of the Incarnation there were one hundred thirty nuns, there was as much tranquility and sanctity there as among the ten or twelve discalced nuns in the monastery of Alba. It was during this time, while she officiated as prioress of the Incarnation, that Teresa under the direction of John of the Cross received the grace of spiritual marriage.

Between Teresa and the Dominican Fernández a deep mutual respect and an easy working relationship developed. More and more Madre Teresa turned to Fernández for her necessary permissions. In June of 1571 Teresa had written to Doña María de Mendoza, sister of the bishop of Avila, about a certain permission: "We can ask for a licence from Father Provincial, and your Ladyship can tell the community to receive them. As an alternative, we can go to Father Visitator, who will give his consent at once. I can work with him better than with Father Provincial, who simply will not answer my letters however often I write to him."

As in the case of the nuns, Fernández also placed Teresa's friars in positions of responsibility, hoping thereby to promote reform. This move, however, was damaging to the new contemplative communities just starting to get on their feet.

Andalusia was another story. Desiring to push reform among the friars of his district, Francisco Vargas wrote in November of 1571 to Fray Ambrosio Mariano, whom Teresa had recruited for the foundation of her friars in Pastrana, and ordered him to make a foundation in Seville like the one they had in Pastrana. This foundation, he decided would be exempt from the jurisdiction of the Carmelite provincial in Andalusia and would receive only those aspirants coming directly from the world. Vargas's orders to Mariano went contrary to the restrictions Rubeo had set up for the contemplative friars. In reality, by turning to Teresa's friars for help in reforming the Carmelite order, both visitators drew them beyond the limits established by the prior general when he allowed for a few houses of contemplative friars.

During the years 1570-1575 seven houses of contemplative friars were founded in addition to the two original ones (Duruelo and Pastrana) in which Teresa played a more direct role. The four new ones in Castile (Alcalá, Altomira, La Roda, and Almodóvar del Campo) were founded with the prior general's permission. The problem arose over those founded in Andalusia (in Seville, Granada, and La Peñuela). These latter three were requested, against Rubeo's orders, by the Dominican visitator Vargas.

By the time the four year term of the Dominican visitators had expired along with Teresa's term as prioress at the Incarnation, the total picture had so changed that the prior general, the provincials, and even Teresa herself were alarmed. Rubeo was alarmed because monasteries were being founded apart from consultation with the prior general and even against his express prohibition; the provincials, because the new Carmelite communities arising within their districts were practically autonomous, with innovations and customs foreign to the order's tradition; Teresa, because she observed the friars going off in a direction different from the one she had envisioned. In her *Foundations* she reveals her feeling when she writes that if it were not for the trust she had in God she would have at times regretted ever having founded the friars. She recognized that they had no leader and laments that they had no constitutions that they all agreed upon. "In each house they did as they saw fit," she disapprovingly comments (23, 12). Without presenting her reasons, which we can only guess at, Teresa at first wanted no foundations of her friars or nuns in Andalusia. When, in fact, she made the foundation in Beas, she thought she was making it in Castile. Not until the deed was done did she discover that, though in the civil province of Castile, Beas belonged to the ecclesiastical jurisdiction of Andalusia.

It was here in Beas that her overwhelming first meeting with "Padre Maestro Fray Jerónimo Gracián de la Madre de Dios" took place. Here was the answer to the Mother Foundress's prayers. A friar with the learning, spirituality, and apparent political skills necessary to salvage what Teresa had begun. Of this elevating experience in Beas she writes: "So during those days I went about with such excessive consolation and happiness that indeed I was surprised at myself" (24, 2). But what was perhaps most remarkable about Gracián was that he actually listened to Teresa's opinions about the friars, their problems, and other matters. Later, Gracián himself wrote enthusiastically about this meeting: "She taught me everything she knew, giving me so many doctrines, rules, and counsels that I could have written a large book about what she taught me."[73] Previous to this fateful meeting, Gracián had been named apostolic visitator of the Carmelites in Andalusia by Vargas. At the time of the appointment, Gracián had been professed little more than a year, having been ordained to the priesthood and having received his doctorate in theology before entering the order.

When the Carmelite order convened in chapter at Piacenza, May 22, 1575, no time was lost in addressing the question of the discalced friars in Andalusia. The chapter reaffirmed in no uncertain terms the position the prior general had thus far taken. Those who had been made superiors against the obedience due superiors within the order itself, or who had accepted offices or lived in monasteries or places prohibited by the same superiors, should be removed. The monasteries of discalced friars in Andalusia were to be abandoned within three days. The friars and nuns were not to go completely barefoot, "since nowhere in the rule is such a thing prescribed." Neither were they to be referred to as "discalced," but as "contemplatives" or "primitives." No rift was to be created in the order by calling some "discalced" and others "of the cloth."

The previous year, on August 13, 1574, Gregory XIII, the new pope, had declared the end of the Dominican visitation and ordained that from then on the Carmelites should be visited by the prior general and his delegates. However, what had been established by the Dominican visitators was to remain in effect. Afterward, the papal nuncio Ormaneto received assurance that the recall of the Dominican visitators in no way affected his own powers as nuncio to visit and reform religious orders. Offended because the visitation had been called officially to a close without a word to him, the king imperiously declared Gregory's papal brief to be invalid because it lacked his royal placet.

It was precisely while Gracián was in Beas that the nuncio, Ormaneto, sent for him in Madrid, and on August 3, 1575, the nuncio not only confirmed Gracián in his present position but extended his authority as reformer and visitator to the friars and nuns of Castile as well. Gracián's motive in accepting arose not so much out of any desire to reform the friars of the observance but to protect Teresa's friars, or the contemplatives, from being undone. Also, during the time of his visitation, he aimed to make more foundations of his own friars so that the group might become well rooted. Others hurled accusations of boldness and ambition at him for accepting the charge.[74]

Previously, while in Beas, Gracián had ordered the Mother Foundress to go deeper into Andalusia against her strong desires and make a foundation in Seville, a rich and sensuous city of thirty thousand inhabitants, looked upon as the gate to the Indies. Teresa resignedly complied, writing: "This is a favor our Lord grants me, to have the opinion that these superiors are right in everything" (24, 4). Indeed, the foundation in Seville turned out to be one of the most trying of all Teresa's foundations. If her brother Lorenzo had not returned at that time from the Indies and offered his assistance, the Madre's foundation might never have succeeded. The people of Andalusia were not at first as interested in helping her as were those in Castile.

An added trial for Teresa now was her fear for Gracián's life. When, as reformer, Gracián returned from Madrid in 1575 to the Carmelite friars' monastery in Seville with his patent letter from the nuncio, the friars demanded that he give it to them so that they could make a copy of it. When Gracián understandably refused to let it out of his possession, a minor revolt took place among the eighty friars. The rumor moved quickly through the city that Gracián's life was in danger. Of course, it made its way to the doors of Teresa's Carmel where the nuns were already in prayer since they knew that this was the day, the feast of Our Lady's Presentation in the Temple (November 21) in which the feared visitation was to begin. They were also familiar with those frightening stories about how, not long before, a reformer of friars in Catalonia had been stabbed to death. As happens with rumors, by the time the tale reached the Carmel, the version told that Gracián had been killed. As a reprisal for the uproar and seeming disobedience, and against Teresa's advice, the young Carmelite visitator excommunicated the friars, thereby bringing more scandal to an already highly scandalized city.

Though Fray Jerónimo had asserted his authority, the quarreling over whether or not he had any did not allow him to begin his visitation until January. As things turned out, though, Gracián was anything but a tyrant to be feared. In the process of his visitation, there were those, in fact, who complained against him that he was not carrying out the visitation with the required severity. These advocates of greater severity were in particular Fray Ambrosio Mariano and Juan Calvo de Padilla, a Castilian priest who worked on the reform of the religious orders and who was esteemed by the king. On the other hand, there were those who resisted Gracián's measured steps for improvement by spreading malicious lies about him, hoping to damage his reputation in Madrid and Rome.

During the period in which some of these perturbing events were taking place, Rubeo, on December 10, 1575, appointed Jerónimo Tostado visitator, reformer, and commissary general of the Spanish provinces. His instructions to Tostado were to enforce the statutes laid down by the visitators of Pius V, those of the general chapter of Piacenza and especially those of Gergory XIII. There were two restrictions made on his powers: he could not grant permission to anyone to join the contemplative friars nor could he allow the contemplatives to make any foundations. Rubeo reserved these rights to himself. Since Tostado's mission was preceded by the rumor that he had come to destroy Teresa's work, Ormaneto advised Tostado to postpone his visitation in Andalusia and go to Portugal first.

The movement among Teresa's friars had now gone so far that it was impossible to reverse the tide. Their numbers came close to three hundred, and they had gained considerable prestige among the people and at the royal court. They were also receiving strong support from Ormaneto. On August 3, 1576, under Gracián's initiative, these friars declared themselves a separate province, which consisted of the ten monasteries of nuns in addition to the nine of friars.

In June of 1575, Teresa herself had already written a worried letter to Rubeo in an attempt to explain everything. She assured him of her love, admiration, and prayers and of the prayers of all the nuns as well. As for the friars, she writes frankly: "They are defending their position, and I really think that they are Your Reverence's faithful sons and desire not to displease you. But still I cannot fail to blame them. It now seems they are beginning to realize that they should have followed a different course so as not to have displeased Your Reverence." After pointing out that the houses were founded by virtue of the apostolic authority of Vargas, she mentions the number of the friars and the esteem they held in the minds of the people and even of the king. She does this so as to warn Rubeo against any drastic measures that would stir up the people and king against the order. Then she

pleads: "As a true father, forget the past and remember that
Your Reverence is a servant of the Virgin and that she will be displeased if you cease to help those who, by the sweat of their brow,
seek the increase of her order." In another plea for peace, in
November of 1575, she urges Gracián to communicate with the
prior general and show him the proper deference: "It is enough
that things are being done against his will without your having
to fail to send him some kind words or to pay any attention to
him. You see, my Father, it is to him we promised obedience,
and nothing can be lost thereby."

In a further effort to explain to Rubeo, in February 1576, she
zealously defends Gracián, describing how he resisted and was
unwilling to undertake the visitation in Andalusia which was imposed on him. In the same vein, she seeks to raise Rubeo's opinion
of his own Andalusian Carmelites: "They have helped us in every
way since we have been here, and, as I wrote to your Reverence, I
have found here men of much talent and learning. I would certainly be happy if we had some like them in our Castilian province." And she adds in her characteristic fashion: "I am not surprised that they are tired of all the visitations and changes."

Turning again to the question of Gracián and Mariano, she
obviously puts all that she has into a plea in their favor: "But let
Your Reverence consider that it is characteristic of children to
err and of parents to pardon and not look at faults. For the love
of our Lord, I beseech your Reverence to do me this favor." She
then puts in a plea for herself, that Rubeo might listen to her
suggestions: "Consider that this would be advisable for many
reasons which perhaps, Your Reverence, being over there, does
not understand as well as I do here, and that, even though we
women are not suited for giving counsel, sometimes we are
right."

Teresa returned from Seville to Castile in June of 1576, and
Gracián concluded his visitation in Andalusia in May of 1577.
Before calling a chapter in the south, Gracián journeyed to Madrid to consult with the nuncio. But an unexpected disaster over-
turned his plans. Ormaneto died in the odor of sanctity on the
night of June 17, 1577, with nothing to his name, having given
all to the poor. Though the king informed Gracián that the lat-

ter's faculties as visitator had not ceased with the death of the nuncio, the new nuncio, Felipe Sega, did not agree and sought to persuade the king to give up the plan of reform initiated by Ormaneto so that the religious orders would be left free to reform themselves. In addition, the nuncio informed Gracián that his faculties had ceased with the death of Ormaneto.

Though Sega had come to Spain with a bias against Teresa and her friars, he wanted first of all to investigate the entire matter to form a better judgment of what was transpiring. The king, who on the contrary was biased in favor of Teresa and her friars, approved but also insisted that the nuncio with the help of assistants obtain correct information about the differences between the two groups of Carmelites.

When the contemplative friars with seeming contempt celebrated a chapter at Almodóvar del Campo, in October of 1578, a chapter that had been decreed two years previously by Gracián when he had been in power, Sega took quick action. On October 16, 1578, he declared the chapter null and void and under pain of excommunication forbade Antonio de Jesús, who had been elected provincial, to act as provincial. Sega for safe measure then placed Teresa's friars and nuns under the jurisdiction of the provincials of Castile and Andalusia, Juan Gutiérrez and Diego Cárdenas respectively. These provincials clamorously asserted their authority, serving notice of it to the contemplative friars and nuns in a rude manner, scandalous to the people. Teresa writes of the nuns' experience when the provincial's emissaries came to St. Joseph's in Avila: "It was a morning of trial: all who were there—justices, lawyers, and gentlemen—were shocked at their lack of proper religious conduct, and I was very distressed. I would have gladly told them what I thought, but we didn't dare speak."[75] These public scenes were repeated in the other Teresian monasteries both in Castile and Andalusia.

The leaders among the Teresian friars, Antonio de Jesús, Ambrosio Mariano, Gabriel de la Assunción, and Gracián were excommunicated and placed under arrest in various monasteries until the investigation could be completed. Gracián was confined to the Carmel of Madrid where, he honestly admits, some of the brethren among the observants treated him very well.

Previous to all of this turmoil, Rubeo had died in September of 1578, at the age of 69, as a result of injuries suffered two years before in a fall from his mule. Teresa wrote sorrowfully of this to Gracián: "On the day I heard it I did nothing but weep and weep and I felt great pain over all the trials we had caused him, which he certainly did not deserve. If we had gone to him about the matter everything would have proceeded smoothly."[76]

While the leaders were in prison, Teresa carried on a campaign in favor of her friars through letters and recommendations to as many influential people as she could think of. She fired off letters to Madrid, Rome, and elsewhere, to the king, to bishops, and to noblemen, to anyone she thought could help.

When the nuncio's investigators learned of the insolent ways in which the provincials were carrying out the visitations of the contemplative houses and of the lies that had been uttered against Gracián, some among them wished first to take care of that matter and leave the investigation, especially of the alleged faults of Gracián, for later. Sega said "No," insisting that first Gracián be punished.

Gracián was in a dilemma. He knew that if he were to deny the accusations made against him and a process in his defense were begun, Teresa's friars would in the meantime lose out. On the other hand, if he submitted to the charges, he would be admitting through his silence to what was not true. Consulting a number of theologians who, as is their custom, came up with different opinions, he decided finally, for the good of the discalced, not to bother defending himself.[77]

The appointed judges became scrupulous about the penalty to inflict on him because they knew he was not blameworthy. Sega accused one of them of trying to be an advocate rather than a judge; the accused judge snapped back that Sega was trying to be an accuser rather than a judge. In the end, Gracián was absolved of all censures, but deprived of active and passive voice, sent to the monastery of the contemplatives in Alcalá, given penances, and forbidden to write or receive letters, especially from nuns, or otherwise interfere in the affairs of the order.

As for Mariano, Teresa confesses in the above-mentioned letter to Rubeo in defense of the impetuous friar, that she herself had suffered again and again from him but learned to pass it over since she knew what a good man he was. When the commission came to investigate Mariano and take his confession, the notary asked him when it was he had last spoken or written to the king. As might have been expected, Mariano's reply was quick and flippant: "not since the last time." When the notary rebuked him for making fun of the nuncio, Mariano defended himself by asserting that the question deserved no other response since it implied that a subject was at fault for speaking or writing to a king as Catholic as Philip. Of course, the king was kept informed of all these happenings. Perhaps he even smiled, a rare accomplishment for Philip II, on hearing the story about Mariano. Understandably, Mariano escaped punishment and set off for Jerez de la Frontera on an engineering project sponsored by the king.[78]

At that point Nicolás Doria entered the scene. When at the end of the fourteenth century Barcelona's leading private banks failed, Italian financiers began to assume the role of principal bankers to the kings of Aragón. Genoa in particular made skillful use of opportunities and gradually succeeded in converting itself into the financial capital of the western Mediterranean. The Genoese settled in Córdoba, Cádiz, and Seville and entrenched themselves at one strategic point after another in the Castilian economy. Nicolás Doria was a Genoese banker who had come to the notice of the king on account of his abilities. But so greatly was he frightened on one occasion in which he almost perished in a shipwreck that he converted completely to God and sacrificed his fortune to the poor, ultimately joining Teresa's friars in Seville at the age of forty-two. It was to Doria that Teresa turned when all the leaders of her friars were under arrest or in exile. The shrewd Genoese banker succeeded in disguising his real reasons for being in Madrid and while living in a monastery of the observant Carmelites managed the affairs of Teresa's friars without raising the least suspicion.

After Gracián received his sentence, a member of the investigating commission resigned, forcing the nuncio Sega to ask the king for a replacement. In response Philip II, "took the initiative to favor us" and appointed Teresa's close friend, the Dominican

Pedro Fernández. Of Fernández, Teresa says: "He knew well the truth about how each group lived, for the desire of us all was nothing other than that this be known." And expressing the relief she felt on hearing the news, she adds: "And so when I saw that the king had named him, I considered the matter taken care of, as by the mercy of God it is" (28, 6). What the commission did was to place Angel de Salazar, a former provincial of the observant Carmelites in Castile, in charge of the contemplatives. He was, in Gracián's view, a gentle and discreet man whose main concern was to console the afflicted and promote peace.[79]

At the beginning of chapter 28 in her *Foundations*, Teresa gives a quick sketch of these events and promises that they will be written up by someone who had more firsthand information about the whole affair than she. This "someone" was Gracián who did later write his account, recently discovered, of the friars' foundations. What Teresa insistently reminds her readers is that in all the sorry conflict, her greatest trial was the displeasure of the prior general. She sums up her dilemma and the unhappy situation in chapter 28:

> "And so that I might not be helping the friars make foundations, he was induced into becoming displeased with me, which was the greatest trial I suffered in the work of these foundations, even though I have suffered many. On the one hand, very learned men who were my confessors would not agree that I should stop and counseled me to help toward the growth of the work, pointing out that I clearly rendered service to our Lord and helped toward the increase of our order; and on the other hand, going against the will of my superior was like a death to me. For apart from the obligation I had toward him because he was my superior, I loved him very tenderly and there were many reasons for obeying him. It is true that even though I wanted to please him by obeying his order, I could not because there were apostolic visitors whom I was obliged to obey" (28., 2).

During the years of these troubles, Teresa was prevented from making any more foundations. Instead, as she points out, "we were all occupied unceasingly in prayers and penances so that our Lord would preserve the houses already founded if doing so would be for His service." Not until four years after the foundation in Seville did she once again, in 1580, take to the road. This was the year in which Teresa's friars were given the permission to form a separate province, "which was all that we were desiring for the sake of our peace and tranquility." Teresa summed up the happy outcome: "Now we are all at peace, calced and discalced; no one can hinder us from serving our Lord. Hence, my Brothers and Sisters, since His Majesty has heard your prayers so well, let us make haste to serve Him" (29, 30-32).

The Last Days

A peasant girl, born in 1549 in Almendral (in the province of Toledo), entered St. Joseph's in Avila at the age of twenty-one and took the name Ana de San Bartolomé. Favored by God with extraordinary mystical graces, this Carmelite, who was beatified in 1917, accepted them with remarkable simplicity, and as a result of these graces felt strong desires to serve others in the community, sometimes taking on three jobs at a time. After Teresa broke her arm on Christmas eve of 1577, she chose Ana to act as both her infirmarian and secretary. Blessed Ana became Teresa's constant companion. It is to her that we owe the straightforward, poignant account of Teresa's last days.[80]

When Madre Teresa left Avila on January 2, 1582, for the foundation in Burgos she took her niece Teresita, the daughter of her brother Lorenzo, with her. Teresita, though still not sixteen, had been living with the nuns in the enclosure with the hope of becoming a member of the community when old enough. The reason Teresa brought her niece to Burgos was to avoid giving some of the unimpressed relatives a chance to pressure the young girl into leaving so that they might gain Don Lorenzo's bequest to the monastery of St. Joseph's. Once the drawn-out resistance of the archbishop of Burgos to the new foundation of nuns wore down and the foundation was established, Teresa eagerly, though still in a precarious state of health, set about plans to return to Avila. The time for Teresita's profession was approaching, and she did not want to be "taking this young girl from one place to another." In addition, Teresa's orders from Gracián were to return to her monastery in Avila to act as prioress there as soon as the foundation in Burgos was made.

Ana de San Bartolomé has pointed out that in the dreadful journey to Burgos with the rains, snow, and flooded roads and bridges, Teresa's health was no better than the weather. So wet were they all on their arrival in Burgos that they stayed before the warm fire that night longer than usual. This caused Teresa so much harm that she began to experience dizziness during the night and to suffer from severe vomitings. Since her throat was already inflamed, these latter caused a bleeding sore. During the three following months, with all their disappointments over prospects for a foundation in Burgos, Teresa was seriously ill, and her throat was so sore that she had to live on liquids.

Finally, at the end of July, she was able to leave Burgos. She stopped off at Palencia and remained there until August 25 when she left for Valladolid. In a letter from Valladolid on August 26, she discloses her plan to be there until September 8, the feast of our Lady, then to proceed to Medina, and finally, "with the help of God, . . . [to] be in Avila by the end of this month."

The Mother Foundress's stay in Valladolid was unpleasant. Some of Teresa's relatives, in particular the mother-in-law of her nephew Francisco, were protesting Don Lorenzo's will, and María Bautista, the prioress of Valladolid, a relative and long-standing friend of Teresa's, favored the protesting relatives. Since the Mother Foundress held out firmly against them, María Bautista became ill-tempered. According to Ana de San Bartolomé, when they were leaving the prioress slammed the door on them telling them to go and never return. Teresa expressed her feelings in a letter to Gracián: "I have had a difficult time here with Don Francisco's mother-in-law. She is a strange woman."[81] She goes on to say that since the claim of the monastery in Avila is sound she trusts in God that the monastery will eventually inherit everything.

Arriving probably September 17 in Medina, with the intention of remaining about ten days and then moving on to Avila, Teresa received a distressing order. Antonio de Jesús who was acting as vicar provincial while Gracián was in Andalusia came to Medina with the news that the Mother Foundress must go to Alba de Tormes because of the election of a prioress that was to take place there and because the duchess of Alba wanted to see her. Still weak from her lingering illness, longing to get back to Avila, Teresa fell into a deep sadness. The vicar provincial's orders and their effect on the Madre remained fixed in Ana's mind. This incident became for the devoted infirmarian a key example of Teresa's virtue. Ana testifies that she had never seen Teresa suffer so much over anything superiors had ordered her.

As for the election of a prioress in Alba, it seems there was little that was edifying in the community. No doubt Father Antonio thought Teresa's presence would inspire better behavior and change some attitudes. In a previous letter, dated August 6, to the founding benefactress, Teresa Layz, Madre Teresa indicated some of the problems of the Alba community and bluntly states her displeasure over the conduct of some of the nuns. She worries that no prioress will want to stay there very long since so many are trying to get out of the office. "If the nuns are what they ought to be," the Madre writes, "what will it matter to them who the prioress is? But these are childish ways and reveal attachments that are far from being appropriate for discalced nuns, nor are they found in other houses." This is the community in which Teresa was to end her days.

But before she left Medina, the Mother Foundress also met with some unpleasant behavior by the prioress there. When she made an observation about something that was not going well, the prioress, Alberta Bautista, took the matter badly, became upset, and went to her room. Teresa, wearied that her remark would be so upsetting to someone who usually showed a good spirit, grew heavy of heart and also went to her cell without eating and without sleeping the entire night. The next morning when they left, Ana tells us, they were sent on their way with nothing to eat for the journey. At one point, near Peñaranda de Bacamonte, Teresa thought she was going to faint, so ill and weak did she feel. There was no food to give her other than some dried figs. Blessed Ana records her own distressed feelings: "When I saw that nothing could be found to buy, I could not look at the Saint without weeping, for judging by her face she seemed half dead. I can never describe the anguish I then felt. My heart seemed to be breaking, and I could only weep when I saw the plight she was in, for I saw her dying and could do nothing to help her."[82]

The travelers arrived in Alba around six in the evening, probably on September 21, the feast of St. Matthias. Greeting the nuns with much happiness and peace, Teresa then told them of her exhaustion, "God help me, how tired I am," and went to bed earlier than she had in years. Ana doubted whether she had a healthy bone in her body.

The Mother Foundress, though, was not yet daunted, and for the next eight days was up and down, receiving Communion daily, even reciting the Divine Office, and attending as well to some business matters in the parlor. One of the visitors to the parlor during these days was the troubled Teresa Layz who undoubtedly wanted to discuss the coming elections and other community problems.

Another of the visitors was Agustín de los Reyes, one of her friars, desirous of convincing Teresa that the nuns in Salamanca should purchase another house in that university town. But Teresa opposed the idea because the desired house was in too noisy a place. After three hours of conversation with the Madre in which he failed to get her to budge, Fray Agustín concluded by telling her that nothing else could be done anyway since the deed was already done. "The deed is done?" asked Teresa, and then she categorically stated, "anything but done, nor will it ever be."[83] Eight days after her death, the negotiations for the new house in Salamanca collapsed.

Also visiting Teresa during these days, perhaps on September 28, was her sister Doña Juana de Ahumada to whom Teresa manifested her desire to move on to Avila. But on September 29 the Madre went to bed never to rise again. She had suffered a hemorrhaging from which it was understood that she would die. Doctors who have studied the remaining descriptions of her last illness believe that the actual cause of Teresa's death was cancer of the uterus.

On October 1, the community held their elections for prioress.

They had attempted to discuss these matters with the Madre but she had refused to get involved.

On October 3, in the morning, the barber-surgeon put the Mother Foundress through the painful ordeal of cupping, a remedy that was prevalent in those times and meant to facilitate the excretion of certain liquids and humors.

At five in the afternoon, Teresa asked that Padre Antonio bring her Communion. Although he wanted to postpone it till the next day, he finally gave in to her wishes. While waiting for the Blessed Sacrament, she asked the Sisters to pardon her for the bad example she had given and to obey the rule and constitutions with much perfection. She begged them not to follow in her footsteps since she had been the worst in observing them.

When the Eucharist was brought in, her countenance changed and grew radiant with a kind of reverent beauty, making her look much younger. The impulses of love became so ardent that it seemed she who had been dying now wanted to leap from the bed to receive her Lord. She spoke aloud fervent words of love: "O my Lord and my Spouse, now the hour has arrived for us to go forth from this exile, and my soul rejoices in oneness with You over what I have so much desired." She also uttered fervent prayers of thanksgiving to God for having made her a daughter of the Church and enabling her to die within it. Confessing that she was a great sinner, she prayed over and over the prayers of psalm 51: "a heart contrite and humbled, O God, you will not spurn"; "cast me not out of your presence"; "a clean heart create for me, O God." At nine in the evening she asked to be anointed and assisted in reciting the psalms and other prayers.

In the testimony given by witnesses, there is a general agreement concerning the themes of the prayers spoken aloud by Teresa on the eve of her death before and after receiving the Eucharist and after receiving the Sacrament of the Sick. On the one hand, she revealed her intense feelings of sorrow at being a sinner, repeating pleas for mercy from God. This she did through verses taken from a psalm and spoken in Latin as she had learned them through choral recitation of the prayer of the Church. On the other hand she revealed her awareness of approaching union with Christ her Bridegroom and her urgent longings for that moment. The words denote an active surge of loving energy and searching rather than an attitude of passive waiting. "Now the hour has struck."

Further, in her thankfulness for being a daughter of the Church, she rejoiced in the thought of her Mother the Church, where she found the deposit of revelation, the norm of faith, the administration of the sacraments, the Christian family; this Church was now to offer her the Blood of Christ, the grace of redemption.

The following day, the feast of St. Francis (the little poor man of Assisi), her face was aglow, and with a crucifix in her hands she remained in prayer, in deep quiet and peace, without speaking or stirring throughout the whole day. In the evening, a couple of hours before she died, Padre Antonio told Blessed Ana who had been continually at her foundress's side to go and get something to eat. But Teresa began looking about, and when Antonio asked her if she was looking for Sister Ana, she gestured affirmatively. When Ana returned, Teresa smiled and with tender love took the humble Sister's arms and placed her head in them. In this manner the saintly Madre remained until she died between nine and ten that evening. She was surrounded by all the nuns in the community. Her niece Teresita, Blessed Ana, Padre Antonio de Jesús, and Padre Tomás de la Asención were also present.

After her death, her countenance turned as white as alabaster and being freed of every wrinkle took on an extraordinary beauty. A powerful and pleasing fragrance began to flow from her body and spread through the entire house, indeed as the truths of her profound writings would one day spread through the world. Hers had been a life unexplainable without God and without the grace that comes through Jesus Christ.

The Autograph

The autograph of *The Foundations*, once finished, was probably left at the monastery of Alba de Tormes. Later it was given to Luis de Leon, the noted Augustinian friar and scholar at Salamanca, who was assigned the task of preparing the first edition of Teresa's writings. In his edition of Teresa's works, published by Guillermo Foquel in Salamanca (1588), *The Foundations* was omitted. The given excuse was lack of time. But few doubt that there were other reasons as well for its omission, including the references to people still alive. There were those praising Doña Casilda de Padilla, who had later left the monastery, and those exalting Padre Gracián who by that time had lost favor with the friars in authority (10, 8-16; 11, 1-11; 23, 1-13; 24, 1-4).

When Fray Luis de León died in 1591, the manuscript passed into the hands of Francisco Sobrino. But the following year, in his overall efforts to enrich his library, Philip II called for the autographs of the Castilian nun, reformer, and mystic. Along with *The Life, The Way of Perfection,* and the short work *On Making The Visitation,* the autograph of *The Foundations* now remains in the library of King Philip's immense royal monastery and palace, the Escorial.

During the two decades in which no printed copy of the work was available, many copies were made. In 1610, two of Teresa's closest friends, Padre Gracián and Madre Ana de Jesús, by then for all practical purposes in exile from Spain, took upon themselves the task of getting the book into print in Brussels. Since Teresa herself had given no title to the work, they named it *The Book of Her Foundations.* But their publication had its deficiencies. One of the most engaging sections of the work, found in chapters 10 and 11, dealing with the strange events surrounding the vocation of Doña Casilda de Padilla was suppressed. In addition, and not unexpectedly, Gracián introduced his own variations and corrections into the text. Finally, an account of the foundation in Granada, written by Ana de Jesús at Gracián's request, was included. This latter foundation was made by Madre Ana and Fray John of the Cross, with Teresa's authorization, at the time of the foundation in Burgos. The publication was not well received in Spain, for the book had been brought out without gaining the required permission from authorities within the order and because the editors depended on defective copies rather than the autograph which was not consulted.

Even in the autograph the industrious Gracián had crossed out some words, but wisely in such a way that usually they can be easily read. He also inserted a number of unnecessary comments in the margins. These were made mainly in the first seven chapters. Later, the Dominican Fray Domingo Báñez crossed out many of Gracián's comments and corrections and rewrote clearly into the text Teresa's original words, reminding us that the Jesuit Francisco de Ribera had also found difficulties with Gracián's corrections in the autograph of the *Interior Castle*.[84] The corrections by Gracián that were not cancelled by Báñez passed into the printed edition of this work. Such had not been the case with Teresa's other works in the edition of Fray Luis de León who ignored Gracián's corrections. The most notable variation in the original, deciphered only in this century by Padre Silverio, is that introduced in the last paragraph of chapter 4. Teresa wrote: "The favors the Lord grants in these houses are so many that if there are one or two nuns in each house that God leads now by meditation all the rest reach perfect contemplation"(4, 8). Gracián crossed out some of the words and emended the text so that it read: "The favors the Lord grants in these houses are so many that though all the nuns are brought by God along the way of meditation, some reach perfect contemplation."

Not until 1880, when Don Vicente de la Fuente published a photocopy of the original did readers have a faithful copy. Padre Silverio in his critical edition of the works of St. Teresa was the first to offer the public a reliable text.[85]

The Book of Foundations may be divided as follows:
1. On founding more monasteries (chs. 1-2)
2. Medina del Campo (ch. 3)
3. Counsels on prayer (ch. 4)
   A. The substance of perfect prayer (ch. 5, no. 2)
   B. How to acquire love (ch. 5, nos. 3-17)
4. Cautions about a form of spiritual absorption (ch. 6)
5. Counsels on melancholy (ch. 7)
6. Counsels on revelations and visions (ch. 8)
7. Malagón (ch. 9)
8. Valladolid (chs. 10-12)
   A. The vocation of Doña Casilda de Padilla (ch. 10, no. 8-ch. 11)

February, 1984

Kieran Kavanaugh, O.C.D.
Carmelite Monastery
Brookline, Massachusetts

Many there are deserving of our gratitude at the completion of this third volume of St. Teresa's works. Again, special thanks go to Padre Tomás Alvarez for permitting us to make use of his Spanish edition of the complete works. Once more, too, we must thank Jean Mallon, our faithful and careful typist. The Carmel in Elysburg has for a third time contributed an excellent index, and the Carmels in Danvers and Indianapolis have provided some beneficial editorial assistance. Of particular help to me in the preparation of this volume was Padre Emilio Miranda, of the Carmelite community in Avila, a specialist with regard to places and objects having to do with Teresa and her times. With much patience and expertise he guided and instructed me in my journey through Spain to all of Holy Mother's foundations. I am grateful as well to Padre Juan Bosco, also from the Carmel in Avila, who assisted me in coming to a better understanding of Spanish culture. Father Steven Payne of the Institute of Carmelite Studies who read over this introduction and offered many useful suggestions deserves a special word of thanks. All the members of the Institute provided continual encouragement, and our business manager, Brother Bryan Paquette, eased our labors with some happy words and delightful new working tools. Finally, thanks must go to my brothers in the monastery here in Brookline who spared me from kitchen duty and gave me the quiet and free time that were necessary to bring this volume to completion.

K.K.

A TERESIAN CHRONOLOGY

1515   March 28, born in Avila.

      April 4, baptized in the parish church of St. John the Baptist.

1522   Attempts to run away with her brother Rodrigo to the land of the Moors.

      (Adrian VI of Utrecht is elected pope; Zwingli begins his reform in Zurich; Luther's translation of the New Testament into the German vernacular is published.)

1528   Doña Beatriz de Ahumada, Teresa's mother, dies.

1531   María de Cepeda, Teresa's older sister, marries and takes up residence in Castellanos de la Cañada. Teresa enters the convent school of Our Lady of Grace.

      (Ulrich Zwingli dies. Francisco Pizarro begins the conquest of Peru.)

1532   In the autumn Teresa leaves the convent school because of an illness.

1533   Spends time convalescing at her uncle's home in Hortigosa and at her older sister's home in Castellanos de la Cañada.

1534   Her brother Hernando leaves for Peru.

      (St. Ignatius and his companions make their vows at Montmartre in Paris. Pope Clement VII, elected in 1523, dies and is succeeded by Paul III.)

1535   Teresa's brother Rodrigo leaves for Rio de la Plata.

      Nov. 2, Teresa leaves home and enters the monastery of the Incarnation.

      (Henry VIII decrees the Act of Supremacy proclaiming himself as head of the Church of England.)

1536   Nov. 2, Teresa receives the religious habit at the Incarnation.

(Erasmus dies. John Calvin publishes *Institutes of the Christian Religion* and takes up the work begun by Zwingli in Switzerland.)

1537   Nov. 3, Teresa makes her religious profession of vows at the Incarnation.

1538   Because of illness she leaves the Incarnation so as to undergo treatment in Becedas. Stops at her uncle's in Hortigosa and her sister's in Castellanos de la Cañada. Reads Osuna's *The Third Spiritual Alphabet* given to her by her uncle.

1539   April, begins to undergo the treatments administered by the quack in Becedas.

   July, returns seriously ill to her father's home in Avila. August, lapses into a coma of four days' duration. She is brought back to the Incarnation with a paralysis which lasts three years.

1540   Nov. 5, her brothers Lorenzo and Jerónimo leave for America in the expedition of Vaca de Castro.

   (St. Ignatius of Loyola's constitutions for the Society of Jesus are approved by Paul III. In 1541, Valdivia establishes Santiago in Chile; Calvin begins to organize his church in Geneva, and John Knox his reform in Scotland.)

1542   Teresa feels cured through the intercession of St. Joseph. She gives up prayer out of a false sense of humility.

   (Paul III publishes the bull convoking the Council of Trent; St. John of the Cross is born in Fontiveros.)

1543   Teresa cares for her sick father and assists him in his death (in December).

1544   Returns to the practice of prayer at the advice of the family confessor, Vicente Barron, O.P.

1546   Jan. 18, the battle of Iñaquito (Peru) in which four of Teresa's brothers fight.

   Jan. 20, her brother Antonio dies from wounds suffered in battle.

   Her brother Agustín leaves for America in the expedition of Pedro de la Gasca.

   (Feb. 18, Martin Luther dies.)

1548   In the spring Teresa makes a pilgrimage to the shrine in Guadalupe for her brothers in America.

1549 Three of Teresa's brothers, Lorenzo, Jerónimo, and Agustín, fight in the battle of Xaquixaguana on the side of Pedro de la Gasca against Pizarro.

   (Paul III dies Nov. 20 and is succeeded by Julius III Feb. 7, 1550.)

1553 Teresa's younger sister, Doña Juana de Ahumada marries Don Juan de Ovalle in Alba de Tormes.

1554 In Lent, Teresa experiences a profound conversion before a statue of the wounded Christ.

   Begins to consult with a Jesuit confessor, Diego de Cetina.

1555 Juan de Prádanos, S.J., becomes her confessor.

   (Julius III dies in March and is succeeded by Marcellus II who dies in May and is succeeded by Paul IV. The Treaty of Augsburg allows rulers of the German states to decide what religion should be professed in their territories.)

1556 May, Teresa receives the grace of spiritual betrothal.

   Baltasar Alvarez, S.J., becomes Teresa's director.

   (Charles V resigns the kingdoms of both Spain and the Spanish overseas empire in favor of his son Philip II. St. Ignatius of Loyola dies in Rome.)

1557 Teresa consults with St. Francis Borgia, S.J., who passes through Avila.

   Her beloved brother Rodrigo crosses the Andes and dies in battle in Chile.

1559 The intellectual visions of Christ begin.

   (Paul IV dies in Rome and is succeeded by Pius IV. The Inquisitor Fernando Valdés publishes for Spain an index of forbidden books.)

1560 Beginning of the imaginative visions of the risen Christ. She is ordered to mock the visions by showing the fig.

   Receives the grace of the wounding of the heart while staying at the house of Doña Guiomar de Ulloa.

   St. Peter of Alcántara arrives in Avila and assures Teresa, and others, that her spiritual favors are the work of God.

   The frightening vision of hell.

   Discussions about a new foundation begin.

Teresa writes the first extant account of her spiritual life for Pedro Ibáñez, O.P.

1561   Aug. 12, St. Clare promises to help her.

End of August, Teresa brings her little nephew Gonzalo back to life.

Christmas, ordered to go to Toledo to stay with Doña Luisa de la Cerda, the widow of Arias Pardo.

1562   January to June, resides in Toledo; meets García de Toledo, O.P.

March, meets María de Jesús and learns about the practice of poverty in the primitive rule.

June, finishes her first redaction of the *Life*. Returns from Toledo to Avila.

July, finds in Avila the apostolic rescript for the foundation of St. Joseph's dated Feb. 7.

Aug. 24, foundation of the new monastery of St. Joseph. Four novices receive the habit. Teresa is called back to the Incarnation.

Aug. 29, the city initiates a lawsuit against the monastery.

Oct. 19, St. Peter of Alcántara dies.

December, Teresa moves to St. Joseph's with permission of the provincial and takes four nuns from the Incarnation with her. Changes her name to Teresa of Jesus.

(The wars of religion begin in France between the Huguenots and Catholics.)

1563   Teresa is named prioress of St. Joseph's succeeding Ana de San Juan (Dávila) who returns to the Incarnation.

She writes the *Constitutions* for St. Joseph's which are approved by the bishop of Avila, Don Alvaro de Mendoza, and by Pius IV in 1565.

(The Council of Trent closes December 4.)

1564   May 21, John Baptist Rossi (Rubeo) is elected prior general of the Carmelite Order.

Oct. 21, the first profession, of four nuns, at St. Joseph's.

(John Calvin and Michelangelo Buonarroti die; Galileo Galilei and William Shakespeare are born.)

1565   January, Teresa's brother Hernando dies in Colombia.

July 17, the bull of Pius IV confirms the practice of poverty of the new monastery and its submission to the bishop.

1566   Teresa finishes the first redaction of *The Way of Perfection* and, probably, the second; she also writes her *Meditations on the Song of Songs*.

The visit of Alonso Maldonado, the Franciscan missionary in Mexico, to St. Joseph's.

(Pius V is elected in January to succeed Pius IV who died the previous month.)

1567   Feb. 18, the prior general Rubeo comes to Avila for his visitation.

April 27, Rubeo authorizes Teresa to found other monasteries.

May 16, in another patent letter the general clarifies that his permission excludes Andalusia.

Aug. 15, the first foundation is made in Medina del Campo.

Aug. 16, Rubeo gives permission for two foundations of Teresian friars provided they are not made in Andalusia.

Teresa meets St. John of the Cross in Medina and convinces him to join her in her work.

1568   January, leaves Medina for Alcalá to visit the new monastery of María de Jesús.

March, goes to Toledo and there agrees to make a foundation in Malagón.

April, makes the foundation in Malagón.

May 19, leaves Malagón for Valladolid, stopping in Toledo, Escalona, Avila, Duruelo, and Medina.

Aug. 15, the foundation in Valladolid.

In Valladolid, Teresa teaches St. John of the Cross about her way of life. He afterward sets out to prepare the house at Duruelo for the first foundation of friars, which is made November 28.

Oct. 31, Teresa receives a letter from St. John of Avila giving approval to what she wrote in her *Life*.

(The Moorish revolt in Granada.)

1569 February, leaves Valladolid; passes through Medina, visits the new friars in Duruelo, and stops in Avila.

March 24, arrives in Toledo.

May 14, the foundation in Toledo.

May 30, leaves Toledo for Pastrana; stops in Madrid for eight days at *Las Descalzas Reales* (discalced Franciscan nuns for members of the nobility); meets Ambrosio Mariano.

June 23, foundation of the nuns in Pastrana.

July 13, foundation of the friars in Pastrana.

Writes her *Soliloquies*.

Aug. 26, two apostolic visitators for the Carmelite order are appointed: Pedro Fernández, O.P., and Francisco Vargas, O.P.

1570 July 10, Teresa attends the profession in Pastrana of Ambrosio Mariano de San Benito and Juan de la Miseria.

Nov. 1, the foundation in Salamanca.

(Pius V excommunicates Queen Elizabeth I of England.)

1571 Jan. 25, foundation in Alba de Tormes.

Oct. 14, Teresa takes possession of the office of prioress at the Incarnation.

(Defeat of the Turkish Armada at Lepanto.)

1572 Arranges to have St. John of the Cross as chaplain and confessor to the nuns at the Incarnation. Jerónimo Gracián enters novitiate.

Writes her *Response to a Spiritual Challenge*.

Nov. 18, receives the grace of spiritual marriage.

(Pius V dies and is succeeded by Gregory XIII; St. Bartholomew's eve, the massacre of the Huguenots; Nicolás Ormaneto arrives in Spain as nuncio.)

1573 Aug. 25, Teresa begins writing her *Foundations*.

1574 March, the journey from Alba to Segovia with St. John of the Cross for the foundation in Segovia on March 19.

April 6–7, the nuns abandon the foundation in Pastrana by order of Teresa and are received in Segovia.

Oct. 6, finishes her term as prioress at the Incarnation.

1575 Feb. 24, foundation in Beas.

April-May, first meetings with Gracián.

May 18, leaves Beas for Seville.

May 24, in the church of St. Ann in Ecija makes a vow to obey Gracián.

May 29, foundation in Seville.

Aug. 12, her brother Don Lorenzo returns from America.

December, she is denounced to the Inquisition of Seville.

Receives orders from the chapter held in Piacenza to retire to one of her monasteries in Castile.

1576 Jan. 1, the foundation in Caravaca made by Ana de San Alberto at Teresa's orders.

Writes accounts of her spiritual life for Rodrigo Alvarez, S.J., who is consultant to the Inquisition in Seville.

May 28, leaves Seville with her brother and his family and stops for some days in Almodovar del Campo and Malagón.

June 23, arrives in Toledo.

August, writes *On Making the Visitation.*

1577 Feb. 6, writes the *Satirical Critique.*

June 2, begins to write *The Interior Castle.*

June 18, the nuncio, Ormaneto, dies.

July, she goes to Avila.

Aug. 29, the new nuncio, Sega, arrives in Madrid.

Nov. 29, Teresa concludes *The Interior Castle.*

Dec. 3, St. John of the Cross is taken prisoner, and the following day Teresa writes a letter to the king pleading for help and justice on the saint's behalf.

Dec. 24, she falls down the stairs at St. Joseph's and breaks her left arm, which is never set properly and leaves her incapacitated.

1578 July 23, Sega issues a counterbrief taking away Gracián's faculties as apostolic visitator.

Aug. 9, the royal council forbids the discalced to obey Sega.

Aug. 17-18, St. John of the Cross escapes from his prison in Toledo.

Oct. 9, the Teresian friars hold a chapter at Almodóvar, against Teresa's better judgment, and elect Antonio de Jesús superior.

Oct. 16, Sega annuls the chapter's decisions and places the Teresian friars and nuns under the authority of the provincials of the observant Carmelites.

Nov. 4, the prior general, Rubeo, dies.

(Don John of Austria dies and is succeeded by Alexander Farnese in the government of the Low Countries.)

1579   April 1, Sega and his counsellors deprive the provincials of authority over the Teresian friars and nuns and appoint Angel de Salazar as vicar general.

June, Teresa begins traveling once more: Medina, Valladolid, Salamanca, Alba, Avila, Toledo.

Nov. 24, arrives in Malagón and engages in speeding up the construction work on the new monastery.

Dec. 8, the nuns move to the new monastery, the only one constructed from its foundations according to Teresa's specifications.

(The Union of Utrecht forms the alliance of northern provinces of the Netherlands and makes protestantism the state religion.)

1580   February, the foundation in Villanueva de la Jara.

March, Teresa leaves Villanueva de la Jara and journeys to Toledo where she becomes seriously ill.

June, leaves Toledo for Segovia, passing through Madrid. Gracián and Diego de Yanguas, O.P., examine and "correct" *The Interior Castle* in the parlor of Segovia in the presence of Teresa.

June 22, the papal brief *Pia consideratione* allows the Teresian friars and nuns to form a separate province.

June 26, Teresa's brother Don Lorenzo dies.

Aug. 8, she arrives in Valladolid and becomes seriously ill.

Dec. 28, leaves Valladolid for Palencia and makes the foundation there the following day.

(King Henry of Portugal dies leaving no successor to the throne. Philip II to assert his rights to the crown orders the Duke of Alba to invade Portugal.)

1581 March 3, opening of the chapter at Alcalá in view of which Teresa wrote letters to Gracián concerning legislation of the nuns.

March 4, Gracián is elected provincial.

June 30, the foundation in Soria.

Sept. 10, María de Cristo renounces her office of prioress in Avila, and Teresa is elected.

Nov. 28, St. John of the Cross arrives in Avila with the desire to persuade Teresa to come to Granada for a foundation there, but she declines.

(Philip II is recognized as king of Portugal. Legazpi and Urdaneta found the city of Manila.)

1582 Jan. 2, Teresa leaves Avila for the last time on the way to the new foundation in Burgos.

Jan. 20, the foundation in Granada is made by St. John of the Cross and Ana de Jesús.

April 19, the foundation in Burgos is finally achieved.

July 26, she leaves Burgos.

Aug. 2, stops off in Palencia.

Aug. 25, arrives in Valladolid.

Sept. 15, leaves Valladolid and arrives in Medina.

Sept. 19, leaves Medina and, at the order of Antonio de Jesús, goes to Alba de Tormes.

Sept. 20, reaches Alba de Tormes at six in the evening.

Sept. 29, goes to bed seriously ill never to get up again; announces that her death is at hand.

Oct. 3, receives the sacraments of reconciliation and of the sick.

Oct. 4, at nine in the evening dies "a daughter of the Church" at the age of sixty-seven.

The Gregorian Calendar was introduced that year so that the day following Teresa's death became October 15.

1614 April 24, she is beatified by Paul V.

1622 March 12, she is canonized by Gregory XV along with Saints Isidore, Ignatius Loyola, Francis Xavier, and Philip Neri.

1970 Sept. 27, she is declared a Doctor of the Church by Paul VI, and becomes the first woman saint to be so recognized.

A N C E

N

TERESA'S FOUNDATIONS AND JOURNEYS

1567: Ávila, Arévalo, **MEDINA,** Madrid, Alcalá

1568: Alcalá, Madrid, Toledo, **MALAGON,**
Toledo, Ávila, Duruelo, Alba, Medina,
VALLADOLID

1569: Valladolid, Medina, Duruelo, Ávila,
TOLEDO, Madrid, **PASTRANA,** Madrid,
Toledo

1570: Toledo, Madrid, Pastrana, Madrid, Toledo,
Ávila, **SALAMANCA**

1571: Salamanca, **ALBA,** Arévalo, Ávila, Medina,
Arévalo, Avila

1572: . . .

1573: Ávila, Alba, Ávila, Salamanca

1574: Salamanca, Alba, Medina, Arévalo,
SEGOVIA, Ávila, Valladolid

1575: Valladolid, Medina, Ávila, Toledo,
Malagón, **BEAS,** Córdoba, **SEVILLE**

1576: Seville, Córdoba, Malagón, Toledo

1577: Toledo, Ávila

1578: . . .

1579: Ávila, Arévalo, Medina, Salamanca, Ávila,
Toledo, Malagón

1580: Malagón, Toledo, **VILLANUEVA DE LA
JARA,** Toledo, Segovia, Ávila, Arévalo,
Medina, Valladolid, **PALENCIA**

1581: Palencia, Burgo de Osma, **SORIA,** Burgo de
Osma, Segovia, Ávila

1582: Ávila, Arévalo, Medina, Valladolid,
Palencia, **BURGOS,** Palencia, Valladolid,
Medina, Alba

0
40   80 miles   160

THE FOUNDATIONS

Prologue

JHS

1. Apart from what I have read in many places, I have seen through experience the great good that comes to a soul when it does not turn aside from obedience. It is through this practice that I think one advances in virtue and gains humility. In obedience lies security against that dread (which for us as mortals living in this life is a good thing) that we might stray from the path to heaven. Here one finds the quietude that is so precious in souls desiring to please God. For if they have truly resigned themselves through the practice of this holy obedience and surrendered the intellect to it, not desiring any other opinion than their confessor's (or, if they are religious, their superior's), the devil will cease attacking with his continual disturbances. He will have seen that he is losing rather than gaining. Also, those restless stirrings within us, which make us fond of doing our own will and which even subdue reason in matters concerning our own satisfaction, come to a stop. Those who practice obedience remember that they resolutely surrendered their own will to God's will, using submission to the one who stands in God's place as a means to this surrender.

Because His Majesty, in His goodness, has given me light to know the rich treasure contained in this precious virtue, I have striven — although weakly and imperfectly — to obtain it. Yet, often the small amount of virtue I see in myself contradicts what I just said. For with some things they command me to do I realize that such striving doesn't suffice. May the divine Majesty provide what is lacking for the accomplishment of this present task.

2. While in St. Joseph's in Avila in the year 1562, the same

year in which that monastery was founded, I was ordered by Fr. García de Toledo, a Dominican, who at the time was my confessor, to write of that monastery's foundation, along with many other things; whoever sees that work, if it is published, will learn there of those events.[1] Now here in Salamanca, in the year 1573, eleven years later, my confessor, a Father Rector from the Society, whose name is Maestro Ripaldo,[2] having seen this book of the first foundation, thought it would be of service to our Lord if I wrote about the other seven monasteries[3] that were since founded through the goodness of the Lord, and also about the first monastery of the discalced Fathers of this ancient order.[4] And so he commanded me to write this. It seems impossible for me to do so because I was so busy, both with correspondence and with other necessary occupations ordered by my superiors. I was recommending myself to God and somewhat distressed for being so useless and in such poor health. Even without this feeling of being useless, it often seemed to me because of my poor health and my lowly natural inclinations that I wouldn't be able to bear doing this work. While I was in this prayer, the Lord said to me: "Daughter, obedience gives strength."

3. May it please His Majesty that this be so, and may He grant me the grace to be able to recount for His glory the favors that through these foundations He has granted this order. One can be certain that this account will be given in all truthfulness, without any exaggeration, in so far as possible, but in conformity with what has taken place. For even in something of very little importance I wouldn't tell a lie for anything in the world. In this work that is being written for the praise of our Lord, any untruthfulness would cause me great scrupulosity. I believe that such a thing would involve not only a waste of time but deception concerning the works of God, and instead of being praised for them He would be offended. It would be a great betrayal. So that I might accomplish this task, may it please His Majesty not to let me out of His hand.

Each foundation will be expressly mentioned. And I will try to be brief, for my style is so heavy that although I may want to be brief, I fear that I will become tiresome and tire even myself. But because of the love my daughters have for me, they who will possess this work after my days are done will be able to put up with the style.

4. I do not seek my own benefit in anything, nor do I have any reason to do so, but only His glory and praise, for many things will be seen for which glory and praise should be given Him. Thus may it please our Lord that anyone who reads this will not think of attributing praise to me, since to do so would be against the truth. Rather, let readers ask His Majesty to pardon me for the poor way in which I have benefited from all these favors. There is much greater reason for my daughters to complain about this defect than to thank me for what has been done through these favors. Let us, my daughters, give all our thanks to the divine goodness for the many favors He has granted us. I ask the reader to recite a Hail Mary out of love for Him that it may help me to leave purgatory and reach the vision of Jesus Christ our Lord, who lives and reigns with the Father and the Holy Spirit, forever and ever, amen.

5. Since I have a poor memory, I believe that many very important things will be left unsaid and that other things will be said that could be omitted. In sum, the work will be in accord with my lack of intelligence and culture and my lack also of the quiet necessary for writing. They also are ordering me, if the occasion offers itself, to deal with some things about prayer and how, by being deceived, those who practice it could be kept from making progress.

6. In all things I submit to what the holy Roman Church holds, with the resolve that before this work reaches your hands, my Sisters and daughters, learned and spiritual persons will see it. I begin in the name of the Lord, taking for my help His glorious Mother, whose habit I wear, although unworthily, and also my glorious father and lord, St. Joseph, in whose house I am, for he is the patron of this monastery of discalced nuns,[5] through whose prayer I have been continually helped.

7. In the year 1573, feastday of St. Louis, king of France, which is August 24.[6] May God be praised!

*Begins With the Foundation of the Carmel of
St. Joseph in Medina del Campo*

Chapter 1

*On the circumstances surrounding the beginning of both this
foundation and the others.*

FROM WHAT I can understand now, the five years I spent in
St. Joseph's in Avila after its foundation[1] seem to me to
have been the most restful of my life, and my soul often misses
that calm and quiet. During those years some young religious
women entered, whom the world, apparently, had already held
in its grasp as was manifested in their display of its elegant and
fashionable dress. Drawing them quickly away from those vanities, the Lord brought them to His house, endowing them with
so much perfection that it was to my embarrassment. He did
this until the number reached thirteen, which had been set as
the maximum number.[2]

2. It was a delight for me to be among souls so holy and pure,
whose only concern was to serve and praise our Lord. His Majesty sent us what was necessary without our asking for it; and
when we were in want, which was seldom, their joy was greater.
I praised our Lord to see so many lofty virtues, especially the detachment they had from everything but serving Him. I, who was
the superior there, never remember worrying about the necessities of life. I was convinced that the Lord would not fail those
who had no other concern than to please Him. And if at times
there wasn't enough food for everyone and I said that what
there was should go to those most in need, each one thought
that she could do without, and so the food remained until God
sent enough for everyone.

3. With respect to the virtue of obedience, to which I am very
devoted (although I didn't know how to practice it until those
servants of God so taught me that I couldn't be ignorant as to
whether or not I possessed it), I could mention many things that
I saw there. One thing comes to mind now, and the incident

came about in the refectory one day when they served us help-
ings of cucumbers. My portion consisted of one that was very
thin and rotten inside. Secretly, I called a Sister, one of those
with greater intelligence and talents, to test her obedience and
told her to go and plant the cucumber in a little vegetable garden we had. She asked me if she should plant it upright or sideways. I told her sideways. She went out and planted it, without
the thought entering her mind that the cucumber would only
dry up. Rather, since she planted it out of obedience, she blinded
natural reason so as to believe that what she did was very appropriate.[3]

4. It occurred to me to charge one of them with six or seven
contradictory duties. She undertook them, remaining silent,
thinking it would be possible for her to do them all. There was a
well with very bad water according to those who tried it, and it
seemed impossible for the water to flow since the well was very
deep. When I called some workmen to dig a new one, they laughed
at me as though I were wanting to throw money away. I asked
the Sisters what they thought. One said that it should be tried,
that since our Lord would have to provide someone to bring us
water as well as food, it would be cheaper for His Majesty to give
us the well on the grounds of the house and that thus He would
not fail to do so. Observing the great faith and determination
with which she said it, I became certain. And, contrary to the
opinion of the one who understood all about founts and water, I
went ahead. And the Lord was pleased that we were able to put
in a conduit which provided enough water for our needs, and
for drinking, and which we now have.[4]

5. I do not present this as a miracle, for there are other things
I could tell, but to show the faith these Sisters had since the
things did happen in the way I tell them. Nor is it my first intention to praise the nuns of these monasteries, for through the
goodness of the Lord, all of them act in this way. And of these
things and many others one could write at length, and with
benefit, for at times those who follow will be inspired to imitate
these Sisters. But if the Lord should desire this to be known, the
superiors will command the prioresses that they write of it.

6. Well now, this wretched one was among these angelic

souls. They didn't seem to me to be anything else, for there was no fault they hid from me, even if interior. And the favors, and ardent desires, and detachment the Lord gave them were great. Their consolation was their solitude. They assured me that they never tired of being alone, and thus they felt it a torment when others came to visit them, even if these were their brothers. The one who had the greater opportunity to remain in a hermitage considered herself the luckiest. In considering the real value of these souls and the courage God gave them to serve and suffer for Him, certainly not a characteristic of women, I often thought that the riches God placed in them were meant for some great purpose. What was later to come about never passed through my mind, because it didn't seem then to be something possible. There was no basis for even being able to imagine it, although my desires to be of some help to some soul as time went on had grown much greater. And I often felt like one who has a great treasure stored up and desires that all enjoy it, but whose hands are bound and unable to distribute it. So it seemed my soul was bound because the favors the Lord was granting it during those years were very great, and I thought that I was not putting them to good use. I tried to please the Lord with my poor prayers and always endeavored that the Sisters would do the same and dedicate themselves to the good of souls and the increase of His Church. Whoever conversed with them was always edified. And these were the things with which my great desires were fully taken up.

7. Four years later, or, I think, a little more than that, a Franciscan friar happened to come to see me, whose name was Fray Alonso Maldonado,[5] a great servant of God, who had the same desires for the good of souls as I, but he was able to transfer them into deeds for which I envied him greatly. He had recently come back from the Indies. He began to tell me about the many millions of souls that were being lost there for want of Christian instruction, and before leaving he gave us a sermon, or conference, encouraging us to do penance. I was so grief-stricken over the loss of so many souls that I couldn't contain myself. I went to a hermitage[6] with many tears. I cried out to the Lord, begging Him that He give me the means to be able to do something to

win some souls to His service, since the devil was carrying away
so many, and that my prayer would do some good since I wasn't
able to do anything else. I was very envious of those who for love
of our Lord were able to be engaged in winning souls, though
they might suffer a thousand deaths. And thus it happens to me
that when we read in the lives of the saints that they converted
souls, I feel much greater devotion, tenderness, and envy than
over all the martyrdoms they suffered. This is the inclination
the Lord has given me, for it seems to me that He prizes a soul
that through our diligence and prayer we gain for Him, through
His mercy, more than all the services we can render Him.

8. Well, going about with such great affliction, while I was in
prayer one night, our Lord represented Himself to me in His
usual way. He showed me much love, manifesting His desire to
comfort me, and said: "Wait a little, daughter, and you will see
great things."

These words remained so fixed in my heart that I could not
forget them. No matter how much I thought about this promise
I couldn't figure out how it would be possible, nor was there a
way of even imagining how it could come about. Nonetheless, I
remained very much consoled and certain that these words would
prove true. But the means by which they eventually did never
entered my mind. Thus another half year, I think, passed, and
afterward there took place what I shall now describe.

Chapter 2

*How our Father General came to Avila and what followed from
his visit.*

OUR GENERALS ALWAYS reside in Rome and none ever came
to Spain.[1] So it seemed impossible that one should come
now. But since nothing is impossible when our Lord wants it, His
Majesty ordained that what had never happened before should
come about now. When I came to know of it, I felt grieved. For
as was already mentioned concerning the foundation of St.
Joseph's, that house was not subject to the friars for the reason

given.[2] I feared two things: one, that our Father General would be displeased with me (and rightly so since he was unaware of how the things had come to pass); the other, that he would order me to return to the monastery of the Incarnation, where the mitigated rule is observed, which for me would have been an affliction for many reasons—there would be no point in going into them. One reason should be enough: that in the Incarnation I wouldn't be able to observe the austerity of the primitive rule, that the community numbers more than 150,[3] and that where there are few there is more harmony and quiet. Our Lord did better than I had imagined. For the general is such a servant of the Lord, and so discreet and learned, that he regarded the work as good; moreover he showed no displeasure toward me. His name is Fray Juan Bautista Rubeo de Ravena, a person very distinguished in the order, and rightly so.[4]

2. Well then, when he arrived in Avila, I arranged that he come to St. Joseph's. And the bishop[5] thought it well that he be given all the welcome that the bishop himself would receive. I gave our Father General an account in all truth and openness, for it is my inclination to speak thus with my superiors, whatever might happen, since they stand in the place of God—and with confessors, the same. If I didn't do this, it wouldn't seem to me that my soul was secure. And so I gave him an account of my soul and of almost my whole life, although it is very wretched. He consoled me much and assured me that he wouldn't order me to leave St. Joseph's.

3. He rejoiced to see our manner of life, a portrait, although an imperfect one, of the beginnings of our order, and how the primitive rule was being kept in all its rigor, for it wasn't being observed in any monastery in the entire order; only the mitigated rule was observed.[6] And with the desire he had that this beginning go forward, he gave me very extensive patent letters, so that more monasteries could be founded, along with censures to prevent any provincial from restraining me.[7] I did not ask for these, but he understood from my way of prayer that my desires to help some soul come closer to God were great.

4. I was not seeking these means; rather the thought seemed

to me foolish because a useless little woman as helpless as I well understood that she couldn't do anything. But when these desires come to a soul, it is not in its power to put them aside. Faith and the love of pleasing God make possible what to natural reason is not possible. And thus in seeing the strong desire of our Most Reverend General that more monasteries be founded, it seemed to me I saw them founded. Remembering the words our Lord had spoken to me,[8] I now perceived some beginning to what before I could not understand. I was very sad to see our Father General return to Rome. I had grown to love him very much, and it seemed to me I was left helpless. He showed me the greatest kindness, and during the times that he was free from his duties he came to speak about spiritual things as one to whom the Lord must grant great favors. In this house it was a consolation for us to hear him. Moreover, before he went away, the bishop, Don Alvaro de Mendoza, very devoted to favoring those who aim after serving God with greater perfection, asked him permission for the foundation in his diocese of some monasteries of discalced friars of the primitive rule. Other persons also asked for this. Our Father General wanted to do so, but he found disagreement within the order. And thus, so as not to disturb the province, he let the matter go for then.

5. After some days passed, I was thinking about how necessary it would be if monasteries of nuns were to be founded that there be friars observing the same rule. Seeing how few friars there were in this province, making me even wonder whether or not they were going to die out, I prayed to the Lord over the matter very much and wrote to Father General. In the letter, I begged him for this permission as best I knew how, giving him the reasons why it would be a great service to God. I pointed out how the difficulties that could arise were not sufficient to set aside so good a work, and suggested to him what service it would render to our Lady, to whom he was very devoted. She must have been the one who arranged it. This letter reached him while he was in Valencia, and from there he sent me the permission for the foundation of two monasteries because he desired the best religious observance for the order.[9] So that there wouldn't be any opposition, he made his permission subject to

the approval, difficult to obtain, of both the present and the former provincial. But since I saw that the main thing was accomplished, I had special hope the Lord would do the rest. And so it happened that through the kindness of the bishop, who took up this matter as his own, both provincials gave their permission.[10]

6. Well then, being consoled in having the permissions, my concern grew in that there was no friar in the province that I knew of who could begin this work, nor any layman who desired to make such a start. I didn't do anything but beg our Lord that he would awaken at least one person. Neither did I have a house or the means to get one. Here I was, a poor discalced nun, without help from anywhere—only from the Lord—weighed down with patent letters and good desires, and without there being any possibility of my getting the work started. Neither courage nor hope failed, for since the Lord had given the one thing, He would give the other. Everything now seemed very possible, and so I set to work.

7. O greatness of God! How You manifest Your power in giving courage to an ant! How true, my Lord, that it is not because of You that those who love You fail to do great works but because of our own cowardice and pusillanimity. Since we are never determined, but full of human prudence and a thousand fears, You, consequently, my God, do not do your marvelous and great works. Who is more fond than You of giving, or of serving even at a cost to Yourself, when there is someone open to receive? May it please Your Majesty that I render You some service and that I not have to render an accounting for all that I have received, amen.

Chapter 3

The circumstances surrounding the foundation of the monastery of St. Joseph in Medina del Campo.

WHILE I WAS HAVING ALL these concerns, the thought came to me to ask help from the Fathers of the Society, for they were well accepted in that place, that is, in Medina. As I have written in my account of the first foundation, they guided my soul for many years. I always feel especially devoted to them because of the great good they did for it.[1] I wrote to the rector in Medina about what our Father General had ordered me to do. The rector happened to be the one who had been my confessor for many years, whom I mentioned, although I did not give his name. His name is Baltasar Alvarez, and at present he is provincial.[2] He and the others said they would do what they could about the matter. They thus did a great deal to secure permission from the people and the bishop,[3] for since the monastery is to be founded in poverty, permission is everywhere difficult to obtain. So there was a delay of several days in the negotiations.

2. A priest went there to attend to these negotiations. He was a good servant of God, very detached from all worldly things and much dedicated to prayer. He was the chaplain in the monastery where I lived. The Lord gave him the same desires that He gave me, and so I was helped very much by him, as will be seen further on. His name is Julián de Avila.[4]

Well, now that I had the permission, I didn't have a house or a penny to buy one with. Furthermore, how could a poor wanderer like myself get credit for a loan unless the Lord would give it? The Lord provided that a very virtuous young lady, who because of lack of room could not enter St. Joseph's, heard that another house was being founded and came to ask if I would accept her in the new one. She had some money which was very little and not enough to buy a house but enough to rent one and to help with the travel expenses.[5] And so we found one to rent. Without any more support than this and with our Father Chaplain, Julián de Avila, we left Avila. Besides myself, there were two nuns from St. Joseph's and four from the Incarnation, the monastery of the mitigated rule where I stayed before St. Joseph's was founded.[6]

3. When our intention became known in the city, there was much criticism. Some were saying I was crazy; others were hoping for an end to that nonsense. To the bishop—according to what he told me later—the idea seemed very foolish. But he didn't then let me know this; neither did he hinder me, for he loved me much and didn't want to hurt me. My friends said a

great deal against the project. But I didn't pay much attention to them. For that which to them seemed doubtful, to me seemed so easy that I couldn't persuade myself that it would fail to be a true success.

Before we left Avila, I wrote to a Father of our order, Fray Antonio de Heredia,[7] asking him to buy me a house, for he was then prior at St. Anne's, the monastery of friars of our order in Medina. He spoke of the matter to a lady who was devoted to him,[8] for she had a house that had completely collapsed except for one room. The house was situated in a fine location. She was so good she promised to sell the house and so they came to an agreement without her asking for any surety or binding force other than his word. If she had asked for any, we would have had no resources. The Lord was arranging everything. This house was so tumble-down that we had rented another to live in while it was being repaired, for there was much to do on it.

4. Well, on the first day, as nightfall was approaching and we were entering Arévalo and tired because of our bad provisions for traveling, a priest friend of ours who had lodging for us in the home of some devout women came out to meet us. He told me in secret that we didn't have a house because the one rented was near a monastery of Augustinian friars who resisted our coming and that a lawsuit would be unavoidable.[9] Oh, God help me! When You, Lord, want to give courage, how little do all contradictions matter! Rather, it seems I am encouraged by them, thinking that since the devil is beginning to be disturbed the Lord will be served in that monastery. Nonetheless, I told the priest to be quiet about it so as not to disturb my companions; especially two of them from the Incarnation, for the others would suffer any trial for me. One of these two was then subprioress there,[10] and the two did much to impede the departure. They were both from good families and were coming against their will because what we were doing seemed absurd to everyone. Afterward I saw that they were more than right. For when the Lord is pleased that I found one of these houses, it seems that until after the foundation is made my mind doesn't admit any reason that would seem sufficient to set the work aside. After the deed is done, all the difficulties come before me together, as will be seen later.

5. When we reached our lodging place, I learned that in the town was a Dominican friar, a very great servant of God, to whom I had confessed during the time that I was in St. Joseph's. Because in writing of that foundation I spoke much about his virtue, I will mention here no more than his name, Fray Maestro Domingo Báñez.[11] He is very learned and discreet. By his opinion I was guided, and in his opinion the foundation was not as troublesome as it seemed to others. The person who knows God better does God's work more easily. And from some of the favors that he knew His Majesty granted me and from what he had seen in the foundation of St. Joseph's, everything seemed to him to be very possible. It was a great consolation to me when I saw him, for with his favorable opinion it seemed to me everything would turn out all right. Well, when he came to see me, I told him in strict secrecy of my plan. To him it seemed that we could bring the matter with the Augustinians to a quick conclusion. But any delay was hard for me to bear because I didn't know what to do with so many nuns. And thus, because inside the lodging place the nuns had been told of the situation, we all passed the night with much apprehension.

6. The first thing in the morning the prior of our order, Fray Antonio, arrived and said that the house he had made an agreement to buy was adequate and had an entrance way which if adorned with some hangings could be made into a little church. We decided to move into that house. At least to me the idea seemed very good, for whatever could be done more quickly is what suited us best since we were outside our monasteries. And also I feared some opposition, since I learned through experience from the first foundation. Thus I desired that we take possession of the house before our intentions be made known, and so we determined to do this at once. Our Father Master Fray Domingo, agreed.

7. We arrived in Medina del Campo on the eve of our Lady's feast in August at twelve midnight. We dismounted at the monastery of St. Anne's so as not to make noise and proceeded to the house on foot. It was by the great mercy of God that we were not struck by any of the bulls being corralled at that hour for the next day's run. We were so engrossed in what we were doing that

we didn't pay any attention. However, the Lord, who always takes care of those who seek to serve Him (and indeed, that's what we were trying to do), kept us from being harmed.

8. When we arrived at the house, we entered the courtyard. The walls looked to me to be quite dilapidated, but not as dilapidated as they looked when daylight came. It seems the Lord wanted that blessed Father to be blinded and thus unable to see that the place was not suitable for the Blessed Sacrament. When we saw the entrance way, it was necessary to clear away the dirt since overhead was nothing but a rustic roof of bare tile. Because the walls were not plastered, the night almost over, and all we had were some blankets—I believe there were three—which for the whole length of the entrance way were nothing, I didn't know what to do. For I saw that the place wasn't suitable for an altar. It pleased the Lord, who wanted the place to be prepared immediately, that the butler of that lady who was the owner had at her house many tapestries belonging to her and a blue damask bed-hanging; and the lady had told him to give us whatever we wanted, for she was very good.

9. When I saw such nice furnishings, I praised the Lord, and so did the others—although we didn't know what to do for nails, nor was it the hour for buying them. We began to look in the walls. Finally, through much effort, a supply was found. With some of the men hanging the tapestries, and we cleaning the floor, we worked so quickly that when dawn came the altar was set up, and the little bell placed in a corridor; and immediately Mass was said. Having Mass was sufficient in order to take possession. But not knowing this, we reserved the Blessed Sacrament,[12] and through some cracks in the door that was in front of us, we attended the Mass, for there was no place else for us to do so.

10. Up to this point I was very happy because for me it is the greatest consolation to see one church more where the Blessed Sacrament is preserved. But my happiness did not last long. For when Mass was finished I went to look a little bit through a window at the courtyard, and I saw that all the walls in some places had fallen to the ground and that many days would be required to repair them. Oh, God help me! When I saw His Majesty placed in the street, at a time so dangerous, on account of those Luther-

ans,[13] as this time in which we now live, what anguish came to my heart!

11. To this anguish were joined all the difficulties that those who had strongly criticized the project could bring up. I understood clearly that those persons were right. It seemed impossible for me to go ahead with what had been begun. Just as previously everything seemed easy to me when I reflected that I was doing it for God, so now my temptation constricted the Lord's power to such an extent that it didn't seem I had received any favor from Him. Only my lowliness and my powerlessness did I have before me. Well now, supported by something so miserable, what success could I hope for? Had I been alone, I think I could have suffered the situation. But to think that my companions, after the opposition with which they had left, had to return to their houses was a painful thing to bear. Also, it seemed to me that since this first attempt had gone wrong, everything that I had understood I must do for the Lord in the future would not come about. Then, in addition, came the fear concerning whether or not what I understood in prayer was an illusion. This latter was not the least suffering but the greatest, for I had the strongest fear of being deceived by the devil.

O my God, what a thing it is to see a soul when You desire to abandon it to suffering! Indeed, when I recall this affliction and some others that I have had in the course of making these foundations, it doesn't seem to me that bodily trials, even though great, are anything in comparison.

12. With all this anguish that kept me truly depressed, I didn't let my companions know anything because I didn't want to cause them more distress than they already had. I suffered with this trial until evening, for then the rector of the Society sent a Father to see me who greatly encouraged and comforted me. I didn't tell him all my sufferings but only those which I felt at seeing us on the street. I began to speak of his finding us a house to rent, cost what it would cost, so that we could move to another one while this one was being repaired. And I began to console myself in seeing the many people who came, and that none of them had any thought that what we did was foolish, which was mercy from God, for it would have been very right if

the Blessed Sacrament had been taken away from us. Now I think back on my foolishness and how no one thought of consuming the Eucharist, though it seemed to me that if it had been consumed, everything would have been undone.

13. Despite our great efforts, no house for rent was found in the whole area. This made me suffer through very painful nights and days. Even though I put some men in charge of always keeping watch over the Blessed Sacrament, I was worried that they might fall asleep. So I arose during the night to watch it through a window, for the moon was very bright and I could easily see it. Many people came during all those days, and not only did they fail to perceive this as wrong but they were stirred to devotion to see our Lord once again in the stable. And His Majesty, as one who never tires of humiliating Himself for us, didn't seem to want to leave it.

14. After eight days had passed, a merchant who lived in a very nice house,[14] told us when he saw our need that we could live on the upper floor of his house and stay there as though in our own. It had a large gilded room that he gave us for a church. And a lady who lived next to the house that we bought, whose name was Doña Elena de Quiroga, a great servant of God, told me she would help so that construction of a chapel for the Blessed Sacrament could be immediately started, and also accommodations made so that we could observe the rule of enclosure. Others gave us many alms for food, but this lady was the one who aided me most.[15]

15. Now with this I began to calm down because we were able to keep strict enclosure, and we began to recite the Hours. The good prior hurried very much with the repair of the house, and he suffered many trials. Nonetheless, the work took two months. But the house was repaired in such a way that we were able to live there in a reasonably good manner for several years. Afterward, our Lord continued bringing about improvements for it.

16. While in Medina, I was still concerned about the monasteries for friars, and since I didn't have any, as I said,[16] I didn't know what to do. So I decided to speak about the matter very confidentially with the prior there[17] to see what he would

counsel me, and this I did. He was happy to know of it and promised me he would be the first. I took it that he was joking with me and told him so. For although he was always a good friar, recollected, very studious, and fond of his cell—in fact, he was a learned man—it didn't seem to me he was the one for a beginning like this. Neither would he have the courage or promote the austerity that was necessary, since he was fragile and not given to austerity. He assured me very much and asserted that for many days the Lord had been calling him to a stricter life. Thus he had already decided to go to the Carthusians, and they had already told him they would accept him. Despite all this, I was not completely satisfied. Although I was happy to hear what he said, I asked that we put it off for a while and that he prepare by putting into practice the things he would be promising. And this he did, for a year passed and during that year so many trials and persecutions from many false accusations came upon him that it seems the Lord wanted to test him. He bore it all so well and was making such progress that I praised our Lord, and it seemed to me His Majesty was preparing him for the new foundation.

17. A little later it happened that a young Father came there who was studying at Salamanca. He came along with another, as his companion, who told me great things about the life this Father was leading. The young Father's name was Fray John of the Cross.[18] I praised our Lord. And when I spoke with this young friar, he pleased me very much. I learned from him how he also wanted to go to the Carthusians. Telling him what I was attempting to do, I begged him to wait until the Lord would give us a monastery and pointed out the great good that would be accomplished if in his desire to improve he were to remain in his own order and that much greater service would be rendered to the Lord. He promised me he would remain as long as he wouldn't have to wait long. When I saw that I already had two friars to begin with, it seemed to me the matter was taken care of; although I still wasn't so satisfied with the prior, and thus I waited a while, and waited also for the sake of finding a place where they could begin.

18. The nuns were gaining esteem in the town and receiving

much affection. In my opinion, rightly so, for they were not interested in anything else than how each one could serve our Lord more. In all matters they lived the same way as at St. Joseph's in Avila since the rule and constitutions were the same.

The Lord began to call some women to receive the habit, and the favors He gave them were so great that I was amazed. May He be ever blessed, amen. In order to love, it doesn't seem that He waits for anything else than to be loved.

Chapter 4

Treats of some favors the Lord grants to the nuns of these monasteries and gives counsel to the prioresses about the attitude one should have toward these nuns.[1]

SINCE I DO NOT KNOW how much time on this earth the Lord will still give me, or how much opportunity to write, and since now it seems I have a little time, I thought that before I go further I should give some counsels to prioresses. Through these, the prioresses will learn both to understand themselves and to guide their subjects so that the souls of these latter will receive greater benefit, even though with less satisfaction.

It should be noted that, when they ordered me to write about these foundations, seven monasteries (leaving aside the first one, St. Joseph's in Avila, of which I wrote at that time) had been founded by the Lord's favor. This takes us up to the foundation of Alba de Tormes, which is the last of them. The reason that more have not been established is that my superiors have tied me down to something else, as will be seen later.[2]

2. Well, in observing what has been happening spiritually during these years in these monasteries, I have seen the need for what I want to say. May it please our Lord that I may manage to do so in accordance with what I see is necessary. If the spiritual experiences are not counterfeit, it's necessary that souls not be frightened. For as I have mentioned in other places, in some little things I've written for the Sisters,[3] if we proceed with a pure conscience and obediently, the Lord will never permit the devil

to have enough influence to deceive harmfully our souls; on the contrary, the devil himself is the one who is left deceived. And since he knows this, I don't believe he does as much harm as our imagination and bad humors do, especially if there is melancholy; for the nature of women is weak, and the self-love that reigns in us is very subtle. Thus many persons have come to me, both men and women, together with the nuns of these houses, who I have clearly discerned were often deceiving themselves without wanting to do so. I really believe that the devil must be meddling so as to trick us. But I have seen very many, as I say, whom the Lord in His goodness has not let out of His hand. Perhaps He wants to exercise them through these deceptions they undergo so that they might gain experience.

3. Things pertaining to prayer and perfection are, because of our own sins, so discredited in the world that it's necessary for me to explain myself the way I do. If even without seeing danger people fear to walk this path of prayer, what would happen if we mentioned some of the danger? Although, truthfully, there is danger in everything, and, while we live, we have to proceed with fear and ask the Lord to teach us and not abandon us. But, as I believe I once said,[4] if some danger can be lacking, there is much less of it for those who turn their thoughts more to God and strive for perfection in their lives.

4. Since, my Lord, we see that You often free us from the dangers in which we place ourselves, even in opposition to You, how can one believe that You will fail to free us when we aim after nothing more than to please You and delight in You? Never can I believe this! It could be that because of other secret judgments God might permit some things that must happen anyway. But good never brought about evil. Thus, may what I have said help us strive to walk better along the road so as to please our Spouse more and find Him sooner, but not make us abandon it; and encourage us to walk with fortitude along a road that has such rugged mountain passes, as does that of this life, but not intimidate us from walking through them. For, in the final analysis, by proceeding with humility, through the mercy of God, we will reach that city of Jerusalem, where all that has been suffered will be little, or nothing, in comparison with what is enjoyed.

5. Well, as these little dovecotes of the Virgin, our Lady, were beginning to be inhabited, the divine Majesty began to show His greatness in these weak little women, who were strong though in their desires and their detachment from every creature. When practiced with a pure conscience, such detachment must be what most joins the soul to God. There is no need to point this out because if the detachment is true it seems to me impossible that one offend the Lord. Since in all their dealings and conversations these nuns are concerned with Him, His Majesty doesn't seem to want to leave them. This is what I see now and in truth can say. Let those fear who are to come and who will read this. And if they do not see what is now seen, let them not blame the times, for it is always a suitable time for God to grant great favors to the one who truly serves Him. And let them strive to discern whether there is some failure in this detachment and correct it.

6. I sometimes hear it said about the first members of religious orders that since they were the foundation the Lord granted them greater favors as He did to our holy forebears; and this is true. But we must always observe that they are the foundation for those who are to come. If we who live now had not fallen from where our forebears were, and those who come after us would live as they did, the edifice would always be firm. What does it profit me that our forebears had been so holy if I afterward am so wretched that I leave the edifice damaged through bad customs? For it is clear that those who come will not so much remember those who lived many years ago as those they see before them. It would be rather amusing were I to make the excuse that I am not one of the first members and at the same time fail to recognize the difference lying between my life and virtue and that of those to whom God granted such great favors.

7. Oh, God help me! What twisted excuses and what obvious deceit! I regret, my God, to be so wretched and so useless in your service; but I know well that the fault lies within me that You do not grant me the favors You did to my forebears. I grieve over my life, Lord, when I compare it with theirs, and I cannot say this without tears. I see that I have lost what they have worked

for and that I can in no way blame You. Nor is it in any way good for persons to complain if they see their order in some decline; rather, they should strive to be the kind of rock on which the edifice may again be raised, for the Lord will help toward that.[5]

8. Well to return to what I was saying,[6] for I have digressed a great deal, the favors the Lord grants in these houses are so many that if there are one or two in each that God leads now by meditation all the rest reach perfect contemplation. Some are so advanced that they attain to rapture. To others the Lord grants a favor of another kind, giving them, along with rapture, revelations and visions that one clearly understands to be from God. There is no house now that does not have one, two, or three who receive this latter favor. Well do I understand that sanctity does not lie in these favors, nor is it my intention to praise only them but to make it understood that the counsels I want to give have a purpose.

Chapter 5

Gives some counsels on matters concerning prayer. This chapter is very beneficial for those engaged in active works.

IT IS NOT MY INTENTION or thought that what I say here be taken for certain and as an infallible rule, for that would be foolish in things so difficult. Since there are many paths along this way of the spirit, it could be that I will manage to say certain useful things about some of them. If those who do not walk along the path of which I'm speaking do not understand what I'm saying, it will be because they are walking by another. And if I do not help anyone, the Lord will accept my desire. He knows that even though I have not experienced all of which I speak, I have seen it in other souls.

2. First, I want to treat, according to my poor understanding, of the substance of perfect prayer. For I have run into some for whom it seems the whole business lies in thinking. If they can keep their mind much occupied in God, even though great ef-

fort is exerted, they at once think they are spiritual. If, on the contrary, without being able to avoid it, they become distracted, even if for the sake of good things, they then become disconsolate and think they are lost. Learned men will not fall victim to these misconceptions, although I have already met learned men who have had some of them. But it is fitting that we women receive advice with regard to all these misunderstandings. I do not deny that it is a favor from the Lord if someone is able to be always meditating on His works, and it is good that one strive to do so. However, it must be understood that not all imaginations are by their nature capable of this meditating, but all souls are capable of loving. I have already at another time written about the causes of this restlessness of our imagination, I think;[1] not all the causes—that would be impossible —but some. And so I am not treating of this now. But I should like to explain that the soul is not the mind, nor is the will directed by thinking, for this would be very unfortunate. Hence, the soul's progress does not lie in thinking much but in loving much.

3. How does one acquire this love? By being determined to work and to suffer, and to do so when the occasion arises. It is indeed true that by thinking of what we owe the Lord, of who He is, and what we are, a soul's determination grows, and that this thinking is very meritorious and appropriate for beginners. But it must be understood that this is true provided that nothing interferes with obedience or benefit to one's neighbor. When either of these two things presents itself, time is demanded, and also the abandonment of what we so much desire to give God, which, in our opinion, is to be alone thinking of Him and delighting in the delights that He gives us. To leave aside these delights for either of these other two things is to give delight to Him and do the work for Him, as He Himself said: *What you did for one of these little ones you did for Me.*[2] And in matters touching on obedience He doesn't want the soul who truly loves Him to take any other path than the one He did: *obediens usque ad mortem.*[3]

4. Well if this is true, from where does the displeasure proceed which for the greater part is felt when one has not spent a

large part of the day very much withdrawn and absorbed in
God, even though we are occupied with these other things? In
my opinion, there are two reasons for this displeasure: The first
and main one[4] is the very subtle self-love that is mixed in here.
This self-love does not allow one to understand what it is to want
to please ourselves rather than God. For, clearly, after a soul
begins to taste how sweet the Lord is,[5] it is more pleasing for the
body to be resting without work and for the soul to be receiving
delight.

5. O charity of those who truly love this Lord and know their
own nature! How little rest they can have if they see they may
play a little part in getting even one soul to make progress and to
love God more, or in consoling it, or in taking away some danger
from it. How poorly would it then rest with this particular rest of
its own! And when it cannot help with deeds, it will do so with
prayer, begging the Lord for the many souls that it is sad to see
being lost. The soul loses its delight and counts the loss as gain,
for it doesn't think about its own satisfaction but rather about
how it can best do the Lord's will, and this it does through obedience. It would be a distressing thing if God were clearly telling
us to go after something that matters to Him and we would not
want to do so but want to remain looking at Him because that is
more pleasing to us. What an amusing kind of progress in the
love of God it is, to tie His hands by thinking that He cannot
help us except by one path!

6. I know personally some individuals (leaving aside, as I
have said,[6] what I have experienced) who brought me to understand this truth when I was greatly distressed to see myself with
so little time. And I thus was sorry for them to see they were so
occupied with so many business matters and things that obedience commanded them. I was thinking to myself, and even said
so, that it wasn't possible in the midst of such commotion for the
spirit to grow, for at that time they didn't have much spirit. O
Lord, how different are your paths from our clumsy imaginings!
And how from a soul that is already determined to love You and
is abandoned into Your hands, You do not want anything but
that it obey, that it inquire well into what is for Your greater service, and that it desire this! There's no need for it to be seeking

out paths or choosing them, for its will is Yours. You, my Lord, take up this care of guiding it to where it receives the most benefit. The prelate who is the superior may not be concerned for what benefits the soul but concerned only that the business he thinks is fitting for the community be attended to. Yet, You, my God, do have concern and go about disposing the soul and the things with which it is dealing in such a way that, without understanding how, we find in ourselves spiritual improvement, so great that we are afterward left amazed.

7. There was a person to whom I spoke a few days ago who for about fifteen years was kept so busy through obedience with work in occupations and government that in all those years he didn't remember having had one day for himself, although he tried the best he could to keep a pure conscience and have some periods each day for prayer. His soul in its inclination is one of the most obedient I have seen, and so he communicates this spirit of obedience to all those with whom he deals. The Lord has repaid him well; for he has found that he has, without knowing how, that same precious and desirable liberty of spirit that the perfect have. In it, they find all the happiness that could be wanted in this life, for in desiring nothing they possess all. Nothing on earth do they fear or desire, neither do trials disturb them, nor do consolations move them. In sum, nothing can take away their peace because these souls depend only on God. And since no one can take Him away from them, only the fear of losing Him can cause them pain. Everything else in this world, in their opinion, is as though it were not; it neither contributes anything nor removes anything from their happiness. Oh, happy obedience and happy the resulting distraction that could obtain so much!

8. This is not the only person, for I have known others of the same sort, whom I had not seen for some, or many, years. In asking them about how they had spent these years, I learned that the years were all spent in the fulfillment of the duties of obedience and charity. On the other hand, I saw such improvement in spiritual things that I was amazed. Well, come now, my daughters, don't be sad when obedience draws you to involvement in exterior matters. Know that if it is in the kitchen, the

Lord walks among the pots and pans helping you both interiorly
and exteriorly.

9. I remember that I met a religious who had resolved and
become very determined never to say "no" to anything his superior commanded no matter how much labor it would cost him.
One day he was completely worn out from work; and when it
was already late and he could no longer stay on his feet and went
to sit down and rest a little, the superior met him and told him
to take the hoe and go dig in the garden. He remained silent; although in his human nature he was indeed afflicted, for he
couldn't help it. He took his hoe and when he was about to enter
a passageway into the garden (I saw the spot many years after he
told me of this, for I managed to found a house in that place),
our Lord appeared to him weighed down with the cross, so tired
and worn that this religious understood clearly that what he
himself was enduring was nothing when compared with what
the Lord endured.

10. I believe that, since the devil sees there is no path that
leads more quickly to the highest perfection than obedience, he
sets up many annoyances and difficulties under the color of
good. Note this well and you will see clearly that I am speaking
the truth. The highest perfection obviously does not consist in
interior delights or in great raptures or in visions or in the spirit
of prophecy but in having our will so much in conformity with
God's will that there is nothing we know He wills that we do not
want with all our desire, and in accepting the bitter as happily
as we do the delightful when we know that His Majesty desires it.
This seems most difficult (not the doing of it, but this being content with what completely contradicts our nature); and indeed
it truly is difficult. But love has this strength if it is perfect, for
we forget about pleasing ourselves in order to please the one we
love. And truly this is so; for even though the trials may be very
great, they become sweet when we know we are pleasing God.
And this is the way by which those who have reached this stage
love persecutions, dishonor, and offenses. This is so certain, so
well known, and so plain that there is no reason for me to delay
over the matter.

11. What I intend to explain is why obedience, in my opin-

ion, is the quickest or best means for reaching this most happy
state. The reason is that since we are by no means lords of our
own will in such a way that we can employ it purely and simply
in God, obedience is the true path for subjecting it to reason.
For this subjection is not accomplished by means of good reasons; human nature and self-love can find so many of them that
we would never arrive at the goal. And often the most reasonable thing seems to us foolish if it is not to our advantage.

12. So much could be said here that we would never finish
dealing with this interior battle and all that the devil, the world,
and our own sensuality do to make us twist reason.

Well, what is the remedy? That in obedience, just as in a very
dubious litigation, a judge is accepted and both sides place the
matter in his hands. Tired of arguing, our soul accepts one who
may be either the superior or the confessor with the determination not to have any more argument or to think any more of its
own case but to trust the words of the Lord who says, *Whoever
hears you hears Me,*[7] and it disregards its own will. The Lord es-
teems this surrender very much, and rightly so, because it means
making Him Lord over the free will He has given us. By exercising ourselves in this surrender, sometimes denying ourselves, at
other times waging a thousand battles since the judgment made
in our case seems to us absurd, we come to be conformed with
what they command us. It can be a painful exercise, but with or
without the pain we in the end do what is commanded, and the
Lord helps so much on His part that for the same reason that we
subject our will and reason to Him He makes us lords over our
will. Then, being lords of ourselves, we can with perfection be
occupied with God, giving Him a pure will that He may join it
with His, asking Him to send fire from heaven so that His love
may burn this sacrifice[8] and take away everything that could
displease him. We have done what we can by placing the sacrifice on the altar, although through much hardship. And, insofar as is in our power, the sacrifice remains on the altar and does
not touch the ground.

13. Clearly, no one can give what he does not have; he must
have it first. Well, believe me that in order to acquire this treasure there is no better way than to dig and toil in order to exca-

vate from this mine of obedience. The more we dig the more we shall find; and the more we submit to men, having no other will than that of our superiors, the more we shall be lords over our will so as to bring it into conformity with God's will.

Observe, Sisters, whether leaving the pleasure of solitude is not well repaid. I tell you that it is not because of a lack of solitude that you will fail to dispose yourselves to reach this true union that was mentioned, that is, to make your will one with God's. This is the union that I desire and would want for all of you, and not some absorptions, however delightful they may be, that have been given the name "union." The absorption will be genuine union if afterward there is present the union just explained. But if after this suspension not much obedience remains, and self-will is present, it seems to me the soul will be united with its self-love rather than with the will of God. May His Majesty be pleased that I act in accordance with what I understand.

14. The second reason,[9] it seems to me, for this displeasure is that since in solitude there are fewer occasions to offend the Lord (for some cannot be lacking because the devils and we ourselves are present everywhere), it seems the soul in its journey is freer from stain. For if it is fearful of offending Him, it finds the greatest consolation in not having anything to make it stumble. And certainly this seems to me reason enough for desiring not to have conversation with anyone unless it's about God's great favors and delights.

15. Here, my daughters, is where love will be seen: not hidden in corners but in the midst of the occasions of falling.[10] And believe me that even though there may be more faults, and even some slight losses, our gain will be incomparably greater. Note that I am always presupposing that these things are done out of obedience or charity. For if these latter are not factors, I always repeat that solitude is better, and even that we must desire it. We must desire solitude even when involved in the things I'm speaking of; indeed, this desire is continually present in souls that truly love God. As for my saying that leaving solitude is a gain, I say this because doing so makes us realize who we are and the degree of virtue we have. For people who are always recol-

lected in solitude, however holy in their own opinion they may be, don't know whether they are patient or humble, nor do they have the means of knowing this. How could it be known whether a man were valiant if he were not seen in battle? St. Peter thought he was very courageous; see how he acted when the occasion presented itself.[11] But he came through that experience not trusting at all in himself, and as a result he trusted in God and subsequently suffered the martyrdom about which we know.[12]

16. Oh, God help me, if only we understood how great our misery is! In everything there is danger if we do not understand this misery. For that reason it is a great good for us if we are ordered to do things that show us our own lowliness. I consider one day of humble self-knowledge a greater favor from the Lord, even though the day may have cost us numerous afflictions and trials, than many days of prayer. Moreover, the true lover loves everywhere and is always thinking of the Beloved! It would be a thing hard to bear if we were able to pray only when off in some corner. I do realize that prayer in the midst of occupations cannot last many hours; but, O my Lord, what power over You a sigh of sorrow has that comes from the depths of our heart on seeing that it isn't enough that we are in this exile but that we are not even given the chance to be alone enjoying You.

17. Here we see clearly that we are His slaves, our wills being sold, out of love for Him, through the virtue of obedience, since through obedience we in some way give up enjoying God Himself. And yet, this is nothing if we consider that He came from the bosom of His Father out of obedience to become our slave. Well, how can one repay this favor or what service render for it? It's necessary to be on one's guard and careful in the performance of good works by having frequent interior recourse to God, even though these works are done in obedience and charity. And let souls believe me that it is not the length of time spent in prayer that benefits one; when the time is spent as well in good works, it is a great help in preparing the soul for the enkindling of love. The soul may thereby be better prepared in a very short time than through many hours of reflection. All must come from His hand. May He be blessed forever.

Chapter 6

*Warns about the harm that can be done to spiritual people if
they do not understand when the spirit must be resisted. Treats
of the soul's desires to receive Communion and of the delusion
that can be present in such desires. There are important things
here for those who govern these houses.*[1]

I HAVE DILIGENTLY TRIED to understand the origin of a great
absorption I have seen in some persons whom the Lord favors much in prayer and who do their best to prepare themselves
to receive these gifts. I am not dealing now with the soul's suspension or rapture given by His Majesty, for I have written
much about this in other places.[2] In a matter like rapture there
is nothing to speak of because if it is genuine we cannot do anything ourselves to prevent it, however much we try. It must be
noted that in rapture the power that takes away our power to be
in control of ourselves lasts but a short while. But frequently it
happens that there begins a kind of prayer of quiet, something
that resembles spiritual sleep, that so absorbs the soul that if we
do not understand how one is to proceed therein much time
could be lost and our strength diminished through our own fault
and with little merit.

2. I would like to know how to explain myself here; it is so difficult that I don't know if I'll succeed. But I do know well that, if
they want to believe me, souls who may be proceeding under
this misconception will understand. I know some souls of great
virtue who remained for seven or eight hours in absorption;
everything seemed to them to be rapture. Any virtuous exercise
so laid hold of them that they soon abandoned themselves to the
absorption,[3] thinking it was not good to resist the Lord. Little
by little such persons can die or become fools if they do not seek
a remedy. What I understand about this occurrence is that since
the Lord begins to give delight, and our nature is very fond of
delight, the soul becomes so occupied in the pleasure that it
does not want to stir or lose that experience for anything. Indeed, the pleasure is greater than any of the world's pleasures.
And when the experience takes place in a weak nature, or comes

from one's own natural inventiveness (or better, imagination), nature will make souls know a thousand delightful lies. In this absorption the imagination does not wander but in apprehending one thing concentrates on it without distraction. Many persons when they begin to think about something, even though the matter may not concern God, are left absorbed or looking at it without adverting to what they are gazing on. They are like people who are slow and who seem, through indolence, to forget what they are about to say. This is what happens in these cases in conformity with the person's nature, or bodily humors, or weakness, or if the individual suffers melancholy; these people end up believing a thousand pleasant lies.

3. A little further on I shall speak of melancholy,[4] but even if this humor is not present, that which I have mentioned[5] happens. And it also happens to persons who are worn out through penance. As I have said,[6] when love begins to give pleasure to the senses these persons allow themselves to be carried away by it. In my opinion their love would be much better if they did not allow themselves to remain in stupefaction, for in this condition of prayer one can easily resist. For just as a person will faint from weakness and be unable to speak or stir, so this is what happens here; for the strength of the spirit lays hold of nature, when this latter is weak, and subjects it.

4. You could ask me what difference there is between this absorption and rapture since the two are the same, at least in appearance—and you would be right as regards appearance but not as regards reality. For in rapture, or union of all the faculties, as I say, the duration is short, and great effects, interior light, and many other benefits are given, and the intellect doesn't work; it is the Lord who works in the will. In the absorption, things are very different, for although the body is captive, the will is not, nor is the memory or the intellect. But these faculties carry on their delirious activity, and if they rest in something they will perhaps go back and forth over it with ifs and buts.

5. I find no benefit in this bodily weakness—for it is nothing else—except that it arises from a good source. It would be a greater help to use this time well than to remain in this absorption so long. Much more can be merited by making an act of love

and by often awakening the will to greater love of God than by leaving it listless. So I counsel the prioresses to make every possible effort to prevent the nuns from spending long periods in this daze. For to remain in such an absorption is nothing else, in my opinion, than to allow the faculties and senses to become crippled and not carry out what the soul commands them. Thus they deprive the soul of the gain that they usually get for it by proceeding carefully. If the absorption is understood to be caused by weakness, take away the fasts and disciplines (I mean those that are not obligatory, and in time it could happen that all of them in good conscience may be taken away), and give these persons duties that will distract them.

6. And even if one does not experience these swoons, this course of action is necessary if the imagination is greatly occupied, even if with very sublime things of prayer. For it happens sometimes that these persons are not in control of themselves. If they have received some extraordinary favor from the Lord or seen some vision, then, especially, will their souls be left in such a condition that they will think they are continuing to see the vision; but this is not so, for the vision was seen no more than once. Whoever finds herself in this absorption for many days should strive to change the subject she is meditating on, for if a subject pertains to the things of God there is no difficulty in dwelling on one more than another since the faculties will be occupied in God. And sometimes one rejoices as much in considering God's creatures and the power He had in creating them as in thinking of the Creator Himself.

7. O hapless human misery that was left in this condition through sin, for even in good things we need rule and measure so as not to ruin our health and become incapable of enjoying them. And indeed what was said is fitting for many persons, especially those with weak heads or imaginations. If one follows this advice one serves our Lord more, and it is very necessary that what I said be understood. If a nun sees that one of the mysteries of the Passion or of the glory of heaven or of any other similar thing comes into her imagination and remains many days and that, although she wants to, she cannot think of something else or take away this absorption, let her understand that it is fit-

ting for her to distract herself insofar as she can. Otherwise, she will in time come to know the harm that will be done and that this absorption stems from what I mentioned: either from great bodily weakness or from the imagination, which is worse. A madman, when he goes into some frenzy, is not the master of himself, cannot divert his attention, or think of anything else, nor are there reasons that can move him to do this because he is not in control of his reasoning power. The same thing could happen here; even though the absorption is a delightful madness — or if she has the humor of melancholy — it can do her very great harm. I don't see how it could be good, for the soul is capable of enjoying God Himself. Well, even if the subject matter is not one of the mysteries that I mentioned,[7] since God is infinite, why must the soul be held captive by just one of His mysteries or grandeurs, for there is so much in which we can be occupied? And the more of His mysteries we might want to consider the more His grandeurs will be revealed.

8. I do not mean that in the course of an hour or a day they should think on many things, for this would perhaps amount to enjoying none of them properly. Since these matters are so delicate, I would not want others to think I'm saying what it doesn't enter my mind to say, or to understand one thing for another. Certainly, it is so important to understand this chapter well that even though writing about such a matter may be a tiresome thing to do, it doesn't tire me. Nor would I want whoever does not at first understand this to grow tired in reading it many times, especially the prioresses and the mistresses of novices who must guide the Sisters in prayer. For the Sisters will see that if they do not walk carefully in the beginning, much time will be required afterward to remedy similar weaknesses.

9. If I were to write all that has come to my attention concerning this harm, they would see that I am right to insist so much on the matter. I want to mention only one instance, and from this one they will be able to deduce everything else. There are in one of these monasteries two Sisters, one a choir nun and the other a lay Sister,[8] both of whom are most prayerful, mortified, humble and virtuous, much favored by the Lord, to whom He communicates His great marvels. They are especially

so detached and taken up with His love that it doesn't seem, however much we desire to catch up with them, that they fail to respond, in conformity with our lowliness, to the favors our Lord grants them. I have dwelt so much on their virtues in order that those who do not have so much virtue will fear more. When they began to experience some great impulses of desire for the Lord that they could not resist, it seemed to them the desire was mitigated when they received Communion. As a result, they obtained from their confessors permission to receive frequently. Their affliction increased so much that if they did not receive Communion each day, it seemed to them they would die. The confessors, since they saw souls like these with such great desires, thought daily Communion was a suitable remedy for the complaint; and the one confessor was a very spiritual man.

10. The matter didn't stop here. In the case of one of the nuns, her longings were so great that she found it necessary to receive Communion early in the morning so as to be able to live; that was her opinion, for the two were not souls that would feign anything, nor for anything in the world would they tell a lie. I was not there, but the prioress[9] wrote to me of what was going on, saying that she could not get anywhere with them and that competent persons held that since nothing else could be done this remedy should be used. I at once, by the grace of God, understood the situation. Nonetheless, I remained silent until I could be present there, for I feared lest I be mistaken; and it would not have been right to contradict the one who approved, until giving him my reasons.

11. He was so humble that as soon as I went there and spoke to him he agreed with me. The other one was not so spiritual, hardly at all in comparison. There was no argument that could persuade him. But I cared little about persuading this one because I was not so obliged to him. I began to speak to the nuns and give many reasons in my opinion sufficient to make them understand that it was their imagination that made them think they would die without this remedy. They had their minds so fixed on receiving Communion as a remedy that nothing sufficed, nor was it enough to bring forth reasons. Now I saw that they were to be excused, and I told them that I too had such

desires and would give up receiving Communion so that they could believe that they wouldn't have to receive except when everyone did. I told them we would all three die, for I thought doing so would be better than to start a custom like this in these houses where there were others who loved God as much as they and would want to do likewise.

12. The harm the custom had caused was so extreme—and the devil must have meddled—that since they did not receive Communion, they truly thought they would die. I showed great severity, because the more I saw that they were not submitting themselves to obedience (because in their opinion they could not do so) the more clearly I saw that the desire was a temptation. They passed through that day with a good deal of difficulty; and another day, with a little less. And so the impulsion continued to diminish in such a way that even if I received Communion, because I was ordered to do so (for the confessor saw them so weak that he didn't give them the same order), they bore this very well.

13. Within a short time both they and everyone else recognized that this had been a temptation. And they realized how good it had been to remedy the situation in time, for a little later more things happened in that house that were disturbing to the superiors (not through the fault of these two nuns—perhaps later I may say something about it); and these superiors would not, in addition, have taken well to a custom like that, nor would they have tolerated it.

14. Oh, how many things of this sort I could mention. I'll mention only one other. It didn't happen in a monastery of ours but in a monastery of Bernardines. There was a nun there who was no less virtuous than those mentioned. Through disciplines and fasts she became so weak that each time she received Communion or had occasion to be enkindled in devotion she would immediately fall to the floor and there remain for eight or nine hours. It seemed to her and everyone else that she was experiencing a rapture. This happened so often that if a remedy had not been provided, much harm would have resulted. The report of the raptures spread through the whole locality. It saddened

me to hear about her experience because, thanks be to the Lord, I understood its nature, and I feared about where it would end up. Her confessor was a close friend of mine, and he came to tell me about it. I told him what I understood and why the absorption was a waste of time and couldn't possibly be a rapture, but the result of weakness. I told him to take away her fasts and disciplines and to distract her. She was obedient; she did as he said. As soon as she began to gain strength there was no more thought of rapture. And if indeed the experience had been one of rapture nothing would have sufficed to prevent it except the will of God, for the force of the spirit is so great that our efforts are not sufficient to resist. And, as I said,[10] a rapture leaves great effects in the soul; this other leaves no more effects than if it had not occurred, but tiredness in the body.

15. Let it, therefore, be understood from this example that anything that so controls us that we know our reason is not free should be held as suspect. Know that liberty of spirit will never be gained in this way. For one of the traits reason has is that it can find God in all things and be able to think about them. All the rest is subjection of spirit and, apart from the harm done to the body, so binds the soul as to hinder growth. The soul here resembles someone on a journey who enters a quagmire or swamp and thus cannot move onward. And, in order to advance, a soul must not only walk but fly. This immobility happens frequently when, as they say (and it seems to them), they are immersed in the divinity and cannot help themselves or find a remedy by diverting their attention because they are suspended.

16. Let them note that I again advise that in an instance of one day or four or eight there is nothing to fear, for it is not unusual for someone naturally weak to remain stunned for a number of days. If the matter goes beyond this, a remedy is necessary. The good in all this is that there is no sinful fault, nor will these souls fail to gain merit. But there are the difficulties I mentioned and many more. In the matter concerning Communion, it will be a very great difficulty, because of the soul's love, if there is no submission in these things to the confessor and the prioress. Even though the soul feels drawn to solitude, it shouldn't go to the extreme of not consulting with them. It's

necessary in this just as in other things that souls mortify themselves and be brought to understand that refraining from doing one's own will is more fitting than the experience of consolation.

17. Our self-love, too, can get mixed in with these experiences. It has happened to me sometimes that when I saw others receiving Communion just after I had received myself (to the point that the sacred species must have been still intact), I would desire not to have received so as to receive again. Since this happened to me so many times, I came afterward to notice (for at the time it didn't seem to me there was anything to give careful attention to) how the desire came more from wanting my own satisfaction than from love of God. Since in receiving Communion we, for the most part, experience tenderness and delight, that desire to receive again was taking hold of me. If its purpose was to have God within my soul, I already had Him; if it was to fulfill the obligation of going to Holy Communion, I had already done so; if to receive the favors that are bestowed with the Blessed Sacrament, I had already received them. Finally, I came to understand clearly that there was no other purpose in the desire than to experience again that sensible delight.

18. I remember that in a place where we had one of our monasteries I knew a woman who was a very great servant of God in the opinion of the whole town, and she must have been. She received Communion daily and did not have a particular confessor; but on one day she would go to one church to receive Communion, and on another day to another. I noted this and wished more that she obey someone than receive Communion so often. She was in a house by herself and, in my opinion, doing whatever she wanted. But since she was good, all that she did was considered good. I told her of this at times, but she didn't pay any attention to me, and with reason, for she was much better than I. But in this matter I didn't think I was mistaken. The holy Fray Peter of Alcántara came to that place, and I arranged that he talk to her. I did not rest satisfied with the account she gave him. But perhaps she had nothing more to tell, for we are so miserable that we are never much satisfied except with those who follow our own way; for I believe that she had served the Lord more and done more penance in one year than I had in many.

19. But to come to the point, she fell sick with a fatal illness and diligently arranged that Mass be said in her house each day and that she receive the Blessed Sacrament. Since the sickness continued, a priest, a good servant of God, who often said the Mass for her, didn't think it was proper that she receive Communion daily in her house. The devil must have tempted her, because that day happened to be her last, the day on which she died. Since she saw the Mass ending and that she was deprived of the Lord, she became so greatly vexed and angry with the priest that he came to me, much scandalized, to tell me about it. I felt very sorry, for I still don't know if she was reconciled; it seems to me she died soon afterward.

20. Hence I came to understand the harm done by following our own will in no matter what; and especially in so important a matter. For it is right that those who approach the Lord with such frequency should so understand their own unworthiness as to refuse to follow their own opinion, but supply, by obedience to a command, that which is lacking in order to approach so great a Lord — and what is lacking must be great. This good soul had the opportunity to humble herself very much, and perhaps she would have thereby merited more than by receiving Communion. It should be understood that the priest was not at fault, but that the Lord, seeing her misery and how unworthy she was, had thus ordained in order to enter so wretched a lodging. This is what a certain person did whom discreet confessors often refused to allow to receive Communion,[11] for she went frequently. This person, though she felt the loss very deeply, desired, on the other hand, the honor of God more than her own and did nothing but praise Him because He had awakened the confessor to look after her and not let His Majesty enter so wretched a lodging. And with these reflections she obeyed, with deep calm in her soul, although with a tender and loving pain. But not for the whole world together would she have gone against what was commanded her.

21. Believe me, it is clear that a love of God (I do not mean that it is really love but that in our opinion it is) that so stirs the passions that one ends up offending the Lord, or so alters the peace of the enamoured soul that no attention is paid to reason,

is in fact self-seeking. And the devil will be on the alert to afflict us when he thinks he can do us more harm, as he did to this woman. For certainly it frightened me very much, although not because I believed it would play a part in hindering her salvation, for the goodness of God is great, but because the temptation came at the worst time.

22. I have mentioned the matter here so that the prioresses might be warned and the Sisters might fear, reflect, and examine themselves on the manner in which they approach to receive so great a favor. If they approach in order to please God, they already know that He is pleased more by obedience than by sacrifice.[12] Well, if this is true and if I merit more, why am I disturbed? I do not say they are left without a humble distress, for not all souls have reached such perfection that they will be freed from suffering distress merely by the fact that they know they are doing what is more pleasing to God. Clearly, if the will is very detached from all self-interest, it will not feel anything. Rather it will rejoice that it is offered an occasion to please the Lord in something so costly, and it will humble itself and be just as satisfied by making a spiritual communion.

23. In the beginning of the spiritual life these great desires to approach the Lord are favors granted by God. This is true also at the end, but I say the beginning because at that time they should be more appreciated. Since in other things pertaining to perfection that I mentioned[13] these beginners are not so advanced, it may be readily granted them that they experience tenderness and feel pain when Communion is taken from them, provided the pain is borne with peace of soul and they draw forth acts of humility as a result. But when these souls experience some disturbance or passion and become angry with the prioress or confessor, they should believe that their desire to receive is an obvious temptation. This also holds true if someone decides to receive Communion even though the confessor says not to receive. I would not want the merit that is thereby derived, for in such matters we must not be the judges of our own case. He who has the keys to bind and loose must be the one to judge.[14] That we might have understanding in things so important, may it please the Lord to give us light; and may His help not fail lest we cause Him displeasure through the favors He grants us.

Chapter 7

How one must deal with the nuns who have melancholy.[1] *This chapter is necessary for prioresses.*

THESE SISTERS OF MINE at St.Joseph's in Salamanca, where I am staying while writing this, have repeatedly asked me to say something about how one must deal with the nuns who have that bodily humor called melancholy. For however much we strive not to accept those who have it, it is subtle and feigns death when it needs to, and thus we do not recognize it until the matter cannot be remedied. It seems to me that in a little book I said something about this;[2] I don't remember. Little is lost in saying something here, if the Lord be pleased that I succeed in doing so. It could be that I said something about this already, at another time; I would mention it another hundred times if I thought I could say something pertinent about the matter. So many are the contrivances that this humor seeks in order to do its own will that there is a need to search them out in order to know how to bear with those who have it and govern them so that no harm is done to the other nuns.

2. It must be pointed out that not all those who have this humor are so troublesome, for those who are humble and good-natured, even though they are disturbed within themselves, do not hurt others, especially if they possess sound intelligence. And also there are greater and lesser degrees of this humor. Certainly, I believe the devil takes melancholy as a means for trying to win over some persons. And if they do not walk with great care, he will do so. For since this humor can subdue reason, what won't our passions do once reason is darkened? It seems that if reason is wanting, madness results, and so it does. But in those of whom we are now speaking, the melancholy doesn't reach the point of madness, which would be much less harmful. But to have to consider someone a rational person and deal with her as such even though she isn't is an unbearable burden. Those who are totally afflicted with this illness are to be pitied, but they do no harm, and if there is a means for bringing them under control, it is to put fear into them.

3. With those in whom this very harmful affliction has just begun, even though it is not so strong, the same remedy is necessary if other attemps prove insufficient. The affliction, in sum, springs from that humor or root and stems from that stock. And it is necessary that the prioress make use of the penances of the order and strive to bring these persons into submission in such a way as to make them understand they will obtain neither all nor part of what they want. For if they come to think that sometimes their cries, and the furies the devil speaks through them in order to bring them to ruin if he can, are sufficient for them to get what they want, they will be lost. And one such person is enough to disrupt the quiet of a monastery. Since the poor little thing has no one to help her defend herself from the things the devil puts before her, it is necessary for the prioress to proceed with the greatest care in governing her not only in exterior but also in interior matters. For since reason is obscured in the sick person, it must be clear in the prioress so that the devil doesn't begin to bring that soul under his control, taking that affliction as a means. Only at intervals does this humor afflict so much as to subdue reason. And then the person is not at fault, just as insane people are not at fault for the foolish things they do. But those who are not insane, whose reason is weak and at other times well, still have some fault. Thus it is a dangerous thing if during the times in which they are ill they begin to take liberties, which is a terrible artifice of the devil. It's necessary that they do not do so; otherwise, they will not be masters of themselves when they are well. If we consider the matter, that which interests these melancholic persons most is getting their own way, saying everything that comes to their lips, looking at the faults of others with which they hide their own, and finding rest in what gives them pleasure; in sum, they are like a person who cannot bear anyone who resists him. Well, if the passions go unmortified, and each passion seeks to get what it wants, what would happen if no one resisted them?

4. I repeat, as one who has seen and dealt with many persons having this affliction, that there is no other remedy for it than to make these persons submit in all the ways and means possible. If words do not suffice, use punishment; if light punishment is

not enough, try heavy; if one month in the prison cell is not enough, try four months; no greater good can be done for their souls. For as I have said[3] and I repeat (and it is important for the afflicted themselves to understand this, even though at times they may be unable to help themselves), since the affliction is not confirmed madness of the kind that excuses one from any fault — although sometimes it may be, but it is not always so — the soul remains in much danger. But sometimes, as I say, reason is so overpowered that those afflicted will be forced to do or say what they did and said when they had no control. It is a great mercy from God toward those suffering this affliction that they may submit to someone who will govern them through this danger that I mentioned,[4] for herein lies all their good. And, for the love of God, if anyone read this let her reflect that perhaps it is a matter of her own salvation.

5. I know some persons who are on the borderline of losing their minds completely. But they are humble and so fearful of offending God that even though they may be dissolving in tears and grieving within themselves, they don't do anything but what they are ordered to do. And they suffer their illness as others do theirs; although this one is a greater martyrdom. Thus they will have greater glory and have their purgatory here in this life instead of the next. But I repeat that those who do not submit willingly should be urged to do so by the prioress. And let them not be deceived with indiscreet pieties lest they end up disturbing all with their confusion.

6. There is another very great harm, leaving aside the danger that was mentioned:[5] Since the afflicted nun appears to be good and the force the illness exercises interiorly is not understood, our nature is so miserable that each one will think that she herself is melancholic and that thus others must bear with her. And, in point of fact, the devil will cause the matter to be thus understood, and he will bring about such havoc that when one comes to recognize the fact there will be difficulty in providing a remedy. This matter is so important that no negligence whatsoever should be allowed. But if the melancholic nun should resist the prelate, who is the superior, she should pay for it in the same way as the healthy nun and should not be pardoned for any-

thing. If she should utter an insulting word to her Sister, the same holds true. So likewise in all similar things.

7. It seems to be unjust to punish a sick person, who can't help it, just as one would a healthy person. Therefore, it would also be unjust to bind and whip the insane, and the just thing would be to allow them to kill everyone. Believe me, I have tried and, in my opinion, attempted many remedies, and I find no other. It absolutely must not be tolerated that the prioress out of pity allow such nuns to begin taking liberties, for when she gets down to remedying the situation much harm will have already been done to others. If the insane are bound and chastised so that they will not kill others, and this is right and even seems to be a very compassionate thing to do since they cannot control themselves, how much more must one be careful not to allow these melancholic persons liberties by which they could harm souls. And I truly believe that this affliction is often, as I have said,[6] found in those whose dispositions are unrestrained, lacking in humility, and poorly disciplined; and the humor doesn't have as much strength as in the insane. I mean that "in some" the humor doesn't have as much strength, for I have seen that when there is someone to fear they do control themselves and they can. Well, why can't they do so for God? I fear that the devil, under the guise of this humor, as I have said,[7] wants to gain many souls.

8. Nowadays the term is used more than usual, and it happens that all self-will and freedom go by the name melancholy. Thus I have thought that in these houses and in all Religious houses, this term should not be uttered. For the term seems to bring along with it freedom from any control. Rather, the condition should be called a serious illness—and how truly it is one—and be cared for as such. For sometimes it is very necessary to reduce the humor by means of medicine in order that it be endured; and the nun must remain in the infirmary and understand that when she comes out and returns to the community she must be humble like all and obey as do all. And she must understand that when she does not do so she may not use the humor as her defense. For the reasons that I have mentioned, and more could be said, this procedure is fitting. The prioress

must, without letting these nuns realize it, lead them with much compassion, like a true mother, and seek whatever means she can to provide a remedy.

9. It seems that I am contradicting myself because up to now I said that these nuns must be dealt with strictly. So I repeat that they must not think they can come out and do what they want, nor should they be allowed out except under the condition that they must obey. For the harm lies in their thinking that they will be free to do whatever they want. But the prioress can refrain from ordering them to do what she sees they will be unable to do because of their not having the strength within themselves. She should lead them with all the skill and love necessary so that if possible they submit out of love, which would be much better, and usually happens. She should show that she greatly loves them and make this known through words and deeds. And she must note that the greatest remedy she has is to keep them much occupied with duties so that they do not have the opportunity to be imagining things, for herein lies all their trouble. And even though they may not perform these duties so well, she should suffer some defects so as not to have to suffer other greater ones that will arise if the melancholy overpowers them. I know that this is the most suitable remedy you can provide. And strive that they do not have long periods of prayer, not even those established in the constitutions, because, for the greater part, their imaginations are weak and the long prayer will do them much harm. Otherwise, they will fancy things that neither they nor anyone who hears them will ever understand. Let her take care that they eat fish only rarely;[8] and also during the fasts, they ought not fast as much as do the others.

10. It seems excessive to give so much advice for this affliction and not for any other, there being so many serious ones in our miserable life, especially when considering the weakness of women. It is for two reasons that I do so: First, it seems these nuns are well, for they don't want to know that they have this affliction. Since it doesn't force them to stay in bed, because they do not have a fever, or to call the doctor, it's necessary for the prioress to be their doctor; for it is a sickness more prejudicial to all perfection than that of those who are in bed and in danger of

death. Second, in the case of other illnesses it happens that either one is cured or one dies; with this illness, very seldom are the afflicted cured, nor do they die from it but they come to lose their minds completely—which is a death capable of killing all the nuns. They suffer more than death in themselves through afflictions, fantasies, and scruples, all of which they call temptations, and so they will have a great deal of merit. If they could come to understand that the illness is the cause of these, they would find much relief provided they paid no attention to them.

Indeed, I have great compassion for them, and it is also right that all those living with them have it. These latter should reflect that the Lord can give this compassion, and they should bear up with them, without letting this be known as I have said.[9] Please the Lord I may have succeeded in pointing out the proper thing to do in regard to so serious an illness.

Chapter 8

Some counsels concerning revelations and visions.

SOME PERSONS SEEM TO BECOME frightened just in hearing the words "visions" and "revelations." I don't understand why they consider this path along which God leads a soul such a dangerous one, or from where this dread comes. I do not want to treat now of which ones are good and which bad, or with the signs for discernment that I have heard from very learned persons; but of what ought to be done by someone who sees herself in this situation, for few are the confessors who will not intimidate her. Indeed, it doesn't cause as much fear or scandal to say that the devil is representing many kinds of temptation, the spirit of blasphemy, and absurd and indecent things as it does to say that an angel appeared or spoke or that our Lord Jesus Christ crucified was seen.

2. Nor do I want to treat at present of the revelations that are from God (for by now the fact that these bring great blessings to the soul goes without saying), but of the representations made by the devil in order to deceive and of how he makes use of the

image of Christ our Lord, or of his saints. I hold that His Majesty
will not give the devil the power to deceive a person by means of
similar figures unless through that person's own fault, but that
the devil himself will be the one deceived. (I mean, he will not
deceive where there is humility).[1] Thus, there is no reason to be
terrified but to trust in the Lord and pay little attention to these
things except for the sake of praising the Lord more.

3. I know a person whose confessors caused her much distress
over similar things; but afterward, from what she could understand through the great effects and good works that resulted,
she judged that her experiences were from God. And she was
very distressed that because of the command they gave her she
had to bless herself and make the fig when she saw a vision.[2]
Later, in talking with a highly learned Dominican,[3] she was told
by him that this was wrong, that no one should do so, for wherever we see the image of our Lord, it is good to pay it reverence,
even if the devil may have painted it. The devil is a great
painter, and in wanting to do us an evil deed, he rather does us a
good one if he paints a crucifix or other image so lifelike that he
leaves it engraven in our heart. This reasoning pleased me
much, for when we see a very good painting, even though we
might know that a bad man did it, we wouldn't fail to esteem
the image that was painted nor would we pay attention to the
painter and lose our devotion. For the good or the evil does not
lie in the vision but in the one who sees it and in whether or not
she profits by it with humility; for if humility is present, no harm
can be done not even by the devil. And if humility is not present,
even if the visions be from God they will be of no benefit. For if
that favor which should humble a nun when she sees she is unworthy of it makes her proud, she will be like the spider that
converts everything it eats into poison; or like the bee that converts it all into honey.

4. I want to explain myself further: Our Lord, through His
goodness, may wish to represent Himself to a soul so that it
might know or love Him more, or that He might show it one of
His secrets, or grant it some particular gifts or favors. And if the
soul, as I have said,[4] considers itself a saint because of a favor
(for it should be confounded and know how little its lowliness

deserves any favor) and thinks that this favor comes to it because of some service it has rendered, clearly the great good that could result is converted into evil, as in the example of the spider. Well now, let us suppose that the devil so as to incite pride causes these apparitions. The soul may think they are from God, humble itself, recognize its unworthiness to receive so great a favor, and strive to serve more. For in seeing itself rich, while not even deserving to eat the crumbs that fall from the table[5] of the persons of whom it has heard that God grants these favors (I mean, not deserving to be a servant of any of them), it humbles itself, begins to force itself to do penance, prays more, and takes greater care not to offend this Lord. For it thinks it is He who grants this favor, and obeys with greater perfection. If it responds in these ways, I am sure the devil will not return, but will be put to shame, and that no harm will be left in the soul.

5. When she is told some things to do, or about the future, the nun should speak about the matter with a discreet and learned confessor, and not do or believe anything other than what he tells her. She can communicate about it with the prioress so that the latter might provide her with such a confessor. And let her be careful, for if she doesn't obey what the confessor tells her and fails to be guided by him, the experience comes from either the bad spirit or dreadful melancholy. Even if the confessor may not be right, she will be more right in not departing from what he tells her, even though it may be an angel of God who speaks to her in the favor. For His Majesty will enlighten the confessor or ordain how the task may be carried out. In following the above advice, there is no danger; in doing otherwise, there can be many dangers and much harm.

6. Let us keep in mind that human nature is very weak, especially in women, and in this way of prayer weakness shows itself more. Thus it is necessary that we don't immediately think that every little thing that comes to our fancy is a vision, and we should believe that when a vision does occur, this will be clearly known. Where some melancholy is present, there is need for much greater care. For in regard to these fancies, things have been told to me that have left me amazed at how it is possible for such persons truly to think that they see what they do not see.

7. Once a confessor, who was much admired, came to see me, for he was confessor to a person who told him that for many days our Lady appeared to her, sat on her bed, and spoke for over an hour telling her about future events and a great deal more. Among many absurdities there were some predictions that turned out to be right, and as a result the apparitions were thought to be true. I understood immediately the nature of the experience, although I did not dare say so. For we are in a world in which it is necessary to consider the opinions others have of us in order that our words take effect. So I told him to wait to see if the prophecies would prove true and to look for other effects and inquire into the life of that person. In the end he came to understand that the whole thing was nonsense.

8. I could tell of so many things like this that would more than justify my advice, that is: that a soul should not believe things at once, but that it wait for time to pass and understand itself well before telling the confessor so that it doesn't deceive him without wanting to deceive him. For if he doesn't have experience of these things, his learning however great will not suffice for him to understand them. Not so long ago (in fact, very recently) there was a man who spoke much nonsense about things like these to some very learned and spiritual men. When he spoke with a person who had experienced such favors from the Lord, she saw clearly that he was suffering from madness together with illusion. Although the illusion wasn't then manifest but very dissimulated, the Lord after a while revealed it clearly; but this person who understood what the cause was had first to suffer much in not being believed.[6]

9. For these reasons and other similar ones it's very necessary for each Sister to speak clearly about her prayer to the prioress. The prioress should carefully consider the temperament and perfection in virtue of that Sister so that she might advise the confessor and provide for better understanding. She should choose a confessor for this particular purpose if the ordinary confessor is not sufficient for such matters. Let the Sisters be very careful that things like these, even though very truly from God, or favors recognized as miraculous, be not communicated to outsiders or to confessors who don't have the prudence to be

silent. This is most important, more so than they may think, and it's important that the Sisters not discuss these things among themselves. And the prioress, with prudence, should always be seen as tending more to praise those who distinguish themselves in matters pertaining to humility, mortification, and obedience than those God leads by this very supernatural path of prayer, even though the latter may have all these other virtues. For if this path is from the spirit of the Lord, it brings with it the humility to like being despised. And the praise of the above virtues will not harm the person who is led by this path and will benefit others. For since the others cannot attain to these things, for God gives to whomever He wants, let them flee sadness and seek to have the other virtues. Although God also gives these other virtues, they can in addition be the objects of our striving, and they are of great value for the Religious life. May His Majesty give them to us since no one who strives for them with effort, solicitude, prayer, and confidence in His mercy will be denied by Him.

Chapter 9

Deals with how she left Medina del Campo for the foundation of St. Joseph's in Malagon.

How far I've wandered from my subject! And yet, it could be that some of these counsels that were mentioned were more opportune than my telling about the foundations.

Well now, while at St. Joseph's in Medina del Campo I observed with great consolation how those Sisters were following in the footsteps of the Sisters of St. Joseph's in Avila through complete religious dedication, sisterly love, and spirituality. I observed, too, how our Lord provided for His house, for the needs of the chapel as well as for those of the Sisters. Some of the new ones entering the monastery it seemed the Lord had chosen as the kind of cement that is suited to an edifice like this. In these beginning stages, all the good, I think, will be for the sake of the future. For since these Sisters find the path, those who are to come will follow it.

2. There was a lady in Toledo, a sister of the duke of Medina-celi, in whose home I had stayed by order of my superiors, as I mentioned more at length in writing about the foundation of St. Joseph's.[1] While I was in her home, she got to like me in a special way, which in turn must have been a means by which this lady was stirred to do what she did. For His Majesty often makes use of means like these that seem fruitless to us who don't know the future. Since this lady knew that I had permission to found monasteries, she began to urge me very much to make a foundation in her town of Malagón.[2] I in no way wanted to accept since the town was so small that we would be forced to have an income in order to support ourselves—something to which I was very much opposed.

3. Both my confessor[3] and other learned men with whom I discussed the matter told me that I was doing wrong, that since the holy Council had given permission to have an income, I shouldn't, because of my own opinion, fail to found a monastery where God could be so much served. To this were added the many urgings of this lady which I could not resist. She provided a sufficient income, for I am always in favor of monasteries being either completely poor or maintained in such a way that the nuns will not need to beg from anyone for their needs.

4. I made every effort I could so that none of the nuns would possess anything, but that they would observe the constitutions in their entirety as in our other monasteries founded in poverty. Having completed all the paper work, I sent for some Sisters to make the foundation, and along with that lady we went to Malagón. When we got there, the house was not yet ready for us to move in. And so we were detained for more than eight days in an apartment of this lady's castle.

5. On Palm Sunday,[4] in the year 1568, with the people of the town, we went in procession to the church, in our white mantles and with veils covering our faces. A sermon was preached there, and from that church the Blessed Sacrament was brought to our monastery. This inspired great devotion in everybody. I stayed there for some days. On one of those days, while in prayer after having received Communion, I understood from our Lord that He would be served in that house. I don't think I was there quite

two months, for my spirit was eager to go and found a house in Valladolid, and the reason was the one I will now mention.

Chapter 10

Deals with the foundation of the house in Valladolid. Its title is The Conception of Our Lady of Mount Carmel.

FOUR OR FIVE MONTHS before this monastery of St. Joseph's in Malagón was founded, I was speaking with a distinguished young gentleman[1] who told me that if I wanted to establish a monastery in Valladolid he would most willingly give me a house he owned with a large and good garden containing a vineyard. He wanted to give away the property immediately; it was very valuable. I accepted his offer, although I wasn't too decided on making a foundation where the property was, since the place was about a quarter of a league outside the city. But it seemed to me that we could move to the city once the possession of a house had been taken in that district. And since he offered it so willingly, I did not want to refuse his good deed or hinder his devotion.[2]

2. Two months later, more or less, he was struck by a sudden illness that took away his speech, and he could not confess well, although he made many signs to ask the Lord's pardon. He died shortly afterward, very far from where I was.[3] The Lord told me that the young man's salvation had been in great jeopardy but that he had received mercy for the service he had rendered to the Blessed Mother in giving that house to be a monastery of her order; however, that he would not leave purgatory until the first Mass was said there, that then he would leave. I was so conscious of the grievous afflictions of this soul that even though I wanted to make a foundation in Toledo, I set it aside for then and hastened as much as I could to found a house in Valladolid.

3. It couldn't be made as quickly as I desired, for I was forced to delay a number of days at St. Joseph's in Avila, which was under my charge, and afterward at St. Joseph's in Medina del Campo, for I passed by there. I was in prayer one day in Medina

when the Lord told me to hurry because that soul was suffering very much. Although I didn't have the means available, I set to work and entered Valladolid on the feast of St. Lawrence.[4] And when I saw the house, I was dismayed; I knew that it would be a foolish mistake for nuns to stay there. The cost to them would be very great. For although the site was most gratifying on account of the garden which was so delightful, the nuns would certainly become sick, for it was near a river.

4. Though tired out, I had to go to Mass at a monastery of our order. I saw that the monastery was at the entrance to the city,[5] and this was so far away that my distress was doubled. Nonetheless, I said nothing to my companions[6] so as not to discourage them. Although weak, I had some faith that the Lord, by whom I had been told what was just mentioned, would provide a remedy. I arranged very secretly for workmen to come and begin building walls to provide for recollection, and other necessary things. With us, were the priest I mentioned, Julián de Avila,[7] and one of the friars mentioned,[8] who desired to be discalced and who was learning about our method of procedure in these houses. Julián de Avila was engaged in seeking to obtain the license from the bishop, who, before I arrived, had given us reason to hope that it would be granted. The license could not be gotten so quickly as to prevent a Sunday from coming along first. But permission was granted to say Mass where the church would be, and thus it was said for us.

5. I had forgotten that what was told to me about that soul would then be accomplished.[9] For, although I was told "at the first Mass," I thought that it would be at the one in which the Blessed Sacrament would be reserved. When the priest[10] came with the Blessed Sacrament to the place where we were to receive Communion and I approached to receive it, the gentleman I mentioned appeared beside him, his face joyful and resplendent. With hands folded, he thanked me for what I had done so that he could leave purgatory and go to heaven. And indeed before the first locution, when I heard that he was on the way to salvation, I had not had such a thing in mind and was consequently much afflicted. It seemed to me that another way of dying would have been necessary in view of the way he had

lived. For although he had performed many good deeds, he was much involved in the things of the world. True, though, he had told my companions that he kept death very much before him. It is important to know that our Lord is pleased with any service rendered to His Mother, and great is His mercy. May He be blessed and praised for everything. For He repays our lowly deeds with eternal life and glory, and He makes them great while they are in fact of little value.

6. Well, when the feastday of our Lady's Assumption arrived, which was August 15, 1568, we took possession of this monastery. We were there only a short while[11] because almost all of us fell very sick. This was seen by a lady from that city, Doña Mariá de Mendoza, who is the wife of Commander Cobos[12] and mother of the marquis of Camarasa. She is a very Christian woman and most charitable. The superabundance of alms she gave away made this clear. When she saw the situation, and before I spoke to her about the matter, she showed me much charity; for she is the sister of the bishop of Avila who was very favorable toward us in the foundation of the first monastery and is still so in all that pertains to our order.[13] Since she is very charitable and saw that we could not remain there without great hardship and also that the site was far from where we could receive alms, as well as unhealthy, she told us to give that house to her and that she would buy us another. And this she did. The one she gave us was worth much more, and in addition she has given all that is necessary up till now, and she will do so as long as she lives.

7. On the feast of St. Blaise[14] we moved there in a large procession, and with great devotion shown on the part of the people; and their devotedness continues even to this day, for the Lord grants many favors in that house. And He has brought souls whose sanctity in due time will be recounted so that He may be praised. For it is by such means that the Lord desires to magnify His works and favor His creatures. In fact, a very young girl entered there and showed what the world is by despising it. It has occurred to me to speak of her here so that those who have great love for the world will be put to shame and that young girls to whom the Lord may give good desires and inspirations will take her example and carry them out.

8.   There is in this place a lady named Doña María de Acuña, a sister of the count of Buendía. She was married to the governor of Castile. When he died, she was left, while still quite young, with a son and two daughters. She began to live so holy a life and rear her children in such virtue that she merited from the Lord that He desire these children for Himself. (I was mistaken, for she was left with three daughters.) The one daughter became a nun immediately. The other one did not want to marry but lived a very edifying life with her mother.[15] The son at an early age began to understand what the world was and felt so intensely God's call to enter religious life that no one was able to prevent him from following it. His mother was so delighted with his vocation that she helped him very much by her prayers to our Lord, although for fear of his relatives she did not show this openly. In sum, when the Lord wants a soul for Himself, creatures have little strength to prevent this. So it happened in this case, for after having been delayed for three years and strongly urged to change his mind, he entered the Society of Jesus.[16] A confessor of this lady[17] told me that he had been informed by her that she had never in her life experienced such joy in her heart as on the day her son made his profession.

9.   O Lord! What a great favor You grant to those children whose parents love them so much as to want them to possess their estates, inheritance, and riches in that blessed life that has no end! It is a great pity the world is now so unfortunate and blind that it seems to parents their honor lies in not letting the dung of this world's goods be forgotten and in not remembering that sooner or later these things will come to an end. And everything that has limits, even though it lasts a while, will eventually come to an end; and little importance should be given to it. Such parents want to sustain their own vanities at a cost to their children, and very boldly take from God souls that He wants for Himself. And they take from these souls a good so great (God inviting them to be His guest) that, even were the good not to last forever, it would still be extraordinary to see oneself freed from the tiresomeness of the world and its laws; and the more goods people possess, the greater the tedium. Open the eyes of parents, my God. Make them understand the kind of love they are

obliged to have for their children so that they do not do these children so much wrong and are not complained about before God in that final judgment where, even though they may not want to know it, the value of each thing will be understood.

10. Well, this gentleman, who was the son of this Doña María de Acuña (his name was Don Antonio de Padilla), at the age of seventeen, more or less, was mercifully drawn by God from the world. Hence, the estates went to the oldest daughter, whose name was Doña Luisa de Padilla. For the count of Buendía had no sons, and Don Antonio was heir to both the earldom and the governorship of Castile. I will not mention the many things Don Antonio suffered from his relatives before going on with his plan, because this is not my purpose in writing. Whoever knows how much value those of the world place on their having an heir to their properties will fully understand.

11. O Son of the Eternal Father, Jesus Christ, our Lord, true King of all! What did You leave in the world? What could we, your descendants, inherit from You? What did You possess, my Lord, but trials, sufferings, and dishonors? You had nothing but a wooden beam on which to swallow the painfully difficult drink of death. In sum, my God, it does not fit those of us who want to be your true children, and hold on to their inheritance, to flee suffering. Your heraldry consists of five wounds. Courage, then, my daughters; this must be our badge if we are to inherit His kingdom. Not with rest, not with favors, not with honors, not with riches will that which He bought with so much blood be gained. O illustrious people! Open your eyes for the love of God; behold that the true knights of Jesus Christ and the princes of His Church, a St. Peter and a St. Paul, did not follow the road you follow. Do you think perhaps there will be a new road for you? Do not believe it. Behold the Lord is beginning to show it to you through such young persons as those of whom we are now speaking.

12. At times I have seen and spoken to this Don Antonio. He would have wanted even many more possessions so as to leave them all. Blessed the young man and blessed the young girl who have merited so much from God that at the age in which people are usually overpowered by the world, they trampled on it. Blessed be He who bestowed on them so much good.

13. Well since the estates were left to the older sister, it happened that she didn't attribute any more importance to them than did her brother. For from the time she was a child she gave herself so much to prayer (which is the place where the Lord gives the light to understand truths) that she esteemed these things as little as did her brother. Oh, God help me, how many trials, torments, litigations, and even risking of lives and honor many would undergo to be heir to this inheritance. She suffered greatly in order to be allowed to renounce it. So goes this world; it would clearly show us its frenzy if we were not blind. Very willingly, so that they might leave her free from this inheritance, she renounced it in favor of her sister — for there was no one else — who was ten or eleven years old. Immediately, in order to perpetuate their miserable family name, her relatives arranged to have this young girl marry an uncle of hers, the brother of her father, and obtained a dispensation from the Supreme Pontiff; and the two were engaged.

14. The Lord did not desire that the daughter of such a mother and the sister of both such a brother and such sisters be left more deceived than they, and thus what I will now relate happened. When the girl began to enjoy the worldly clothes and finery that, in accord with her status, would attract the fancy of a girl at that tender age (two months had not yet gone by from the time of her engagement), the Lord began to give her light, although she was not then aware of what He was doing. Once at the close of a day she had spent most happily with her fiancé, whom she loved more intensely than her age warranted, she became extremely sad at seeing how the day came to an end and that likewise all days would come to an end. Oh, greatness of God! That very happiness that the joys of perishable things gave her, she came to abhor! She began to experience such great sadness that she couldn't hide it from her fiancé, nor did she know how to tell him, nor could she, even though he was questioning her.

15. At that time she had to go on an unavoidable journey to a place far from where she lived. She felt very sorry since she loved him so much. But soon the Lord revealed to her the cause of her affliction; it was, in fact, that her soul was inclined toward that

which would have no end. She began to consider how her brother and sister had chosen the safer path and left her amid the world's dangers. This, on the one hand; on the other hand, the fact that it seemed there was no remedy was exhausting her (for she wasn't aware, until she asked, that even though she was engaged it was still possible for her to become a nun). And above all, the love she had for her fiancé did not allow her to come to a decision. So she was suffering much distress.

16. Since the Lord wanted her for Himself, He gradually took away this love she had for her fiancé and increased her desire to give up everything. At this time she was moved only by the desire to be saved and to seek the best means. For it seemed to her that in the midst of the things of the world she would forget to seek that which is eternal. This is the wisdom God infused in her at so early an age; to seek how to gain that which is without end. Fortunate soul that so early in life freed itself from the blindness in which many old people die! Once she saw that her will was free, she resolved to occupy it completely in God. Until that time she had remained silent; now she began to speak of the matter to her sister. Her sister, thinking it was a childish trifle, tried to dissuade her and told her some things about how she could be saved even though married. The young girl responded by asking her sister why she herself had given up marriage. Some days passed, and her desire went on increasing. She didn't say anything to her mother, but perhaps it was the mother who through her prayers was causing this battle in her daughter.

Chapter 11

Continues the subject that was begun about how Doña Casilda de Padilla attained her holy desires of entering religious life.

A T THIS TIME THE HABIT WAS RECEIVED by a lay Sister in this monastery of the Immaculate Conception about whose vocation I should perhaps say something.[1] Although she is from a different background (a little peasant girl), she is so virtuous, because of the great favors God has granted her, that she deserves to be remembered here in praise of Him. And when Doña Casilda (the name of this girl beloved of the Lord) went with her grandmother,[2] who was her fiancé's mother, to this lay Sister's reception of the habit, she felt intensely drawn to this monastery, thinking that since it was small and the nuns were few they could serve the Lord better. But she still had not reached the decision to leave her fiancé, which, as I said,[3] was what most held her back.

2. She recalled how before she was engaged she used to spend periods of time in prayer. Her mother in her goodness and holiness had brought her children up this way, for once they reached the age of seven she would make them enter an oratory from time to time, and she taught them how to reflect on the Passion of the Lord and made them go to confession frequently. And thus she witnessed this happy outcome of her desires, that her children belong only to God. She told me herself that she had always offered them to God and begged Him to take them out of the world, for she was already disillusioned and knew how little it should be esteemed. I sometimes reflect on the accidental joy that will be hers when she sees them rejoicing in eternal joys and that she was the means, and on the gratitude they will have toward her, and how on the contrary those parents who did not bring their children up as children of God (for they are children more of God than of their parents) will find themselves, together with their children, in hell, and the maledictions they will spew forth and the despair they will experience.

3. Well, to return to what I was saying, since Doña Casilda realized that she was now reluctant even to recite the rosary, she had great fear that things would always get worse. It seemed to her she saw clearly that by coming to this house her salvation would be assured. And thus she reached an unwavering decision. One morning when she came here with her sister and mother, the occasion arose for their entering inside the monastery; indeed without any worry that the young girl would do what she did. Once she saw herself inside, no one was able to get her to leave the house. So many were the tears and words with which she begged them to allow her to stay that all were fright-

ened. Her mother, although interiorly rejoicing, feared the relatives and did not want her to remain in this way lest they say that the daughter had been persuaded by her mother. And the prioress,[4] too, felt like this, for it seemed to her that the girl was but a child and that more testing was needed. This took place in the morning. They had to stay until evening, and they sent for the girl's confessor and for Father Maestro Fray Domingo (the Dominican whom I mentioned in the beginning),[5] who was my confessor, although I was not here then.[6] This Father understood at once that it was the Spirit of the Lord. He helped her very much, suffering a good deal from her relatives, promising to help her so that she could return another day. (That is the way all those who seek to serve God must act. They must strive not to consider human prudence so much when they see a soul called by God.)

4. After a great deal of persuasion, and so that blame would not be placed on her mother, she came out this time. Her desires continued to increase. Her mother began to inform her relatives secretly so that the fiancé would not learn of it. They said her desire was a childish whim and that she should wait until she was of age, for she wasn't yet twelve years old. She asked why, since they found her old enough to be married and left to the world, they didn't find her old enough to give herself to God. The things she said made it appear that it wasn't she who was speaking.

5. The matter couldn't be kept so secret that her fiancé was not informed. Since she knew about this, it seemed to her that she couldn't bear waiting for him to give his consent to her entering religious life. On the feast of the Immaculate Conception, when she was in the house of her grandmother (who was also her mother-in-law to be), who didn't know anything about her desires, she begged to be allowed to go to the country with her governess to relax a while. Her grandmother, to please her, allowed her to go, in a carriage along with her servants. Giving one of the servants some money, the girl asked him to wait for her at the entrance of this monastery with some bundles of twigs or vine branches. She arranged to go in a roundabout way so that they would pass by this house. When she arrived at the en-

trance, she told the servants to ask at the turn for a jug of water and not to tell who it was for, and she quickly got down from the carriage. The servants told her not to get down, that they would bring the water to her, but she refused. The bundles were already there. She told them to tell the nuns to come to the door to get those bundles, and she stood waiting there. When the nuns opened, she entered inside and went and embraced the statue of our Lady, weeping and begging the prioress not to throw her out. The shouts of the servants were loud as was also their pounding on the door. She went to speak to them at the grille and told them that she would by no means come out and that they should go and tell her mother. The women that had gone with her broke into loud laments. She made little of it all. Her grandmother, when told the news, decided to go at once.

6. In sum, neither the girl's grandmother, nor her uncle, nor her fiancé (who came to the grille and tried to get her to change her mind) could do any more than torment her when with her, and afterward she would be stronger in her resolve. Her fiancé, after much moaning, told her that she could serve God more by giving alms. She answered that he could give them. And, in response to his other arguments, she told him that she was more obliged to seek her salvation and that she saw she was weak and that she could not be saved amid worldly occasions of sin, and that he should not complain about her because she hadn't left him except for God, and that because of this she was not offending him. Once she saw that nothing satisfied him, she got up and left him.

7. He made no impression on her; rather, she felt totally displeased with him. When God enlightens the soul with truth, temptations and stumbling blocks set by the devil help it more. For it is His Majesty who fights for the soul, and thus she saw clearly here that it was not she who was speaking.

8. Since her fiancé and relatives saw how little they accomplished in trying to get her to leave willingly, they turned to force. Thus, they obtained a court order to take her out of the monastery and that the nuns allow her to leave. During the whole time, from the feast of the Immaculate Conception to that of the Holy Innocents[7] (when they took her away), she re-

mained in the monastery, without receiving the habit, but following all the religious observances as though she had received it, and with the greatest happiness. On the day the law officers took her away she was brought to the house of a gentleman. She was in tears, asking why they were tormenting her since it would be of no avail. In the gentleman's house men religious as well as other persons tried hard to persuade her. Some thought it was all childish, others wanted her to enjoy the married state. I'd have to go on at great length if I were to tell about the arguments she was confronted with and the way she got out of them all. She left them astonished by the things she said.

9. Since they saw they were getting nowhere, they brought her to her mother's house so as to detain her there for a while. Her mother was now tired of seeing so much disturbance, but did not by any means help her; rather, from what appeared, she was against her. It could be that she was against her so as to test her further. At least that's what she told me afterward, and she is so holy one cannot but believe what she says. But the girl did not know this. Moreover, the girl's confessor was extremely opposed. As a result, she had only God, and one of her mother's maids, who was one in whom she confided. Thus she underwent much trial and hardship until her twelfth year, when she learned that, since they couldn't get her to give up the idea, they were planning to bring her to be a nun at the monastery where her sister was,[8] for not so much austerity was practiced there.

10. Knowing about this, she was determined to strive through every means she could to obtain her happiness by going ahead with her own plan. And thus, one day when she went to Mass with her mother, her mother went to confess in one of the confessionals. Doña Casilda then asked her governess to go to one of the Fathers and ask him to say a Mass. When she saw that the governess was gone, she placed her chopines in her sleeves, lifted her skirt and hastened as quickly as she could to this monastery, which was quite far away. Her governess, when she didn't find her, went after her; once she got near, she asked a man to catch hold of her. He said afterward that he wasn't able to move, and so he let her get away. The girl entered the first gate of the monastery, closed it, and began to shout; when the governess

arrived, this young girl was already inside the monastery. They gave her the habit immediately. And thus she fulfilled the good inspirations the Lord had placed within her. His Majesty began very shortly to repay her with spiritual favors, and she to serve Him with the greatest happiness, humility, and detachment from everything.

11. May He be blessed forever! For thus, through the rough, woolen dress of the poor He gives pleasure to one who was so attached to very costly and elegant clothes; although the dress of the poor played no part in hiding her beauty. For the Lord distributed natural graces to her as well as spiritual: a temperament and intelligence so agreeable as to awaken all to praise His Majesty. May it please Him that there be many who will thus answer His call.[9]

Chapter 12

Tells about the life and death of a religious, Beatriz de la Encarnación, whom our Lord brought to this same house. Her life was one of high perfection, and her death was of a kind that makes it fitting for us to remember her.[1]

SOME YEARS BEFORE, A YOUNG girl, Doña Beatriz, a distant relative of Doña Casilda, entered this monastery to become a nun.[2] She amazed all when they saw the great virtues the Lord was forming in her. And both the nuns and the prioress affirmed that they had never noticed in any aspect of her life anything they would consider an imperfection. Nor did they ever see any other expression on her face than a modest happiness that well revealed the inner joy of her soul. With an untroubled quiet she kept strict silence in such a way that nothing singular was noticed about it. Never was she known to have spoken a reprehensible word, nor was any obstinacy seen in her, nor did she ever make an excuse, even though, as is the custom in these houses in order to practice mortification, the prioress to test her tried to blame her for something she had not done. Never did she complain about anything, or of any Sister. Nor by her expression or word did she in the office she held give displeasure to anyone or occasion to attibute some imperfection to her. Neither was any reason found for accusing her of some fault in chapter,even though the defects the monitors would point out during chapter were very minute.[3] In all events her interior and exterior composure was unusual. This arose from her keeping eternity very much in mind and the end for which God created us. She always bore the praises of God on her lips and the greatest spirit of gratitude; in sum, hers was a perpetual prayer.

2. In matters of obedience she was never at fault, but showed a readiness, perfection, and joyfulness in all that she was ordered to do. She practiced the greatest charity toward her neighbor—this was shown in such a way that she said that she would allow herself to be broken into a thousand pieces to keep any soul from being lost and so that thus all souls might find joy in their Brother, Jesus Christ (which is how she referred to our Lord). As for her trials, which were very severe, there were terrible illnesses, as I shall say afterward,[4] with intense pain, and she suffered them with the greatest willingness and happiness, as if they were choice favors and delights. Our Lord must have given her spiritual favors and delights, for otherwise it would have been impossible for her to bear her illnesses as cheerfully as she did.

3. It happened that in this city of Valladolid some men were going to be burned because of their great crimes. She must have known that these men were not approaching their death with as good a disposition as was fitting, and this caused her the greatest affliction; with much anguish she went to our Lord and begged Him very earnestly for the salvation of those souls. And in exchange for what they deserved (or that she might obtain that grace—I don't remember the precise words), she promised to give her whole life, all the trials and sufferings she could bear. That same night the first fever struck her, and until she died she was always suffering. The condemned men, in turn, died well; hence it seems that God heard her prayer.

4. She was next afflicted with an intestinal abscess causing the severest suffering. The patience the Lord had placed in her soul was indeed necessary in order for her to endure it. This ab-

scess was so internally located that the medicines they gave were of no help until the Lord willed that it come to a head and drain, and thus she improved somewhat from this illness. With that desire for suffering given to her, she was unable to be satisfied with little, and thus once, while she was listening to a sermon on the feast of the Cross, her desire so increased that when the sermon was over she went in a tearful impulse and threw herself on her bed. When they asked her what was the matter, she answered that they should beseech God to give her many trials and that with this she would be content.

5. She spoke with the prioress about all these interior matters and in this practice found comfort. Throughout her illness, she never gave the least trouble to anyone, nor did she do anything but what the infirmarian wanted, even if it was something as slight as drinking a little water. It is very common for souls who practice prayer to desire trials when they do not have any. But when they do and are in the midst of these very trials, it is not common for them to rejoice. And thus, once when she was afflicted, though the affliction did not last long, and suffering extreme pain from an abscess in her throat so that she could not swallow, she told the prioress in the presence of the Sisters (since the prioress's duty was to console and encourage her to bear so much sickness) that she had no pain and that she would not change places with any of the Sisters who were very well. She kept the Lord, for whom she was suffering, so present before her that she tried to cover up her suffering as much as possible that others would not know how great it was. And thus, except when the pain grew intense, she complained very little.

6. It seemed to her there was no one on earth as wretched as she; thus, insofar as one could understand, her humility was great. In speaking of the virtues of other persons, she was very joyful. In matters concerning mortification she was persistent. Without letting it be noticed, she avoided what afforded her recreation, for unless one were watching closely, this would not be known. It didn't seem she lived or conversed with creatures, so little did she care about anything. However things went, she bore them with peace. She was always composed; so much so that once a Sister said to her that she seemed to be like one of

those persons of nobility so proud that they would rather die from their hunger than let anyone outside know about it. For they couldn't believe that she failed to feel some things, although it hardly seemed so.

7. She performed all her work and duties with the goal of not losing any merit, and so she used to say to the Sisters: "The smallest thing when done for the love of God is priceless; we should set our eyes, Sisters, only on this goal of love and on pleasing Him." She never meddled in things that were not her responsibility; thus she found fault with no one but herself. So strongly did she feel that no good should be said of her that she was careful not to speak well of others in their presence so as not to cause them pain. She never sought consolation (neither by going to the garden nor in any created thing), for she said it would be rude to seek relief from the sufferings that our Lord gave her. Thus she never asked for anything, but got along with what was given her. She also said that it would be a cross for her to find consolation in anything that was not God. The fact is that when I inquired from those in the house, no one had seen in her anything other than what would be seen in someone of great perfection.

8. Well, when the time arrived in which our Lord desired to take her from this life, the sufferings increased; so many illnesses came upon her together that others, in order to praise our Lord at observing the happiness with which she bore them, went at times to see her. The chaplain especially, who is the confessor in that monastery and a true servant of God, had a great desire to be present at her death. Being her confessor, he considered her a saint. God was pleased to grant him this desire. For since she was in so much pain, and although she had already been anointed they called him in case there would be need that night for her to be reconciled or helped to die. A little before nine while all were with her (and he too), about a quarter of an hour before she died, she raised her eyes, and a happiness like a shining light came over her countenance. She remained as would someone gazing on an object that gives profound joy, for she smiled twice. All those who were there, and the priest himself, received so much spiritual delight and happiness that they didn't know

what else to say than that it seemed to them they were in heaven. And with this happiness that I mention, her eyes fixed on heaven, she died, looking like an angel. Thus we are able to believe, according to our faith and according to her life, that the Lord brought her to rest in payment for the many things she had desired to suffer for Him.

9. The chaplain affirms, and has told many persons, that at the time of her burial he perceived an extremely sweet fragrance coming from her body. The Sister sacristan also affirms that despite all the candles that burned at the funeral and burial, not one of them grew smaller in size. All this can be believed as coming from the mercy of God. In speaking of these things with a confessor of hers from the Society of Jesus with whom for many years she discussed her soul, I was told that they didn't amount to much; and he said he was not surprised because he knew that our Lord communicated a great deal with her.

10. May it please His Majesty, my daughters, that we know how to profit from companionship as good as this and from many other persons whom our Lord gives us in these houses. It may be that I will say something about them so that those who are a bit lukewarm will be strengthened and that we may all praise the Lord who in this way lets His magnificent riches show forth in us weak, little women.

Chapter 13

Treats of how and by whom in the year 1568 the first house for the observance of the primitive rule by discalced Carmelite friars was founded.

BEFORE MAKING THE FOUNDATION of Valladolid, I had already agreed with both Father Fray Antonio de Jesús, who was then prior of the Carmelite monastery of St. Anne in Medina, and Fray John of the Cross, as I have already mentioned,[1] that they would be the first to enter if a monastery for discalced friars were founded for the observance of the primitive rule. Since I had no resources for acquiring a house, I did nothing but commend the matter to our Lord. For, as I have said, I was now satisfied with these Fathers.[2] The Lord had indeed exercised Father Fray Antonio de Jesús in trials during the year since I had spoken with him; and he suffered them with much perfection. As for Father Fray John of the Cross, no trial was necessary. Even though he had lived among the calced friars, those of the cloth,[3] he always lived a life of great perfection and religious observance. Since the Lord had given me the chief requirement for a beginning, which was friars, He was pleased to arrange the rest.

2. A gentleman from Avila, named Don Rafael,[4] with whom I had never spoken, found out, I don't know how (for I don't remember), about my desire to make a foundation for discalced friars. He came and offered me a house he owned in a little town[5] of very few inhabitants (I don't think even twenty, but I don't remember now). He kept the house there for an administrator who collected the revenue from his grain fields. Although I imagined how it might look, I praised our Lord and thanked this gentleman very much. He told me it was on the direct route to Medina del Campo and that since I had to pass by there to make the foundation in Valladolid I could see it. I told him I would, and indeed that is what I did. I left Avila with a nun companion and with Father Julián de Avila, the chaplain at St. Joseph's in Avila, the priest I mentioned who helped me in these travels.

3. Although we left in the morning, we got lost because we didn't know the road; and since the place is little known, we couldn't get much information about where it was. Thus, our traveling that day was very trying and the sun was very hot. When we thought we were near, we discovered we had just as far to go. I always remember the tiredness we felt and the wrong roads we took on that journey. The result was that we arrived shortly before nightfall.

When we entered the house it was in such a state that we dared not remain there that night; it wasn't at all clean and was filled with vermin. It had a fairly good entrance way, a room double in size, a loft, and a small kitchen. This was all we had for our monastery. I figured that the entrance way could serve as the chapel, the loft as the choir, which would adapt well, and the room for sleeping.

My companion, although much better than I and very fond of penance, couldn't bear the thought of my planning to found a monastery there and said to me: "Surely, Mother, there isn't a soul, however good, that could put up with this. Don't even consider it." The Father who came with me, although he agreed with my companion, did not oppose me since I had told him my intentions.[6] We went to spend the night in the church, although not in vigil because we were exhausted.

4. When we arrived in Medina, I spoke immediately with Father Fray Antonio, and I told him what took place and that if he would have the courage to stay there for a while, I was certain God would soon provide a remedy, and that the important thing was to begin. It seems to me I was most aware of what the Lord had done and was feeling sure, so to speak; just as I do now from what I see and even much more so because of what up till now I have seen, for at the time of my writing this there are, through the goodness of God, ten monasteries of discalced friars.[7] And I told him he should realize that neither the provincial at that time nor the previous one would give permission—for the foundation needed their consent, as I said at the beginning —if we were seen living in a well established house.[8] This was apart from the fact that we did not have the means for such a house. And I pointed out that in that little place and house the foundation would not attract attention. God had given him more courage than He had given me. And so Fray Antonio told me that he would be willing to live not only there but in a pigsty. Fray John of the Cross was of the same mind.

5. Now what remained was to obtain the consent of the two Fathers I mentioned because this was the condition under which our Father General granted the permission.[9] I hoped in our Lord to obtain it, and so I told Father Fray Antonio to take care to do all he could to gather something together for this house. I went with Fray John of the Cross to the foundation of Valladolid about which I have written.[10] And since we spent some days before establishing the enclosure on account of the workmen who were getting the house ready, there was an opportunity to teach

Father Fray John of the Cross about our way of life so that he would have a clear understanding of everything, whether it concerned mortification or the style of both our community life and the recreation we have together. The recreation is taken with such moderation that it only serves to reveal the Sisters' faults and to provide a little relief so that the rule may be kept in its strictness. He was so good that I, at least, could have learned much more from him than he from me. Yet this is not what I did, but I taught him about the lifestyle of the Sisters.[11]

6. It pleased God that the provincial, Fray Alonso González, from whom I had to obtain approbation, was there. He was elderly, good natured, and without malice. I told him many things, and reminded him of the account he would have to give if he hindered a work as good as this when asked by God to carry it out. His Majesty, wanting the foundation, put him in the right disposition, for he mellowed very much. When Doña María de Mendoza and the bishop of Avila, her brother (who is the one who always favored and protected us) came, they convinced both him and Father Fray Angel de Salazar, the previous provincial, the one from whom I feared all the difficulty. Moreover, a certain need arose at the time for which the latter provincial had need of assistance from Doña María de Mendoza. This fact, I believe, helped a great deal, although even if this opportunity had not been present, our Lord would have moved the provincial's heart just as He did the heart of Father General which was anything but inclined to the idea.

7. Oh, God help me, how many obstacles I have seen in these business matters that seemed impossible to overcome, and how easy it was for His Majesty to remove them. And how ashamed I am not to be better after seeing what I have seen. For now as I am writing, I am growing fearful and want our Lord to make known to everyone how in these foundations we creatures have done next to nothing. The Lord has directed all by means of such lowly beginnings that only His Majesty could have raised the work to what it now is. May He be always blessed, amen.

Chapter 14

*Continues to speak of the foundation of the first monastery of
discalced Carmelite friars. For the honor and glory of God, tells
something about both the kind of life lived there and the good
our Lord began to do in those surroundings.*

HAVING THE PERMISSION OF these two provincials, I now
figured that nothing was lacking. We arranged that
Father Fray John of the Cross would go to the house and get it
ready so that, in spite of all, it could be lived in. For me, what
was most urgent was that the friars begin, for I was very fearful
lest some obstacle would come along our path. And this they
did. Father Fray Antonio had already gathered some of the
things necessary. Insofar as we could, we helped him; although
our help amounted to little. He came to Valladolid with great
happiness to speak to me and told me what he had collected,
which was very little. It was only with clocks that he was well
provided, for he had five of them; this greatly amused me. He
told me they were meant as a help to follow the daily schedule,
which he wanted well fixed; I don't think he even had any bed
yet to sleep in.

2. Although they had wanted to do a great deal with the
house, not much time was required to prepare it because there
was no money. When it was ready, Father Fray Antonio happily
renounced his priorship and promised to observe the primitive
rule. Although he was told to try the new way of life first, he did
not want to. He went to his little house with the greatest happiness in the world. Fray John was already there.

3. Father Fray Antonio has told me that when he first came
near the little place he felt a great inner joy, and it seemed to
him that he was now through with the world by leaving it all and
placing himself in that solitude. Neither of the two found the
house unfit; rather, it seemed to them they were living in the
midst of great pleasures.

4. Oh, God help me! What little these buildings and exterior
comforts do interiorly. Out of love for Him, I ask you my Sisters
and Fathers, that you never fail to be very moderate in this mat-

ter of large and mangificent houses. Let us keep before us our
true founders, those holy fathers from whom we descend, for we
know that by means of that path of poverty and humility they
now enjoy God.

5. Truly I have seen that there is more spirituality and even
inner happiness when suitable accommodations for the body are
seemingly lacking than afterward when the house is large and
the accommodations good. What benefit is it to us that the house
be large since it is only one small room that each one habitually
uses? That it be well designed—what help is that to us? Indeed,
if it isn't well designed, we won't then have to go around looking at the walls. By considering that the house will not be ours
forever, but ours only for as short a time as this life lasts, even
though that may be long, everything will be easy for us. We will
see that the less we have here below, the more we will enjoy in
eternity, where the dwelling places will be in conformity with
the love with which we have imitated the life of our good Jesus.
If we say that these are the beginning steps in order to renew the
rule of the Virgin, His Mother, our Lady and Patroness, let us
not be so offensive to her or to our holy fathers of the past as to
fail to live as they did. Since, because of our weakness, we cannot do so in every way, in matters that are not essential for sus-
taining life, we must proceed very carefully. For it is all a matter
of but a little effort, and that becomes delightful, as was the
case with these two Fathers. And once we are determined to undergo this effort, the difficulty passes, for all the pain is but a little in the beginning.

6. On the First or Second Sunday of Advent (I don't remember which of these Sundays it was), in the year 1568, the first
Mass was said in that little stable of Bethlehem, for it doesn't
seem to me the house was any better.[1] The following Lent, while
on my way to the foundation in Toledo, I passed by there.[2] When I
arrived in the morning, Father Fray Antonio was sweeping the
doorway to the church with that joyful expression on his face
that he always has. I said to him: "What's this, my Father; what
has become of your honor?" Telling me of his great happiness,
he answered with these words: "I curse the day I had any."

When I entered the little church, I was astonished to see the spirit the Lord had put there. And it wasn't only I, for the two merchants, my friends from Medina who had accompanied me there, did nothing else but weep. There were so many crosses, so many skulls! I never forget a little cross made for the holy water fount from sticks with a paper image of Christ attached to it; it inspired more devotion than if it had been something very expertly carved.

7. The choir was in the loft. In the middle of the loft the ceiling was high enough to allow for the recitation of the Hours, but one had to stoop low in order to enter and to hear Mass. There were in the two corners facing the church two little hermitages, where one could do no more than either lie down or sit. Both were filled with hay because the place was very cold, and the roof almost touched one's head. Each had a little window facing the altar and a stone for a pillow; and there, too, the crosses and skulls. I learned that after the friars finished Matins they did not leave the choir before Prime but remained there in prayer, for their prayer was so deep that when it came time to say Prime their habits were covered with snow without their having become aware of the fact. The two Fathers recited the Hours with another Father from among those of the cloth who went to stay with them (although he didn't change his habit because he was very sickly) and another young, unordained brother who was also there.[3]

8. They used to go preach in many of the neighboring towns where the people were left without any instructions in Christian doctrine. On this account also I rejoiced that the house had been founded there. For I had been told that there was no monastery nearby nor any place from which the people could get instructions, which was a great pity. In a short time the reputation the Fathers had was so great that I experienced the deepest consolation when I learned of it. For their preaching, as I say, they journeyed barefoot a league and a half, or two, for at that time they did not yet wear sandals (afterward they were ordered to wear them), and in much snow and cold. When finished with their preaching and confessing, they returned very late to their house for supper. In their happiness, all they did seemed small to them.

9. As for food, they had a surplus, for the people in the neighboring towns provided them with more than they needed. And some gentlemen from those towns came there to confession and offered them better houses and sites. Among those gentlemen was a Don Luis, lord of five towns.[4] This particular gentleman had built a church to honor an image of our Lady, which was indeed worthy of being venerated. His father had sent it through a merchant from Flanders to his grandmother or mother (I don't remember which). The merchant liked it so much that he kept it for many years, and afterward at the hour of his death ordered that it be sent to Don Luis. It is a large altarpiece; I haven't seen anything better in my life—and others say the same. Father Fray Antonio went to that place at the request of this gentleman and saw the image; he liked it so much, and rightly so, that he agreed to transfer the monastery there. This town is called Mancera.[5] Although there was no well in that place, nor did it seem that any could be found there, this gentleman built the friars a monastery, small and in keeping with their profession, and gave them furnishings. He did everything very well.

10. I don't want to fail to mention the way, considered to be miraculous, in which the Lord gave them water. One day after supper, while the prior, Father Fray Antonio, was talking in the cloister with his friars about the need for water, he rose and took a staff he was holding in his hands and made a sign of the cross on one part of it (I think he made the sign of the cross, although I don't remember well whether he did or not); but anyway he pointed with the stick and said: "Now, dig here." After they had dug only a little, so much water came out that it is now even difficult to drain the well so as to clean it. The water is very good for drinking, and all that was needed for the remaining construction work was taken from there, and never, as I say, does the well empty out. After they had enclosed a garden with a wall, they sought to get water for the garden and made a water wheel and went to much expense; up till now, they have not been able to find any more, not even a little.

11. I couldn't thank our Lord enough when I saw that little house,[6] which shortly before was uninhabitable, with such a

spirit that everywhere I looked I found something edifying. And by the way they were living, I learned of the mortification, prayer, and good example they were giving. A gentleman and his wife, whom I knew and who lived in a nearby town, came to see me there, and they never stopped telling me about the sanctity of these Fathers and the great good they were doing in those towns. I experienced the greatest interior joy, for it seemed to me that I saw a beginning that would be of much benefit to our order and service to our Lord. May it please His Majesty that things will continue as they are now, and that my plan will indeed be realized.

The merchants who had accompanied me told me that not for all the world would they have missed having gone there. What a thing virtue is, for that poverty pleased those merchants more than all their riches, and their souls were left satisfied and comforted.

12. After conversing with those Fathers, I spoke of some things and begged them especially — since I am weak and wretched — not to be so rigorous in penitential practices, for what they were doing was severe. Since it had cost me so much in desire and prayer for the Lord to give me some friars to begin with and I saw such a good start, I feared lest the devil would attempt to put an end to this beginning before what I hoped for could be accomplished. As one who is imperfect and of little faith, I did not observe that this was God's work and that His Majesty would carry it forward. Since they engaged in practices in which I did not, they paid little attention to my words about giving them up. And thus I went away greatly consoled, although I did not give God the praise so great a favor deserved.

May it please His Majesty, in His goodness, that I be able to serve somehow for the very many things I owe Him, amen. For, indeed, I understood that this foundation was a much greater grace than the favor He granted me to found houses of nuns.

Chapter 15

Treats of the foundation of the monastery of the glorious St. Joseph made in the city of Toledo in 1569.

I N THE CITY OF TOLEDO there was a merchant, a respected man and servant of God, who never wanted to marry but lived a very good Catholic life of great trustworthiness and virtue. Through honest trade he went about increasing his wealth with the intention of using it for some work very pleasing to the Lord. He was struck with a fatal illness. His name was Martín Ramírez[1]. A Father from the Society of Jesus named Pablo Hernández,[2] a confessor of mine when I was in Toledo arranging for the foundation of Malagón, was very eager that one of our monasteries be founded in Toledo. So he went to speak with the man and told him of the great service such a foundation would give our Lord and how the fund for chaplains and chaplaincies[3] that he wanted to establish could be left for this monastery and that the certain feast days and everything else he had resolved to leave to the care of a parish in that city would be taken care of by such a monastery.

2. The merchant was so sick that he saw there was no time to make such arrangements, and he left the whole matter in the hands of his brother, whose name was Alonso Alvarez Ramírez; once this was done, God took him. The right decision had been made, for this Alonso Alvarez is a very discreet God-fearing man, truthful and charitable in almsgiving, and open-minded. As one who has had many dealings with him, I can as an eyewitness say this in all truthfulness.

3. When Martín Ramírez died, I was still involved with the foundation at Valladolid. There I received a letter from Father Pablo Hernández of the Society and from Alonso Alvarez himself, giving me an account of what had happened and advising me that if I wanted to accept this foundation I should come quickly. So, shortly after the house in Valladolid was put in order, I left for Toledo. I arrived on the eve of Our Lady of the Incarnation[4] and went to the house of Doña Luisa, which is where I stayed at other times. She was the foundress of Malagón. I was

received with great joy, for she loves me very much. I brought with me two nuns from St. Joseph's in Avila, who were great servants of God.[5] We were immediately given a suite of rooms, as was that lady's custom, where we remained with as much recollection as in a monastery.

4. I immediately began to take up the business matters with Alonso Alvarez and a son-in-law of his, named Diego Ortiz. The latter, although very good, and a theologian, was more unyielding in his opinion than Alonso Alvarez. He did not readily soften his demands. They began to ask for many conditions that I didn't think I could easily agree to. While engaged in these negotiations, I was looking for a house to rent so as to establish possession of the new foundation. But I was never able to find one that was suitable, although a great deal of searching had been done. Nor was I able to get the ecclesiastical administrator to give me the license (for at that time the archbishop was not there),[6] although this lady in whose house I was staying tried hard, as did also a nobleman, a canon in this church, whose name was Don Pedro Manrique, son of the governor of Castile. Don Pedro was a very good servant of God, and still is (for he is alive, though he had poor health). Some years after this house was founded, he entered the Society of Jesus where he is now.[7] He was an important person in this city because he is very intelligent and trustworthy. Nonetheless, he was unable to get me the license. For when the governor softened in his resistance, those on the council did not. To add to this, Alonso Alvarez and I couldn't come to an agreement because of his son-in-law to whom he gave much power. We ended up by disagreeing on everything.

5. I didn't know what to do, for I hadn't come for any other reason, and I saw that if I went away without making a foundation, the fact would be much publicized. Nonetheless, I was saddened more over their not giving me the license than by all the rest. I knew that once possession of the foundation was established, the Lord would provide as He had in other places. So I resolved to talk to the governor, and I went to a church that was next to his house and sent someone to beg him to be kind enough to speak with me. More than two months had passed in trying to obtain the license, and each day the matter got worse. When I

saw him, I told him that it was hard to accept the fact that there were women who wanted to live with so much austerity, perfection, and withdrawal from the world while those who would bear nothing of this but lived in comfort wanted to hinder these works that were of such service to our Lord. These and many other things I told him with a great determination which was given me by the Lord. The governor's heart was so moved that before I left he gave me the license.

6. I went away very happy. It seemed to me I now had everything without having anything, for I must have had only about three or four ducats. With these I bought two paintings done on canvas[8] (for I didn't have anything with an image to put on the altar), two straw mattresses and a woolen blanket. As for the house, we forgot about it since I was not in agreement with Alonso Alvarez. A merchant in the same city, a friend of mine named Alonso de Avila[9], who had never wanted to marry and who thinks only of doing good for those in prison — and he does many other good works as well — told me not to be afflicted, that he would find a house for me; but he took sick. Some days before, a very holy Franciscan friar named Martín de la Cruz had come to that place. He was there for some days, and when he left he sent me a young man named Andrada[10] (by no means rich but very poor), asking him to do everything I told him. One day when Andrada was attending Mass in a church, he came to speak to me and tell me what he had been told by that blessed man and that he was certainly ready to do everything he could for me; although only with his personal service could he help us. I thanked him and was amused, and my companions even more so, to see the kind of help that saintly man had sent us. The clothes this young man had on were not the kind one would wear when going to speak with discalced nuns.

7. Having the license but no one who would help me, I didn't know what to do or whom to entrust with the task of seeking a house for me to rent. I remembered the young man that Fray Martín de la Cruz had sent me and mentioned him to my companions. They laughed very much at me and told me not to do such a thing, that it would serve for no more than to make the secret plan public. I didn't want to listen to them. Since he was

sent by that servant of God, I trusted that there was something for him to do and that his offer to help had a mystery about it. Thus I sent for him and told him, placing him under all the secrecy I could, what was happening and asked that with this in mind he look for a house for me and that I would provide a guarantor for the rent. The guarantor of the rent was the good Alonso de Avila who, as I mentioned,[11] took sick. The task seemed a very easy one to Andrada and he told me that he would look for one. Right away, the day after the next, while I was attending Mass at the house of the Society of Jesus, he came to speak to me and said that he already had the house, that he had the keys, that it was nearby and that we should go to see it. And this we did. It was so nice that we stayed in it for almost a year.[12]

8. Frequently, when I reflect on this foundation, I am amazed by the designs of God. For almost three months—at least more than two, but I don't remember exactly—very wealthy persons had made the rounds of Toledo looking for a house for us and were never able to find one, as though there were no houses in the city. And then this youth comes along, not rich but very poor, and the Lord desired that he find one immediately. And though it could have been found without trouble if an agreement had been reached with Alonso Alvarez, not only did we fail to reach one but were far from doing so. Thus in God's design the foundation had to be made in poverty and with trial.

9. Well then, since the house pleased us, I gave the order at once to take possession before anything was done in it, lest some obstacle arise. Indeed, in a short while Andrada, who was mentioned, came to tell me that the house was being vacated that day, that we should bring our furniture. I told him there was little to do, for we had nothing but two straw mattresses and a blanket. He must have been surprised. My companions regretted that I told him and said that since I had mentioned this to him and he thereby saw how poor we were, he would not want to help us. I had not thought of this, but he paid little attention to it. For the One who gave him that desire had to advance the work until it was completed. And indeed I don't think we ourselves could have done better than Andrada in preparing the

house and getting workmen. We borrowed the things necessary for saying Mass, and, in order to take possession of the house, went with a workman at nightfall; and we brought a bell that is used at the elevation of the Blessed Sacrament, for we had no other. With much fear on my part, we spent the whole night getting everything in order. There was no place for a church except in one of the rooms of another little house next to this one and occupied at the time by some women; the owner had also rented this little house to us.

10. Since we had everything ready by dawn and we had not dared say anything to the women lest they reveal what we were doing, we began to make a door through a thin partition wall which led on to a very tiny patio. When the women, still in bed, heard the pounding, they got up terrified. We had all we could do to calm them down; but it was already time for Mass, and although they were hard to deal with, they did not do us any harm. And when they saw what our intention was the Lord pacified them.

11. Afterward, I realized how poorly we had proceeded; for at the time, with the absorption God gives in the work so that it will get done, one does not think of the difficulties. Well, when the owner of the house found out that it was made into a church, the trouble began, for she was the wife of an heir to an entailed estate and was very much opposed to this. The Lord was pleased that when she learned we would buy the house if we were satisfied with it, she was appeased. But, when those on the council learned that the monastery, for which they had never wanted to give a license, was founded, they became very angry and went and complained to the canon (whom I had secretly informed), boasting to him that they would do everything in their power to destroy it. Since the ecclesiastical administrator had gone on a trip after having given me the permission and was not in the city, they went to complain to the canon I mentioned, astonished at such boldness that a useless little woman should found a monastery against their will. He pretended that he knew nothing and pacified them as best he could, telling them that she had done so in other cities and with due authorization.

12. After I don't know how many days, they sent us a notice

of excommunication so that no Mass could be said until I presented the documents giving me authorization for what was done. I answered very meekly that I would do what they ordered, although I was not obliged to obey in that matter. And I asked Don Pedro Manrique, the gentleman I mentioned,[13] to go and speak to them and show them the documents. He appeased them since the deed was already done; otherwise, we would have been in deep trouble.

13. For some days we had no more than the straw mattresses and the blanket, and even that day we didn't have so much as a stick of wood to make a fire to cook a sardine. And I don't know who it was the Lord moved to leave a little bundle of wood in the church to help us. The nights were quite cold; but with the blanket and the woolen mantles we wore, we kept ourselves warm, for these mantles often help us. It will seem impossible that though we had stayed in the house of that lady who loved me so much,[14] we had to enter the new foundation in so much poverty. I don't know the reason, except that God wanted us to experience the good that lies in this virtue. I did not ask for help, because I don't like to be a bother; and she perhaps wasn't aware. Moreover, I am indebted for what she was able to give us.

14. The experience was very good for us; the interior consolation and happiness we felt were so great that I often think about what the Lord keeps stored up within the virtues. It seems to me this lack we experienced was the cause of a sweet contemplation. But this poverty did not last long, for soon Alonso Alvarez himself as well as others were providing us with more than we needed. And, true to say, my sadness was such that it resembled that of discovering that many gold jewels in my possession were taken away and I left poor. Thus I felt sorry that they were bringing our poverty to an end, and my companions felt the same. Since I saw they were sad, I asked them what troubled them, and they answered: "What else could it be, Mother, for it no longer seems we are poor."

15. From then on my desire to be very poor increased. And I felt freedom in having so little esteem for temporal goods, for the lack of these goods brings an increase of interior good. Cer-

tainly, such a lack carries in its wake another kind of fullness and tranquility.

During those days in which I was discussing the foundation with Alonso Alvarez, there were many persons to whom the plan seemed wrong — and they told me so — since that family was not from the nobility, although the family was very good, regardless of its social status, as I have said.[15] They thought that in a city as important as Toledo I would not lack comfort. I did not pay much attention to this, because, glory to God, I have always esteemed virtue more than lineage. But so much was said to the ecclesiastical administrator that he gave me the license under the condition that I make the foundation as in other places.

16. I didn't know what to do, for after the foundation was made they again took up the negotiations. But since the house was already founded, I arranged to let them become the patrons of the large chapel and settled things in such a way that they would have no connection with what pertained to the monastery, as is now the case. There was already someone who wanted the large chapel, an important person; and there were many opinions about this so that I didn't know what to decide. Our Lord desired to give me light in this matter, and so at one time He told me that lineage and social status mattered not at all in the judgment of God. He gave me a severe reprimand for listening to those who spoke to me about this; concerns of this sort were not for those of us who had already despised the world.

17. With these and other reasons I was very humbled, and I resolved to settle what had been begun and give them the chapel. I never regretted it, for we have seen clearly what poor assistance we would have received as far as buying a house goes. But with the help of Alonso Alvarez we bought a house in the place where we are now. It is one of the nicest in Toledo, and cost twelve thousand ducats. Since, according to the contract, so many Masses and feasts are to be celebrated, the nuns as well as the people are much consoled. Had I paid attention to the vain opinions of the world, it would have been impossible, from what we can understand, for us to be so well provided for, and I would have offended the one who with so much good will did this charitable deed for us.

Chapter 16

Treats of some of the things that have taken place, to the honor and glory of God, in this monastery of St. Joseph's in Toledo.

IT HAS OCCURRED TO ME to say something about what some of the nuns put into practice in the service of the Lord so that those who follow may strive to imitate the good things that were done in the beginning.

Before the house was bought, a nun named Ana de la Madre de Dios entered here at the age of forty. Her whole life had been spent in serving His Majesty. Although her house and way of life lacked no comfort because she lived alone and was well-to-do, she wanted instead to choose the poverty and submission of our order, and so she came to speak with me. Her health was poor. But since I saw she was so good and determined a soul, I thought she would be helpful for the beginning of the foundation; so I admitted her. God was pleased to give her much more health in the practice of austerity and submission than she had in her freedom and comfort.[1]

2. What edified me, and the reason I am recording this here, is that before she made her profession she offered everything she owned—and she was very rich—as an alms to the house. I was not happy about this and did not want to consent, telling her that perhaps afterward either she would be sorry she entered or we might not want to admit her to profession. And I added that what she did was imprudent, although we would not have let her go without giving the money back. But I wanted to overstate the point: first, so that there would be no occasion for temptation; second, in order to test her spirit. She answered that if this were to happen she would beg for the money out of love of God. And I was unable to make her change her mind. She lived very happily and with much better health.

3. The mortification and the obedience that were practiced in this monastery were great. As a result, the several times that I was there the prioress had to be careful[2] about what she said. For even when she said something only casually, they would immediately carry it out. Once they were looking at a pond that

was in the garden, and she said to a nun standing nearby: "But what would happen if I were to say, 'jump in'?" Hardly was this said, and the nun was in the pond and got so soaked that she had to change her clothes. At another time, when I was present, the nuns were going to confession, and one who was waiting for the other to finish came to speak to the prioress.[3] She asked her why she was doing that and if it was a good way to recollect herself and told her to go stick her head in a well that was nearby and there think of her sins. The nun thought she was to jump into the well and went so quickly to do so that if they hadn't hurried to hold her back she would have done so thinking she was doing God the greatest service in the world. Other similar things, requiring much mortification, were done. This made it necessary for learned men to restrain the nuns and explain to them the matters in which they were obliged to obey. For these nuns did some things that were imprudent, so that if their good intention had not redeemed them, they would have lost rather than gained merit. The above is true not only of this monastery, but it occurred to me to speak of the matter here. Rather, in all the others there are so many things happening that I wish I had not a part in them so that I could freely tell about some of them for the praise of our Lord in His servants.

4. It happened that while I was here a fatal illness struck one of the Sisters. After receiving the sacraments and being anointed, her happiness and joy were so great that, as though she were going to another country, we were able to talk to her about how she should recommend us to God when in heaven and to the saints to whom we were devoted. A little before she died, I went to her room to be with her, for I had just gone before the Blessed Sacrament to beg the Lord to give her a good death. And when I entered I saw His Majesty at the head of the bed. His arms were partly opened as though He were protecting her, and He told me that I could be certain He would protect all the nuns that die in these monasteries and that they should not fear temptation at the hour of death. I was left very consoled and recollected. After a little while I began to speak to her, and she said to me: "O Mother, what great things I am going to see." Thus she died, like an angel.[4]

5. And I have noticed that some who have died since this occurred have done so with quiet and calm as though they were in rapture or in the prayer of quiet, without showing the least sign of any temptation. Thus I hope in the goodness of God that He will be merciful to us at the moment of death through the merits of His Son and those of His glorious Mother whose habit we wear. Therefore, my daughters, let us strive to be true Carmelites, for soon the day's journey will end. And if we were to know the affliction that many experience at the hour of death and the cunning deceit with which the devil tempts them, we would highly esteem this favor.

6. One thing occurs to me now that I want to tell you, for I knew the person, and indeed he was almost a relative of my relatives. He was a great gambler, who had taken some theology by which the devil tried to deceive him, making him believe that the purpose of amendment at the hour of death was worth nothing. He had this so fixed in his mind that others could in no way get him to confess. Nor did anything suffice, though the poor man was extremely afflicted and repentant of the evil life he had lived. But he asked why he should confess since he saw that he was condemned. A learned Dominican friar who was his confessor did nothing but argue with him, but the devil taught him so many subtleties that the friar's arguments were insufficient. Thus for some days the confessor didn't know what to do; and, along with others, he must have recommended the matter urgently to the Lord since he had compassion on the man.

7. When the illness, which involved pain in the side, was beginning to afflict the man greatly, the confessor returned. He must have thought up other arguments, but they would have been of little benefit if the Lord had not taken pity on that man and softened his heart. And when the confessor began to speak to him and give him reasons, the man sat up in bed as though he were not sick at all and said to him: "What, in short, do you have to say that could help me benefit from my confession? For I want to make it." And he sent for a secretary or notary (I don't remember which) to record his testimony, and made a very solemn oath not to gamble any more and to amend his life. He confessed very well and received the sacraments with such devotion that from what we can understand according to our faith he was

saved. May Our Lord be pleased, Sisters, that we live our lives as true daughters of the Blessed Virgin and keep our vows so that He may grant us the favor He has promised us. Amen.

Chapter 17

Treats of the foundation of the two monasteries in Pastrana, one for the nuns and one for the friars. They were made in 1570, I mean 1569.

AFTER THE FOUNDATION OF THE HOUSE IN TOLEDO, during the fifteen days preceding Pentecost, the little church, the grates, and other things had to be prepared. There was a great deal to do, for as I have said we remained in this house for almost a year. I was tired after those days from going about with the workmen. When the vigil of Pentecost came, all the work was done. That morning as we sat in the refectory to eat, great consolation came over me in seeing that I no longer had anything to do and that I could enjoy some time with the Lord on Pentecost; I was almost unable to eat so consoled did my soul feel.[1]

2. I did not deserve to have this consolation very long, for while I was in the midst of it, they came to tell me that a servant sent by the princess of Eboli, the wife of Ruy Gómez de Silva, was there. I went to meet him and learned that the princess was sending him for me since I had been in communication with her for some time about the foundation of a monastery in Pastrana. I didn't think it was to come about so quickly. The idea made me uneasy because it would have been dangerous to leave a monastery founded so recently and in the midst of opposition. So I resolved not to go, and said so. The servant told me that this would not be acceptable, because the princess was already in Pastrana and had not gone for any other reason, that she would take a refusal as an insult. Despite all this, I had no thought of going, and so I told him to go get something to eat and that I would write to the princess; and then he left. He was a very honorable man, and though he did not like it that I refused, once I explained the reasons to him, he went along with them.

3. Moreover, the nuns who were to make up the new community had just arrived, another reason why I did not see how I could leave so soon.[2] I went before the Blessed Sacrament to beg the Lord to help me write in such a way that the princess would not grow angry. That would have been very bad for us since the friars were then just beginning and, above all, it was good to keep in the favor of Ruy Gómez who had such strong influence with the king and with everyone. But I don't remember if I recalled the latter, although I know well that I did not want to displease Ruy Gómez.[3] While I was praying to the Lord, He told me not to fail to go, that I was going for more than that foundation and that I should bring the rule and constitutions.

4. Since I heard this—although for myself I saw serious reasons for not going—I didn't dare but do what I usually do in similar instances, which was to follow the counsel of my confessor. And so I sent for him. I did not tell him what I had heard in prayer.[4] In this way I am always left more satisfied, for I beg the Lord to give my confessors light in conformity with what they can know naturally. And when His Majesty wants something to be done, He puts it in their heart. This has happened to me many times. So it happened this time, for after considering everything, he thought I should go, and with that I decided to leave.

5. I set out from Toledo the second day after Pentecost traveling by way of Madrid. There my companions and I went for lodging to a monastery of Franciscan nuns, with a lady, who had founded it and lived in it, named Doña Leonor Mascareñas.[5] She had been the king's governess and is a very good servant of our Lord. I had lodged there at other times when on certain occasions I had to pass by, and she always showed me much kindness.

6. This lady told me she was happy I had come at that time because a hermit was there who eagerly desired to meet me[6] and that it seemed to her the life he and his companions were living was very similar to that of our rule. The thought came to me that if this were so it would be a good thing since I had only two friars, and so I begged her to arrange for us to speak. He was staying in a room given him by this lady. He was there with another young brother named Fray Juan de la Miseria, a great servant of

God and very simple with regard to the things of the world.[7] While we were speaking together, this hermit told me that he wanted to go to Rome.

7.　Before going on, I want to mention what I know about this Father, named Mariano de San Benito. He was Italian, a doctor, and very intelligent and talented. While he was living as the supervisor of the entire household of the queen of Poland, our Lord called him to leave all so as to better obtain his salvation. He had not been inclined to marry, but was a knight of the Order of St. John of Jerusalem. He had undergone some trials in which he had been falsely accused of being involved in a man's death and thus put in prison for two years. While there, he didn't want to be defended by any learned man or anyone else, but only by God and His justice, for there were witnesses who said that he had ordered them to kill the man. Resembling the old men in the story about Saint Susanna,[8] when each was asked where the accused was at the time, one said that he was seated on a bed; and the other, at a window. In the end they confessed to having calumniated him. And he assured me that he had spent much money to free them so that they would not be punished, and that certain information had come into his possession against the one who had caused him the trouble and that he likewise did as much as he could not to do that one any harm.

8.　Through these and other virtues—for he is a clean-living and chaste man, unwilling to have any dealings with women— he must have merited from our Lord knowledge of what the world is so that he would strive to withdraw from it. And thus he began to think about which religious order to join. And, from what he told me, in thinking about the different orders, he found in each one some difficulty for his temperament. He learned that near Seville some hermits had come together to live in a desert called El Tardón, under a very holy man, named Padre Mateo,[9] whom they took as their superior. Each one lived apart in a cell. They did not recite the divine office together but did gather in an oratory for Mass. They had no fixed income; neither did they want to receive alms, nor did they. But they supported themselves by the work of their hands, and each one ate alone and very poorly. When I heard about this, it seemed to me to be a living picture of the life of our own holy fathers. Father Mariano had spent eight years in this manner of life. When the holy Council of Trent came and took away authorization for the eremitical life, he wanted to go to Rome to seek permission that they might continue as they were, and this was his intention when I spoke to him.[10]

9. Well now, when he told me the manner of his life, I showed him our primitive rule and told him that without so much trouble he could observe all of that since his life was the same as that prescribed in the rule, especially living by the work of one's hands. He was very much inclined to the latter and told me that the world was lost because of greed and that this was why religious life was not valued. Since I felt the same, we quickly agreed in this and even in everything else. When I gave him reasons about how much he could serve God in this habit, he told me that he would think over the matter that night. I already saw that he was nearly decided, and I understood that what I had learned in prayer (that I was going to Pastrana for more than the foundation of a monastery of nuns)[11] referred to this. The thought gave me the greatest happiness since it seemed to me that the Lord would be much served if this hermit were to enter the order. He was so moved that night by His Majesty, who desired this, that the next day he called for me, now very determined and even very surprised to see how quickly he himself had changed, especially through the instrumentality of a woman, for even now he sometimes mentions this to me, as though what I said were the cause and not the Lord who can change hearts.

10. Great are God's judgments. Mariano had gone many years without knowing what to decide concerning his state, for the life he had been living was not that of a religious, since the hermits did not make vows or take on any obligation other than to remain there in solitude. And God quickly moved him and revealed how much His Majesty would be served by him in this state and the need for him in order to carry on what had been begun. For he has helped a great deal, and up to now it has cost him many trials. And by what can be seen from the opposition the followers of this primitive rule now experience,[12] the work will cost him more until it is firmly established. For through his

talent, intelligence, and good life he is influential with many persons who favor and defend us.

11. Well then, he told me how Ruy Gómez had given him a good hermitage and site in Pastrana, the place where I was going, for a settlement of hermits and that he wanted to accept it for this order and receive the habit. I thanked him and praised our Lord greatly. For of the two monasteries for which our Most Reverend Father General had sent permission, only one had been founded.[13] From there I sent a message to the two Fathers that were mentioned, the present provincial and the previous one,[14] begging them to give me permission since the monastery could not be founded without their consent. And I wrote to the bishop of Avila, Don Alvaro de Mendoza, who was very favorable toward us, to try to get them to grant it.

12. God was pleased that they look favorably on my request. It seemed to them that in a place so isolated the foundation could do them little harm. Mariano gave me his word that he would go there when the permission came. Thus, I was extremely happy. Once there, I met the princess and the prince, Ruy Gómez, who received me very cordially. They gave us a separate apartment, where we stayed longer than I had expected. For the house where we were to live was so small that the princess had ordered much of it to be torn down and many things built anew, but not the walls.

13. I spent three months[15] there during which many trials were suffered, since the princess asked me to do things that were not fitting for our form of religious life, and so I decided, rather than make the foundation, to leave. The prince, Ruy Gómez, with both his common sense, which was very great, and his reasonableness, got his wife to agree with us. And I bore with some things because I was more desirous that the monastery of friars be founded than that of the nuns. I knew how important this was, and the importance afterward became clear.

14. At this time Mariano with his companion (the two hermits that were mentioned)[16] came, and when the permission arrived, the prince and princess were glad to agree that the hermitage they had given him for hermits be used by discalced friars. I sent

for Father Fray Antonio de Jesús, who was the first discalced and was in Mancera so that he might get the foundation started. I made habits and white mantles and did all I could so that they might take the habit at once.

15. At this time I had sent to Medina del Campo for more nuns, for I had brought only two with me. There was a Father in Medina, about middle-aged, not too old, not too young, and a very good preacher, whose name was Baltasar de Jesús.[17] Since he knew that the monastery was being founded, he came with the nuns and desired to become a discalced. This he did after he arrived, and when he told me, I praised God. He gave the habit to Father Mariano and his companion. Both of them became lay brothers, for Father Mariano did not want to become a priest, but wanted to be the least of all; nor could I convince him otherwise. Afterward, by order of our Most Reverend Father General, he was ordained a priest.[18] Once the two monasteries were established and Father Fray Antonio de Jesús had come, novices began to enter, of whom I shall give some examples later on. And they began to serve our Lord so authentically that, if He be pleased, someone more capable than I of telling about it, will put it in writing. For such a task, I would fall short.

16. As for the nuns, the monastery there received much kindness from the prince and princess. And the princess favored them and treated them well until the prince, Ruy Gómez, died.[19] Tempted by the devil, or perhaps because the Lord permitted it—His Majesty knows why—the princess in the intense emotion felt from her husband's death entered to be a nun. With the affliction she was experiencing, the practices of enclosure to which she was not accustomed could only displease her, and because of the holy Council the prioress could not give the liberties the princess wanted.

17. The princess came to dislike both the prioress and all the rest of the nuns along with her. Such was her dislike that even after she discarded the habit and lived in her own house she caused them trouble. And the poor nuns were so disturbed that I strove in every way I could, begging the superiors, to move the monastery from there and found one in Segovia. As will be said later,[20] they did move to Segovia, and left behind all that the

princess had given them, but brought along some nuns she had ordered them to accept without any dowry. The beds and other little things that the nuns had brought there with them they also took along. Their departure left the townspeople very sorry. As for me, seeing the nuns in peace left me with the greatest happiness in the world. For I was very well informed that they were in no way at fault for the displeasure of the princess. On the contrary, they served her as much when she had the habit as they did before she received it. The only occasion for her displeasure was the one I mentioned[21] plus the hardship both she and the servant she had brought with her experienced. For, from what is known, she was entirely at fault. In sum, the Lord permitted it. He must have seen that it was not proper for that monastery to be there, for His judgments are great and beyond all our understanding. I, on my own account, would not dare do anything without consulting learned and holy persons.

Chapter 18

Treats of the foundation of the monastery of St. Joseph in Salamanca in the year 1570. Deals with some important counsels for prioresses.

AFTER THESE TWO FOUNDATIONS WERE MADE, I returned to the city of Toledo, where I remained some months until the house, which I mentioned, was bought and everything was left in order.[1] While I was engaged in these things, a rector of the Society of Jesus wrote me from Salamanca, telling me that it would be very good to have one of these monasteries there, giving me reasons for this.[2] But since the town was very poor, I resisted founding a monastery there in poverty.[3] In considering that Avila is just as poor, and the monastery there is never in want, nor do I believe that God will fail those who serve Him, if they live as moderately as we do, and that the nuns are so few and help themselves through the labor of their hands, I decided to make the foundation. And going from Toledo to Avila, I sought there to obtain permission from the bishop who was then . . .[4] Since the Father Rector had informed him about our order and that the foundation would render service to God, he responded very favorably and gave the permission without delay.

2. It seemed to me that once I had permission from the ordinary, the monastery was as much as founded, so easy did the rest seem to me. Thus, I immediately sought to rent a house that a lady, whom I knew,[5] would let me have. But this was a difficult thing to do because the time was not the proper one for renting and the student occupants agreed to leave only when the new occupants arrived. They did not know who the new ones would be, for I took the greatest care so that nothing would be known until I took possession of the foundation. I already have experience of what the devil stirs up to hinder one of these monasteries. And although with this one God, desiring it to be founded, did not allow him to cause trouble in the beginning, the trials and contradictions were so great afterward that they are still not completely overcome — and some years have passed between the time it was founded and my writing this account.[6] Thus, I believe that God is served very much in it since the devil cannot bear it.

3. Well now, having obtained the permission and being certain of a house to rent, I left for Salamanca. I trusted in the mercy of God because there wasn't a person there who could in any way help me with the great deal that had to be done in order to make the proper adaptations in the house. For the sake of secrecy, I took with me only one other nun as companion,[7] for I found this to be better than bringing the nuns before taking possession. I had learned from experience through what had happened to me in Medina del Campo; there I got myself into much trouble.[8] Thus, if there were some obstacle, I could undergo the trial alone, with no one other than the one required companion. We arrived on the vigil of All Saints.[9] The previous night we had travelled a good deal before coming to a place to sleep. The weather was cold; and I, very sick.

4. I am not recording in these foundations the great hardships endured in the traveling: the cold, the heat, the snow (once it didn't stop snowing the whole day); sometimes getting lost, and at other times, being very sick and having a fever (for, glory to God, I usually have poor health). But I saw clearly that

our Lord was giving me strength. It happened to me at times when a foundation was being planned that I would be so sick and have so many pains that I would get very anxious. It seemed to me that I wasn't even able to remain in my cell without lying down. I would turn to our Lord, complain to His Majesty, and ask how He desired me to do what I couldn't. Afterward, although I still felt the hardship, His Majesty gave me strength, and with the fervor and solicitude he gave, it seems I forgot about myself.

5. From what I now remember, fear of the hardship involved never prevented me from making a foundation even though I felt strong aversion to the traveling, especially the long journeys. But once we got started, the journey seemed easy to me, and I considered for whose service it was made and reflected that in that house the Lord would be praised and the Blessed Sacrament reserved. This is a special consolation for me: to see one more church, particularly when I recall the many that the Lutherans are suppressing. I don't know what trials, however great, should be feared if in exchange something so good comes about for Christianity. For although we often do not take note, it ought to be a great consolation for us that Jesus Christ, true God and true man, is present in the most Blessed Sacrament in many places. Certainly I am very often consoled in the choir when I see these very pure souls praising God, for one cannot help but recognize their holiness in many things, seeing their obedience, the joy so much enclosure and solitude give them, and their happiness when some opportunities for mortification come along. In places where the Lord gives the prioress more grace in exercising them in mortification, I see greater happiness. And the result is that the prioresses tire more easily in thus exercising them than these souls do in obeying, for never in this matter of mortification do the desires of these nuns cease.

6. Although this subject is foreign to the one concerning the foundation that I began discussing, some things are coming to my mind now about this matter of mortification. Perhaps, daughters, they will be important for the prioresses, and so lest I forget I'll mention them now. For since the prioresses have different talents and virtues, they seek to lead their nuns along

their own way. The one who is very mortified thinks that anything she commands is easy to submit to, as it would be for her, but perhaps it would be very harmful for the nun to whom she gives the orders. We must be careful about this. If for ourselves something would be harsh, we must not order others to do it. Discretion is an important aspect of government, and very necessary in these houses. I would say much more necessary than in other houses, for the account one must render concerning one's subjects is greater. This applies in interior as well as exterior matters.

Other prioresses, who are very spiritual, would like to reduce everything to prayer; in sum, the Lord leads souls by different paths. But the prioresses must remember that they are not there for the purpose of choosing a path for others according to their own liking but so as to lead subjects by the path of the rule and constitutions even though they themselves might desire and feel urged to do something else.

7.   Once I was living in one of these houses with a prioress who was fond of penance; she led all the others along this path. She once had the entire community take the discipline while reciting the seven penitential psalms with their accompanying prayers, and things of this sort. Thus it happens that if a prioress is absorbed in prayer, even though the hour is not one set apart for prayer, but after Matins, she keeps the whole community there even though it would be much better if the Sisters went to bed. If, as I say, she is fond of mortification, everyone has to follow suit, and these little sheep of the Virgin keep silent like little lambs; as for me, certainly, it causes much devotion, and embarrassment, and, at times, much temptation. The Sisters don't understand, for they are all absorbed in God. But I fear for their health and would want them to observe the rule, for with that there is plenty to do; and the rest should be done with gentleness. This is especially important in what pertains to mortification. For love of our Lord, the prioresses should be attentive in this, for discretion and knowledge of each one's talents are very important in these matters. If the prioresses are not carefully attentive, they will do the nuns much harm and leave them disturbed instead of helping them.

8. They must reflect that this mortification is not a matter of obligation; this is the first thing they must consider. Although mortification is very necessary in order that the soul gain freedom and high perfection, it is not accomplished in a short time. Rather, little by little, the prioress should help each one according to the spirituality and amount of intelligence God gives. It might seem to prioresses that intelligence is not necessary for this mortification, but they are mistaken. For with some nuns, much time will pass before they come to understand perfection and even the spirit of our rule (and perhaps they will afterward be the holiest), for they will not know when it is good to excuse oneself, and when not, or other trifling matters that if they understood they would perhaps carry out with ease. And such nuns do not completely understand, nor does it seem to them that these are matters pertaining to perfection, which is worse.

9. There is a nun in one of these houses who is among the best servants of God in them, insofar as I can tell. She has a deep spirituality, receives favors from His Majesty, and has a spirit of penance and humility; yet, she does not completely understand some points in the constitutions. The accusation of faults in chapter[10] seems to her uncharitable, and she wonders how anyone can say anything against the Sisters and similar things and says that she could say some things against some Sisters who are very good servants of God; and in other matters I see that she is ahead of those who understand this well. The prioress must not then think that she understands a soul at once. Let her leave this to God, for it is He alone who can understand it. Rather, the prioress should strive to guide each nun along the way His Majesty is leading that one, provided that the nun is not failing in obedience or in the more essential matters of the rule and constitutions. That virgin martyr, from the eleven thousand, who hid herself did not fail to be a saint; on the contrary, by coming alone afterward to offer herself to be martyred, she perhaps suffered more than the rest of the virgins.[11]

10. Now, then, let us return to the subject of mortification. The prioress may ask something of a nun in order to mortify her, and although it is a little thing it may be a heavy burden to the nun. And even though the Sister does it, she is left so dis-

turbed and tempted that it would have been better had she not been told to do it; I mean, to do it right away. The prioress should take heed not to try to make such a one perfect by force but should allow her to proceed gradually until the Lord does the work in her. For that which is done to help her advance shouldn't be for her a cause of disturbance and spiritual distress, which is a very terrible thing, for she will be a very good nun without that perfection. Observing the others, she will gradually do as they do, as we have seen. And if she doesn't, she will be saved without this virtue of mortification. For I know one of these nuns who all her life practiced great virtue, and for some years now has served our Lord in many ways, and she often experiences some feelings and imperfections that she cannot do anything about, and she complained about them to me and is aware of them. I think that God allows her to fall into these sinless faults (for there is no sin in them) so that she might humble herself and realize that she is not totally perfect.

Therefore, some nuns will suffer great mortifications, and the greater the mortifications they are ordered to perform the more they will enjoy them because the Lord has given them the strength of soul to surrender their wills. Others will not suffer even little ones; and to impose mortifications on them would be comparable to loading a child down with two sacks of wheat. Not only will the child be unable to carry them, but he will bow under the weight and fall to the ground. Therefore, my daughters — I am speaking with prioresses — pardon me, for the things I have seen that happen to some make me to go on at greater length in this matter.

11. Another counsel I give you, and it is a very important one. Do not give any order that could be a sin (even venial) if carried out, and not even if you do so just to test obedience. (I've heard that some things would have involved mortal sin if done.) At least the nuns, because of their innocence perhaps, are without blame; but not the prioress, beause there is no order she gives that they will not carry out immediately. And since they hear and read about what the saints of the desert did, everything seems to them well done if ordered by obedience, at least in their own case. And also let subjects be advised that anything

that would be a mortal sin when not ordered by the superior would still be one if the superior orders it, unless the matter involves omitting Mass or the Church fast, or things like that, in which the prioress may have reasons for dispensing. But something like jumping into the well and things of that sort are wrong to do. No one should think that God must work miracles, as He did with the saints; there are many other things in which perfect obedience may be practiced.

12. All the mortification in which these dangers are not present, I praise. Once a Sister in Malagón asked permission to take a discipline, and the prioress (she must have been asked more than once) answered: "Don't bother me." Since the nun persisted, the prioress said: "Go on, keep walking; don't bother me." With great simplicity, the nun went walking for several hours until another Sister asked her why she was walking so much, or something like that. And she replied that she had been ordered to do so. When the bell was rung for Matins and the prioress asked where she was, the other nun told her what had taken place.

13. Thus it's necessary, as I have mentioned at another time, that the prioresses be careful about what they do with souls that they see are so obedient. For another Sister showed a nun one of those very large worms, telling her to observe how pretty it was. The prioress said to the nun jokingly, well, let Sister eat it. The Sister went and fried it very well. The cook asked her why she was frying it. She told her she was frying it so that she could eat it, and this she wanted to do. And the prioress, being very careless, could have done her much harm. I find I'm happier that they go to excess in matters of obedience because I am particularly devoted to this virtue, and so I have put down all I could so that the nuns might possess it. But it would profit me little to do so if the Lord through His supreme mercy had not given the grace for all in general to be inclined toward this virtue. May it please His Majesty to continue to give this grace long into the future. Amen.

Chapter 19

Continues the account of the foundation of the monastery of St. Joseph in the city of Salamanca.

I HAVE DIGRESSED MUCH. When something presents itself that by the Lord's will I come to understand through experience, it bothers me not to give advice about it. It could be that what I think about the matter is worthwhile. Always inquire, daughters, from those who are learned, for through them you will learn how to advance along the way of perfection with discretion and in truth. If prioresses want to fulfill their duties well, they have great need to go to confession to a learned man (and if they don't, they will make many mistakes in the interests of sanctity); and they should strive also that their nuns confess to a learned man.

2. Well, on the vigil of All Saints, in the year that was mentioned,[1] we arrived at noon in the city of Salamanca. From an inn I sought to find out through a good man there if the house was free. He was a great servant of God, named Nicolás Gutiérrez,[2] to whom I had entrusted the task of making sure that it would be unoccupied. This man had won from His Majesty through his good life a great peace and happiness in the midst of trials, for he had undergone many trials. Having once enjoyed great prosperity, he was left very poor, but he bore the poverty with as much joy as he did the riches. The good man worked very hard for this foundation, with much dedication and willingness. When he came, he told me that the house was occupied, that he hadn't been able to get the students to leave. I told him how important it was that they vacate immediately, before my presence in that city became known, for I am always afraid lest some obstacle arise, as I have said.[3] He went to the one who owned the house and insisted so much that it was vacated that afternoon. When it was almost night, we entered.

3. It was the first monastery I founded without reserving the Blessed Sacrament, for I had previously thought that a foundation was not official until the Blessed Sacrament was reserved. And I had now learned that this wasn't necessary. That was a

great consolation to me, for the house was in bad condition because of those students who had previously occupied it. Since they must not have had a gift for cleanliness, the whole house was in such a state that we did no small amount of work that night. The next morning the first Mass was said, and I arranged for more nuns to come from Medina del Campo.[4] My companion and I spent the night of All Saints alone. I tell you, daughters, I have to laugh when I recall the fear of my companion, who was María del Sacramento, a nun older than I and a great servant of God.[5]

4. The house was very large, was in a mess, and had many garrets. My companion couldn't get the students out of her mind, thinking that since they were so angry for having had to leave the house, one of them may have hidden there. They could have done this very easily, for there were many possibilities. We locked ourselves in a room where there was some straw, which was the first thing I provided for the founding of the house, because in having straw we would have a bed. We slept there that night with two borrowed blankets. The next day some nuns that were nearby, who we thought would be very displeased, lent us furnishings for our companions, who were to come, and sent us alms.[6] Their monastery was called St. Isabel's, and all the time we were there they gave us alms and did many favors for us.

5. Once my companion was locked in that room, it seems she calmed down a little with regard to the students, although she didn't do anything but look about from side to side, still fearful. And the devil must have helped by bringing to her mind thoughts about the danger. Her thoughts then began to disturb me, for with my weak heart, not much was needed. I asked her why she was looking around since no one could get in there. She answered: "Mother, I was wondering what would happen if I were to die now; what would you do here all alone?" If that had happened it would have been a hard thing for me to take. And I began to think a little about it and even become afraid. Because as for dead bodies, although I am not afraid of them, my heart gets weak even when I'm not alone. And since the tolling of the bells helped matters along, for, as I said, it was the vigil of All

Souls,[7] the devil had a good means of making us squander our thoughts on trifles. When he sees that one has no fear of him, he looks for other devices. I said to her: "Sister, when this happens, I'll think about what to do; now, let me sleep." Since we had just spent two bad nights, sleep came soon and took away our fears. The next day more nuns arrived, and with them present, the fears left.

6. The monastery was in this house for about three years—I don't recall whether or not it was four, for I don't remember well since they sent me to the Incarnation in Avila.[8] I never would, or did, leave any monastery until it was in fit condition, had a spirit of recollection, and was adapted according to my wishes. In this matter God greatly favors me, for when there was question of work to be done I enjoyed being the first. And as though I were to live in that house for the rest of my life, I sought to obtain everything, even the smallest thing that would contribute to the tranquility suitable for the life, and so it gave me great happiness to see that everything was in good shape. I very much regretted to see what these Sisters suffered, although not from a lack of sustenance (I took care of this from where I was, for the house was not located in a place suitable for receiving alms), but from a location that was unhealthy because of the humidity and cold. Since it was so large a house it could not be repaired. And, what was worse, the Blessed Sacrament was not reserved, which is a great affliction when so much enclosure is practiced. The Sisters were not unhappy but bore everything with a joy that moved one to praise God. Some told me that they thought it would be an imperfection to desire a house, that they were as happy there as they would be if they had the Blessed Sacrament.

7. Well, when the superior[9] saw their perfection and the trial they were undergoing, he was moved with pity and ordered me to come from the Incarnation. They had already reached an agreement with a gentleman there who was going to sell them a house.[10] But it was in such condition that they would have had to spend a thousand ducats before entering it. It belonged to an entailed estate, but the gentleman decided to allow us both to occupy it without first obtaining permission from the king and

to put up partition walls. I got Father Julián de Avila,[11] who is the one I said came with me on these foundations, and we looked at the house so as to decide what had to be done, for experience has taught me much about these things.

8. We went in August and hurried as much as we could. The nuns were able to stay where they were until the feast of St. Michael, the time when houses were rented there. But the house was still far from being finished. Since we had not rented for another year, the one in which we were staying had another renter already. We were in a great hurry. The whitewashing of the church was about finished. The gentleman who had sold us the house was not there. Some persons who wished us well told us that we had done wrong in coming so soon, but where there is need one takes poorly any advice that doesn't provide some help.

9. We moved on the eve of St. Michael, a little before dawn. The news had already been spread that the Blessed Sacrament would be reserved on the feast of St. Michael and that a sermon would be preached.[12] Our Lord was pleased that on the afternoon of the day we moved it rained so hard that it was most difficult to bring the things we needed. The chapel had been newly fixed up, but the roof was so poorly tiled the rain came through most of it. I tell you, daughters, I felt very imperfect that day. Since the news had already been spread about, I didn't know what to do. I became so distressed that I said to the Lord, almost complaining, that either He not order me to get involved in repair works or He help me in this need. The good man Nicolás Gutiérrez, with his equanimity, as though nothing had happened, told me very meekly not to be disturbed, that God would provide a remedy. And so it happened. On the feast of St. Michael, when it was time for the people to come, the sun began to shine, which filled me with devotion, and I saw how much better that blessed man had done by trusting in our Lord than I with my disturbance.

10. There were many people, and there was music, and the Blessed Sacrament was reserved with great solemnity. Since this house is in a good location, the people began to know about it and be devoted to it. In particular, the countess of Monterrey,

Doña María Pimentel,[13] favored us, as well as a lady, whose husband was the magistrate there, whose name was Doña Mariana. The very next day, as though to temper our happiness in having the Blessed Sacrament, the gentleman to whom the house belonged came. He was so furious that I didn't know what to do with him. And the devil made sure that he couldn't be reasoned with, for we had fulfilled all that we had agreed upon with him. There was little use in trying to explain to him. When some other persons spoke to him, he was a little appeased; but afterward he changed his mind again. I had already decided to leave the house. He didn't want this either, because he wanted to be given the money at once. His wife to whom the house belonged had desired to sell it in order to provide for two daughters, and this was the reason given in asking for the license to sell it. The money had already been deposited with a person chosen by the husband.

11. The fact is that even though this happened more than three years ago, the purchase of the house is not finalized, nor do I know whether the monastery will remain there; and this is why I have mentioned these things.[14]

12. What I do know is that in none of the monasteries of the primitive rule that up to now the Lord has founded did the nuns come near to suffering trials as great as these. Through the mercy of God, those who are there are so good, for they bear everything happily. May it please His Majesty to lead them on, for whether or not they have a good house matters little. Rather, it gives us great pleasure to find we are in a house that we can be thrown out of, for we remember how the Lord of the world didn't have any. It has happened to us at times in these foundations that we were in a house that we didn't own, and the truth is that I never saw a nun distressed about that. May it please His Majesty that through His infinite goodness and mercy we will not be in want of the eternal dwelling places, amen, amen.

Chapter 20

*Treats of the foundation of the monastery, Our Lady of the An-
nunciation, in Alba de Tormes. It was made in the year 1571.*

TWO MONTHS HAD NOT YET PASSED since the feast of All Saints
(the day on which possession was taken of the house in
Salamanca) when I received an urgent request from the administrator for the duke of Alba and his wife that a monastery be
founded in the town of Alba. I was not too keen about the idea
because the town was a small one, which would make it necessary for us to have an income, and my inclination was not to
have one. Father Master Fray Domingo Báñez (who had been
my confessor, whom I consulted when beginning these foundations) happened to be in Salamanca, and he reprimanded me
and told me that since the Council had given permission it
would not be right to forego the foundation of a monastery because of a need for an income.[1] He said further that I failed to
understand that whether the monastery had an income or not
made little difference in regard to nuns being poor and very
perfect.

Before I say more, I shall mention who the foundress was and
how the Lord moved her to make the foundation.

2. The foundress of the monastery, Our Lady of the Annunciation, was Teresa de Layz, a daughter of noble parents, hidalgos of pure blood.[2] Since her parents were not as rich as would
be expected considering the nobility of their lineage, they had
their house in a place called Tordillos, which is two leagues
from the said town of Alba. It is a great pity that the world is so
influenced by vanity that people would prefer to remain in thes?
little villages where there is a lack of Christian doctrine and of
many other things that are means to the enlightenment of souls,
than to fail even one iota in those punctilios that accompany
what they call honor. Since the parents already had four daughters when Teresa de Layz was born, they were much distressed
to see that she also was a daughter.

3. Certainly, it is something to be much wept over that
human beings do not know what is best for them and are totally

ignorant of the judgments of God and of the great blessings that
can come to them through daughters or of the great sufferings
that can come from sons. It doesn't seem they want to leave this
matter to the One who creates their children and understands
everything, but they kill themselves over what should be making
them happy. As people whose faith is asleep, they do not reflect
or recall that it is God who thus ordains, and so they do not leave
everything in His hands. And being so blind that they do not do
this, they suffer great ignorance in not understanding how little
these afflictions help them. Oh, God help me! How differently
will we understand these ignorances on the day when the truth
about all things shall be understood. And how many fathers and
mothers will be seen going to hell because they had sons and also
how many will be seen in heaven because of their daughters.

4. Well, to return to what I was saying, things came to the
point that on the third day after her birth they left their baby
girl alone and forgot about her for the entire day, from morning
until night, as though she mattered little to them. One thing
they had done well was to have her baptized by a priest as soon
as she was born. When at night, a woman came who was taking
care of the baby and knew what was going on, she hastened to
see if the child was dead. Some other persons who had gone
there to visit the mother were also witnesses to what I shall now
tell. Weeping, the woman took the baby into her arms and complaining of the cruelty said: "How is it, my daughter, are you
not a Christian?" The baby girl lifted her head and answered,
"Yes, I am," and spoke no more until reaching that age at which
all children begin to speak. Those who heard her were amazed,
and her mother began to love and cherish her from then on, and
she often said that she would like to live to see what God would
do with this child. She reared her daughter in keeping with high
moral standards and taught her everything about virtue.

5. When the time came that her parents wanted her to marry,
she refused, nor did she have any desire at all to get married.
She happened to find out that Francisco Velázquez, now her
husband, who is also the founder of this house, was seeking her.
In hearing his name, she decided to marry if she could marry
him, never having seen him in her life. But His Majesty saw that

this was fitting so that the good work both of them did in order to serve Him could be done. Besides being a virtuous and rich man, Francisco Velázquez loves his wife so much that he seeks to please her in everything. And rightly so, for all that one can seek in a married woman the Lord gave to him in great abundance. Along with the diligent care she takes of her household, her goodness is so great that when her husband brought her to his native town of Alba and the duke's housing administrators happened to arrange that lodging be given in her house to a young gentleman, she was very upset and began to abhor the town.

For being youthful and attractive in appearance, she could have been the victim of some evil deed since the devil began to put bad thoughts in that gentleman's mind.

6. Aware of this, but without saying anything to her husband, she asked him to take her away from there. He did so and brought her to Salamanca where she lived very happily, surrounded by much of the world's goods, since he held a position that made others want to please and flatter him.[3] They had but one sorrow, that God had not given them children. That He might give them, she offered many devotions and prayers. And she never begged the Lord for anything else but that He give her offspring so that after her death her children could continue the praise of His Majesty, for it seemed to her unfortunate that this praise would end with her and that there would be no one after her days to praise Him. And she told me that there wasn't any other desire that came to her mind. And she is a woman who is so truthful and good a Christian and virtuous, as I have said, that it often makes me praise our Lord to see her works and her great desires never to fail to use her time well and to please Him always.

7. Well, then, living many years with this desire and recommending it to St. Andrew, who, she was informed, is a patron of such causes, and after many other devotions that she had offered, she was told one night while lying down: "Do not desire children, for you will be condemned." She was left frightened and fearful. But not for this reason did the desire leave her, for it seemed to her that since her purpose was so good there would

be no reason for her to be condemned. So she continued to beg our Lord. Especially, she carried out a particular devotion to St. Andrew. Once, while experiencing this desire, though she doesn't know whether she was awake or asleep (whatever may be the case, it is clear that the vision was true from what followed), it seemed to her that she was in a house where on the patio beneath the gallery was a well. And she saw in that place a green meadow with white flowers, so beautiful she wouldn't be able to describe what she saw. Near the well, St. Andrew appeared in the form of a very venerable and handsome person, for it gave her great delight to look on him, and he said to her: "These are children other than those you desire." She did not want the great consolation she felt in that place to end; but it did not last. And she understood clearly that the vision was of St. Andrew, without anyone telling her; and also that our Lord willed that she found a monastery. Hence it can be understood that the vision was an intellectual as well as an imaginative one, nor could it have been either a whim or an illusion caused by the devil.

8. First, the vision was not a whim; this can be deduced from its great effect, for from that point on she never more desired children. She remained so convinced in her heart that this was God's will that she no longer asked for or desired them. Thus she began to think about the way in which she could do what the Lord wanted. Nor was it an illusion caused by the devil. This can be discerned from the fact that a monastery is now founded where our Lord is much served, for the devil of himself cannot do good. In addition, this took place more than six years before the monastery was founded, and the devil cannot know the future.

9. Very surprised by this vision, she told her husband that since God did not desire to give them children they should found a monastery of nuns. Being so good and loving her so much, her husband was happy with the idea and began to consider where they might found one. She wanted it in the town where she had been born. He put up legitimate objections to convince her that her town would not be a good place for it.

10. While they were discussing this, the duchess of Alba called for him. When he arrived, she ordered him to return to Alba to

undertake duties in her house, and he accepted the office even though it was a less important one than the office he had held in Salamanca.[4] When his wife heard about it, she was very distressed because, as I said, she abhorred Alba. Being assured by her husband that they would not accept guests any more, she was somewhat appeased; although she was still very troubled since Salamanca was more to her liking. He bought a house and sent for her. She came with great weariness and felt wearier when she saw the house. For although the location was very good and the property extensive, the house did not have enough rooms; thus she was very troubled that night. The next morning, when she walked onto the patio, she saw on the same side the well where she had seen St. Andrew. And she saw everything else, no more nor less than what had been shown to her—I mean the place, not the saint or the flowers or the meadow, although she did have and still has them well imprinted in her imagination.

11.   When she saw these things, she became troubled and resolved to found the monastery there. She did this now with great consolation and tranquility, without wanting to go somewhere else, and they began to buy more houses nearby until they had ample land. She was concerned about which order they would ask, for she wanted the nuns to be few and strictly enclosed. In discussing the matter with two religious from different orders, who were very good and learned men, she was told by both that it would be better to do some other good works because nuns are usually unhappy. And she was told many other things, for since the project saddened the devil he wanted to prevent it, and thus he made them think that the reasons they gave her were very sound. Since they presented so many as to why it wouldn't be good, and the devil presented more in order to hinder it, she became fearful and disturbed and decided not to go ahead. This she told to her husband, and the two of them felt that since such men had told her that it would not be good and her intention was to serve our Lord they should forget about it. Thus they agreed to arrange for a marriage between a niece on her husband's side and a nephew of hers, who was very virtuous and still young and whom she loved very much, and give them a great part of their estate, keeping the rest for their own spiritual well-

being. They were both left feeling certain and serene about this decision.

12. But since our Lord had ordained something else, their agreement was of little benefit. In less than fifteen days, the nephew became so seriously ill that within a very few days our Lord brought him to Himself. She became so convinced that the cause of her nephew's death had been her decision to set aside what God wanted her to do, in order to leave the estate to him, that she felt great fear. She recalled what happened to Jonah the prophet for not having wanted to obey God,[5] and it seemed to her that God had punished her by taking away that nephew whom she loved so much. From that day on she was determined not to let anything make her fail to found the monastery, and her husband was also; although they didn't know how to go about it. It seemed to her that God had put into her heart what has now been accomplished. Those whom she told about the monastery, and to whom she described how she wanted it, laughed over the matter since they thought she would not find the things she was looking for; this was true especially of a confessor of hers, a Franciscan friar, a distinguished man of learning. She was very dejected.

13. At that time, this friar happened to go to a certain town where he was told about these monasteries of Our Lady of Mt. Carmel that were now being founded. Very well informed about them, he returned and told her he had now discovered how she could found the monastery she desired. He told her what had happened and that she should try to speak with me about it. This she did. We underwent much difficulty in trying to come to an agreement. For in the case of monasteries founded with an income, my goal always was that they have enough to keep the nuns from dependence on relatives, or on anyone, and that food and clothing and everything necessary be given to them in the house, and that the sick be very well cared for. For when necessities are lacking, many troubles arise. In founding many monasteries in poverty, without an income, I never lack courage or confidence; I am certain that God will not fail them. In founding them with an income that is small, everything fails me; I find it better that they not be founded.

14. She and her husband finally became reasonable and offered enough revenue to provide for the number of nuns. And what I highly appreciated, they left their own house in order to give it to us and moved into one that was in a dilapidated condition. The Blessed Sacrament was reserved and the foundation was made on the feast of the Conversion of St. Paul, in the year 1571,⁶ for the glory and honor of God. In this foundation, in my opinion, His Majesty is very much served. May it please Him to protect it always.

15. I began to say some particular things about some of the Sisters in these monasteries thinking that when this would be read those now living in them would not be alive and that those who come after would be inspired to carry on in the tradition of such a good beginning. Afterward, it has seemed to me, there will be someone who will tell these things better and in more detail and without having the fear that I have had of giving the impression of being partial.⁷ And so I have left out many things considered miraculous by those who have seen or known of them, for such things are supernatural. I have not wanted to say anything about them or of what our Lord has been clearly seen to do through the nuns' prayers.

In the account of the dates on which these monasteries were founded I suspect that I am sometimes mistaken, although I try diligently to remember.⁸ Since these dates are not of great importance, because they can be corrected afterward, I put them down according to what I can remember; it makes little difference if there is some error.

Chapter 21

Treats of the foundation in Segovia of the Carmel of the glorious St. Joseph. It was founded on the very feast of St. Joseph in 1574.

I HAVE ALREADY MENTIONED how after I founded the monasteries of Salamanca and Alba and before we had our own house in Salamanca, the Father Maestro Fray Pedro Fernández,

who was then the apostolic commissary, ordered me to go to the
Incarnation in Avila for three years.[1] I also mentioned that
when he saw the need of the nuns in Salamanca for a house, he
ordered me to go there so that they could move into one of their
own.[2] One day while I was there in prayer, our Lord told me to
go to Segovia and make a foundation. This seemed impossible to
me, for I could not go unless ordered to do so, and I had learned
from the apostolic commissary, the Father Maestro Fray Pedro
Fernández, that he did not want me to make any more foundations. I also saw clearly that since the three years I was to stay in
the Incarnation were not over, he had great reason for not wanting any more foundations. While I was thinking about this, the
Lord told me to tell him and that He Himself would bring this
foundation about.

2. At the time, I was in Salamanca. From there I wrote to His
Paternity reminding him that he already knew I had a command from our most Reverend Father General to make a foundation when I saw that there was an opportunity for doing so. I
mentioned that one of these monasteries had been accepted in
Segovia by both the city and the bishop, that if His Paternity
would give the order I would found it, that I was pointing this
out to him to satisfy my conscience, and that I would feel confi-
dent and content with whatever he ordered. I believe these were
the words, more or less, and I added that it seemed to me the
monastery would render service to God. I think, indeed, that
His Majesty wanted it, because the apostolic commissary said
immediately that I should found it, and he gave me permission.
From what I had known about him in regard to these matters, I
was very much amazed. And from Salamanca I arranged that
they rent me a house, for after the experience in Toledo and
Valladolid I had learned that it was better to rent a house and
take possession first and then look for one to buy. This was so for
many reasons, the principal one being that I didn't have a cent to
buy one with. Once the monastery was founded, the Lord would
then provide; also, a more appropriate site could be chosen.

3. There was a lady there who had been the wife of the owner
of an entailed estate. Her name was Doña Ana de Jimena. She
had once come to see me in Avila. She was a good servant of God,

and her calling had always been to be a nun. Thus after the founding of the monastery, she and one of her daughters, who was living a devout life, entered it. And the Lord took away the unhappiness she had experienced both while married and as a widow and gave her a double measure of happiness in the religious life. Both mother and daughter had always been very recollected and faithful servants of God.[3]

4. This good lady acquired the house and provided for everything she saw we needed, both for the church and for ourselves. As a result, I had little work to do. But there is never a foundation in which there is not some trial. And the trial came in addition to the fact that I went there while suffering from a high fever and nausea, and from interior ills of very great dryness and darkness of soul, and from bodily complaints of many kinds, the intensity of which lasted three months. And for the half year that I was there, I was always sick.

5. On the feast of St. Joseph, we reserved the Blessed Sacrament. Although we had permission from both the bishop and the city, I did not want to enter except on the eve of the feast, secretly, and at night. Much time had passed since the permission had been given, but because I had been at the Incarnation and did not have our Father General for superior, but someone else,[4] I had not been able to make the foundation. The permission I had received from the bishop of that place—when he agreed—was in word. He gave it through a gentleman named Andrés de Jimena who was looking for a house for us. But this gentleman didn't bother about getting the permission in writing, nor did this seem to me to matter. I was mistaken, for when the vicar general learned that the monastery had been founded, he came at once, very angry, and did not allow Mass to be said any more and wanted to take prisoner the one who said it, a discalced friar, who came with both Father Julián de Avila and another servant of God, who came with me, named Antonio Gaytán.[5]

6. This latter was a gentleman from Alba. He was called by the Lord some years before while very much involved in the world. He so trampled it under foot that all he thought about was how to serve the Lord more. In the foundations that will be dealt with from here on, mention will have to be made of him,

for he helped me much and did a great deal of work for me. I have told who he is, and if I should have to tell of his virtues, I would not finish very quickly. What mattered most to us was that he was so mortified, for there was no servant from among those who came with us who was as ready as he was to do all the necessary things. He is a man of deep prayer, and God has granted him so many favors that everything others would consider a burden made him happy and was easy for him to accept. This is the way he is in all the work that he has done for these foundations. For it indeed seems that God called both him and Father Julián de Avila for this purpose, although Father Julián de Avila was with us from the first foundation. By giving me company like this, our Lord must have desired that everything turn out well for me. It was Father Julián's characteristic while traveling to speak of God and to teach those who traveled with us or whom we met, and thus in every way he served His Majesty.

7. It is only right, my daughters, that those of you who read these foundations should know what you owe to these two (for without any self-interest they labored so much for this good that you enjoy, of being in these monasteries) in order that you might recommend them to our Lord and they might receive some benefit from your prayers. For if you knew the bad nights and days they suffered, and the trials on the roads, you would do so very willingly.

8. The vicar general did not want to go away without leaving a guard at the door of the church. I don't know why; it served to frighten a little those who were there. As for me, I was never much bothered by what happened once possession of the foundation had taken place; all my fears came before. I sent for some persons, relatives of a companion I brought from among my sisters,[6] who were renowned in that place that they might speak to the vicar general and explain to him that I had permission from the bishop. He knew this very well, as he said afterward, but he thought we should have informed him. I believe that had we done so, things would have been much worse. Finally, they got him to agree to let us stay in the monastery, but he removed the Blessed Sacrament. This didn't matter to us. We remained thus for some months until a house was bought;[7] along with it came

many lawsuits. We had lawsuits with the Mercedarians and, because the house had an annuity attached to it, with the cathedral chapter. Before this we had many difficulties with the Franciscan friars because of a house we tried to buy near them.

9. O Jesus! What a trial it is to have to contend with many opinions. When the litigation would seem to be over, it would begin anew because it wasn't enough to give them what they asked for; there was at once some other difficulty. Explained in this way, it all seems like nothing; but going through it was much different.

10. A nephew of the bishop did all that he could for us, for he was the prior and canon of that church;[8] and so, too, did the licentiate Herrera, a very great servant of God. Finally, after we gave much money, the lawsuit came to an end. We were left with the lawsuit of the Mercedarians, for in order to move to the new house great secrecy was necessary. When they found out that we were there, for we had moved a day or two before the feast of St. Michael,[9] they thought it would be good to settle for a sum of money. The greatest suffering that these obstacles caused me was that in no more than seven or eight days my three years as prioress at the Incarnation were to come to an end, and I necessarily had to be there.

11. Our Lord was pleased that everything should turn out so well that no contention remained, and within two or three days I was at the Incarnation.[10] May His name be ever blessed who has always granted me so many favors, and may all creatures praise Him. Amen.

Chapter 22

Treats of the foundation named after the glorious St. Joseph of the Saviour and made in the town of Beas on the feast of St. Matthias in the year 1575.[1]

WHEN I WAS SENT, as mentioned, from the Incarnation to Salamanca,[2] a messenger came there from the town of Beas with letters for me from a lady in that area and from the curate beneficiary there. The letters contained both the offer of a benefice from that town and requests from other persons asking me to come and found a monastery. They already had a house; all that was needed was to go and make the foundation.

2. When questioned by me, the man recounted wonderful things about the land, and rightly so, for it is very delightful and has a good climate. But in considering the distance, many leagues from here, the notion of making a foundation there seemed to me foolish. Especially so, since I was under the orders of the apostolic commissary, who, as I mentioned,[3] was opposed to, or at least not in favor of, my making foundations. So I wanted to answer that I was unable, and avoid asking permission of the apostolic commissary about it. Afterward, it seemed to me that since he was present at that time in Salamanca and I had received the order from our Reverend Father General not to fail to make foundations,[4] it would be unwise to refuse without getting his opinion.

3. When he saw the letters brought to me by the messenger, he sent word that he didn't think it would be good to disappoint them, that he had been edified by their devotion, that I should write telling them that when they had permission from the Order of Knights of that town, provisions would be made for the foundation.[5] He was certain that the council of the Order of Knights would not give the permission, for he had known from elsewhere that in many years no one had been able to receive such a permission from it, and he did not want my answer to sound like a refusal. Sometimes I think about this and how that which our Lord wants, even though we may not want it, comes about in such a way that without our being aware we are the instruments of it. In this case the instrument was the Father Maestro Fray Pedro Fernández, who was the commissary. And so when they received the permission from the council, he couldn't refuse. The foundation was made in this way.

4. This monastery of the blessed St. Joseph was founded in the town of Beas on the feast of St. Matthias in the year 1575. It came about for the honor and glory of God in the following way.

There was in this town a gentleman named Sancho Rodríguez de Sandoval, of noble lineage and having many temporal possessions. He was married to a lady named Doña Catalina Godínez. Among the children that our Lord gave them were two daughters, those who founded this monastery. The older[6] was fourteen when our Lord called her to His service. Up to this age she was far from ready to leave the world; on the contrary, she had such a high estimation of herself that all that her father sought for her in marriages seemed of small account.

5. One day while in a room next to the one in which her father was lying down, she happened to read on a crucifix the inscription that is placed over the cross. Suddenly when she read it, the Lord worked a complete change in her: She had been thinking of a marriage that was being sought for her, which was better than she could have hoped for, and saying to herself: "With what little my father is content, that I become connected with an entailed estate; I am thinking of becoming the origin of a new line of descendants." She was not inclined toward marriage, for she considered it demeaning to be subject to someone; nor did she know where this pride came from. The Lord knew how it could be remedied. Blessed be His mercy.

6. The moment she read the inscription, it seemed to her that just as sunshine enters a dark room, a light came into her soul by which she understood the truth. With this light she set her eyes on the Lord who was on the cross shedding blood, and she thought about how badly He was treated and of His great humility and about how different the road of pride was that she was following. There must have been some space of time in which the Lord suspended her. There His Majesty gave her a deep knowledge of her own misery, and she desired that all might know of it. He gave her so great a desire to suffer for God that all that the martyrs suffered she desired to suffer with them. She experienced such profound humiliation and self-abhorrence that were it not an offense against God, she would have wanted to be a very dissolute woman so that all might abhor her. Thus she began to despise herself with great desires for penance, which afterward she put into effect. She at once promised chastity and poverty and wanted to see herself so subject that she would have rejoiced to be carried off then to the land of the Moors and remain there. All of these virtues lasted in

her in such a way that the experience was clearly seen to be a supernatural favor from our Lord, as will be said later, so that all might praise Him.

7. May You be blessed forever and ever, my God, for within a moment You undo a soul and remake it. What is this, Lord? I would want to ask here what the apostles asked You when You cured the blindman, whether it was his parents who had sinned.[7] I mean, who could have merited so sublime a favor? She certainly did not, for it was already mentioned what thoughts You took away from her when You granted that favor. Oh, great are Your judgments, Lord! You know what You are doing, but I do not know what I am saying since Your works and judgments are incomprehensible. May You be ever glorified, for You have the power to do even more. What would become of me if this were not so? But, did the merit in some way come from her mother? For so great was her mother's practice of Christianity that it would be possible that Your goodness, being merciful, would desire that she see within her lifetime this great virtue in her daughters. Sometimes I think You grant similar favors to those who love You, and You do them so much good that You give them that by which they may serve You.

8. While she was in this state, such a loud noise came from the room above that it seemed everything was falling down. It seemed that all of that noise was coming down in the corner where she was, and she heard some roars that lasted quite a while. They were such that her father who although he had not yet got up, as was mentioned,[8] became so frightened he began to tremble. As though beside himself, he took a robe and his sword and entered there and very much shaken asked her what that noise was. She told him that she hadn't seen anything. He looked in the next room further and since he saw nothing told her to go stay with her mother and informed her mother about what he had heard and not to let their daughter be alone.

9. This indeed explains what the devil must feel when he sees a soul already considered to be his own loosed from his power. Since he is so hostile toward what is good for us, I am not surprised that in seeing our merciful Lord grant so many favors all at once he should become frightened and make such a show of

his feeling. This was especially so, because he understood that on account of the riches that were left in that soul he had to remain without any that could be considered his. For I hold that our Lord never grants so great a favor to a person without allowing others to share in it as well. She never said anything about this. But she was left with the strongest desire to embrace religious life and frequently sought permission from her parents to do so. They would never give their consent.

10. After three years had gone by in which she frequently sought permission, she began, on the feast of St. Joseph,[9] to dress in a simple manner since she saw that they did not want her to be a religious. She told only her mother from whom it would have been easy to obtain the permission to be a nun. As for her father, she did not dare ask, but she went to the church so that once the townspeople had seen her in this dress, she could be sure her parents would not take it away. And this is what happened, for they let the matter go. During those three years, she observed hours of prayer and mortified herself in every way she could, for the Lord taught her. She used to enter the courtyard and throw water on her face and then expose it to the sun so that because of the resulting ugly appearance her parents would give up the idea of a marriage for her, for she was still being urged to marry.

11. She no longer had any desire to give orders to anyone. Since she had charge of her father's house, it happened that when she realized that she had given orders to the housemaids, for she couldn't do otherwise, she would wait until they were asleep and kiss their feet, anxious because they, though better than she, were serving her. Since during the day she was busy with her parents, when it was time for sleep, she would spend the whole night in prayer. Thus, she often went with so little sleep that it would have been impossible for her to do so without supernatural aid. The penance and the disciplines were many because she had no one to guide her nor did she speak with anyone. Among other things, one Lent she wore her father's coat of mail next to her flesh. She used to go to a secluded place to pray, where the devil heaped ridicule on her. Often she began prayer at ten at night and was absorbed in it until daylight.

12. She spent about four years in these exercises. Then, desiring that she serve Him through other greater ones the Lord gave her most serious and painful illnesses. Thus she suffered from continual fever, dropsy, heart trouble, and a breast tumor which was removed. In sum, these illnesses lasted almost seventeen years; there were but few days in which she felt well. Five years after she had received the above favor from God, her father died.[10] Her sister, when fourteen (one year after Doña Catalina had made this change) also put on a simple garb, for she had been fond of fine clothes, and began as well to practice prayer. Her mother helped them in all their good practices and desires. She thought that it was good for them to become occupied in a very virtuous work, one that was far out of harmony with their status: teaching girls needlework and reading, without any fee, but only for the opportunity to instruct the girls in prayer and doctrine. Their work was very fruitful because many girls were helped, and even now the good habits these girls learned when small are visible. The good work didn't continue for long because the devil, saddened by it, made the parents of the little girls feel that it was an affront for their daughters to be taught free of charge. This along with the beginning of the illnesses that afflicted her caused her to discontinue the work.

13. Five years after the father of these young ladies died, their mother died. Doña Catalina had always felt called to be a nun, but she could not get her parents' consent. She now wanted to go away at once to be a nun. Since there was no monastery in Beas, her relatives counselled her that since they had the sufficient means they should strive to found a monastery in their own town, that this would be of greater service to our Lord. Since the town is a commandery of the Order of the Knights of Santiago, permission was necessary from the council of this order, and so she diligently sought to obtain it

14. It was so difficult to obtain that they spent four years in which they underwent many trials and expenses; and until a petition was sent to the king himself, nothing proved helpful. And it happened that because the difficulty became so great, her relatives began to tell her that the idea was foolish and that she should forget about it. Since she was almost always in bed with

such serious illnesses, as was mentioned, they said that no monastery would accept her as a nun. She answered that if within a month our Lord gave her health they should understand thereby that He would be served by the monastery and that she would go to the royal court herself to obtain the license. When she said this, it had been more than half a year that she had not got out of bed; and for almost eight years she had hardly moved from it. During those eight years she suffered from a continual fever, consumption, tuberculosis, dropsy, and an inflammation of the liver. This latter could be felt, and it so burned that even her clothes were affected by it and her chemise scorched. This seems incredible, and I myself inquired of the doctor about these illnesses that she had at that time, for I was amazed. She also suffered from gout and sciatica.

15. On the eve of the feast of St. Sebastian, which was a Saturday,[11] our Lord gave her such complete health that she didn't know how to conceal it and prevent the miracle from being known. She says that when our Lord desired to cure her He gave her an interior trembling that made her sister think that her life was coming to an end. And she saw within herself the greatest change, and in her soul, she says, she felt another change which was beneficial to her. Because of her health she was able to attend to the business of the monastery, and this made her happier than did her feeling of good health. From the beginning when God called her, He gave her an abhorrence of self, for she made little of all. She says she was left with so powerful a desire to suffer that she begged God earnestly to exercise her in suffering in every way.

16. His Majesty did not fail to fulfill this desire. During those eight years they bled her more than five hundred times, without counting the many cuppings; the body shows them clearly. They put salt in the wounds, for the doctor said it was good for drawing the poison from a sore on her side; they did this more than twenty times. What is more amazing is that as soon as she was told that the doctor prescribed one of these remedies, she fearlessly longed for the time to come in which they would carry it out, and she encouraged the doctors to apply the cauteries, which were used often for a breast cancer and other purposes.

She says that what made her want this was the desire to prove whether or not the longings she had for martyrdom were authentic.

17. Since she found that she had suddenly become well she discussed with both her confessor and doctor the possibility of being brought to another town so that they could say the change of environment had caused the cure. They did not want to do so; on the contrary, they spread the news. They had already judged her to be incurable because the blood she was spitting up was so putrefied that they said it contained part of the lungs. She remained in bed for three days, not daring to get up lest the miracle of her health become known. But since it could be no more disguised than could her illness, the attempt to hide it was of little benefit.

18. She told me that the previous August while begging our Lord either to take away her great desire both to be a nun and to found a monastery or give her the means to do so she was convincingly assured that she would be well in time to go, during Lent, to obtain the license. Thus, she says that at that time even though the illnesses weighed more heavily on her, she never lost the hope that our Lord was going to grant her this favor. Even though she was anointed twice (one time she was so close to the end that the doctor said there would be no reason to go for the oils, that she would be dead before they arrived), she never stopped trusting in the Lord that she would die a nun. I don't mean that they anointed her twice between August and the feast of St. Sebastian, but before that.

When her brothers and relatives saw the favor and miracle that the Lord had performed in giving her health so suddenly, they did not dare prevent her from going, although it seemed foolish. She was at the royal court for three months, and in the end the license was not given. When she presented this petition to the king and he learned that it was for discalced Carmelite nuns, he ordered that it be given at once.[12]

19. When the time came to found the monastery, it seemed obvious that she had obtained this from God, for the superiors accepted it even though the town was so far away and the income small. What His Majesty desires cannot be set aside. Thus

the nuns came at the beginning of Lent in 1575. The people of the town received them with a solemn procession and great joy. The happiness was so universal that even the children showed that our Lord would be served by this work. The monastery was founded under the patronage of St. Joseph of the Saviour this same Lent on the feast of St. Matthias.[13]

20. On the same day the two sisters received the habit with much joy.[14] The health of Doña Catalina continued to improve. Her humility, obedience, and wish to be despised show clearly that her desires had been authentic and for the service of our Lord. May He be glorified forever and ever, amen.[15]

21. This Sister told me, among other things, that almost twenty years ago she went to bed one night longing to find the most perfect religious order there was on earth so as to be a nun in it. She began to dream, in her opinion, that she was walking along a very straight and narrow road, very dangerous in that one could fall into some deep ravines that appeared. She met a discalced friar. (Seeing Fray Juan de la Miseria,[16] a little friar, laybrother of the order who was in Beas while I was there, she said that he seemed to be the same one she had seen in the dream.) He said to her, "Come with me, sister," and brought her to a house with a great number of nuns in which there was no other light than that coming from some candles they were carrying. She asked what order this was; all remained silent, and then they lifted their veils and their faces were joyous and they were laughing. And she declares that she saw the faces of the same Sisters she now sees, and that the prioress took her by the hand and said to her, "Daughter, I want you here," and showed her the constitutions and the rule. When she awoke from this sleep, she felt a happiness that made her think she had been in heaven, and she wrote down what she remembered from the rule. Much time passed in which she didn't tell her confessor or anyone, and no one knew anything about this religious order.

22. When a Father from the Society[17] who knew of her desires came there, she showed him the paper and told him that if he found that religious order she would like to enter it. He knew of these monasteries and told her how what was written was taken from the rule of the order of Our Lady of Mount Carmel; although

he didn't explain things to her so clearly, but just spoke of the monasteries that I was founding. Thus she arranged to send me a messenger as was mentioned.[18]

23. When they brought her the reply, she was so sick that her confessor told her to be calm and that even if she were in the monastery they would dismiss her, how much less would they accept her now. She was terribly distressed and turned to our Lord with great anxieties and said to Him: "My Lord and my God, I know through faith that You are He who can do all things; well, then, Life of my soul, either take away these desires or give me the means to carry them out." She said this with extreme confidence, begging our Lady through the sorrow she felt when she beheld her dead Son in her arms, to intercede for her. She heard a voice within her say: "Believe and hope for I am He who can do all things; you will be healthy, for He who had the power to prevent so many illnesses, each deadly in itself, from bringing about their effect will more easily take them away." She says that these words came with such force and certitude that she couldn't doubt that her desire would be granted, even though many more illnesses weighed her down until the Lord gave her the health we have mentioned. Certainly, what she has suffered seems incredible. Had I not been informed by the doctor and those who were in the house, or by other persons, being as wretched as I am, it would not have been unusual for me to think that some of this was exaggerated.

24. Although she is weak, she is now healthy enough to keep the rule. She is a good subject and has a very happy disposition and, as I have said,[19] is humble in everything, which makes us all praise our Lord. The inheritance of each of them was given to the order without any conditions, so that even if they were not admitted to profession the money would still belong to the order. The detachment she has from both her relatives and property is great. And she always has the strong desire to move far away, and thus she begs this of her major superiors very much, although her obedience is so great that she is happily willing to remain there. And in this same spirit she received the white veil; for there was no way of getting her to become a choir Sister, but she wanted to be a lay Sister. This was so until I wrote to her

telling her many things, scolding her because she wanted something other than what was her Father Provincial's will.[20] I told her that wanting to be a lay Sister was not more meritorious, and I mentioned other things, and dealt with her harshly. And this is her greatest happiness, to be spoken to harshly. As a result she submitted, very much against her will, to becoming a choir Sister. I don't know anything about this soul that does not have to do with her trying to be more pleasing to God, and all the nuns feel the same way. May it please His Majesty to keep her in His hands and increase the grace and virtues He has given her for His greater service and honor. Amen

Chapter 23

Treats of the foundation of the monastery of the glorious St. Joseph of Carmel in Seville. The first Mass was said on the feast of the most Blessed Trinity in 1575.[1]

WHILE I WAS IN THIS TOWN OF BEAS waiting for the license from the Council of the Order of Knights for the foundation in Caravaca, a Father from the discalced of our order named Maestro Jerónimo Gracián de la Madre de Dios came to see me.[2] A few years before he had received our religious habit while in Alcalá. Throughout his life he has been a man of much learning, intelligence, and modesty along with other great virtues. It seems, while he was in Alcalá, that he was chosen by our Lady for the good of this primitive order without his having the remotest idea of receiving our habit, although he had considered entering the religious life. His parents had other intentions because of his great talent and their good standing with the king,[3] but he was far from being inclined toward their plans for him. From the time he began school, he was urged by his father to take up the study of law. Yet, while still very young, he felt so strongly the desire to study theology that by force of tears he got his father to allow him to do so.

2. After graduating with a master's degree, he took steps to enter the Society of Jesus, and they had accepted him. But for a

certain reason they told him to wait several days. He tells me that he was tormented by all the enjoyments in his life and that he didn't think they constituted a safe path to heaven. He always set aside the hours for prayer and was extremely recollected and upright.

3. At this time a close friend of his entered the monastery in Pastrana to become a friar in our order. This friend's name was Fray Juan de Jesús, and he, too, had a master's degree.[4] I don't know how the interest began, whether it did so because of a letter Fray Juan wrote about the greatness and antiquity of our order or in some other way; for Father Gracián enjoyed very much reading everything about the order and verifying, through important authors, what was asserted. He says that he often had scruples about failing to study other things because he was unable to set these studies aside, and he occupied his hours of recreation in this way. O wisdom and power of God! How impossible for us to flee from His will! Our Lord truly saw the great need there was for a person like this to carry on the work that He had begun. I often praise Him for the favor He granted us in this matter. Had I very much desired to ask His Majesty for a person to organize all the things pertaining to the order in these initial stages, I would not have succeeded in asking for all that He in fact gave in Father Gracián. May the Lord be blessed forever.

4. Well then, while not having the slighest thought of taking the habit of this order, he was asked to go to Pastrana to speak to the prioress of our monastery there—for it had not yet been abandoned—that she might accept a nun.[5] What means the divine Majesty takes! For had Father Gracián decided to go there to take the habit, he would perhaps have met with so much opposition that he might never have done so. But the Blessed Virgin, our Lady, to whom he is extemely devoted, wanted to repay him by giving him her habit. So I think she was the mediatrix through whom God granted him this favor. And this glorious Virgin was the reason he received it and became so fond of the order. She did not want one who desired to serve her so much to lack the occasion for putting this desire into practice. It is her custom to favor those who want to be protected by her.

5. While still a boy in Madrid, he often went to pray before an image of our Lady to whom he had great devotion. I don't remember where it was; he called her "his love," and his visits were very frequent.[6] She must have obtained for him from her Son the purity in which he always lived. He says that sometimes it seemed to him his eyes were swollen from weeping over the many offenses committed against her Son. As a result there arose in him a strong impulse and desire to help souls, and he felt it very deeply when he saw offenses committed against God. He has so great an inclination toward the good of souls that any hardship becomes small to him if he thinks that through it he can produce some fruit. I have seen this myself in the many trials that he has undergone.

6. Well, the Virgin brought him to Pastrana as though by tricking him into the thought that he was going there in order to request the habit for a nun. And God brought him there in order to give him the habit. Oh, secrets of God! But how true that without our desiring it, He disposes us so as to give us favors. And this soul was repaid for the good deeds that he did, for the good example that he had always given, and for his great desire to serve the Lord's glorious Mother. His Majesty must always repay this latter with wonderful rewards.

7. Well, when he arrived in Pastrana, he went to speak to the prioress that she might accept the nun; and it seemed as though he had asked her to pray to the Lord that he himself might enter. For he is a very pleasant person so that generally he is loved by those who have dealings with him—it is a grace our Lord gives—and thus he is extremely loved by all his subjects, both friars and nuns. Yet he doesn't let any fault go by, for he is extraordinarily careful in looking out for the welfare of the religious life. In his actions he is so gentle and pleasant that it seems no one is able to complain about him.

8. Well, when this prioress saw him, that which happened to others happened to her; she felt a strong desire that he enter the order and told the Sisters how important it was to get him to join, for at the time there were very few, or almost none like him.[7] And she told them all to beseech our Lord not to let him go without his receiving the habit.

This prioress is a very great servant of God. By her prayer alone I think she would have been heard by His Majesty; how much more would the prayers of nuns as good as those that were there be heard. All of them took the matter very much to heart and with fasts, disciplines, and prayer begged His Majesty continually. Thus He was pleased to grant us this favor. For since Father Gracián went to the monastery of the friars and saw so much religious observance and opportunity to serve our Lord and above all that it was the order of the Lord's glorious Mother whom he so much desired to serve, his heart was moved not to return to the world. The devil set before him many difficulties, especially the pain this would bring his parents. They loved him very much and had great trust that he would help provide for their children, for they had many daughters and sons.[8] He left this care to God for whom he left all, and decided to be a subject of the Virgin and take her habit. So they gave it to him amid the great happiness of all, especially of the nuns and the prioress. The nuns gave much praise to our Lord, thinking that His Majesty had granted them this favor through their prayers.

9. He spent the year of probation with the humility one would find among the youngest novices. His virtue was especially tried at a time when the prior was absent. A very young friar was in charge who had no learning, very little talent, and no prudence for governing. He was without experience since he had only recently entered. The manner in which he guided them was excessive as well as were the mortifications he made them perform. Every time I think of them I am amazed at how Father Gracián was able to suffer them, especially how he could put up with persons like that. The spirituality God gave him was necessary for this suffering. It was clearly seen afterward that this young friar was the victim of much melancholy, and nowhere was he free of it.[9] Even as a subject, he's a source of trouble, how much more so when he governs! The humor has much control over him, for he is a good religious, and God sometimes permits this mistake of putting such persons in office so as to perfect the virtue of obedience in those He loves.

10. So it must have happened that as a reward God has given Father Fray Jerónimo de la Madre de Dios the greatest light in

matters of obedience so that as one who had such a good initiation into its practice he might teach it to others. And that he might not lack experience in all the things we need to know about, he underwent the most severe temptations for three months prior to his profession. But as the good captain of the sons of the Virgin that he was to become, he defended himself well against these temptations. For when the devil harassed him most to get him to give up the habit, he defended himself by promising to make his vows and not give it up. He gave me a certain work that he wrote while undergoing those great temptations. It inspired me with much devotion, and the fortitude the Lord gave him is clearly seen.

11. It will seem inappropriate that he should have informed me of so many personal matters about his soul. Perhaps the Lord wanted this that I might record it here, and He might be praised in His creatures. For I know that neither to any confessor nor to any other person has this Father manifested so much about himself. At times he had reason for so doing because he thought that on account of my age and from what he had heard about me I had some experience. It was while we were speaking about other matters that he told me about these things and additional ones that cannot be suitably put in writing, for I would be going on at much greater length.

12. Certainly, I have used much restraint so that if this work should ever get into his hands he won't suffer pain. I couldn't help it, nor did it seem to me (for if this work is to be seen, it won't be for a long time yet) that one who did so much good for the renewal of the observance of the primitive rule should be forgotten. Although he was not the one who first began, he came along at the right moment. For sometimes I would have regretted[10] ever having begun had it not been for the great confidence I had in the mercy of God. I'm referring to the houses of the friars, for those of the nuns, through God's goodness, have so far always gone well. Those of the friars were not going badly, but the basis was there for a very quick collapse. Since the discalced didn't have their own province, they were governed by the calced. Those who could have governed, such as Fray Antonio de Jesús, the one who began the renewal,[11] were not given

the power to do so. Nor did the friars have constitutions given by our most Reverend Father General.[12] In each house they did as they saw fit. Until the day comes in which they can govern themselves they will have much trouble because some think one way and others another. At times I found them very tiring.

13. Our Lord provided a remedy through the Father Maestro Fray Jerónimo de la Madre de Dios, because they made him apostolic commissary and gave him authority and rule over the discalced friars and nuns.[13] He drafted constitutions for the friars, for we already had ours from our most Reverend Father General, and so he did not draw up any for us. But he did draw them up for the friars through the apostolic power he had and the talents that the Lord has given him as I have mentioned. In his first visitation of the friars, he arranged everything with such moderation and harmony that it indeed seemed he was helped by the Divine Majesty and that our Lady had chosen him to help her order. I begged her very much to intercede that her Son always favor this Father and give him grace to advance far in His service. Amen.

Chapter 24

Continues with the foundation of St. Joseph of Carmel in the city of Seville.

WHEN, AS I MENTIONED,[1] the Father Maestro Fray Jerónimo Gracián came to see me at Beas, we had never previously met although I had very much desired to meet him. (Yes, at times, we had corresponded.) I was extremely delighted when I learned he was there, for I greatly desired to meet him on account of the good reports given me concerning him. But much greater was my happiness when I began speaking with him, for it seemed from the way he pleased me that those who had praised him had hardly known him at all.

2. Since at that time I had so many difficulties, it seems that when I saw him the Lord showed me the good that was going to come to us through him. So during those days I went about with such excessive consolation and happiness that indeed I was sur-

prised at myself. At that time he did not have authority outside Andalusia. It was when he was in Beas that the nuncio sent to see him and then gave him authority over the discalced friars and nuns of Castile.[2] So much joy did my spirit feel that I couldn't thank our Lord enough those days, nor did I want to do anything else.

3. At this time they had brought the license for the foundation in Caravaca. The permission granted did not correspond with my proposal, and so it was necessary to petition the royal court again. For I had written to the foundresses that the foundation would in no way be made unless a certain missing detail were asked for, and so it was necessary to appeal again to the court.[3] It cost me a great deal to wait there so long, and I wanted to return to Castile. But since Father Fray Jerónimo was there, to whom that monastery was subject, and since he was the commissary for the whole province of Castile,[4] nothing could be done without his approval; so I talked to him about it.

4. He thought that if I were to leave, the foundation in Caravaca would fail, and also that a foundation in Seville would render great service to God. It seemed to him this latter would be very easy, for some well-to-do people had asked him and were able and wealthy enough to provide a house at once. The archbishop of Seville[5] so favored the order that Father Fray Jerónimo believed a foundation would render the order a great service. So it was arranged that the prioress and the nuns who were to go to Caravaca would instead go to Seville, although for certain reasons I had always strongly refused to found these monasteries in Andalusia. If when I went to Beas I had known that it was in Andalusia, I would by no means have gone. The mistake was that although the land was not yet within Andalusia, which I believe begins five or six leagues further, the ecclesiastical province was.[6] Since I saw that a foundation in Seville was the resolve of my major superior, I immediately submitted, although I had decided on another foundation and had some very serious reasons against going to Seville. (This is a favor our Lord grants me, to have the opinion that these superiors are right in everything.)

5. Preparations were immediately begun for the journey be-

cause it was beginning to get very hot. Father Apostolic Commissary, Gracián, responding to a call from the nuncio left for a meeting with him,[7] and we for a journey to Seville with my good companions, Father Julián de Avila, Antonio Gaytán, and a discalced friar.[8] We journeyed in wagons well covered, which was our mode of traveling, and when we reached an inn we took whatever room was available, good or bad. And one Sister received what we needed at the door, for not even those who journeyed with us entered the room.

6. Although we hurried along on our journey, we did not reach Seville until the Thursday before Trinity Sunday,[9] after having endured scorching heat. Even though we did not travel during siesta time, I tell you, Sisters, that since the sun was beating on the wagons, getting into them was like stepping into purgatory. Sometimes by thinking of hell, at other times by thinking that something was being done and suffered for God, those Sisters journeyed with much happiness and joy. The six souls who were with me were of the kind that made me think I was daring enough to go off with them to the land of the Turks and that they had the fortitude, or better, our Lord gave them the fortitude, to suffer for Him; for this was the subject of their desires and conversations. They were very experienced in prayer and mortification. Since they had to remain so far away, I chose those who seemed to me to be the most apt.[10] And this was all necessary because of the trials that were suffered. Some of the hardships, and the greatest, I won't mention because another person might be involved.

7. One day before Pentecost, God gave them a severe trial by sending me a very high fever. I believed that their cries to God were enough to prevent the sickness from getting worse. Never before in my life had I experienced a fever like this without its growing worse. It made me think I had sleeping sickness so withdrawn did it make me. They threw water on my face, but being so hot from the sun, the water provided little refreshment.

8. I don't want to fail to mention the bad inn at which we stayed when I was in this condition. We were given a small room with just a bare tile roof. It had no window, and when the door was opened, the sun poured in everywhere. You must remember

that the sun in that region is not like it is in Castile, but much more annoying. The bed on which they made me lie down was such that I would have fared better on the ground. One part was so high and the other so low that one didn't know how to stay in it; it was like lying on sharp stones. What a thing sickness is! For when we're healthy, it's easy to put up with all kinds of inconveniences. Finally I decided it would be better if I got up and we left. It seemed better to me to suffer the sun in the field than in that little room.

9. What will it be like for the poor ones who are in hell? Never will there be any change at all, for even a change from one trial to another brings with it some relief. It has happened to me that when after suffering from very severe pain in one place I experienced other pain elsewhere, the change seemed to provide some relief even though the pain was just as great; so it was in this instance. As for me, insofar as I remember, it didn't cause me any distress that I was sick; the Sisters suffered much more than I. The Lord was pleased that the severity of the fever did not last beyond that day.

10. A little before this—I don't know whether it was two days—something else happened to us which got us into a tight spot while we were crossing the Guadalquivir on a barge. When it was time for the wagon to cross, it was not possible to make a straight crossing where the rope was, but they had to wind their way across; the rope from the other shore was of some help by flowing with the barge. However, it happened that those who were holding the rope let it go, or I don't know what happened, for the barge went off with the wagon and without rope or oars. I felt much more concern in seeing the anxiety of the boatman than I did about the danger. We were all praying; the others were all screaming.

11. A gentleman watching us from a nearby castle was moved with pity and sent someone to help, for the barge then had not yet broken loose and our brothers[11] were pulling, using all their strength; but the force of the water dragged them along to the point that some fell to the ground. Indeed, the boatman's son caused in me feelings of great devotion, which I never forget—he must have been ten or eleven years old—for the way he was

working so hard upon seeing his father in this difficulty made me praise our Lord. But as His Majesty always gives trials in a compassionate way, so He did here. It happened that the boat got stuck on part of a sand bar where there was not much water; thus a rescue was made possible. Since nightfall had come, we would not have known how to continue our journey if someone from the castle had not come to guide us.

I had not thought of dealing with these things because they are of little importance, and I could have mentioned many bad incidents that occurred on our journeys. But I have been urged to enlarge on my account of this trip.

12. A much greater trial for me than those mentioned was what happened to us on the second day after Pentecost. We were hurrying to reach Córdoba in the morning so as to hear Mass without being seen by anyone. For the sake of greater solitude, they led us to a church located on the other side of a bridge. When we were about to cross the bridge, we found that on account of the wagons we needed a license which is issued by the magistrate. This took more than two hours since he was not up yet, and many people approached to find out who we were. This didn't bother us much because, since the wagons were well covered, the people were unable to do so. When the license finally came, we found that the wagons wouldn't fit through the gate of the bridge. It was necessary to saw them, or I don't know what, which took another while. When we finally reached the church where Father Julián de Avila was to say Mass, it was filled with people. The church was dedicated to the Holy Spirit, which we had not known, and thus they were celebrating an important feast in which a sermon was to be preached.

13. When I saw this I was very sorry. It seemed to me better to go without hearing Mass than to enter such turmoil. It didn't seem so to Father Julián de Avila. And since he was a theologian, we all had to follow his opinion. My other companions perhaps would have followed mine, and it would have been ill-advised, although I don't know if I would have trusted only in my opinion. We got out near the church, and although no one was able to see our faces, since we always wore large veils in front of them, it

was enough for the people to see us with the veils, the white, coarse woolen mantles we wore, and our sandals of hemp for them to get all stirred up; and that's what happened. The shock was certainly a great one for me and for all, and it must have taken away my fever completely.

14. As we entered the church, a friendly man approached me so as to hold off the people. I pleaded with him to bring us to some chapel. He did so and closed it and did not leave us until we left the church. After a few days, he came to Seville and told a Father of our order that he thought God had rewarded him for the good deed he had performed, for the Lord had provided him with, or given him, a large estate about which he had forgotten.

I tell you, daughters, although it may perhaps seem to you to be nothing, this incident was for me one of the really bad moments I went through. From the uproar of the people you would think that a herd of bulls had come into the church. Thus, I couldn't wait to get out of that place. Since there was nowhere nearby to take siesta, we took it under a bridge.

15. When we reached Seville and the house that Father Fray Mariano had rented for us, which he had been told about, I figured that everything was done. As I say, the archbishop favored the discalced and had at times written to me manifesting much love.[12] That wasn't enough to keep him from causing me much trouble, for God so desired it. The archbishop is very much opposed to monasteries of nuns founded in poverty, and he is right. The trouble was that he hadn't been told; or rather, that was to the advantage of this foundation, for had he been told I am certain he would not have agreed to it. Since Father Commissary and Father Mariano (for whom also my arrival had been the source of the greatest happiness) were most certain that by my coming I would be doing the archbishop an enormous favor, they did not tell him beforehand. And, as I say, while thinking they were right, they could have been making a great mistake. With the other monasteries, the first thing I did was to obtain the license from the ordinary of the place as the holy Council requires.[13] In this case, not only did we consider the license as given, but also, as I say, we thought the monastery would be a

great favor to him, as it truly was, and this he came to understand afterward. But the Lord desired that no foundation be
made without some trial in one way or another.[14]

16. Well, when we arrived at the house which, as I say, they
had rented for us, I thought we could immediately take possession, as was my custom, so that we could say the Divine Office.
But Father Mariano began to procrastinate—he was the one
who was there—and so as not to cause me any grief, he did not
want to tell me everything. Since he didn't have sufficient reasons, I understood where the difficulty lay, which was that the
license had not been granted. The archbishop told me that it
would be good if the monastery were founded with an income,
or something like that, for I don't remember. Finally, he told
me that he didn't like to grant permission for monasteries of
nuns, and that since he had been archbishop he had never done
so for any. He had been there many years, as well as in Córdoba,
and he is a great servant of God. Especially, he didn't like giving
a license for a monastery to be founded in poverty and said that
he would not do so.

17. This amounted to saying that the monastery must not be
founded. First, it would have seemed to me wrong to found in
the city of Seville a monastery with an established income even
though I could have done so. The places where I did agree to
make foundations with an income were small and required that
either I found the monastery with an income or not at all since
without one there would be no means of sustenance. Secondly,
not a cent was left from the expenses of the journey, and we
hadn't brought anything with us except what we were wearing
and some tunics and toques, and what was necessary in order to
cover the wagons and travel comfortably in them. In order that
those who came with us could return, they had to look for a way
of borrowing. One of Antonio Gaytán's friends who was there
lent them what they needed. And Father Mariano looked for
what was necessary to furnish the house; nor did we have a
house of our own. Thus, it was an impossible situation.

18. Through what must have been persistent pleading on the
part of the said Father we were allowed to have Mass, which was
the first, on the feast of the most Blessed Trinity.[15] But word was

sent that the bell should not be rung; neither was it to be put up, although it had already been put up. We were in this situation more than fifteen days. I know that if it had not been for Father Commissary and Father Mariano, I would definitely have returned with my nuns, and with very little regret, to Beas for the foundation in Caravaca. Much greater was the regret I actually experienced those days; since I have a bad memory, I do not remember, but I believe this lasted more than a month. For it was more difficult to return now after the monastery was known than it would have been immediately after our arrival. Father Mariano never allowed me to write to the archbishop, but instead went about gradually trying himself to convince him, making use also of letters from Father Commissary who was in Madrid.

19. As for me, one thing was calming and prevented me from feeling great scruple; it was that Mass had been said with the archbishop's permission, and we always said the Divine Office in choir. The archbishop did not fail to send a visitor with the message that he would see me soon, and an assistant was sent to say the first Mass. Hence I saw clearly that there was no point in my being disturbed. Yet, I felt distressed, not because of me or my nuns, but because of the anxiety Father Commissary experienced. Since he had ordered me to come, he felt very bad and would have been pained were something unfortunate to have happened, and he had many reasons for worrying about that.

20. At this time the calced Fathers came in order to inquire concerning the authority by which the foundation had been made. I showed them the patents I had from our most Reverend Father General.[16] With this they were calmed. But if they had known what the archbishop was doing, I don't think the documents I showed them would have sufficed. However, this was not known, and everyone thought the foundation pleased the archbishop very much and made him happy. Finally, God was pleased that he come to see us. I told him about the harm he was doing us. In the end, he told me that the monastery could remain and in the way I wanted it. From then on, he always favored and supported us in everything that occurred.

Chapter 25

Continues telling about the foundation named after the glorious St. Joseph in Seville and about what we suffered in order to get our own house.

N O ONE WOULD HAVE THOUGHT that in a city as wealthy as Seville and with so many rich people there would be fewer opportunities for a foundation than in any of the other places I had gone to. There was so much less help that I sometimes thought that it would not be good for us to have a monastery in that place. I don't know if the climate itself of that territory is the reason. I have always heard it said that the devils have greater leeway there to tempt souls, for God must grant it to them. They certainly afflicted me there, for I never felt more pusillanimous or cowardly in my life. Indeed, I didn't recognize myself, although the confidence I usually have in our Lord did not leave me. But in my human nature I felt very different from the way I usually do after taking part in these things. I figured that the Lord partly withdrew His hand so that my human nature might be left to itself and I might see that my courage did not come from me.

2. Well then, I stayed there from this time of which I am speaking until a little after Lent.[1] There was not a chance of buying a house, nothing either with which to buy one, nor even anyone who would lend to us as there were in other places. Those women who had often told Father Apostolic Visitator[2] that they would enter our community and had asked him to bring nuns there, afterward thought we were too strict and that they would not be able to endure the life. Only one person, about whom I shall speak later, entered.[3] The time, then, came in which I received orders to leave Andalusia because there were other business matters for me to attend to up here.[4] It distressed me deeply to have to leave the nuns without a house, although I saw clearly that I wasn't accomplishing anything there. For the favor God grants me up here of having people to help me in these works, I did not have there.

3. God was pleased at that time that my brother, Lorenzo de

Cepeda, return from the Indies where he had been for more than thirty-four years.[5] Feeling worse than I that the nuns would be staying there without having their own house, he helped us a great deal, especially in procuring the house in which they now live. For my part, I pleaded with our Lord, begging Him that I not have to go away and leave the nuns without a house. I had the Sisters ask Him as well as the glorious St. Joseph for this favor and we offered many processions and prayers to our Lady. Along with this, seeing my brother determined to help us, I began discussing the purchase of some houses. Just when it seemed that everything was starting to work out, it all came to naught.

4. One day, while I was in prayer beseeching our Lord to give them a house since they were His brides and had such desire to please Him, He told me: "I have already heard you; leave it to Me." I was left feeling very happy since it seemed I already had the house. And this was so. His Majesty prevented us from buying one that because of its nice location was pleasing to all. But the house itself was so old and run down that only the site was being bought and for not much less than was paid for the house we have now. Though all was agreed upon and only the contract remained to be drawn up, I was by no means satisfied. This didn't seem to be in accord with the words I had heard in prayer; for those words, I believed, were a sign that a good house would be given to us. And thus the Lord was pleased that the owner, even though he was making a great profit, should raise a difficulty about signing the contract at the established time, and we were able, without any fault, to get out of the agreement. This was a great favor from our Lord, for there was so much work to be done on the house that the Sisters living there would never in all their lives have been able to do it; and their means were few.

5. Much help was given to us by a servant of God who, from almost as soon as we arrived, began to come each day to say Mass, since he knew that we did not have a celebrant, even though his house was far away and the weather was extremely hot. His name is Garciálvarez.[6] Highly esteemed in the city on account of his good works, he is never occupied with anything but them. And had he been wealthy, we would not have lacked

anything. Knowing all about the house, he thought it would be very foolish to give so much for it. Thus, each day he told us so and managed to get us to speak of it no more. He and my brother went to see the house in which the nuns now live. They got to like it so much, and rightly so—and our Lord wanted this—that in two or three days the contract was signed.[7]

6. What we had to go through before moving in was no trifle. The occupant did not want to leave, and the Franciscan friars, since they were nearby, came at once trying to persuade us that we should by no means move in. If the contract had not been so firmly signed, I would have praised God that it could be broken, because we found ourselves in danger of paying six thousand ducats for a house we were unable to move into. This was not how the prioress viewed the matter.[8] She praised God that the contract could not be broken, for in regard to that house, His Majesty gave her more faith in Him and courage than He did me; just as in everything else, for she is much better than I.

7. This trouble lasted more than a month. God was finally pleased that we move, the prioress with myself and two other nuns, in great fear, at night so that the friars would not be aware until we took possession. Those who came with us said that every shadow they saw seemed to be a friar. When morning came, the good Garciálvarez, who was with us, said the first Mass, and then our fears left us.

8. O Jesus! How many fears I have suffered before taking possession of these foundations! I reflect on the fact that if one can feel so much fear in doing something good, for the service of God, what must be the fear of those who do evil, deeds that are against God and against neighbor? I don't know what they can gain or what satisfaction they can find as a counterbalance to all that fear.

9. My brother was not there yet since he had sought sanctuary on account of a certain error made in the contract which was drawn up so hastily. The error was very harmful to the monastery, and since he was the guarantor of the loan they wanted to arrest him.[9] And because he was an outsider, there was the possibility that they would harass us, and in fact they did, for

until he put up collateral there was trouble. Afterward the negotiations went well, although there was some contention at times so that we might suffer greater trial. We were enclosed in some rooms on the ground floor, and he was there all day with the workers, and he provided us with food as he had been doing before. Since we were in what had been a private home, not everyone knew it was a monastery, and thus there were few alms save for those of the saintly old prior of Las Cuevas, a Carthusian monk and very great servant of God from the Pantoja family in Avila.[10] God gave him so much love for us that from the time we arrived he did not cease helping in every way, and I think he will continue doing so until he dies. We owe a great deal to this saint. I put this down here, daughters, so that if you read it you will pray for the one who helped us so much, and it is right that you pray for him and for all those, living or dead, who have helped us.

10. My brother stayed with us more than a month, I think. (On this subject of time, I have a poor memory and so I could be mistaken; always understand me to be saying "more or less" since it doesn't matter.) During this month he worked a great deal in constructing the church out of some rooms in the house and adapting everything so that we didn't have to do anything.

11. After all the work was finished, I wanted to have the Blessed Sacrament reserved without any noisy display, for I am much opposed to causing any bother if it can be avoided, and so I mentioned this to Father Garciálvarez. He spoke about it with the Father Prior of Las Cuevas, for they were looking after our affairs as they would their own. Their opinion was that in order to make the monastery known in Seville the Blessed Sacrament would have to be reserved with solemnity, and they went to the archbishop. All agreed that the Blessed Sacrament should be brought with much solemnity from a parish, and the archbishop ordered that the clerics and confraternities gather for the occasion and that the streets be decorated.

12. The good Garciálvarez decorated our cloister which then, as I mentioned, looked on to the street. And in decorating the church he went to every extreme with many very nice altars and some other contrivances. Among these latter was a fount

having orange-flower water which we neither requested nor even wanted; although afterward it did give us much devotion. And we were consoled to see that our festival was celebrated with such solemnity, with the streets highly decorated, and a great deal of music and many musical instruments. The saintly prior of Las Cuevas told me that he had never seen anything like this before in Seville, that it was evidently the work of God. He himself walked in the procession, which he was not accustomed to doing. The archbishop reserved the Blessed Sacrament.[11]

Here you see, daughters, the poor discalced nuns honored by all. A little earlier it didn't seem that there would even be any water for them, although there is a great deal in the river. The number of people that came was extraordinary.

13. One thing that happened, according to all who saw it, is worth noting. Since after the procession there was much shooting of artillery and firecrackers, the people had the urge to continue, for it was almost night. And I don't know how, but some powder caught fire, and it was a great wonder that the person who had it didn't get killed. A huge flame leaped up as high as the cloister. The people thought that the taffeta hangings covering the arches would all be reduced to ashes. But no damage was done to them at all, though they were yellow and bright red. What was frightening is that the stone of the arches, under the hangings, was blackened by the smoke, but the taffeta hangings were left unmarred as if the fire had not reached them.

14. All were amazed when they saw it. The nuns praised the Lord that they didn't have to pay for new taffeta. The devil must have been so angry at seeing another house of God and the solemnity that was demonstrated that he wanted somehow to get revenge. But His Majesty did not allow this; may He be blessed forever, amen.

Chapter 26

Continues the account of the foundation of the monastery of St. Joseph in the city of Seville. Tells some very noteworthy things about the first nun who entered there.

YOU CAN EASILY UNDERSTAND, my daughters, the consolation we had that day. For my part, I can tell you that it was very great. I was especially consoled to see that I was leaving the Sisters in a house that was so good and well located, and that the monastery was known, and that there were enough new nuns to pay for the greater part of the cost of the house. Thus, those who in the future, before the established number is reached, may want to enter can do so no matter how little the dowry they bring with them, and the debt can still be paid off. Above all, I was happy for having shared in the trials, and when there was opportunity for a little rest, I left. This festival took place the Sunday before Pentecost in the year 1576, and immediately on Monday, the following day, I departed,[1] for the extremely hot weather was beginning to come and I wanted to be in Malagon before Pentecost and not have to travel on that day. I would have liked to have delayed a day or so, but for the above reason I left in a hurry.

2. The Lord was not pleased that I be there even one day to hear Mass in the chapel. The nuns' happiness was greatly spoiled by my departure.[2] They felt it very keenly, for we had gone through so many trials together in that year. As I have said,[3] I am not recording the worst ones here. In my opinion, aside from the first foundation in Avila (for with that one there is no comparison), none of the other foundations cost me as much as this one did in which the trials were for the most part interior ones. May it please the Divine Majesty that He always be served there, as I hope He will be, for then everything else is of little importance. His Majesty began to draw good souls to that house. As for the five who remained, out of the six I brought with me, I have already told you how good they were; that is, something of what can be told, which is the least. I wish to speak now of the first nun who entered there since her story is something you will enjoy hearing about.

3. She was the young daughter of very Christian parents. Her father was from the mountain region. She was still young, around seven, when her aunt, who had no children, begged her mother to allow her to stay with her. When she was brought to the house, her aunt must have shown her much love and affection as was natural. The maids had been hoping they would get the aunt's inheritance, but now it was clear that since the aunt loved the child she would leave it to her. The maids decided together to remove that obstacle through a diabolical plot, inventing a calumny against the child, saying that she wanted to kill her aunt. And in order to carry this out they gave one from among them I don't know how much money to buy some corrosive sublimate. When they told the aunt, she believed them at once because they all said the same thing. And the child's mother did too, for she is a very virtuous woman.

4. She took the child and brought her home thinking that she might turn out to be a very bad woman. Beatriz de la Madre de Dios,[4] for that is her name, tells me that for more than a year they spanked, punished, and made her sleep on the floor so that she would confess that she had planned to do something so evil. Since the girl denied that she had done it and said that she didn't know what corrosive sublimate was, her mother thought she was much worse since she was stubborn enough to deny it. The poor mother was so afflicted to see her daughter so headstrong in her refusal to admit she had done anything that she thought her daughter would never make amends. It's amazing that the girl didn't admit she was guilty just to free herself from so much punishment. But since she was innocent, God sustained her so that she continued to uphold the truth. And since His Majesty defends those who are without fault, He sent two of those maids an illness so bad that it seemed they had caught the rabies. Secretly they sent for both the little girl and her aunt and begged pardon from them, and finding themselves at the point of death they retracted. The other maid did likewise before dying in childbirth. In sum, all three of them died agonizing deaths in payment for what they had made that innocent girl suffer.

5. I did not learn this solely from her, for her mother, after

she saw that her daughter had become a nun, grieved over the bad treatment they had given her, and told me about it along with other things, for the girl's martyrdoms were many. And God permitted that, without it being her fault, the mother, who was a good Christian and loved her daughter, become her daughter's executioner. This mother is a woman of great honesty and deep Christian spirit.

6. While reading a book on the life of St. Anne, the child, when a little more than twelve years old, became very devoted to the saints of Carmel. For the author of the book says that St. Anne's mother—I believe her name is Merenciana—often went to speak to those saints. The effect this reading had on the girl was one of great devotion to the order of our Lady, for she then promised to become a nun in that order and also made a promise of chastity. When she could, she gave much time to solitude and prayer. In this solitude God and our Lady granted her many great and special favors. She would have liked to become a nun at once but she didn't dare because of her parents. Nor did she know where to find this order; which is surprising, for there was a monastery of the mitigated rule in Seville. But she had never heard of it until she heard of our monasteries many years later.

7. When she reached the marriageable age, though she was still but a girl, her parents came to an agreement on whom she should marry. She was their only child. Although she had had other brothers, they had all died, and she, the less loved by her parents, was left. (When what I mentioned[5] happened one of her brothers was alive, and he defended her saying that the calumny should not be believed.) Once the marriage was arranged, her parents didn't think she would have any objection, but when they told her she answered that she had made a vow not to get married and that no scheme whatever on their part, even if they were to kill her, would get her to do so.

8. Because either the devil blinded the parents or God permitted this so that she would be a martyr, they thought she had done something wicked and that for that reason she did not want to get married. Since they had already given their word and their not following through on it would have been taken as an affront by the other party, they gave her so many whippings,

inflicted on her so many punishments, even to the point of wanting to hang her, for they were choking her, that it was fortunate they didn't kill her. God who desired her for greater things saved her. She tells me that in the end she hardly felt anything because she recalled what St. Agnes had suffered, that the Lord had brought it to her mind, that she was pleased to suffer something for Him, and that she did nothing but offer herself to Him. They thought she would die, for she was in bed three months, unable to stir.

9. It seems very strange that the parents of this young maiden, a girl who never left her mother's side and whose father was very circumspect, should think so much evil of their daughter. She was always holy and virtuous, and very dedicated to almsgiving; all that she could obtain she gave away in alms. If our Lord wishes to grant someone the favor of suffering, He has many means; although, for some years our Lord had been revealing to her parents the virtue of their daughter so that they gave her all she wanted for distributing alms, and the former persecutions were changed into tokens of affection. Nonetheless, because of her longing to be a nun everything was a hardship for her; thus, according to what she told me, she went about dejected and troubled.

10. It happened that thirteen or fourteen years before Father Gracián went to Seville (when nobody had even heard of discalced Carmelites), while she was with her father and mother and two other women who were neighbors, a discalced friar of our order dressed in the coarse wool habit these friars now wear entered their house. They say his face was both fresh and venerable, although he was so old that his beard seemed made of silver threads, and it was long. He approached her and began to speak to her a little in a language that neither she nor anyone else understood. When he finished, he blessed her three times saying: "Beatriz, may God make you strong." And then he went away. No one stirred while he was there, but all remained as though stupefied. Her father asked her who he was. She had thought that her father had known him. They got up at once to go and look for him, but he was seen no more. She remained very consoled, and all the others very amazed, for they considered

this to be something from God, and so they then began to esteem her highly as was said.[6] After this, all those years passed, I believe they were fourteen, while she was ever serving our Lord, beseeching Him to fulfill her desire.

11. She was very weary by the time Father Maestro Fray Jerónimo Gracián arrived there. Going one day to hear a sermon in a church in Triana, which is where her father was living, without knowing who the preacher would be—it was the Father Maestro Gracián—she saw him go up to receive the blessing. When she saw the habit and that he was discalced, she at once recalled the one whom she had seen, for the habit was the same; although the face and the age were different, for Father Gracián was not yet thirty years old. She tells me that her joy was so great she almost fainted, for although she had heard that a monastery was founded there in Triana she had not known to which order it belonged.[7] Immediately, from that day she began to try to confess to Father Gracián. Yet God desired that even that would cost her much, for she tried more than, or at least as many as, twelve times, but the Father never wanted to hear her confession. Since she was young and attractive in appearance—for she must have been no more than twenty-seven—he avoided conversation with her; he is very circumspect.[8]

12. Finally, one day while she was in the church weeping (being also very reserved), a lady asked her what the trouble was. She told her that she had been trying for a long time to speak with that Father who was then in the confessional and that she had not succeeded. The lady brought her to the confessional and begged him to hear the young girl's confession, and thus this girl was able to make a general confession to him. When he saw what a virtuous soul she was, he was greatly consoled, and he consoled her, telling her that perhaps discalced nuns would come there and that he would arrange that they accept her immediately. And that is what happened. The first command he gave me was that she be the first to be admitted, for he was satisfied with her soul. And he informed her of this after we had arrived there. He insisted that she not let her parents know because otherwise there would be no possibility of her entering. And thus on the feastday of the Holy Trinity[9] she took leave

from some women who accompanied her to the church. (Her mother did not go with her when she went to the monastery of the discalced friars for confession, which is where she always went, for it was far away. And she, and her parents through her, gave many alms to the monastery.) She had arranged with a woman who was a very good servant of God to bring her and told the women who were accompanying her that she would soon return. And they allowed her to go since the woman companion was very well known in Seville as a servant of God who did great works of mercy. She put on her habit and mantle of coarse wool; I don't know how she was able to move, except that the happiness she felt made everything seem easy. Her only fear was that someone might recognize her behind this heavy habit, so different from her usual mode of dress, and stop her. What wonders the love of God works! Since she was no longer concerned about her honor and thought of nothing but how to realize her desire, we opened the door at once. I sent word of this to her mother. Her mother came to the monastery as though out of her mind; but she said that she already saw the favor God was granting her daughter. And although she was grieved, she overcame it courageously and did not go to the extreme of not speaking to her daughter as others do. She gave us many alms.

13. This bride of Christ began to enjoy the happiness she had so much longed for and was so humble and fond of doing all there was to do that we could hardly get the broom away from her. Whereas in her own home she had been so pampered, here she found all her rest in working. In her great happiness she began to put on weight. This pleased her relatives so much that they were now content to see her there.

14. In order that she would not enjoy so much good without suffering, she experienced very severe temptations two or three months before the time in which she was to make her profession;[10] not because she had decided against making it, but because it seemed to her a very serious step to take. The devil, making her forget all those years in which she had suffered to attain this blessing, was so tormenting her that she could not overcome the temptation. Nevertheless, by absolutely forcing herself, she defeated him in such a way that in the midst of these torments

she made the plans for her profession. Our Lord, who must not have been waiting for anything more than the testing of her fortitude, visited and consoled her in a very special way three days before the profession and put the devil to flight. She remained so consoled that during those three days it seemed as though she was outside herself with happiness; and rightly so because the favor had been great.

15. A few days after she entered the monastery, her father died. Her mother took the habit in the same monastery and gave all she possessed in alms.[11] Both mother and daughter experience the greatest happiness, edifying all the nuns and serving Him who granted them so wonderful a favor.

16. A year had not passed before another young lady, against the will of her parents, entered. And thus the Lord continues to fill this house of His with souls so desirous of serving Him, for neither austerity nor enclosure deters them. May He be blessed and praised forever and ever, amen.

Chapter 27

Treats of the foundation made in the town of Caravaca. The Blessed Sacrament was reserved on New Year's Day, 1576. The monastery is under the patronage of the glorious St. Joseph.

WHILE I WAS AT ST. JOSEPH'S IN AVILA about to leave for the foundation in Beas that was mentioned[1]—for the only thing we had still to prepare was the means of transportation—a private messenger arrived from a lady in Caravaca named Doña Catalina.[2] After hearing a sermon preached by a Father from the Society of Jesus, three young ladies went to her house determined not to leave until a monastery was founded in that town.[3] This action must have been something they had already discussed with this lady who is the one who helped them make the foundation. They belonged to the most important families of that town. The father of one of them was Rodrigo Moya, a very great servant of God and a man of much prudence.[4] Among the three of them they had enough resources to seek to accomplish a project like this. They learned from the Fathers of the Society of Jesus, who have always favored and helped this work, of what our Lord has done in founding these monasteries.

2. Since I saw the desire and fervor of those souls and that they went so far looking for the order of our Lady, I was moved with devotion and there arose in me the desire to help them carry our their good intention. Learning that Caravaca was close to Beas, I took with me a greater number of nuns than I usually do. My intention was to go there after completing the foundation in Beas. According to the letters these ladies sent, it seemed to me we could come to an agreement. But since the Lord had disposed otherwise, my plans were of little help, as was said when speaking of the foundation in Seville. For they had obtained the license from the council of the Order of Knights in such a way that even though I had made up my mind to go, I had to give up the idea.[5]

3. The truth of the matter is that when I learned in Beas where Caravaca is and saw that it was so out of the way and the road for those who would have to visit the nuns was so bad and that the superiors would be displeased, I had little enthusiasm for making the foundation. But since I had raised the hopes of those ladies, I asked Father Julián de Avila and Antonio Gaytán to go there to see what the place was like and, if they so decided, to cancel the plans. They felt lukewarm toward the project not because of the three who wanted to be nuns but because of Doña Catalina who was mainly responsible for the foundation, for she kept these ladies in a separate room by themselves as though they were already enclosed.

4. These nuns, or better, these who were about to become nuns, especially two of them, were so convinced of their vocation that they knew how to gain the goodwill of Father Julián de Avila and Antonio Gaytán. Before returning, these latter two signed the documents of agreement[6] and returned leaving the young ladies very happy. They came back so enthused about these women and the place that they never stopped talking about it, nor did they stop talking about the bad road. Since I saw that the agreement had been reached but that the license was delayed in coming, I sent the good Antonio Gaytán there again who for love

of me underwent all the hardship willingly. He and Father Julián de Avila were eager that the foundation be made. The truth of the matter is that they are the ones who should be thanked for this foundation. If they hadn't gone there and reached an agreement, I would not have bothered about it.

5. I sent Antonio Gaytán to put up the turn and the grille in the house where the nuns were going to live until finding another suitable one. This was the house of Rodrigo de Moya, who, as I mentioned,[7] was the father of one of these ladies, and very willingly allowed them to use a part of his house. Antonio Gaytán remained there doing this work for many days.

6. When they brought the license and I was about ready to depart for Caravaca, I learned from the license that the house would have to be subject to the council of the Order of Knights and obedience given to them, which is something I could not do because we belonged to the Order of Our Lady of Mount Carmel.

And thus, another license was asked for that would not have this condition, for otherwise neither there nor in Beas would a foundation be possible. When I wrote to the king, who at present is Don Philip, he granted me the great favor of issuing orders that the license be granted.[8] The king is so fond of favoring religious who he knows are faithful to their profession that once he had learned of the manner of life in these monasteries and that we follow the primitive rule, he favored us in everything. And thus, daughters, I beg you that special prayer be always offered for his majesty, as is done by us now.

7. Since they had to petition again for the license, I departed for Seville by order of Father Provincial, who was then, and still is, Father Fray Jerónimo Gracián de la Madre de Dios, as was said.[9] And the poor young ladies were enclosed there until the following New Year's Day. It had been around February when they had sent me a messenger in Avila. The license, then, was obtained in a short time, without any delay. But since I was so far away and involved in so many troubles, I was not able to help them. And I felt most sorry for them, for they wrote to me frequently very distressed, and so I could not bear making them wait any longer.

8. Since it was impossible for me to go because I was so far away and the foundation in Seville was not completed, Father Maestro Fray Jerónimo Gracián, who was the apostolic visitor, as was mentioned, ordered those nuns to go, even though I could not go with them, who had been chosen for the foundation and who were waiting at St. Joseph's in Malagón. I arranged for someone to be prioress who I trusted would fulfill the office very well, for she is far better than I.[10] And taking with them all the provisions, they left with two discalced Fathers of our order.[11] Father Julián de Avila and Antonio Gaytán had already returned home some time before, so I did not want them to accompany the Sisters because they were too far away and the weather was so bad, for it was the end of December.

9. When the nuns arrived in the town, they were received with great joy by the people and especially by those women who had been living an enclosed life. They founded the monastery, reserving the Blessed Sacrament, on the feast of the Holy Name of Jesus, in the year 1576.[12] Two of the women immediately took the habit. The other one suffered very much from melancholy. It must have been bad for her to live an enclosed life, and how much more so when it was so strict and penitential. She decided to return home to live with one of her sisters.[13]

10. Reflect, my daughters, on the judgments of God and on our obligation to serve Him who has allowed us to persevere until making profession and to live always in the house of God and be daughters of the Virgin. For His Majesty benefited by the good will of this young lady and by her property so that the monastery could be founded, and when the time came for her to be able to enjoy what she had so desired, she was lacking in fortitude and became subject to the melancholic humor. This latter, daughters, we often blame for our imperfections and inconstancy.

11. May it please His Majesty to give us abundant grace, for with this, nothing will prevent us from advancing ever in His service. And may He protect and favor all of us so that this excellent beginning, which He was pleased to initiate in women as miserable as we, may not be lost through our weakness. In

His name I beg you, my daughters and Sisters, that you always ask our Lord for this and that each one who enters in the future bear in mind that with her the observance of the primitive rule of the order of the Virgin, our Lady, begins again and that she must in no way consent to any mitigation. Consider that through very little things the door is opened to very big things, and that without your realizing it the world will start entering your lives. Remember the poverty and hardship that was undergone in obtaining what you now quietly enjoy. If you note carefully, you will see that in part these houses, most of them, have not been founded by men but by the powerful hand of God and that His Majesty is very fond of advancing the works He accomplishes provided we cooperate. From where do you think a useless woman like me, subject to obedience, without even a maravedi, with no one to help me in any way, could get the power for such great works? For this brother of mine, who helped with the foundation in Seville and had the means, courage, and goodness of soul to help, was in the Indies.[14]

12. See, my daughters, see the hand of God. Well, it could not be because I am from the nobility that He has given me such honor. In whatever way you want to look at this you will recognize that it is His work. It would not be right for us to undermine it in any way. We must not do so even if it cost us our life, honor, and tranquility. Moreover, we have everything here, for to have life is to live in such a way that there is no fear of death or of any of life's happenings, to have an habitual happiness, as you now all have, and to enjoy this prosperity that cannot be surpassed when there is no fear of poverty, but on the contrary desire for it. Well, to what can the interior and exterior peace that you always enjoy be compared? It is in your power to live and to die with this peace, as you have witnessed in those you have seen die in these houses. For if you always ask God to foster this way of life and you trust not at all in yourselves, He will not deny you His mercy. And if you have confidence in Him and have courageous spirits—for His majesty is very fond of these—you need not fear that He will fail you in anything. Never refuse to accept because they are not wealthy those who ask to become nuns provided they are virtuous and you are pleased with their desires

and talents, and they do not come merely as a remedy for their social situation but come to serve God with greater perfection. God in other ways will provide doubly for that which you might lack because of doing this.

13. I have much experience of this. His Majesty knows well that insofar as I can remember I have never refused to accept anyone because of lack of money, provided I was satisfied with all the rest. The witnesses to this are the many who have been received only for God, as you know. And I can certify that when I received those who brought much wealth I did not feel as great a joy as I did with those I accepted only for God. On the contrary, I had fear about those with wealth, but the poor filled and enlarged my spirit with a happiness so great I wept for joy. This is the truth.

14. Well, if when we had to buy and build houses we got along so well following this procedure, why shouldn't we do so now that we have a place to live? Believe me, daughters, the means by which you think you are accumulating are those by which you will be losing. When the person about to enter has wealth, without any other obligation, it is good that she give it to you as alms instead of giving it to others who have no need of it. For I confess that it would seem to me a lack of love if she didn't do this. But always bear in mind that the one who is about to enter should dispose of her possessions in conformity with what learned men advise her is for the greater service of God. It would be very bad if we were to look for any other good from those who enter this service. We gain much more when she does what she ought for God—I mean with greater perfection—than from all that she brings with her, for none of us is aiming after anything else. Nor may God allow this to happen, but only that His Majesty be served in all and through all.

15. And although I am wretched and miserable, I say this for the honor and glory of God and so that you may rejoice in how these houses of His were founded. Never in any business related to these foundations, nor in anything that happened relative to them, did I do anything or would I have done anything—I mean with regard to these foundations—that I understood to go contrary to the will of God in even one point, and this, too, when I

thought that in order to succeed I would have to cover up my intentions. I proceeded according to what my confessors advised me, for since I have been working on these foundations, my confessors have always been very learned men and great servants of God, as you know. Nor, insofar as I remember, did anything else pass through my mind than to proceed in this way.

16. Perhaps I am mistaken and have done many things wrong without realizing it; and the imperfections are countless. Our Lord who is the true judge knows that my intentions were good, insofar as I could discern concerning myself, I mean. Also, I see clearly that this good did not come from me but from God who willed that this work be done, and because it was His work He favored me and granted this gift. The reason why I'm telling you this, my daughters, is that you may understand how obliged you are and know that so far nothing offensive has been done to anyone. May He who has done everything be blessed and may charity be awakened in the persons who have helped us. May it please His Majesty to protect us always and give us His grace so that we will not be ungrateful for so many favors, amen.[15]

17. You have seen, daughters, that we have undergone some trials, although I believe I have written about the least part of them. For it would be tiresome if I had to describe in detail the roads, the rain and snow, and getting lost and, above all, frequently, my very poor health. With regard to this latter it happened to me—I don't know if I mentioned it—that on the first day of our journey from Malagón to Beas I was traveling with a fever and so many illnesses all together that while considering the distance we still had to travel and seeing myself in this condition I remembered our Father Elijah when he was fleeing from Jezebel, and said: "Lord, how can I suffer this? You take care."[16] The truth is that when His Majesty saw me so weak, He suddenly took away my fever and illness. This so happened that afterward when I thought about it I figured that perhaps it was because a priest, a servant of God, was going to enter the order there;[17] at least the exterior and interior illnesses were suddenly taken away. When I had good health, I underwent the bodily hardships with joy.

18. Well, putting up with the many different personalities

one necessarily finds in every town caused no small amount of trouble. And to leave my daughters and Sisters when going from one place to another, was not the smallest cross, I tell you, since I love them so much; especially when I thought I was not going to return to see them again and I saw their great sadness and tears. Even though they are detached from other things, God has not given them the gift to be detached from me, perhaps so that it might be a greater torment to me, for I am not detached from them either, even though I forced myself as much as I could so as not to show it and I reprimanded them. But this was of little help since their love for me is great, and in many ways it is obvious that this love is true.

19. You have heard how it was not just with the permission of our Most Reverend Father General that these foundations were made but that I was ordered under obedience by him afterward to do so.[18] And not only this, but he used to write to me about the great joy each new house that was founded gave him. Assuredly, the greatest relief I experienced in the midst of the trials was to see the happiness this work gave to him, for it seemed to me that by giving him this happiness I was serving our Lord since he is my major superior, and besides this I love him much.

20. That which came about next did so either because His Majesty desired to give me some rest or because the devil was displeased that so many houses were being founded where our Lord was being served. (It was easy to understand that what came about was not the will of our Father General because he had written me not many years before in answer to my request not to found any more houses that he would not stop ordering me to do so because he wanted me to make as many foundations as I had hairs on my head.) Before I came back from Seville, a general chapter was held. In a general chapter one would think they would be concerned about the expansion of the order, but instead the definitory gave me a command not merely to make no more foundations but not to leave the house in which I chose to reside, which would be a kind of prison, for there is no nun who for necessary matters pertaining to the good of the order cannot be ordered by the provincial to go from one place to another, I mean from one monastery to another. And what was

worse and what made me sad was that our Father General was displeased with me, without any reason at all, because of information given by biased persons.[19]

Along with this I was told of two other serious calumnies that were raised against me. I tell you, Sisters, so that you will see the mercy of our Lord and how His Majesty does not abandon the one who desires to serve Him. For these calumnies not only failed to make me sad but gave me so great an accidental joy[20] that I could not restrain myself. As a result, I'm not surprised at what David did when he went before the ark of the Lord,[21] because of my joy which I didn't know how to conceal I wanted to do nothing else at the time. I don't know the reason, for this has never happened to me in all the other great criticism and opposition I have received. Moreover, one of these two calumnies spoken against me was most serious. But the command not to make foundations — aside from the displeasure of our Most Reverend Father General — brought me great tranquility and was what I was often desiring: to end my days in quiet. But this was not what those who devised this were intending. They wanted to inflict on me the greatest sorrow in the world, and perhaps they may have had other good intentions.

21. On occasion, also, the strong opposition and criticism (sometimes offered with good intentions and at other times for other purposes) that I received in making these foundations gave me great joy. But I don't ever remember, no matter how much the hardship, experiencing happiness as great as I did in this instance. For I confess that at other times any one of these three things that came all together would have been a severe trial for me. I believe that my main joy came from my thinking that since creatures repaid me like this I was pleasing the Creator. For I am convinced that he who looks for joy in earthly things or in words of praise from men is very much mistaken, without mentioning the little advantage there is in them. Today people will think one thing, tomorrow another; at one time they will speak well of something; soon they will speak badly of it. May You be blessed, my Lord and my God, for You are unchangeable forever and ever, amen. The one who serves unto the end will live without end in Your eternity.[22]

22. I began to write about these foundations by order of Father Maestro Ripalda of the Society of Jesus, as I said at the beginning,[23] for he was then the rector of the College in Salamanca and my confessor. While I was in the monastery of St. Joseph in that city in 1573, I wrote about some of these foundations. But because of my many duties I set the work aside. I did not want to continue, for Father Ripalda was no longer my confessor, and we lived in different places, and also because of the great hardship and trials that what I have written cost me; although since I was always ordered to do so under obedience, I consider them well worthwhile. Though I was determined to write no more, the apostolic commissary, who is now Maestro Fray Jerónimo Gracián de la Madre de Dios, ordered me to finish the account of these foundations. Being wretched in the practice of obedience, I told him of the little opportunity I had and other things that came to my mind and also that the task was very tiring for me on top of all the other things I had to do. Nonetheless, he ordered me to finish them little by little as best I could. This I did submitting in everything to what those who know about these things might want to delete. What is poorly expressed, let them delete, for perhaps what seems to me better will sound bad to them.

I have finished today, the vigil of St. Eugene, the fourteenth day of the month of November in the year 1576 in the monastery of St. Joseph in Toledo. This is where I now reside by order of Father Apostolic Commissary, Maestro Fray Jerónimo Gracián de la Madre de Dios, whom we now have as superior for the discalced friars and nuns of the primitive rule, and who is also visitator for those of the mitigated rule living in Andalusia. May this work contribute to the honor and glory of our Lord Jesus Christ who reigns and will reign forever, amen.

For the love of our Lord, I beg the Sisters and Brothers who might read this to recommend me to our Lord that He might have mercy on me and free me from the pains of purgatory, if I should be there, and let me enjoy Him. Since you will not see this while I am living, may the weariness I experienced in writing it as well as the great desire I had to say something that would be consoling to you, if you are allowed to read it, be of some benefit to me after my death.[24]

Chapter 28

The foundation of Villanueva de la Jara.[1]

THE FOUNDATION IN SEVILLE, made more than four years ago,[2] was the last one. It was the last because of the great persecutions that broke out unexpectedly against the discalced friars and nuns. Although there had been many persecutions before, they were not so extreme. Now the whole undertaking was at the point of collapse. It was clearly seen how much the devil resented this holy beginning, which our Lord had initiated, and also that this was the Lord's own work since it was growing. The discalced friars suffered very much, especially the superiors, from serious false testimony and opposition on the part of almost all the calced Fathers.[3]

2. These Fathers informed our Most Reverend Father General[4] in such a way that even though he was a holy man and had given permission for all the monasteries (with the exception of St. Joseph's in Avila, which was the first, for this was founded with the permission of the pope), he was urged to oppose strongly any new foundations among the discalced friars. Toward the monasteries of the nuns, he was always well disposed. And so that I might not be helping the friars make foundations, he was induced into becoming displeased with me, which was the greatest trial I suffered in the work of these foundations, even though I have suffered many. On the one hand, very learned men who were my confessors would not agree that I should stop and counseled me to help toward the growth of the work, pointing out that I clearly rendered service to our Lord and helped toward the increase of our order; and on the other hand, going against the will of my superior was like a death to me. For apart from the obligation I had toward him because he was my superior, I loved him very tenderly and there were many reasons for obeying him. It is true that even though I wanted to please him by obeying this order, I could not because there were apostolic visitators whom I was obliged to obey.[5]

3. A holy nuncio died who greatly promoted virtue and, as a result, esteemed the discalced. Another nuncio arrived who it

seems had been sent by God to test us in suffering. He was a distant relative of the pope, and he must be a servant of God, but he began to take seriously to favoring the calced[6] and in conformity with the information they gave him about us he was convinced that the right thing to do was to put a stop to these foundations. Thus, he began to act with the greatest severity, condemning those he thought could oppose him by imprisoning them or sending them into exile.

4. Those who suffered most were: Father Fray Antonio de Jesús, who was the one who started the first monastery of discalced friars; Father Fray Jerónimo Gracián, whom the former nuncio made apostolic visitator to the Fathers of the cloth[7] and with whom the new nuncio was greatly displeased; and Father Mariano de San Benito. I have already mentioned who these Fathers are in writing of the preceding foundations. On other friars, among the more outstanding ones, he imposed penances, although not so severely. He issued many censures to prevent them from carrying on any business.

5. It was obvious that all this came from God and that His Majesty permitted it for a greater good and so that the virtue of these Fathers would be better known. The nuncio appointed a superior from the Fathers of the cloth to visit the monasteries of our friars and nuns,[8] which would have been a great hardship for us if what he thought was going on had been a fact. Still, the hardship that was suffered was very great. This will be recorded in writing by someone who knows better how to write about it. I am only touching on the matter so that the nuns that are to come will know how obliged they are to advance in perfection, since from that which has cost so much to those who are now living they will benefit free of trouble. For some of the nuns now living have suffered very much in these times from serious false testimony, which grieved me far more than what I was undergoing, for this latter was rather a great delight for me. It seemed to me that I was the cause of this storm, and that if they would have thrown me into the sea, as they did Jonah, the tempest would have stopped.[9]

6. May God who favors truth be praised! And this is what happened here, for since our Catholic king, Don Philip, knew of what was going on and was informed of the life and religious ob-

servance of the discalced, he took the initiative to favor us. Thus, he did not want our cause to be judged by the nuncio alone but gave him four counselors, responsible persons, three of whom were religious, so that our rights would be carefully looked after.[10] One of these was the Father Maestro Fray Pedro Fernández, a person of very holy life, great learning and intelligence. He had been apostolic commissary and visitator of the Fathers of the cloth in the Castile province, and we discalced had also been subject to him. He knew well the truth about how each group lived, for the desire of us all was nothing other than that this be known. And so when I saw that the king had named him, I considered the matter taken care of, as by the mercy of God it is. May it please His Majesty that this all be for His honor and glory.

Although there were many noblemen and bishops who made haste to inform the nuncio of the truth, all this would have benefited little if God had not chosen the king to intervene.

7. We are all very much obliged in our prayers to our Lord, Sisters, to recommend the king and those who have helped this cause. It is the Lord's cause and our Lady's, the Blessed Virgin's, and so I urge you to do this. Well you can imagine, Sisters, what little possibility there was for making any foundations. We were all occupied unceasingly in prayers and penances so that our Lord would preserve the houses already founded if doing so would be for His service.

8. I was in Toledo when these great trials started, which described so briefly will seem small to you but when suffered for so long a time were very great. I had arrived there from the foundation in Seville in 1576. A priest from Villanueva de la Jara brought me letters from the town council there. He came to negotiate with me and ask that I accept as a monastery a shrine in that town dedicated to the glorious St. Anne where nine women were living together. This shrine has a little house nearby where for some years these women were living with so much recollection and holiness that the whole town was moved to seek to help them attain their desires to become nuns. I also received a letter from a doctor, the priest in this town, named Agustín de Ervías,[11] a learned man of great virtue. Because of his virtue he was moved to help this holy work as much as he could.

9. It seemed to me that for the following reasons it would have been completely unsuitable to accept this foundation: First, there were so many women, and it seemed to me it would be very difficult for them to adapt to our way of life when they were used to their own. Second, they had almost nothing to live on, and the population of the place is little more than a thousand which is not much help for living on alms. (Although the town council offered to support them, it didn't seem to me to be a stable offer.) Third, they didn't have a house. Fourth, the place was far from where these other monasteries were located. Fifth, although I was told that these women were very good, I had not seen them and so could not verify whether they had the qualities we require for these monasteries. Thus I decided to turn down the proposal entirely.

10. Before doing so, I wanted to speak with my confessor who was Doctor Velázquez, a canon and professor in Toledo, a very learned and virtuous man, who is now bishop of Osma.[12] For it is always my custom never to do anything on my own but rather to seek the opinion of persons like him. When he saw the letters and understood the matter he told me not to turn the proposal down but to answer in a friendly manner, for when God has joined so many hearts for the sake of something, one may suppose that He will be served by it. This I did, for I neither accepted it entirely nor turned it down. They continued entreating and getting influential persons to intercede with me until this year of 1580. My opinion was always that it would be foolish to agree to this request. When I responded I could never give a completely negative answer.

11. It happened that when Father Fray Antonio de Jesús completed his time of exile at the monastery of our Lady of Succor,[13] he went to preach in Villanueva which is three leagues away. And the present prior of this monastery, Father Fray Gabriel de la Asunción, a person of very good judgment and a servant of God, also came often to this town,[14] for he and Father Antonio were friends of Doctor Ervías, and they began to converse with these holy Sisters. Becoming admirers of their virtue and persuaded by the townspeople and the doctor, they took this matter upon themselves as their own and through letters

tried very hard to persuade me. And while I was at St. Joseph's in Malagón, which is more than twenty-six leagues from Villanueva, this prior came to speak to me about the foundation, giving me an account of what could be done and how after it was made Doctor Ervías would give three hundred ducats income from what he received from his benefice; that permission would be obtained from Rome.

12. This looked very unsure, since it seemed to me that after the foundation was made they would drag their feet saying that the little the Sisters had was quite enough. And then I put forth many reasons, in my opinion sufficient, to convince Father Prior that it would not be suitable to make a foundation, and I said that he and Father Antonio should consider these carefully; and I left the matter on their conscience, thinking that what I had said sufficed for refusing to make the foundation.

13. After he had gone, I considered how much in favor he was of the foundation and that he would persuade the superior we now have, who is Fray Angel de Salazar, to accept it. I wrote to the latter with haste begging him not to give this permission and telling him the reasons. From what he wrote to me afterward, he would not have wanted to give the permission unless the foundation seemed to me a good thing.

14. A month and a half went by, or perhaps a little more. When I thought I had put a stop to the matter, a messenger came with letters from the town council, which took on the obligation to provide for the needs of the monastery, from Doctor Ervías who obliged himself to what I mentioned, and—very enthusiastic ones—from these two reverend Fathers. I found myself very confused. On the one hand, I had great fear of admitting so many Sisters thinking that as usually happens they would band together against those others who would join them; and on the other hand, I did not see a sure means for their support, because that which was offered amounted to nothing very impressive. Afterward I understood that my confusion was from the devil, for even though the Lord had given me so much courage, I had become fainthearted to the point that it doesn't seem I was trusting God at all. But the prayers of those good souls in the end prevailed.

15. One day after I received Communion I was recommending this matter to God as I often used to do. For what made me answer them somewhat favorably was the fear of hindering spiritual progress in souls, for my desire is always to be some means by which our Lord may be praised and that there be more to serve Him. While I was praying in this way, His Majesty reprimanded me sternly, asking me with what treasures that which had been done so far had been accomplished and telling me that I should not hesitate to accept this house, that it would be for His great service and the spiritual progress of souls.

16. Since these locutions from God are so powerful, not only does the intellect understand them but it is enlightened so as to understand the truth, and the will is disposed to the desire to carry them out; and this is what happened to me. For not only was I glad to accept the foundation but it seemed to me that I had been at fault in delaying so long and being tied to human reason when the works I had seen His Majesty do for this sacred religious order were so beyond reason.

17. Having decided to accept this foundation, it seemed to me necessary, for many reasons that occurred to me, that I go with the nuns who were to live there. My human nature resisted very much, for I had arrived in Malagón[15] very sick and have always been so. But since I thought the foundation would serve our Lord, I wrote to my superior to order me to do what he thought best. He sent the license for the foundation and the command that I go personally and bring the nuns of my choice. This latter worried me a great deal since the nuns would have to live with those women who were already there. Praying to our Lord very much over this matter, I took two from the monastery of St. Joseph's in Toledo, one of them for prioress, and two from Malagón, one of them for subprioress.[16] Since we had prayed so much to His Majesty, things turned out very well, which to me was no small matter; for in the foundations that we begin by ourselves alone, the nuns adapt to each other well.

18. Father Fray Antonio de Jesús and Father Fray Gabriel de la Asunción came for us. Given an assurance of help from the town, we left Malagón on the Saturday before Lent, the thirteenth of February in 1580. God was pleased to make the weather

so good and give me such health that it seemed to me I had never been sick. I was surprised and reflected on how very important it is not to consider our weak state of health or any opposition that occurs when we understand that something serves the Lord since God is powerful enough to make the weak strong and the sick healthy. And when our Lord does not do this, suffering will be the best thing for our souls; and fixing our eyes on His honor and glory, we should forget ourselves. What is the purpose of life and health save that they be lost for so great a King and Lord? Believe me, Sisters, you will never go astray in following this path.

19. I confess that my wretchedness and weakness have often made me fear and doubt. But I don't remember that from the time the Lord gave me the habit of a discalced nun, and some time before this, He ever failed to grant me the favor, solely out of His mercy, to conquer these temptations and throw myself into what I understood to be for His greater service however difficult it was. I understand clearly that what I did for my part was little, but God wants no more than our determination so that He may do everything Himself. May He be forever blessed and praised, amen.

20. We had to go to the monastery of our Lady of Succor, already mentioned,[17] which is three leagues from Villanueva, and stay there so as to inform the town that we were coming, which had been agreed upon with these Fathers, and it was right that in everything I obey these Fathers with whom we were traveling. This house stood in a delightfully isolated and solitary spot. And as we approached, the friars came out in procession to meet their prior. Since they were discalced and wore their poor, coarse woolen mantles, they inspired us all with devotion and moved me to tender feelings since it seemed to me that I was present in that flourishing time of our holy Fathers of old. In that field, they appeared to be like white fragrant flowers, and indeed I believe that before God they are, for in my opinion He is authentically served there. They entered the church singing the *Te Deum* with voices very restrained. The entrance to it is underground, as though through a cave, which represented that of our Father Elijah.[18] Certainly, I was feeling so much in-

terior joy that I would have considered a longer journey well worthwhile. I regretted very much that the saintly woman through whom our Lord founded this house was now dead. I didn't deserve to see her, although I had desired to do so very much.[19]

21. It seems to me that it would not be an idle thing to tell something here about her life and the means by which our Lord desired that this monastery be founded there. It has been of such benefit to souls in the surrounding area, as I have been told. On seeing the penance that was done by this holy woman, may you realize, my Sisters, how far behind we are and may you try harder to serve our Lord. There is no reason that we should do less, for we do not come from such noble and refined family descent. Although this is not important, I am mentioning it because she had lived a comfortable life in keeping with her status in society, for she was a descendant of the dukes of Cardona and thus she was called Doña Catalina de Cardona.[20] After she had written to me a few times, she signed her letter with only the words, "the sinner."

22. Those who will write about her life will recount more in detail the many things that could be said about it before the Lord began to grant her such great favors. But in case you might not come to know of it, I will tell here what some trustworthy persons who knew her told me.

23. While this saintly woman was living among the nobility, she was always very concerned about her soul and did penance. The desire for penance greatly increased in her and also the longing to go where she could be alone to enjoy God and dedicate herself to doing penance without any hindrance. She spoke of this with her confessors, but they did not give their consent. I am not surprised that this seemed madness to them, since nowadays the world is very rooted in discretion and has almost forgotten the great favors God granted to the many holy men and women who served Him in the desert. But since His Majesty always favors authentic desires, enabling one to carry them out, He ordained that she go for confession to a Franciscan Father whose name is Fray Francisco de Torres. I know him well and consider him a saint. For many years he has been living a life of

intense fervor, penance, and prayer, and been suffering many persecutions. He must know well the favors God grants to those who strive to receive them, and thus he told her not to give up but to follow the calling His Majesty granted her. I don't know if these were the exact words, but they must have been something like this since she carried them out at once.

24. She disclosed her plans to a hermit who was living in Alcalá and, without ever telling anyone about them, asked him to accompany her.[21] They arrived at the place where the monastery now stands, and there she found a tiny cave hardly large enough for her; here he left her. But what love must have been hers since she wasn't worried about what there might be to eat or about the dangerous things that could happen to her, or about the bad reputation she would have when it was discovered that she had disappeared. How inebriated must have been this holy soul, so absorbed in not letting anyone prevent her from enjoying her Spouse. And how determined she was not to love the world, since she thus fled from all its satisfactions.

25. Let us consider this well, Sisters, and reflect on how with one blow she conquered everything. For although what you do by entering this holy religious order, offering your will to God, and professing so continual an enclosure may not be less, I wonder whether, in the case of some, a part of this initial fervor does not pass away and out of self-love we make ourselves subject again to some things. May it please the divine Majesty that this not be so, but that since we imitate this holy woman in desiring to flee from the world we may interiorly stay far away from it in all things.

26. I have heard many things about the harsh austerity of her life, and what is known must be the smallest part of it. She must have treated her body terribly because she lived for many years in that solitude with such great desires to do penance and no one to restrain her. I will mention what some persons heard from her directly as well as what the nuns at St. Joseph's in Toledo heard. She went to visit these latter and spoke with them as candidly as with her own sisters. She spoke thus with other persons, too, for her simplicity and humility must have been great. And as one who was convinced that she had nothing of herself, she

was far removed from any kind of vainglory and she enjoyed telling about the favors God granted her so that through them His name might be praised and glorified. Doing this would be dangerous for those who have not reached this state, for, at least, it will seem that they are praising themselves. But her candidness and holy simplicity must have freed her from this fault, for I never heard anyone accuse her of it.

27. She said that she had been living in that cave eight years and that on many days she ate only herbs and roots from the field, for after the three loaves of bread given her by the hermit who accompanied her were gone, she had no more until met by a little shepherd who was passing by. Afterward, he provided her with bread and flour, with which she made small cakes baked over the fire. This was all she ate, and she did so only on each third day. This fact is very certain, for even the friars who are there testify to it, and this went on after she was already very thin and wasted. Sometimes when she went to speak with the friars about how to found a monastery they made her eat a sardine, or other things,[22] and rather than benefit from this she was harmed. She never drank wine as far as I know. She took the discipline with a heavy chain, and it used to last often two hours or an hour and a half. The chains she wore were extremely sharp, for a person told me (a woman)[23] that in going there on pilgrimage she remained for the night and feigning sleep she saw her taking the chains off and cleaning them since they were full of blood. But according to what she told the nuns I mentioned,[24] that which she underwent with the devils was greater, for they appeared to her as huge dogs, and jumped up on her shoulders, and at other times as snakes. She had no fear at all of them.

28. After the monastery was built, she still used to go to her cave, sleep there, and remain there except when she attended the Divine Office. And before the monastery was founded she used to go for Mass to that of the Mercedarians,[25] which was a quarter of a league away; and sometimes she went on her knees. Her garb was made of coarse cloth, and her inner tunic of rough wool,[26] made in such a way that she was thought to be a man.

After these years that she lived there in such solitude, our

Lord desired that her way of life become known, and the people began to venerate her so much that she could not get away from them. She spoke to everyone with great charity and love. As time went on, a greater concourse of people came; and those who were able to speak to her considered themselves lucky. She was so worn out from this that she said they were killing her. There were days when the whole field was almost filled with wagons. After the friars came there, there was no other remedy than for them to have her lifted up high so that she could bless all the people, and with that they were freed of them. After eight years in which she lived in the cave (which was now larger, for it had been made so by those who had gone there), she became so sick that she thought she was going to die, and she suffered it all in that cave.

29. She began to have desires that a monastery of friars be founded there, and these persisted for some time without her knowing from which order they would come. Once while praying before a crucifix she always carried with her, our Lord showed her a white mantle, and she understood that they would come from the discalced Carmelites, and she had never known that there were friars like this in the world. At that time only two monasteries of friars had been founded, Mancera and Pastrana. After this experience, she must have inquired. When she learned there was a monastery in Pastrana and since she had been in the past a close friend of the princess of Eboli, wife of Prince Ruy Gómez, to whom Pastrana belonged, she went there to find out how she might make this foundation which she had been desiring so much.

30. There at the monastery of Pastrana, in the church of St. Peter, for this it is called, she received the habit of our Lady,[27] although not with the intention of being a nun or of making profession, for she was never inclined toward being a nun since our Lord was leading her by another path. It seemed to her that if she professed obedience her plan to live in harsh austerity and solitude would be frustrated. All the friars were present when she received the habit of our Lady of Mt. Carmel.

31. In their company was Father Mariano, whom I mentioned in these foundations.[28] He told me that he himself had

experienced at the time a suspension or rapture that carried him completely out of himself and that while in this state he saw many dead friars and nuns. Some were beheaded, some had their arms and feet cut off as though they were martyred, for martyrdom is what this vision was pointing to. And he is not the type of man who would tell what he had not seen, nor has his spirit ever been accustomed to these suspensions, for God does not lead him by such a path. Pray to God, Sisters, that this vision will come true and that we will merit in our times to see so great a blessing and be ourselves among the martyrs.

32. From here, that is, from Pastrana, the holy woman of Cardona began to seek the means to found her monastery and for this purpose she went back to the court which she had so eagerly left before. Doing this must have been no small torment; it was a place where she underwent much criticism and trial. When she left the house where she was staying, she wasn't able to protect herself from the crowd. This happened wherever she went. Some cut pieces from her habit, others from her mantle. She then went to Toledo where she stayed with our nuns. All of them have affirmed to me that the odor of sanctity emanating from her was so great that it permeated even her cincture and habit, which she exchanged for another given her by the nuns; it was something to praise God for. And the closer they came to her the greater was this fragrance, even though her manner of dress, because of the intense heat, would rather have caused a bad odor. I know that they wouldn't say anything but the complete truth, and thus they were left with great devotion.

33. In the court and elsewhere they gave her the means for the monastery, and once she obtained the license, it was founded. The church was built at the place where her cave was. Another cave was made for her further away in which she had a tomb carved out,[29] and she remained there most of the day and night. She lived this way only a short time, for about five and a half years after the monastery was built. That she lived even as long as she did seemed supernatural because of her harsh, austere life. Insofar as I can remember, she died in 1577. Her funeral services were held with greatest solemnity, for a gentleman named Fray Juan de León[30] had great devotion to her and ar-

ranged it all with much care. She is now buried temporarily in a chapel of our Lady, to whom she was extremely devoted, until a church larger than the one they have now will be built to keep her blessed body as is fitting.

34. Great is the devotion they have to her in this monastery, and it seems it remained there and in the surrounding area, especially when they beheld that solitude and cave in which she lived. The friars have testified to me that before she decided to found the monastery, she became so wearied and afflicted at seeing the large number of people coming to see her that she wanted to go to another place where no one would know of her. She sent for the hermit who brought her there so that he might bring her elsewhere, but he was dead. And our Lord who was resolved that this house of our Lady be founded there did not allow her to leave, for as I have said,[31] I know He is served very much there. The friars have all that is necessary for their way of life, and it is clear that they like to be isolated from people; especially the prior,[32] for God also drew him away from a life of much luxury and has repaid him with spiritual consolation.

35. The prior was very charitable toward us. The friars contributed to our foundation from what they had in the church, for since this holy woman was much loved by so many noble persons, their church was well provided with sacred furnishings. I was very much consoled during the time I was there, although this was accompanied by much shame which continues. I saw that the one who had done such harsh penance there was a woman like me, but more delicate because of her background, and not so great a sinner as I. For in this matter there is no comparison between us, and I have received much greater favors of many kinds from our Lord, and that I am not in hell because of my sins is among the greatest of favors. The desire alone to imitate her, if I could, consoled me; but not much, for all my life has passed in desires, but the deeds I do not perform. May the mercy of God help me. In Him I have always trusted through His most sacred Son and the Virgin, our Lady, whose habit I wear through the goodness of the Lord.

36. One day when I had just received Communion in that holy church, very great recollection came over me with a sus-

pension that drew me out of myself. In this suspension, through an intellectual vision, this holy woman appeared in a glorified body and some angels with her. She told me not to grow weary but that I should strive to go ahead with these foundations. I understood, although she did not indicate this, that she was helping me before God. She also told me something else but there is no reason to put it here in writing. I was left very much consoled and with a great desire to work hard, and I hope in the goodness of the Lord that with help as good as are these prayers of hers I will be able to serve Him in some way.

You can see here, my Sisters, how her trials have now come to an end, but the glory she enjoys will have no end. Let us now force ourselves for love of our Lord, to follow this sister of ours. Holding ourselves in abhorrence as she abhorred herself, we will finish our day's journey, for it goes by so quickly and all comes to an end.

37. We arrived in Villanueva de la Jara on the first Sunday of Lent, the feast of St. Barbaciani,[33] the vigil of the feast of the Chair of St. Peter, in the year 1580. On this same day at the time of the high Mass, the Blessed Sacrament was reserved in the church of the glorious St. Anne.[34] The city council and some others along with Doctor Ervías came out to receive us, and we got down from our wagons at the church in the town, which was quite far from St. Anne's. The joy of the whole town was so great. It gave me much consolation to see the happiness with which they received the order of the Blessed Virgin, our Lady. We had heard from afar the peal of the church bells. Once we were inside the church, they began the *Te Deum*, one verse sung by the choir and the other played by the organ. When it was finished, they carried the Blessed Sacrament on one portable platform and a statue of our Lady on another, and crosses and banners. The procession proceeded with much pomp. We were in the middle near the Blessed Sacrament with our white mantles and our veils covering our faces, and next to us were many of our discalced friars from their monastery and Franciscans from the monastery of St. Francis that was located there, and one Dominican who happened to be present (even though he was alone it made me happy to see that habit there). Since the distance was great, there were many altars set up along the way. From

time to time the procession stopped and some verses were recited in honor of our order which moved us to great devotion. So did the sight of all of them praising the great God present in our midst and the fact that because of Him they paid so much honor to us seven poor, little discalced nuns who were there. While I was engaged in all these reflections, I became very ashamed in recalling that I was among them and that if they were to do what I deserved they would all turn against me.

38. I have given you so long an account of this honor that was rendered to the habit of the Virgin so that you might praise our Lord and beg Him that he be served in this foundation. I am happier when there is much persecution and many trials, and I tell about them more eagerly. The truth is that these Sisters that were here suffered persecution and trial for almost six years, at least for the five and a half years that they were in this house of the glorious St. Anne. They suffered these in addition to the great poverty and hardship they had in earning their food, for they never wanted to ask for alms. The reason for the latter was that they didn't think the purpose of their being in the monastery was that others might give them to eat. Furthermore, they did great penance, both by fasting often and eating little, and by their uncomfortable beds and very small house, which was a great hardship because of the strict enclosure that they always observed.

39. Their greatest trial, they told me, came from their intense desire to see themselves clothed with the habit. This was a terrible torment to them day and night since they thought they might never see the desire fulfilled, and thus all their prayers, frequently accompanied by tears, were that God might grant them this favor. And whenever some delay came along, they became extremely distressed and increased their penance. They deprived themselves of food in order to pay from their earnings the messengers sent to me and also for the gifts of gratitude, in their poor way, to those who were able to help them in some way. After having spoken with them and seen their holiness, I well understand that it was through their prayers and tears that they obtained the favor to be admitted into the order. And thus I considered it a far greater treasure to have souls like these in

the order than to have a good deal of income, and I hope that the house will prosper.

40. Well when we entered the house, all were inside at the door. Each one was dressed in her individual way, as she was when she entered, and they never wanted to wear the habit of *beatas*[35] since they were hoping for this foundation, although what they were wearing was very simple. It appeared from their indifferent manner of dress that they took little care of themselves, and almost all were so thin that their life of great penance was evident.

41. They received us with many tears of great joy. It was obvious that these were not feigned, nor were their great virtues, their joy, humility, and obedience to the prioress. They don't know how to please enough those nuns who came to make the foundation. All their fear was that we might turn around and go back when we saw their poverty and the small size of their house. None of them had acted as superior, but with much sisterly love each of them worked as much as she could. The two oldest took care of business matters when necessary; the others never spoke with anyone, nor did they want to. They had no lock for the door but only a bolt; none of them dared to go to the door; only the oldest answered. They slept very little so as to earn their bread and not lose time for prayer in which they spent many hours — on feast days the whole day.

42. They guided themselves with books by Fray Luis de Granada and Fray Peter of Alcántara. They recited the Divine Office most of the time despite their little ability to read, for only one of them read well. And they did not have identical breviaries. Some used old roman breviaries that were given by priests who no longer used them; others used whatever they could find. And since they did not know how to read, they spent many hours at this. They did not recite the Office in a place where they could be heard by outsiders. God must have accepted their good intention and effort, for they must have said little that was correct. When Father Fray Antonio de Jesús began to guide them, he ordered them to recite only the Office of our Lady. They had their own oven for baking bread. And they did everything with as much harmony as they would have done under a superior.

43. All this made me praise our Lord, and the more I dealt with them the happier I was that I had come. It seems to me that however many the hardships I would have had to go through, I would not have wanted to fail to console these souls. My companions who remained there told me that on the very first days they experienced some opposition, but as they got to know these new Sisters better and learn of their virtue, they felt very happy to remain with them and loved them very much. Great is the power of holiness and virtue. The truth is that even though they met with many difficulties and trials these Sisters bore them well, with the favor of the Lord, because they desired to suffer in His service. And the Sister that does not feel within herself this desire should not consider herself a true discalced nun, for our desires must not be for rest but for suffering in order to imitate in something our true Spouse. May it please His Majesty to give us grace for this, amen.

44. The origin of this shrine of St. Anne was as follows. There lived in this town of Villanueva de la Jara a priest born in Zamora who had been a friar of our Lady of Mt. Carmel. He was a devotee of the glorious St. Anne. His name was Diego de Guadalajara, and he built near his house this shrine in which Mass could be heard. And in his great devotion he went to Rome and brought back a bull with many indulgences for this church or shrine. He was a virtuous and recollected man. He stipulated in his will that after his death this house and all his possessions be used for a monastery of nuns of our Lady of Mt. Carmel and that if this could not be done a chaplain be appointed to say some Masses each week and that if and when the monastery were built there would be no obligation to say the Masses.

45. The property so remained, with a chaplain, for more than twenty years, and the estate diminished in value. When the women began living in the house, they received only the house. The chaplain was in another house that belonged to the same chaplaincy which he will now leave to them along with the rest of the estate which amounts to very little. But the mercy of God is so great that He will not fail to favor the house of His glorious grandmother. May it please His Majesty that He be

always served in it, and may all creatures praise Him forever and ever, amen.

Chapter 29

Treats of the foundation of St. Joseph of Our Lady of the Street in Palencia. It was made in the year 1580 on the feast of King David.[1]

HAVING RETURNED FROM THE FOUNDATION of Villanueva de la Jara, the major superior[2] ordered me to go to Valladolid at the request of the bishop of Palencia, Don Alvaro de Mendoza. This was the bishop who had accepted and favored the first monastery, St. Joseph's in Avila,[3] and always favors whatever pertains to this order. Since he was transferred from the diocese of Avila to that of Palencia, our Lord inspired him with the desire to found there another monastery of this sacred order. When I reached Valladolid, I was struck down with so bad an illness that they thought I was going to die.[4] I felt so listless and so unable even to think of doing anything that I could not be persuaded even though the prioress of our monastery in Valladolid who desired this foundation very much was pressing me to go ahead with it.[5] But neither could I find any basis for doing so because the monastery had to be founded in poverty, and they told me that it could not be sustained because the city was very poor.

2. For almost a year this foundation had been a subject of discussion along with that of Burgos. Previously, I had not been so opposed to it, but now, even though I had not come to Valladolid for any other purpose, I found many obstacles. I don't know whether this was due to my severe illness and the resulting weakness or to the devil who wanted to hinder the good that was done afterward. Indeed, I am surprised and saddened. Often I complain to our Lord about how much the poor soul shares in the illness of the body. It seems the soul can do nothing but abide by the laws of the body and all its needs and changes.

3. One of the great trials and miseries of life, I think, is this

helplessness experienced when there is no strong spirit to bring the body into submission. For if the soul is alert, I don't consider the suffering of illness and pain a problem, even though this may be a trial, for the soul is praising God and accepting this as coming from His hand. But it is a terrible thing on the one hand to be suffering and on the other not to be doing anything. This is especially true if the soul has experienced great desires not to rest interiorly or exteriorly but to occupy itself completely in the service of its great God. It has no other remedy here than patience, knowledge of its misery, and abandonment of itself to the will of God who makes use of it for what He wants and in the way He wants. This is the condition I was in then, although I was already convalescing. But, nonetheless, the weakness was so great that I lost even the confidence God usually gives me when I begin one of these foundations. Everything looked impossible to me. If I had met some person at the time to encourage me, this would have been a great help. But some only added to my fear; others, even though they gave me some hope, did not encourage me enough to help me overcome my faintheartedness.

4. It happened that a Father from the Society came there, named Maestro Ripalda, who had been my confessor some time before and was a great servant of God.[6] I told him about my situation, that I wanted to consider him to be standing in God's place, and asked him to tell me what he thought about the foundation. He began to encourage me very much. He told me that I was growing old and that this was the reason for my cowardice. But I saw clearly that this was not the reason, for I am older now and do not experience such timidity. And he too must have understood this, but he scolded me so that I wouldn't think God was behind it. I was then considering the foundations of Palencia and Burgos together, and I had nothing for either of them. But this was not the cause of the way I felt, for I am used to beginning with less. He told me that I should by no means give them up. I had been told the same thing a little previously by a provincial from the Society, named Baltasar Alvarez,[7] but at that time I was well.

5. His words were not enough to get me to make the decision

to go ahead, although they were very helpful. I did not make up my mind completely because either the devil, or as I said,[8] the illness held me bound; but I felt much better. The prioress at Valladolid assisted me as much as she could because she greatly desired the foundation of Palencia. But since she saw me so lukewarm about it, she too was afraid. Now let the true ardor come, for neither the nations nor the servants of God suffice! Therefore, it is often made clear that it is not I who do anything in these foundations, but the work is His who is all powerful in everything.

6. One day just after having received Communion and in the midst of this vacillation and indecision about making any foundation, I begged the Lord to enlighten me so that I might do His will in everything. The lukewarmness was not of the kind that could ever take away as much as one iota from this desire. Our Lord answered in a kind of reprehensive way: "What do you fear? When have I failed you? I am the same now as I was before. Do not neglect to make these two foundations." O great God! How different are your words from those of men! I was thereby left with such determination and courage that the whole world would not have been enough to oppose me. I began at once to make arrangements for them, and our Lord began to give me the means.

7. I took two nuns with me to go and buy the house. Now even though they told me it was impossible to live on alms in Palencia, I may as well not have been told, because I already saw that it was impossible at that time to make a foundation that could have an income. I knew that since God said I should found one, His Majesty would provide. Thus, although my health had not returned entirely, I decided to go despite the harsh weather. I left Valladolid on the feast of the Holy Innocents in the year that I mentioned,[9] for a gentleman had given us a house he had rented in which we could live from the beginning of the new year until the feast of St. John the Baptist, for he had gone to live elsewhere.

8. I wrote to a canon of this city even though I did not know him.[10] But a friend of his told me that he was a servant of God, and I became convinced that he would be a great help to us. For

the Lord Himself, as seen in the other foundations, chooses in each place someone to help Him. His Majesty already knows the little that I can do. I sent a message to beg this gentleman to have the house vacated as secretly as possible, for it was occupied, and not to tell the occupant who was coming. For even though some of the nobility showed their good will and the bishop was very eager for the foundation, I saw that the safest thing was to keep it from being known.

9. Canon Reinoso, for that is the name of the one to whom I wrote, did so good a job that not only did he have the house vacated but he provided beds and a plentiful supply of things. We needed them because the weather was very cold and the previous day had been a troublesome one with fog so thick we could hardly see each other. Indeed, we had little rest until we had prepared a place to say Mass the following day, because before anyone was aware of it we had arrived. I have found that this quiet way of arriving is more fitting, for if we begin discussing opinions, the devil disturbs everything; even though he cannot gain, he stirs unrest. This is what we did, for early in the morning, almost at dawn, a priest who came with us, named Porras, a very good servant of God, said Mass. Also with us was another friend of the nuns of Valladolid, named Agustín de Victoria, who had lent me money to furnish the house and with much care had assisted me on the journey.[11]

10. There were five of us nuns who went to Palencia. With us, as well, was a lay Sister, a companion who has for some time been going about with me. She is a great and discreet servant of God who can help me more than others who are choir Sisters.[12] That night we slept little, although, as I say, the journey had been laborious because of the heavy rains.

11. I was very pleased that the foundation was made on that day since the Office was of King David to whom I am devoted. Immediately that morning I sent word to His Excellency, the bishop, who did not know yet that I was arriving that day. He came at once with the great charity he has always shown us. He told us that he would give us all the bread we needed, and he ordered his administrator to provide many things for us. There is so much that this order owes him, that whoever reads about

these, its foundations, is obliged to recommend him, whether living or dead, to our Lord, and this I ask out of charity. The joy of the people was so great and universal that there was not even one person who disapproved, which was something very unusual. Their knowing that the bishop wanted it contributed greatly to this since he was much loved in that place. The people are among the most gentle and noble that I have ever seen, and so every day I rejoice more in having made that foundation there.

12. Since the house was not ours, we immediately began to negotiate to buy another, for even though this one was up for sale, it was in a very bad place. And with the help I had from the nuns who came, it seemed that we could buy something. Although the amount was small, for that city it was a lot. But if God had not given us the good friends that He did, all would have been to no avail. For the good canon Reinoso brought a friend of his, named Canon Salinas,[13] of great charity and understanding, and they were both as concerned as if the matter were their own—even more so, I believe—and they were always concerned about that house.

13. There was in the town a shrine that inspired much devotion to our Lady called Our Lady of the Street. The devotion to her in the city and the entire region is great, and many people go there. It seemed to His Excellency and to all the people that it would be good for us to be near that church. It did not have a house attached to it, but there were two nearby which, if we bought, would be enough for us along with the church. The church had to be given to us by both the cathedral chapter and some members of the confraternity, and thus we started to try to obtain it. The cathedral chapter made us a gift of it at once, and although the negotiations with the confraternity were more difficult, the members also agreed. As I have said,[14] if I have ever seen virtuous people in my life, they are the people of this town.

14. Since the owners of the houses saw our interest in them, they began to value them more, and rightly so. I wanted to go to see the houses, and they looked so bad to me that I didn't want them at all, nor did those who came with us. Afterward, it was clearly seen that the devil had a great role to play because it

upset him that we would be there. The two canons who were negotiating about it thought that the houses were far from the cathedral, as they were, but in a more populated area of the city. We finally all decided that those houses were unsuitable for us and that we should look for another. This is what the two canons began to do those days. And they did so with such care and diligence, without failing to look at anything they thought might be suitable, that it made me praise our Lord. They became pleased with one house whose owner was named Tamayo. Some parts of the house were just right for our needs, and it was near the house of a noble gentleman, named Suero de Vega, who helps us very much.[15] He as well as other persons in the district were eager that we make the foundation there.

15. That house was not large enough, but they offered us another along with it, although this other was not the kind that could be easily adapted to the first. In sum, from the information they gave me about it, I desired that we go ahead. But the canons did not want to do so until I saw the houses first. I am so reluctant to go into the town, and I trusted so much in them that they couldn't get me to go. Finally, I went to see them and also those of our Lady of the Street, although not with the intention of buying these latter but only so that the owner of the others would not think that we had no other choice. And they had looked so bad to me, as I have mentioned,[16] and to those who had come with me that now we are surprised that we could have thought them so bad. After that, we went to the other place, determined that those houses would be the ones for us. Although we found many difficulties, we accepted them. Yet the houses were not easy to fix up, for in order to make a church, and even then not a large one, all the good space for living quarters would have had to be taken away.

16. It is a strange thing to be resolved about something. Indeed, it was providential that I trusted little in myself, although that time I was not the only one who was mistaken. In sum, we already had it in mind to buy the houses and no other and to pay what was asked for them, which was high, and write to the owner, who was not in the city but nearby.

17. That I have gone into such detail about the buying of the

houses will seem pointless until it is seen that the devil's aim was
to prevent us from buying those of Our Lady of the Street. Every
time I think of it, it makes me fear.

18. We were all determined, as I have said,[17] not to buy any
other. One day while I was at Mass I became very worried as to
whether I was doing the right thing, and a restlessness came over
me that left me almost no quiet during the whole Mass. I went to
receive the Blessed Sacrament, and immediately after receiving
it I heard these words: "This is the one that suits you." They
were such that they made me resolve definitely not to buy those I
was thinking of but those of Our Lady of the Street.

I began to consider what a difficult thing it would be to do
this since the business deal had been much discussed and was so
dear to those who had looked after it with such care. The Lord
answered me: "They do not understand how much I am offended
there, and this will be a great remedy." It occurred to me that
perhaps this locution might be false, although I could not believe
this, for I recognized clearly from its effects that it was from the
Spirit of God. The Lord said to me at once: "It is I."

19. I was left very peaceful and the disturbance I had before
was taken away, although I did not know how to remedy what
had been done and the many bad things that had been said
about the houses, or what to say to my Sisters to whom I had
stressed how bad the condition of them was and that we should
in no way move there without seeing them. Yet this did not concern me so much, for I already knew that the Sisters would be
agreeable to whatever I might do. But I was concerned about
the others and their desire. It seemed to me they would take me
to be vain and unstable since I changed my mind so quickly,
something I greatly abhor doing. All these thoughts were not
enough to move me either much or little to give up going to the
houses of our Lady, nor did I think about their bad condition.
Provided the nuns could prevent as much as one venial sin, the
rest was of little importance; and in my opinion any of them
knowing what I knew would have agreed with me.

20. I had recourse to the following: My confessor was Canon
Reinoso, one of the two who was helping me. I was not confid-
ing to him spiritual matters of this sort because the occasion had

not arisen in which there was need to do so. Since it has always been my custom in these matters, so as to walk along a more secure path, to do what the confessor advises me, I decided to tell him under much secrecy, even though I could not renounce doing what I had heard without feeling much distress. But, in the end, I told him I trusted our Lord would do what I saw at other times, for His Majesty changes the mind of the confessor who is of another opinion so that what He wants is done.

21.   I told him first of how the Lord was accustomed to teaching me often in this way and that up to that point many things had happened by which it was understood that these experiences were from His Spirit. I recounted what took place but told him that I would do whatever he thought, even if it would be painful for me. He is very discreet, holy, and shows good judgment in everything, even though he is young. [18] Although he saw that there would be unfavorable comment, he decided not to go against what had been heard. I told him that we should wait for the messenger, [19] and he agreed, for I trusted that God would take care of things. And so it happened, for even though we had agreed to all that the owner wanted and had requested, he asked for another three hundred ducats, which seemed foolish because we were already paying more than enough. In this we saw the hand of God because the sale was very good for the owner, and since the agreement had been made there was no sense to his asking for more.

22.   What he did helped matters very much, for we said there would be no end to this. But it didn't help completely, because it was clear that if the house was suitable for conversion into a monastery, three hundred ducats wasn't reason enough to forgo the house. I told my confessor that if he thought we should buy the house of Our Lady of the Street he shouldn't worry about my reputation but tell his companion that I was determined to buy Our Lady of the Street whether it was expensive or cheap, in miserable condition or good. Since his companion is very intelligent and alert, I believe that in seeing so quick a change he suspected something about my experience even though nothing was said to him about it, and so he did not press me any further.

23.   Afterward we all saw clearly the big mistake we would

have made in buying the other one. For now we are surprised to see the great advantages the one has over the other, not to mention the main advantage, for it is clearly seen that our Lord and His glorious Mother are served there and that many occasions of sin are being removed. In fact, many night vigils were held there, and since nothing more was there than the shrine, many things could be done that the devil was sad to see taken away. And we were happy to be able to serve in some way our Mother, Lady, and Patroness. And it was very wrong to have done otherwise previously, for we should not have considered any other house. Obviously, the devil was causing blindness in many matters, for there are many conveniences in Our Lady of the Street that would not have been found elsewhere. And all the townspeople were overjoyed for they had been desiring that the monastery be there, and even those who had wanted us to go to the other house were now very pleased with this one.

24. May He who enlightened me in this regard be blessed forever and ever. And He enlightens me thus in anything I manage to do well, for each day I am more amazed at the little talent I have for anything. And don't think that what I'm saying comes from humility, for each day I see it more clearly. It seems our Lord desires me and all others to know that it is only His Majesty who does these works, and that as He gave sight with mud to the blind man, He wants someone as blind as I to do something worth more than mud.[20] Certainly, in this whole matter there were things, as I have said,[21] involving great blindness, and each time I recall it, I would like to praise our Lord again for it. But even for this I'm no good, nor do I know how He puts up with me. Blessed be His mercy, amen.

25. Well these holy canons, friends of the Virgin, immediately made haste to negotiate a contract for the houses and, in my opinion, they got them at a low price. They worked hard, for in each of these foundations God desires that those who help will merit. And I am the one who does nothing, as I have said at other times; and I would never want to stop saying this, because it is the truth. For they worked very hard in getting the house ready, and also gave money for it, because I didn't have any, and together with this they became the guarantors. In other

foundations I had to undergo some anxiety before I found a guarantor, and not for so large an amount as in this instance. And that was understandable; the guarantors had to trust the Lord, for I didn't have a cent. But His Majesty has always granted me a favor which I consider very great; no one has ever lost anything by being a guarantor for me, nor was there any failure to pay back in full.

26. Since the owners of the houses were not satisfied with the two guarantors, the two went to look for the administrator of the diocese whose name was Prudencio. (I don't know if I remember correctly. They tell me this now, for since at that time we called him the administrator, I did not learn his name).[22] He is so charitable with us, for we owed him much and still do. He asked them where they were going; they answered they were looking for him to have him sign that guarantee. He laughed and said: "Well now, you ask for a guarantee for so much money in a way like this?" And he signed it at once while sitting on top his mule, which nowadays is something worth pondering.

27. I would not want to fail to sing the praises of the charity that I found in Palencia both in general and in particular. Truly, it seemed to me like being in the early Church, at least it is not usual now to see such a thing in the world. We had no income and they had to provide us with food, and not only were they not opposed to the foundation but they said that God was doing them the greatest favor. And if considered in the light of faith, what they said was the truth, for just to have one more church where the Blessed Sacrament is reserved is a great deal.

28. May He be blessed forever, amen. For as time goes on it is becoming clearly understood that our Lord is served by the fact that the foundation is in that place and that some inappropriate things must have been done there that are no longer done. Since many people went there for the night vigil and the shrine was in an isolated spot, not everyone went out of devotion. The situation is getting better. The statue of our Lady had been displayed with very little reverence. The bishop, Don Alvaro de Mendoza, had a chapel made in the shrine for it, and little by little things are being done for the honor and glory of this glori-

ous Virgin and her Son. May He be praised forever, amen, amen.

29. Well, when the house was ready for occupation by the nuns, the bishop wanted this to take place with great solemnity. And so it did, one day during the octave of the feast of the Blessed Sacrament.[23] He came himself from Valladolid, and the cathedral chapter, the religious orders, and all the people of the city joined him in the procession. There was much music. We all, with our white mantles and veils covering our faces, went in procession from the house where we were staying to a parish that was close to our Lady's house where the statue was brought to meet us, and from there we took the Blessed Sacrament and had it reserved in the church with great and well-organized solemnity. It caused much devotion. Other nuns who were on their way to the foundation in Soria came with us, all carrying candles. I believe that the Lord was very much praised that day in that city. May it please Him that He be praised forever by all creatures, amen, amen.

30. While I was in Palencia, God willed that the discalced Carmelites be separated from the calced. This was done by letting the discalced form their own province, which was all that we were desiring for the sake of our peace and tranquility. At the request of our Catholic king, Don Philip, a very long brief was obtained from Rome for this purpose.[24] And thus his majesty by obtaining this brief favored us as much as he did in the beginning. The chapter was held in Alcalá presided over by a reverend Father named Fray Juan de las Cuevas who was then prior of Talavera. He belongs to the Dominican order and was appointed by Rome after having been nominated by his majesty. He is a very holy and prudent man, which was necessary for such a task. The king paid for their expenses, and at his orders the entire university of Alcalá helped them. With much peace and harmony the chapter was held in the College of St. Cyril, that of our discalced friars. They elected Father Maestro Gracián de la Madre de Dios as provincial.[25]

31. Because these Fathers will write elsewhere about what took place, there is no reason for me to deal with it. I have mentioned the matter because it was while I was engaged in the work

of this foundation that our Lord brought to a conclusion an endeavor that was so important for the honor and glory of His glorious Mother since it concerned her order. She is our Lady and our Patroness. And this for me was one of the great joys and satisfactions of my life. It would take a long time to tell of the trials, persecutions, and afflictions that I have had to undergo during the past twenty-five years, and only our Lord can understand them. Save for anyone who knows the trials that were suffered, one cannot grasp the joy that came to my heart at seeing the matter concluded and the desire I had that everybody praise our Lord and that we pray for this our holy king, Don Philip. By means of him God brought the matter to a happy ending. Had it not been for the king, the devil was so cunning that everything would have collapsed.

32. Now we are all at peace, calced and discalced; no one can hinder us from serving our Lord. Hence, my Brothers and Sisters, since His Majesty has heard your prayers so well, let us make haste to serve Him. Let those in the present who are eyewitnesses, consider the favors He has granted us and the trials and disturbances from which He has delivered us. And those who are to come, when they find everything running smoothly, let them, for love of our Lord, not neglect anything relating to perfection. May that which is said of some orders that praise their beginnings not be said of them. Now we are beginning, and let them strive to advance always from good to better. Let them beware, for the devil through very small things drills holes through which very large things enter. May it not happen that those who are to come say:"These things are not important; don't go to extremes." Oh, my daughters, everything that helps us advance is important.

33. For love of our Lord I beg you to remember how soon everything comes to an end, to remember the favor our Lord has granted us in bringing us to this order and the great punishment that will befall anyone who might introduce some mitigation. Rather, fix your eyes always on the ancestry from which we come, those holy prophets. How many saints we have in heaven who have worn this habit! Let us adopt the holy presumption that with the Lord's help we will be like them. The battle will be

brief, my Sisters, and the end is eternal. Let us set aside these things that in themelves are nothing, using only those that lead us to this end without end, so as to love Him and serve Him more, for He will live forever and ever, amen, amen. Thanks be to God.

Chapter 30

Begins to treat of the foundation of the monastery of the Blessed Trinity in the city of Soria. It was founded in 1581. The first Mass was said on the feast of our Father St. Elisha. [1]

WHILE I WAS OCCUPIED with the foundation in Palencia, which was mentioned, they brought me a letter from the bishop of Osma, named Doctor Velázquez.[2] While he was canon and professor at the cathedral in Toledo and I was still experiencing some fears, I sought to consult him because I knew he was a very learned man and a servant of God. I entreated him urgently to guide my soul and hear my confession. Although he was very busy, I asked him to do so for the love of our Lord. He saw my need and responded so willingly that I was surprised. And I consulted and confessed to him all the time that I was in Toledo, which was a long time. I spoke to him about my soul with complete openness as I usually do. This did me so much good that from then on my fears began to lessen. True, there was another reason for consulting him which I won't go into here. But, in fact, he was very helpful to me because he assured me with passages from Sacred Scripture, which is what suits me most when I am sure that one knows it well. I knew he did and that he lived a good life.

2. This letter was written from Soria where he was at that time. He told me how a lady, a penitent of his there, spoke to him about a foundation of our nuns, which she thought would be a good thing, and that he had told her he would try to convince me to go there to make the foundation. He said I should not disappoint him and that if I thought the foundation was fitting I should let him know and he would send for me. I was very happy

because, in addition to the fact that the place was good for a foundation I wanted to see him and tell him some things about my soul. I had grown to love him very much because of the great progress my soul made under his guidance.

3. The name of this lady who wanted the foundation was Doña Beatriz de Beamonte y Navarra because she is a descendant from the kings of Navarra and is a daughter of Don Francés de Beamonte who was of a noble and pure lineage.[3] She was married for some years and had no children, but was very wealthy and for a long time had it in mind to provide for a monastery of nuns. She spoke of this with the bishop and he informed her about the discalced nuns of this order of our Lady. What he told her pleased her so much that she greatly urged him to have the foundation made.

4. She is a mild-mannered person, generous and penitent; in sum, a very great servant of God. She owned a good house that was well-constructed and in a good location in Soria. She told us that she would give it to us along with all that was necessary for a foundation, and this she gave together with a five hundred ducat annuity at twenty-five per thousand.[4] The bishop promised to give us a very good church with a vaulted ceiling. The church was a parish church[5] but so close by that we were able to make use of it by means of a covered passageway. The bishop was easily able to make this offer — for he was poor — because there were many churches there, and so he moved the parish to another church. He gave me an account of all this in his letter. I discussed the matter with Father Provincial who was there at the time.[6] He and my friends thought I should write through a personal messenger. The foundation in Palencia was completed, and I was very happy about the one in Soria for the reasons mentioned.[7]

5. I began to gather the nuns I was going to bring with me. There were seven, for that lady desired that there be more rather than less, in addition to a lay Sister, my companion, and myself. Somebody came for us with a stagecoach, which met our needs, for I had told the bishop that I had to bring two discalced Fathers with me.[8] And so I brought with me Father Nicolás de Jesús María, a man of great perfection and discretion, a native of Genoa. He was over forty when he received the habit, I think

—at least he's forty now, and it's only a short while since he took the habit—but he has advanced so far in a short time that it seems clear our Lord chose him so that he might help the order during these very troublesome times of persecution.[9] He has done a good deal. With respect to the others who could have helped, some were exiled, others imprisoned. Since he had no office, little attention was paid to him. For as I mentioned, it was only a short time that he was in the order. Or, God allowed this that there might be some help left for me.

6. He is so discreet that while he was staying in the monastery of the calced Carmelites in Madrid, as though for other business reasons, he dealt with the affairs of the discalced friars in such a disguised manner that the calced friars never knew about it, and so they didn't bother him. We corresponded frequently, for I was in the monastery of St. Joseph's in Avila, and we dealt with a suitable course of action, for this consultation gave him satisfaction. Hence it can be seen what need the order was in since so much attention was paid to me for want, as they say, of good men.[10] It was during this time that I had experience of his perfection and discretion. Thus he is among those in this order whom I love much in the Lord and esteem highly.

7. Well, he and his laybrother companion accompanied us. He had little to do on this journey, for the one sent by the bishop conducted us in much comfort and was a help in finding good inns. When we entered the territory of the bishop of Osma, the people loved the bishop so much that when told that this was one of his projects they directed us to the good inns. The weather was fine. The daily journeys were not long. Thus, little hardship was suffered on this trip; rather, it was a happy one, for hearing the people's praise of the bishop's holiness brought me the greatest joy. We arrived in El Burgo de Osma on the Wednesday before the octave day of the feast of the Blessed Sacrament.[11] We received Communion there the following day, which was Thursday, the octave day. Since we could not reach Soria that day we stopped to eat along the way and passed that night in a church, which was not a bad place, because there was no other inn. The next day we heard Mass there and arrived in Soria around five in the afternoon. The holy bishop stood at a

window in his house and blessed us from there, for we passed right by. This was no small consolation for me, since a blessing coming from a bishop and a saint is something to be highly esteemed.[12]

8. That lady, the foundress, was waiting for us at the door of her house, where the monastery was to be established. We were anxious to get inside because of the large number of people. The crowd was nothing new, for everywhere we go there is much curiosity. The world is so fond of novelty that were it not for the veils we wear over our faces, these crowds would be a great trial. But with these veils, we can put up with them. That lady had decorated very well a large hall in which Mass was to be said, for the covered passageway leading to the church given us by the bishop had to be constructed.[13] On another day, the feast of our Father St. Elisha, Mass was said.[14]

9. That lady had prepared perfectly everything we had need of, and she let us use that hall, which was conducive to recollection, until the feast of the Transfiguration[15] when the covered passageway was completed. It was on this feast that the first Mass in the church was said with great solemnity and in the presence of a large congregation. A Father from the Society preached the sermon, for the bishop had returned to El Burgo de Osma.[16] The bishop never loses a day or an hour without working; although his health was not good, for he had lost his vision in one eye. This was my affliction in Soria, for it saddened me that the vision that was so beneficial in the service of the Lord should be lost. These are God's judgments. He must have allowed this so that His servant might gain, for the bishop did not work any less than before, and so as to test His servant's conformity with His will. The bishop told me it caused him no more distress than if it had happened to his neighbor and that sometimes he reflected that it would not grieve him if he lost sight in the other eye as well because this would allow him to live in a hermitage serving God without any other obligation. And at times he used to tell me that before becoming a bishop he had always felt called to be a hermit, and he had almost decided to give up everything and go off to become one.

10. I could not bear the thought of this since I thought he was

of great benefit to the Church of God, and so I wanted him to have the office he now holds, although the day in which he was appointed bishop I felt a very great disturbance, since he sent me word immediately, as though I saw him weighed down with a heavy burden. I could neither help myself nor find peace, and I went to the choir to recommend him to the Lord. His Majesty gave me peace at once, telling me that He would be very much served by him, and this is what is really happening. Despite the illness in his eye and many other very painful illnesses and his everyday work, he fasts four days a week, and does other penances. His table consists of little that is gratifying. When he makes his visitations, he always goes on foot. His servants find this hard to put up with and complained to me about it. They must either be virtuous or not stay in his house. He has little trust in allowing important business to be handled by his administrators, and even, I think, any business; but he handles everything himself. In the beginning, for two years, he underwent the most savage persecutions there from false testimony. I was amazed because in matters of justice he is a man of integrity and rectitude. Now these persecutions are diminishing, although his persecutors had gone to the royal court and wherever they thought they could do harm. Since the good he is doing throughout the whole diocese is becoming known, these persecutions have little effect. And he has borne all of this with such perfection that he has confounded his persecutors, doing good to those he knew were doing evil to him. However much he has to do, he always finds time for prayer.

11. It seems I am becoming absorbed in praising this holy man, but I have said little. Nothing has been lost since I have mentioned this in order that it be known who is responsible for the foundation of the Blessed Trinity of Soria and also for the consolation of those who are to come, for those who are now here know the story well. Although he did not provide the income, he gave us the church and inspired this lady with the idea of the foundation, and, as I have said,[17] she has a great christian spirit and is virtuous and penitential.[18]

12. Well, then, once we had taken possession of the church and prepared what was needed for the enclosure, it was neces-

sary for me to go the the monastery of St. Joseph in Avila, and thus I departed immediately in the midst of very great heat along a road that was unfit for wagons.[19] A prebendary from Palencia, named Ribera, accompanied me.[20] He was the one who had been a great help in the work involving the covered passageway and in everything. The reason for this was that Father Nicolás de Jesús María left immediately after drawing up the contract, for there was great need of him elsewhere. This Ribera had certain business to attend to in Soria, and so he came with us. From then on, God gave him so much willingness to do good for us that he can be recommended to His Majesty as a benefactor of the order.

13. I didn't want anyone else to come with my companion and me,[21] because this Ribera is so solicitous that he was enough for me, and the less noise there is on my journeys the better I feel. On this journey I paid well for the good trip I had in going to Soria, for, although the guide knew the way to Segovia, he did not know the wagon route. Thus, he led us into places in which we often had to get down from the wagon, and they almost had to carry it past some steep precipices. When we hired guides, they led us along the good roads and then, saying they had other things to do, abandoned us shortly before we came upon the bad roads. Prior to our arrival at an inn, about which we had not been sure, we had undergone much from the hot sun and from the many incidents in which the wagon turned over. I felt sorry for the prebendary who came with us. For now that we were told we were on the right road, we had to turn back and undo what we had done. But he was so rooted in virtue that it doesn't seem to me I ever saw him angry, which amazed me very much and made me praise our Lord, for when one is rooted in virtue, the occasions of sin are of little consequence. I praise the Lord for how He was pleased to bring us safely through that journey.

14. We arrived at St. Joseph's in Segovia on the vigil of St. Bartholomew.[22] Our nuns had been worried because of the delay, for since the roads were so bad, the delay was long. There they provided us with every comfort, for God never gives me a trial without repaying for it immediately, and I rested for eight

days or more. But this foundation was made with so little hardship that there is no reason to pay any attention to the hardship of this return journey, because it was nothing. I came back pleased since it seemed to me, and I hope in His mercy, that Soria is a place where God will be served because the foundation is there, as is already becoming evident. May He be blessed and praised from age to age, amen. Thanks be to God.

Chapter 31[1]

Begins to treat in this chapter of the foundation of the glorious St. Joseph of Saint Anne in the city of Burgos. The first Mass was said April 19, the octave day of Easter, in 1582.

FOR OVER SIX YEARS some members of the Society of Jesus, very conscientious, experienced, learned, and spiritual, were telling me that our Lord would be greatly served if a house of our sacred religious order were founded in Burgos. The reasons they gave for such a foundation made me begin to desire it. On account of the many trials within the order and in the other foundations, there had been no opportunity to attempt a foundation in Burgos.

2. In the year 1580, while I was in Valladolid, the Archbishop of Burgos passed through. Having been bishop in the Canary Islands, he was afterward appointed to the diocese of Burgos and at the time was going there.[2] I asked the bishop of Palencia, Don Alvaro de Mendoza, to ask him to give us permission for a foundation, and he said he would gladly ask him. Since he thinks our Lord is served in these houses, he is very pleased when one is founded. I have already spoken of how much Don Alvaro favors this order, for while bishop of Avila he accepted the first monastery of St. Joseph and always afterward has shown us much favor and considered the affairs of this order as his own, especially those about which I consult him.[3]

3. The archbishop did not want to enter the city of Valladolid but stayed in the monastery of St. Jerome.[4] There the bishop of Palencia had a great feast prepared for him and went to dine

with him and invest him with a cincture, or I don't know what the ceremony was, that would make him an archbishop.[5] It was there that Don Alvaro asked of him the permission for me to found a monastery in Burgos. The archbishop said that he would grant it gladly because even when he was in the Canary Islands he had desired and tried to get one of these monasteries, for he knew me personally and came from a place where one of our monasteries was located, and thus he knew how our Lord was served in them. As a result, the bishop of Palencia told me the foundation would not fail for want of a license, for the archbishop had been very pleased about the project, and that since the Council requires the permission of the bishop but not that it be given in writing, the license could be considered as granted.[6]

4. In speaking previously of the foundation of Palencia, I mentioned the great reluctance I had to making a foundation at that time because of the serious illness from which I was suffering. They had thought I would not live, and I had still not recovered.[7] Yet illness does not usually affect me so much when I see that something is for the service of God, and thus I don't know the reason for my feeling so much repugnance as I then did. For if the reason had been scarcity of means, I had fewer in other foundations. To me, after I had seen what was to take place, the cause seemed to be the devil. And what has happened each time that there has been some trial in one of these foundations is that our Lord has always helped me with locutions and with deeds since He knows how miserable I am. I have thought, at times, how in some foundations in which there have been no trials, His Majesty didn't warn me about anything. The former is what happened here, for since He knew what I would have to undergo He immediately began to encourage me. May He be praised for everything! Thus, in respect to this foundation, as was mentioned in regard to that of Palencia,[8] for both foundations were being discussed together, He asked, as though making a reprimand, what I was afraid of and when He had failed me: "I am the same; do not fail to make these two foundations." Since the courage these locutions have left in me has been mentioned, there is no reason for mentioning it again here. Immediately, all hesitation was taken from me. This makes it seem that

the cause was not illness or old age. Thus I began to make plans for both, as was mentioned.

5. It seemed better to make the foundation in Palencia first, since it was closer, the weather was harsh, Burgos was so cold, and so as to please the good bishop of Palencia; and this is what was done, as was mentioned.[9] Since, while in Palencia, the request came for a foundation in Soria, it seemed better — for in Palencia everything was finished — to go there first and then to Burgos.[10]

The bishop of Palencia thought that an account should be given to the archbishop of what was taking place, and I begged him to do so. After I went to Soria, the bishop sent a canon, named Juan Alonso, from Palencia to the archbishop for no other purpose than that. And the archbishop wrote to me with much love of how he desired my coming, discussed the matter with the canon, and wrote to the bishop of Palencia submitting the matter to him, saying that what he did was because he knew the people of Burgos and knew that their consent was necessary in order to make the foundation.

6. In short, his conclusion was that I should go there and discuss the matter first with the city and that if the city would not give the permission he would give it to me because he was not going to let them tie his hands; and that he had witnessed the foundation of the monastery in Avila, which was the first, and remembered the great turmoil and opposition there[11] and that he wanted to prevent this from happening in Burgos; and that it was not suitable to found a monastery unless with an income or with the consent of the city; that it would not be expedient for me and that that was why he was mentioning this.

7. The bishop considered that the deed was as good as done, and rightly so because the archbishop said I should come, and thus he sent me word that I should go. But my impression was that the archbishop lacked enthusiasm. I wrote to him thanking him for the favor he granted me but telling him that it seemed to me it would be worse to make a foundation against the will of the city than without asking them permission for it and that this would put His Excellency into more conflict (it seems I guessed the little help I would get from him if there were some opposi-

tion), and that I would try to obtain the permission from the city even though I knew this would be difficult because of the contradictory opinions usually held in matters like this. And I wrote to the bishop of Palencia begging him that since summer was almost over and my illnesses were too many for me to be living in so cold a place we should let the idea rest for the time being. I did not express my doubts about the archbishop because the bishop was already displeased with him on account of the obstacles he was setting up after having shown so much willingness, and I did not want to cause some discord between them, because they were friends. Thus I went from Soria to Avila very unconcerned about going to Burgos so soon, and my going to the house of St. Joseph in Avila was very necessary for certain reasons.[12]

8. There lived in this city of Burgos a holy widow named Catalina de Tolosa, a native of Vizcaya. I could go on at length telling about her virtues, her penance as well as her prayer, her generous almsgiving and charity, her good intelligence and courage.[13] She had given two of her daughters as nuns to our monastery of the Conception in Valladolid, I believe four years ago, and two others to Palencia, for she had been waiting that this latter foundation be made, and she brought them before I left.

9. All four turned out as one would expect of daughters brought up by such a mother, for they seemed to be no less than angels. She gave them good dowries and a full supply of other things, for she is very generous. Everything she does, she does to perfection; and she can do it because she is rich. When she came to Palencia we were so certain of the permission of the archbishop of Burgos that it didn't seem there would be any reason to delay, and thus I asked her to look for a house to rent for me so that we could make the foundation and that she provide us with some grilles and turns and charge everything to me. The thought never passed through my mind that she would spend anything of her own but only lend to me. She desired the foundation so much that she was extremely sorry to see it being set aside for awhile. And thus I returned to Avila, as I have said,[14] and was very unconcerned about dealing with the foundation at

that time, but she was not so unconcerned. Thinking that all that was needed was permission from the city, she began to try to get it without telling me anything.

10. She had two neighbors, a mother and daughter, persons of high social status and very good servants of God who desired the foundation greatly. The mother, whose name was María Manrique, had a son who was a magistrate and whose name was Don Alonso de Santo Domingo Manrique. The daughter's name was Doña Catalina. Both mother and daughter discussed the matter with him so that he might seek permission from the city council. He spoke to Catalina de Tolosa asking what he should say about financial backing, for they wouldn't give the permission if there were none. She said, and this she did, that she would take on herself the obligation of giving us a house, if we had none, and also food. With this promise he presented a petition signed in his name. Don Alonso presented it with such skill that he obtained the permission from all the magistrates and from the archbishop, and he brought her the license in writing. As soon as she had begun dealing with the matter, she wrote to me that she was negotiating about the foundation. I thought she was joking because I know how reluctant people are to accept a monastery founded in poverty, and since I did not know, nor did it enter my mind, that she had obligated herself to provide for it, I thought that much more was needed.

11. Nevertheless, one day within the octave of St. Martin while I was recommending the foundation to our Lord, I thought that it could be made if the license were obtained. I couldn't bear the thought of going to a place as cold as Burgos with so many illnesses which would be aggravated by the cold. It would have been rash to make such a long journey just after finishing such a rough one, as I have said,[15] in coming from Soria; nor would Father Provincial allow me to do so. I was reflecting that the prioress of Palencia could easily go,[16] for since everything was in order, there was now nothing to do. While I was thinking about this and very determined not to go, the Lord spoke to me in the following words in which I saw that the license was already given: "Don't pay attention to the cold weather for I am the true warmth. The devil uses all his strength to hinder that

foundation; use yours with my help so that it may be realized and do not fail to go in person, for great good will be done."[17]

12. With these words I changed my mind again, for although my human nature sometimes finds these trials distasteful, my determination to suffer for this great God does not lessen. Thus I told Him not to pay any attention to my feelings of weakness when He orders me to do what would please Him, for with His help I would not fail to do it. There was cold weather and snow at the time. That which daunted me most was my lack of health, for when I have my health everything seems easy to me. This lack of health was what very often tired me out on this foundation. The cold was not bad, at least from what I felt, for in truth it seems I felt as much when I was in Toledo. The Lord had well fulfilled His words about this cold.

13. Within a few days they brought me the license, along with letters, from Catalina de Tolosa and her friend Doña Catalina,[18] urging me to hurry, for they feared lest some mishap might occur. At that time the order of the Victorines[19] came there to make a foundation; and the calced Carmelite friars were there for a long time trying to make a foundation; afterward, the Basilians came. That so many of us had come together at the same time was a great obstacle and something to keep in mind, but also something to praise our Lord for because of the great charity of this city. For the city gave them the licenses very willingly even though it was not enjoying its usual prosperity. I have always heard the charity of this city praised, but I had never thought it was as great as it is. Some favored some orders; others favored others. But the archbishop considered all the troubles that could arise and opposed these other foundations thinking that they would be harmful to the orders founded in poverty which would then be unable to survive. Perhaps these very orders influenced him or the devil invented this so as to remove the great blessing that God brings about wherever there are many monasteries, for God has the power to sustain many as well as few.

14. For this reason, these holy women were urging me so much that I would have gone at once were it not for the business I had to attend to. I was considering how much more obligated I was to these women who were so diligent, and not to lose this opportunity through my own fault.

The locution I had heard implied that there would be much opposition. I could not understand from where it would come, for Catalina de Tolosa had already written me assuring us of the house in which she was living for our foundation and that the city was in accord and the archbishop also. I could not understand from whom this opposition to be stirred up by the devils would come, for I never doubted that the words I heard were from God.

15. In short, His Majesty gives more light to superiors, for when I wrote to Father Provincial about the foundation of which I had heard in the locution, he did not forbid me but asked if I had got permission from the archbishop in writing.[20] I wrote about this to Burgos. They answered that they had spoken with him of how they had asked permission from the city and that he was pleased. With this and all the things he had said concerning the foundation, it didn't seem there was any reason to doubt.

16. Father Provincial wanted to accompany us on this foundation. He did so partly because he was unoccupied at the time, since he had finished preaching the Advent series, and had to visit Soria which he had not seen since its founding and which was not much out of the way; and partly because he wanted to look after my health on the journey, for the weather was harsh, and I, old and sick; and they think my life is somewhat important. Certainly this was the providence of God, for the roads were so flooded from the heavy rains that he and his companions were very necessary to guide us along the way and help pull the wagons out of the mire. This was especially so on the trip from Palencia to Burgos, which was a very daring one to make at that time. True, our Lord told me that we could go without harm, that I should not fear, that He would be with us; although I did not tell this then to Father Provincial. But these words consoled me in the great hardships and dangers that we were going through. There was special danger in a river crossing near Burgos called Paso de los Pontones. The rain had been so heavy and had lasted so long that the water flooded the bridge. As a result, the bridge could not be seen nor could we see where to pass, but all was water, and everywhere it was very deep. In sum, it was a great imprudence to cross there, especially with wagons, for just by veering a little from the course all would have been lost. In fact, one of the wagons did get into a dangerous situation.[21]

17. We had hired a guide in an inn who knew that crossing; but, certainly, it was a very dangerous one. And, oh! The inns! There was no possibility of making a full day's journey in one day because of the bad roads. The wagons usually got stuck in the mud and other mules had to be used to help pull the wagons out. The Fathers who came with us had to undergo a great deal because it happened that the muleteers we hired were young and careless. Going with Father Provincial was a great relief because he took care of everything and has such a peaceful disposition that it seems no hardship weighs him down. Thus, what was difficult he made so easy that it seemed to be a small matter—although not the crossing of the bridge, which frightened us all very much, for if seeing us enter this world of water without a road or a barge made me fear after all the strength our Lord had given me, what must have been the fear of the nuns who accompanied me? We were eight nuns: two who will return with me, and five who are to remain in Burgos, four of them choir Sisters and one lay Sister.[22] I don't think I've yet mentioned Father Provincial's name. His name is Frày Jerónimo Gracián de la Madre de Dios.[23] I have spoken of him at other times. I was making the journey with a severe sore throat, which I caught on my way to Valladolid, along with a fever that had not left me.[24] Eating was very painful. This prevented me from enjoying the good things that happened during the journey. This illness has remained with me until now, the end of June, although considerably less severe, but still very painful. All the nuns were happy on the journey; once the danger was over, they found recreation in talking about it. For those who usually practice obedience as do these nuns, it is a great thing to suffer in obeying.

18. It was through this rough journey and heavy rain that we reached Burgos. Before entering the city, our Father wanted us to go first to visit the holy crucifix[25] and recommend our foundation to the Lord and wait for nightfall, for it was early when we arrived. It was a Friday, January 26, the day after the feast of the Conversion of St. Paul. It had been decided that the foundation be made immediately, and I had brought my letters from Canon Salinas for his relatives and friends strongly urging them to favor this foundation. (Canon Salinas, the one I men-

tioned in discussing the foundation in Palencia,[26] comes from this city and from an important family. He worked just as hard for this foundation as for that of Palencia.)

19. And favor it, they did. Immediately, the next day, the whole city council came in a body to see me, for they did not regret the permission they had given but rather were glad that I came and wanted me to tell them what they could do for me. If we had any fear, it was of the city. Thus we considered that now everything would go easily. Although no one knew of our coming, we thought of making it known to the archbishop so that the first Mass could be said at once as was done in almost all the other foundations. But because of the very heavy rain that was falling when we reached the house of the good Catalina de Tolosa, we did not do so.

20. That night we rested in the great comfort that this holy woman provided for us. But it proved troublesome for me. She had a large fire so as to dry us out. Although there was a chimney, the fire caused me so much harm that the next day I couldn't raise my head. So, through a window with a grate covered by a veil, I spoke with those who came to visit me. Since it was a day in which I had to attend to business matters, I was very embarrassed.

21. Early that morning, Father Provincial went to seek the blessing of His Excellency, for we thought there would be nothing more to do. He found that the archbishop was very disturbed and angry because I had come without his permission, acting as though he had not ordered me to come or had never discussed anything about the foundation. Thus he spoke to Father Provincial extremely angry at me. When finally he conceded that he had ordered me to come, he said that he meant I should come alone to discuss the matter—but that I came with so many nuns! God deliver us from the distress it caused him! There was little use telling him that once we had the permission of the city, as he had asked of us, nothing else was left to be done than simply make the foundation and that the bishop of Palencia had told me (for I had asked him if it would be good that I come without letting the archbishop know) that there was no reason for asking the permission because the archbishop had

already said how much he desired the foundation. This is the way the things happened, and they did happen in this way because God wanted the house to be founded. The archbishop himself acknowledged this afterward. If we had openly informed him, he would have told us not to come. He ended the visit with Father Provincial by telling him that if we did not have an income and our own house he would in no way grant the license; we could easily return to where we came from. And the roads were so good and the weather so beautiful!

22. O my Lord, how certain it is that anyone who renders You some service soon pays with a great trial! And what a precious reward a trial is for those who truly love you if we could at once understand its value! But we did not then want this reward because it was making everything impossible. The archbishop made still more demands: that what would be used for income and buying the house could not be taken from what the nuns brought with them. Since a thought like this had never even entered our mind—especially in these times—everybody thought that there was no chance whatever for the foundation. But not I, for I was always certain that everything was working for the best, that the devil was setting snares so as to hinder it, and that God would accomplish his designs. Father Provincial returned, nonetheless, very happy, for he was not at that time disturbed. God so provided, and He provided also that Father Provincial would not be annoyed with me for not having obtained the archbishop's permission in writing as he had told me to do.[27]

23. Some of the friends and relatives to whom Canon Salinas had written, as I mentioned,[28] had come to see me, and some of them had come right away. They thought the archbishop should be asked for permission to have Mass in the house so that we would not have to go out into the streets, which were very muddy; and for us to go out discalced was thought to be inappropriate. There was in the house, which had been used for ten years by members of the Society of Jesus when they first came to Burgos, a suitable room that had served as a chapel. With this we thought no obstacle would stand in the way of taking possession there until we had a house. Never were we able to get the archbishop to let us have Mass there, even though two canons went to beg

him for it. The most they got from him was that once we had an income, the foundation could be made there until we bought a house. And he said that in order to buy a house we would have to have guarantors who would pay and that we would have to leave the place where we were staying. These guarantors we found at once, for the friends of Canon Salinas offered to do this, and Catalina de Tolosa provided the income for the foundation.

24. It took more than three weeks to decide on the amount of money, how and from where it would come. During this time we could not hear Mass; only very early on feast days. And I, with a fever and very ill. But Catalina de Tolosa did everything so well, because she was so generous and showed so much good will, that she provided us all, in a room where we were secluded, with food for a month, as though she were the mother of each one. Father Provincial and his companions were given lodging in a house of one of his friends, named Doctor Manso,[29] who had been a classmate and was now the canon preacher at the cathedral. Our provincial was very impatient about being detained there so long, but he did not know how he could leave us.

25. Once there was an agreement about the guarantors and the income, the archbishop ordered that the document be given to his administrator, and said that the matter would be taken care of at once. The devil could not leave off tempting the administrator. We thought there would be nothing to cause a delay and that, after we spent almost a month in trying to meet the demands of the archbishop, the administrator would be pleased with what had been done. After examining the document very carefully, the administrator sent me a memorandum saying that the license would not be given until we had a house of our own and that the archbishop did not want the foundation to be made in the house in which we were staying because it was damp and there was too much noise in the street. And with regard to the guarantees made on the property, I don't know what complications and other things he brought up, as though we were just then beginning the whole matter. And he said that he would have no more to say about this, and that the house must satisfy the archbishop.

26. When Father Provincial saw this, he was very upset as

were all the nuns. In order to buy a site for a monastery much time is obviously required, and he was annoyed at seeing us go out for Mass. Even though the church was not far[30] and we heard the Mass in a chapel without anyone seeing us, this situation was a very great hardship for His Reverence and us. By that time, I think, he had made up his mind that we should go back. I could not bear the thought of this when I remembered that our Lord told me that as His instrument I should try to make the foundation, and I was so certain that it would be made that almost nothing caused me distress. My only distress was for Father Provincial. Since I didn't know how much his friends were going to help us, as I shall mention later, I was very sorry that he had come with us. While I was experiencing this affliction (and my companions were also very afflicted, but I didn't mind theirs as much as I did Father Provincial's), but not engaged in prayer itself, our Lord spoke these words to me: "Now Teresa, hold fast." With these words, I tried with more spirit to get Father Provincial to leave and let us remain (and His Majesty must have given him the same spirit), for Lent was approaching and he had to go to preach.[31]

27. He and his friends gave orders that some rooms in the hospital of the Conception be given to us, for the Blessed Sacrament was reserved there and Mass was said each day. This made the provincial somewhat satisfied. But there was no small struggle in getting this, for one of the rooms, which was a good one, had been rented by a widow of this city, and she did not want to let us use it even though she was not going to move there for another half year. It also upset her that one of the rooms they had given us on the top floor, which had only the bare tiles of the roof for a ceiling, had an entrance to her room. She was not satisfied with having the key to the lock on the outside but she also nailed up the entrance from the inside. Furthermore, the hospital confraternity was afraid that we were going to take over the hospital, which was something absurd, but God wanted us to merit more. They made Father Provincial and me promise before a notary that if they told us to leave we would have to do so at once. It was this promise that was the most difficult thing for me to do, for I feared the widow, who was rich and had relatives,

that she would make us leave on one of her whims. But Father Provincial, who was more circumspect, wanted us to do all they asked so that we could go there immediately.

28. They gave us no more than two rooms and a kitchen. But a great servant of God, named Hernando de Matanza, was in charge of the hospital and gave us two other rooms for a parlor. He showed us great charity, and he does so to all, for he does much for the poor. Francisco de Cuevas,[32] who is the postmaster of this city, also showed us great charity, for he was much involved with this hospital. He has always helped us when there was need.

29. I have mentioned the names of those who were our first benefactors because it is right that the nuns living now, and those who are to come after, remember them in their prayers. The founding benefactors should be remembered even more. Although at first it was not my intention to count Catalina de Tolosa among these latter, nor did it enter my mind, she has merited by her good life in the service of our Lord that He so ordain things that the title of founding benefactress cannot be denied her. Apart from her paying for the house, for we would have had no means of doing so, she bore the indescribable cost of all these rebuffs of the archbishop. Her deepest affliction was the thought that the foundation might not be made, and she never tired of doing good for us.

30. This hospital was very far from her house. She visited us almost every day with great charity and sent us all that we needed. Because of this, the people never stopped making critical comments to her, so that if it were not for her courage, these would have been enough to make her give up the whole thing. To see what she was suffering caused me great pain. Even though she hid it most of the time, at other times she could not conceal it, especially when these comments affected her conscience. She is so conscientious that, however great were the occasions of sin that some persons provided for her, I never heard her speak a word that was offensive to God. They told her that she was on her way to hell and asked how she could do what she was doing since she had children. Everything she did was with the advice of learned men. Even if she would have wanted to do otherwise,

I would not have consented for anything in the world to her doing something she should not do, even if it would have meant my giving up a thousand monasteries, to say nothing of just one. But since the business matters concerning the foundation were kept secret, I am not surprised at what was in the minds of the people. She answered with prudence, for she has a great deal of it, and suffered the remarks in such a way that it truly seemed God was teaching her and gave her the ability to please some and bear with others. And He gave her the courage to put up with everything. How much more courage for doing great things do the servants of God have than do those of high nobility if they are not His servants; although she, being of noble descent, is not without much nobility in her background.

31. Well to return to what I was dealing with,[33] once Father Provincial had us in a place where we could hear Mass and observe enclosure, he had the heart to go to Valladolid where he was to preach. Yet he was distressed at not seeing in the archbishop any hopeful sign that the license would be granted. Although I always insisted that it would be given, he could not believe this. And, certainly, there were many reasons for his not believing this which need not be mentioned here. If he had little hope, his friends had less, and they made him more discouraged.

I was more relieved to see him gone because, as I have said,[34] the greatest suffering I had was to see his. He left us the instructions to find a house that we could own, which was something very difficult because until then not even one house was found that was for sale. Our friends, especially those of Father Provincial's,[35] were given greater charge over us, and all agreed not to speak a word to the archbishop until we had a house. The archbishop always said that he desired this foundation more than anyone. And I believe it, because he is such a good Christian that he wouldn't speak anything but the truth; but in his deeds it didn't appear that he desired this since he demanded things that seemed impossible for us to comply with. This was the devil's scheme to prevent the foundation. But, O Lord, how obvious it is that You are powerful, for the very scheme the devil used to prevent it, You used to do something better. May You be blessed forever.

32. From the vigil of St. Matthias, when we began living in the hospital, until the vigil of St. Joseph[36] we were conferring about this and that house. There were so many obstacles that we could not buy any of those that were for sale. I was told of one house owned by a gentleman, which had been up for sale for many days, and even though so many religious were looking for a house, God was pleased that none of them found it suitable. Now, they are all surprised, and some really sorry about this. Two persons had spoken to me about the house. But there were so many who spoke badly of it, that I paid no attention to it, thinking it would be unsuitable.

33. One day I was speaking with Doctor Aguiar, who I said was a friend of our Father Provincial's.[37] He was looking very carefully for a house for us. He said that he had looked at some but that nothing appropriate could be found in the whole city and that it didn't seem possible to find any, as others were telling me. I then remembered the one I mentioned that we had disregarded. I thought, even though it's as bad as they say we can take care of our present need and later on sell it. I told Doctor Aguiar about it and asked him if he would do me the favor of looking at it.

34. To him, this didn't seem to be a bad plan. He had not seen the house, and even though it was a stormy and rough day, he wanted to go there at once. There was an occupant in it who had little interest in its being sold and did not want to show it to him, but its location and the little he could see pleased him greatly, and thus we decided to to try to buy it. The gentleman who owned it was not here but the power to sell it had been given to a priest, a servant of God whom His Majesty inspired with a desire to sell it to us and deal with us very honestly.[38]

35. It was arranged that I go to see it. It pleased me to such an extreme that if they had asked for twice as much as they did, it would have seemed cheap to me. I am not exaggerating, because two years before they were offering the owner that much, and he did not want to sell it. The next day a priest[39] and Doctor Aguiar went there, and when the latter learned of the amount of money that would be acceptable, he wanted to sign the contract at once. I had informed some of my friends, and they had

told me that if I gave this amount I was giving five hundred ducats too much. I told Doctor Aguiar, but he thought the price was cheap if I gave what was asked for. I was of the same mind. I myself would not have hesitated because it seemed to me like a gift, but since the money belonged to the order, I had some scruple. We met about this before Mass on the vigil of the feast of our glorious Father St. Joseph. I told them that after Mass we should meet again and come to a decision.

36. Doctor Aguiar is a very intelligent man and saw clearly that if our desire were made public we would either have to pay much more for the house or not buy it. Thus he was very careful and made the priest promise to come back there after Mass. We nuns went to recommend the matter to God, who said to me, "Do you hesitate over money?" letting me know that the house was suitable for us. The Sisters had prayed very much to St. Joseph that they might have a house by his feastday, and although there was no thought of having it so soon, he heard their prayers. Everyone urged me to conclude the contract. And thus it was done, for Doctor Aguiar found a notary at the door,⁴⁰ which seemed ordained by the Lord, and came with him and a witness and told me it was opportune to sign the contract. Having closed the door of the room so that nothing would be known (for this was Doctor Aguiar's fear), we concluded the sale, in accord with all the legal demands, on the vigil of the glorious St. Joseph,⁴¹ as I have said. It came about through the careful diligence and intelligence of this good friend.

37. No one thought the house would be sold for so little.⁴² Thus, as the news spread, the buyers began to appear and say that the priest who sold it gave it away practically and that the sale should be nullified because of the great fraud. The good priest suffered very much. They immediately informed the owners, a gentleman, as I said,⁴³ and his wife, both from the nobility. They were so happy that their house was being made into a monastery that they approved, although there was nothing else they could now do. Immediately, the next day, the deed was drawn up, and a third of the price was paid. Everything was done according to the requests of the priest. Although some things in the agreement were onerous to us, we accepted everything for his sake.

38. It may seem pointless that I spent so much time in telling about the buying of this house, but indeed those who considered the things in detail thought it was no less than a miracle, both in the price, which made the house seem like a gift, and in the fact that many from religious orders were so blinded that after looking at it did not want to buy it, as though it had never been in Burgos. Those who saw it were amazed and blamed the religious and called them fools. And a monastery of nuns (even two monasteries—one had been recently founded; the other had moved here from elsewhere after their former house had burned down) had looked at it a little while ago. So too did a wealthy person who is trying to found a monastery. They all let it go, and now they are very sorry.

39. Such was the outcry in the city that we saw clearly how right the good Doctor Aguiar was to keep the whole matter secret and in being so diligent about this. Indeed, we can say that, after God, it was he who gave us the house. Good intelligence is a great help in everything. And since he has so much, God moved him and brought this work to completion through him. For more than a month he helped and advised us on how to adapt the house well and with little cost. It seemed as though our Lord had kept it for Himself, for almost everything seemed to be already done. Indeed, as soon as I saw it and how everything was as though made to order for us and done so quickly, it seemed like a dream. By bringing us to such a paradise, our Lord repaid us generously for what we had suffered. Because of the garden, the view, and the water, the property is nothing else but that. May He be blessed forever, amen.

40. The archbishop learned of it immediately and rejoiced in our success, thinking that his obstinacy had been the reason, and he was very right. I wrote to him that I was happy he was pleased and that I would hurry to adapt the house so that he could give us his final permission. Once I told him this, I made haste to move in because I was told that they wanted to keep us where we were until the deed or I don't know what was signed. Thus we moved into one room even though an occupant was still living in the house,[44] for there was also some trouble in getting rid of him. They told me that the archbishop was very angry

about our moving in. I tried to appease him as much as I could, for, because he is good, even though he does get angry, he soon gets over it. He was also angry when he learned that we had the grates and the turn, for he thought that I wanted to go ahead at all costs. I wrote to him that this was not the case, but that in a house for persons living a life of recollection these are customary, that I hadn't even dared to put up a cross so as not to appear to be going ahead before having permission, and this was true. Notwithstanding all the good will I showed, there was no way of getting him to grant the license.

41. He came to see the house and was very pleased with it and showed us much kindness but did not give us the permission, although he offered more hope. There were still I don't know what contracts to be made with Catalina de Tolosa. Everyone was very afraid that he would not give it. But Doctor Manso, whom I mentioned,[45] as the other friend of Father Provincial's, was too good a friend of the archbishop's to be waiting for the proper time before reminding him and urging him. It was very distressing to Doctor Manso to see us going about as we were. For even though there was a chapel in this house, which was never used except for saying Mass for the owners, the archbishop never allowed Mass to be said for us in the house. On feastdays and Sundays we had to go out to a church in order to hear Mass.[46] Fortunately it was nearby, although between the time we moved and the time the foundation was made, a month more or less passed by. All the learned men said there was sufficient reason for allowing Mass in the chapel. The archbishop who is a very learned man understood this too. So it seems there is no other explanation than that our Lord wanted us to suffer. Although I bore it better, there was a nun who in seeing herself out on the street trembled from the distress she felt.

42. In drawing up the contracts there was no little trouble, because one minute they were satisfied with the guarantors, the next minute they wanted the money; and they made many other vexing demands. In this, the archbishop was not so much to blame but one administrator who was very hostile to us. If in God's providence it had not been necessary for this administrator to go on a trip and another take his place, it seems we would

never have obtained the license. Oh, what **Catalina de Tolosa** had to suffer in all this is impossible to say! She bore everything with a patience that amazed me, and she did not tire of providing for us. She gave all the furnishings we needed to set up the house, such as beds and many other things, for she had a well supplied house. It seemed that we were lacking no necessity, even if she lacked it in her own house. Other founding benefactors of our monasteries have given much more in property and wealth, but for none of them was the cost as much as one-tenth of what she went through. And if she had had no children, she would have given all that she could. She desired so much to see the work completed that everything she did toward this end seemed to her little.

43. Seeing so much delay, I wrote to the bishop of Palencia begging him to write again to the archbishop. The bishop was disgusted with him, for everything the archbishop did to us the bishop took as done to him. And what amazed us was that the archbishop never thought he was offensive to us in anything. I begged the bishop to write again to the archbishop saying that since we had the house and had done what he had wanted that he should bring the matter to a close. The bishop sent me an open letter for the archbishop written in such a way that if I had given it to him we would have ruined everything. Thus Doctor Manso, my confessor and adviser, did not want me to give it to him. Although it was very courteous, it spoke some truths that, given the temperament of the archbishop, were enough to annoy him, for he was already annoyed by some of the messages the bishop had sent to him, and they were close friends. The bishop used to tell me that just as through the death of our Lord enemies had become friends so through me friends had become enemies. I told him that from this he could see what I was. I had taken special care, in my opinion, so that they would not become angry with each other.

44. I begged the bishop again, with the best reasons I could think of, that he write another very friendly letter to the archbishop and remind him of the service the monastery would render to God. He did what I asked him, which was no trifle. But since he saw that writing the letter was for the service of God

and a favor to me, which he has always been ready to grant, he finally forced himself. He wrote to me afterward that of all the things he had done for the order nothing compared with his having had to write this letter. In short, this letter was so effective, together with the diligence of Doctor Manso, that the archbishop gave us the license.[47] He sent it with the good Hernando de Matanza, who arrived with no little joy. On this day the Sisters had been more distressed than ever, and the good Catalina de Tolosa so much so that she could not be consoled. It seems that the Lord at the time when He was about to give us the joy wanted to afflict us more. Even I, who had not been lacking in confidence, was lacking in it the night before. May His name be blessed without end and praised forever and ever, amen.

45. The archbishop gave Doctor Manso permission to say the first Mass the next day and to reserve the Blessed Sacrament. And the Father Prior of San Pablo, who belongs to the Dominican order (to which our order owes so much as well as to the Society of Jesus), said the high Mass with much solemnity provided by musicians who came unrequested with their wind instruments.

All our friends were very pleased and so too was almost the whole city, for they had felt very sorry to see us in such a situation. They were so critical of what the archbishop was doing that I sometimes felt more sorry at what I heard people were saying about him than I was about what we ourselves were going through. The joy of the good Catalina de Tolosa and of the Sisters was so great that it inspired me with devotion and I said to God: "Lord, what do these your servants seek other than to serve you and see themselves enclosed for You in a place they will never leave?"

46. No one but those who experience it will believe the joy that is felt in these foundations once we are enclosed where no secular person can enter, for however much we love them it is not enough to take away this great consolation in finding ourselves alone. It seems to me comparable to taking many fish from the river with a net; they cannot live until they are in the water again. So it is with souls accustomed to living in the running streams of their Spouse. When taken out of them and caught up in the net of worldly things, they do not truly live un-

til they find themselves back in those waters. This I always observe in each of these Sisters; this I know from my own experience. Nuns who see in themselves the desire to go out among seculars and converse with them a great deal should fear that they have not discovered the living water of which the Lord spoke to the Samaritan woman[48] and that their Spouse has hid it from them, and rightly so since they are not satisfied in being with Him. I am afraid that this latter stems from two causes: either they did not embrace the religious state for Him alone; or, after having embraced it, they do not recognize the great favor God has granted them in choosing them for Himself and freeing them from being subject to a man who is often the death of them and who could also be, God forbid, the death of their souls.

47. Oh, my Spouse, true God and true man! Should this favor be taken so lightly? Let us praise Him, my Sisters, because He has granted it to us and let us not tire of praising so great a King and Lord, who has prepared for us a kingdom without end in exchange for some little troubles which will end tomorrow and which come wrapped in a thousand joys. May He be blessed forever, amen, amen.

48. A few days after the house was founded, it seemed to Father Provincial[49] and me that in the endowment Catalina de Tolosa had provided for this house there were certain difficulties that could have given rise to a lawsuit and cause her some worry. And we wanted more to trust in God than to be the occasion for giving her any suffering. For this and some other reasons, with the permission of Father Provincial, we nullified in the presence of a notary the contracts concerning the money she had given us and returned all the documents. This was done in great secrecy so that the archbishop wouldn't know of it, for he would have been hurt. But doing this also hurt the house. When it is known that a monastery is founded in poverty, there is nothing to fear because everyone helps. But when people think it has an income, to be without one is dangerous and the monastery will be left temporarily without means. Catalina de Tolosa has provided for a remedy that will become possible after her death. She has arranged that her two daughters, who were to

make profession in our monastery of Palencia that year, would transfer to this house their inheritance that would have been promised to Palencia at their profession. And to another daughter, who desired to receive the habit here, she has left the family estate which amounts to as much as the income she wanted to provide.[50] The only drawback is that these goods cannot be used at once, but I have always held that we will not be in want. The Lord who provides that alms be given to our other monasteries founded in poverty will awaken some to give them here, or will provide the means by which nuns can support themselves. Since no monastery had been founded under such conditions, I sometimes begged the Lord that since He had desired that this foundation be made He ordain that it be helped and have what is necessary, and I had no desire to leave here until I saw whether someone wanting to be a nun would enter.

49. While I was thinking about this one day after Communion, the Lord said to me: "Why do you doubt? Everything is now finished; you are free to go." He thereby let me know that they would not lack what was necessary. These words so impressed me that I had no more worry than I would have if I had left the nuns with a very good income. I immediately began to plan my departure, for it seemed to me I was no longer doing anything else here than enjoy myself in this house, for it suited me perfectly, and I could have been a greater help, although with much more hardship, in other monasteries.

The archbishop and the bishop of Palencia remained good friends. Soon the archbishop began to show us much kindness and gave the habit to Catalina de Tolosa's daughter[51] and to another nun who within a short time entered here. Up to the present, there are some persons who have been looking after us. Nor will our Lord allow his brides to suffer if they serve Him as they are obliged. May His Majesty give them the grace for this through His great mercy and goodness.

[*Epilogue*]

JHS

I T HAS OCCURRED TO ME to record here how the nuns of the first monastery that was founded, St. Joseph's in Avila, about which I wrote in another work and not in this book,[1] transferred their obedience to the order after having first professed it to the bishop.

2. When the monastery was founded, Don Alvaro de Mendoza was bishop, the one who is now bishop of Palencia. All the time that he was in Avila he was extremely helpful to the nuns. And with regard to our giving obedience to the bishop, I heard from our Lord that it would be expedient to give it to him.[2] This was borne out afterward, for in all the disagreements with the order and in many other things that happened we clearly found great support in him. Never did he allow any priest to make a visitation nor did he do anything more in that monastery than what I asked him. This arrangement lasted seventeen years, a little more or less, for I don't remember,[3] nor did I ever intend that this jurisdiction be changed.

3. When those years were over, the bishop of Avila was transferred to the diocese of Palencia.[4] At that time I was in the monastery of Toledo, and our Lord told me that it was fitting for the nuns of St. Joseph's to give their obedience to the order, that I should try to bring this about because in not doing this there would soon be a relaxation of observance in that house. Since I had heard in a former locution that it was good to give it to the bishop, it seemed the Lord was contradicting Himself.[5] I didn't know what to do. I told my confessor who is now bishop of Osma and who is a very learned man.[6] He told me there was no contra-

diction, that formerly the one way was necessary and that now another was and that he thought it would be better if the monastery in Avila were united with these others than alone; and that this was true has been clearly seen in many ways.

4. He made me go to Avila to discuss the matter. I found the bishop of a completely different opinion, for in no way would he agree to this. But since I told him some of the reasons for the harm that could come to the nuns, and he loved them very much and has very good intelligence, and God helped, he thought of some other weightier reasons than the ones I had given him and decided to allow the transfer of jurisdiction. Even though some priests told him that this was not a good thing to do, he did not change his mind.

5. It was necessary to submit the matter to the vote of the nuns. For some of them the change was a very painful one to make. But since they respected me, they accepted my reasons, especially when they realized that now that the bishop, to whom the order owed so much and whom I loved, was gone, they could no longer have me with them. This made a strong impression on them, and thus this important matter was concluded. All the friars and nuns have seen clearly how lost that house would have been in doing the contrary. Blessed be the Lord who so carefully looks after the affairs of His servants! May He be blessed forever, amen.

CONSTITUTIONS

INTRODUCTION

THE CONTRIBUTION of St. Teresa to spiritual literature has received universal recognition. As a mother foundress, she also stands out for her practicality and talent in having maintained the highest spiritual life amid everyday conflicts, conflicts that arose particularly from the material and personal needs of the nuns in her new communities. But one of her accomplishments revealing another facet of her talents and that might escape notice is her work as legislator for her new Carmels.

When Teresa petitioned Rome for the faculty to found the monastery of St. Joseph, she had only a general plan in mind. In the reply from Rome, February 7, 1562, the brief granted her the power to make licit and respectable statutes and ordinances in conformity with canon law. It also granted her the faculty to change these for the better or also abrogate them, entirely or in part, according to the condition of the times and to make other new ones.[1] Teresa needed these powers because the constitutions in use at her monastery of the Incarnation would not have served for the kind of life she envisioned in which the primitive rule of Carmel was to be observed. Neither did there exist within the order any other constitutions drafted for monasteries of nuns observing the primitive rule.

If one looks for an indication of the first steps taken toward the drawing up of constitutions, one may find them in Teresa's account of her first foundation presented in her *Life*. She writes: "Now although there is some austerity because meat is never eaten without necessity and there is an eight-month fast and other things, as are seen in the first rule, this is still in many respects considered small by the Sisters; and they have other observances which seemed to us necessary in order to observe the rule with greater perfection."[2] These words were written after some three years of experience with the new life at St. Joseph's. The other observances referred to, and introduced so as to keep the rule with greater perfection, formed no doubt the nucleus of the constitutions. The first years, then, must have served partly as experimental ones. María de San José supports such a surmise when she points out that Teresa preferred first to experiment before presenting anything to visitators and superiors for approval as law.[3] Another of the early nuns, María de San Jerónimo, testified that if any religious introduced some practices of penance or mortification, Teresa wanted to be the first one to try them out.[4] Finally, by the time the Mother Foundress wrote her first draft of the *Way of Perfection*, in 1566, the year after she had completed her *Life*, she was able to refer explicitly to the constitutions,[5] which leads to the conclusion that by that time at least some constitutions existed in written form.

When, in 1567, the prior general Rubeo visited Avila, Teresa was able to show him the text of her constitutions and seek his approbation of them. The provincial of the Carmelites in Castile, Angel de Salazar, has left us explicit testimony that Rubeo did see and approve Teresa's constitutions.[6] This approval came as the culmination, in a way, of those most quiet and restful years of Teresa's life,[7] the first five years at St. Joseph's.

The text shown to Rubeo unfortunately has not come down to us. The Teresian constitutions that have been preserved legislate not merely for the single monastery in Avila but for a number of Carmels. Some idea, however, of the first text can be got from the constitutions for the friars that were followed in Duruelo. These constitutions were obviously copied, with certain adaptations, from Teresa's first constitutions. This can be deduced from the brevity of the text and from the occasional lapses in which the redactor failed to change the gender from feminine to masculine. These constitutions for the friars were sent to the prior general for his approval and consequently have been preserved in the general archives of the Carmelites of the Observance in Rome. The text is simple and sparse, indicating that she who when speaking of prayer was often extravagant with words was frugal with them when writing laws.

As for Teresa's constitutions for her nuns, the oldest text that is preserved is an expansion of the first constitutions and speaks of Carmels in the plural and of lay Sisters, who were not envisioned at the beginning. It represents a stage in an evolving process. The autograph of this text, which had been conserved in the general archives of the Spanish congregation of discalced Carmelites in Madrid, was lost in the last century at the time of the exclaustration. It bore the title: *Constitutions for the Sisters of the Order of Our Lady of Mount Carmel of the First Rule Without Relaxation, Given by the Most Reverend General of the said Order Fray Juan Bautista Rubeo.* Fortunately a copy of this lost autograph had been made for the general archives of the Portuguese congregation.

Another copy of these early constitutions is preserved in the monastery of nuns of the primitive rule of Carmel founded by María de Jesús in Alcalá.[8] A third copy comes from one of the first historians of the order, Jerónimo de San José. From various ancient copies of these constitutions, Padre Jerónimo constructed his own text which he published in his *Historia del Carmen Descalzo* in 1635.

Editors of Teresa's works have made different choices with respect to these copies. Vicente de la Fuente chose the copy that is in Alcalá for his edition of the works of St. Teresa published in 1861.[9] Padre Silverio chose for his critical edition of 1919 the copy that was made from the autograph for the Portuguese Carmelites. Padre Efrén opted for the copy published by Padre Jerónimo.[10] The variant readings in these texts may represent different moments in the evolving process as well as, in the case of Jerónimo, some meddling.

When compared with what one can estimate concerning the first text for St. Joseph's alone, this later text shows an increase in length of little over a half. But the increase is due mainly to the long penal code that was added to the text and of which Teresa was certainly not the author. This code, with its boring, interminable categories of faults and penalties, makes up one half of the text of these later constitutions. A comparison of this penal code with the one contained in the constitutions of the Incarnation published by Silverio leaves no doubt that the code in

Teresa's constitutions was taken from some version of already existing Carmelite constitutions. But whether, in fact, the constitutions published by Silverio are those of the Incarnation at Avila or of some other Carmelite monastery of nuns with the same name is uncertain. The entire section, then, on faults and penalties (nos. 43–56) represents neither Teresa's mentality nor her style; she simply accepted it without attempting to write a penal code of her own. We have placed this code in the notes so as not to detract in any way from what flows directly from the Foundress's pen.

The Teresian constitutions, then, contain two major sections: the first deals with the daily schedule and way of life of the new family; the second, with the penal discipline required in religious codes of the time. These two sections are followed by a brief epilogue after which come two more prescriptions which are out of place and were probably drafted at a later date.

The first part, written by Teresa, is simple and balanced. With no intention of inserting her spiritual message into her laws, she merely drew up some general guidelines for the community life. The spiritual commentary on her constitutions must be sought principally in the *Way of Perfection* if one is to avoid the temptation to judge by the letter alone.

What stands out in these guidelines for the Teresian life is balance. We find an interweaving of eremitism and cenobitism, of work and contemplation, of liturgical and extra-liturgical prayer. Even the apostolic life is integrated into the contemplative life, in conversations (no. 18), in prayers, and penances (no. 58). The practice of asceticism and enclosure are tempered by a family spirit and by gardens and pleasant views. In receiving and educating novices stress must be placed on prayer and virtues, only persons of prayer should be admitted to the postulancy.

In tracing out her program of contemplative life, Teresa without doubt took into consideration the primitive Carmelite rule as well as the Carmelite constitutions and ordinal then in force, but she did so independently, refusing to tone down the new spirit that issued from her own extraordinary life of prayer. In fact she reacts against a whole gamut of practices observed in her former monastery. Even with regard to prescriptions of the Carmelite rule, she allows herself a certain freedom, as with the law seemingly as important as that of the great silence, which she reforms so as to make room for evening recreation. "Almost everything," she qualifies, "is set up in conformity with our rule" (no. 31), thereby intimating her own conscious role as legislator.

The legislator herself was the prioress, and thus understandably "the Mother Prioress should be the first on the list for sweeping" (no. 22). As for her own method of governing and the spirit in which she wrote her laws: "these things should be done with a mother's love" (no. 34).

As Teresa went on founding her new Carmels, she met with situations in which she had to make exceptions to rules. Because the town of Malagón, for example, was too small for the nuns to live on alms, the monastery had to be endowed with a fixed income rather than founded in poverty as required in Teresa's own constitutions. Nor was fish available in that area, a situation calling for dispensation from the abstinence prescribed by the primitive rule. And in Seville, the unbearable heat demanded some changes in the kind of material prescribed for clothing.

As Carmels multiplied, copies of the constitutions multiplied, and as these multiplied fidelity to the original text diminished. There were prioresses who found no problem at all in adding and omitting whatever seemed suitable to them.[11] There were also new historical circumstances offering the occasion for additions to the legislation. The appointment in 1569 of apostolic visitators for the Carmelite order soon had repercussions in a series of decrees affecting Teresa's Carmels as well. Teresa refers to these as "the Acts."[12] Not all of these decrees are known. Nor did they always please Teresa, as she indicates in a letter to Gracián: "If it seems all right to you, remove the ruling of Padre Fernández where he says that they should not eat eggs or have bread at collation, for I was never able to keep him from imposing this rule. It is sufficient to fulfill the obligation set by the Church without imposing another on top of it, for the nuns tend to get scrupulous, and this does them harm; some don't think they have a need when they in fact do."[13]

When in September of 1576 Padre Juan Roca was named

monitor for the friars at their chapter in Almodóvar, which meant that he had the task of promoting the spiritual life in each house, Teresa learned that he was monitoring the houses of her nuns as well. She reacted strongly in a letter to Gracián: "This is what my nuns fear: that overbearing superiors will come along who will crush them. . . . It is a strange thing that visitators do not think they have accomplished their task unless they make regulations." And as for Padre Roca's regulations: "Just reading them tired me out; what would I do if I had to follow them?"[14]

On the whole, it must be admitted, the apostolic visitators respected Teresa's views and consulted with her, issuing no new orders without her prior knowledge. This was true as well with respect to regulations made by Gracián.

In addition to the "Acts" of the visitators, one had to consider what came from the Holy See. The Church was in a state of reform after the Council of Trent, and the religious orders had to incorporate the new laws that had been drawn up, one example being the new prescriptions regarding cloister.

All this additonal legislation, arising from different sources, at times dealing with a point already provided for, resulted in some obscurity and ambiguity when the time came for a practical application. No one is surprised, then, if Teresa desired a clearer presentation of all this legislation. Her chance came with the brief *Pia consideratione,* June 22, 1580, which gave the provincial to be elected in a coming chapter, at which the discalced Carmelites would separate into their own province, the faculty to legislate for the discalced nuns. The letters that Teresa writes to Gracián before this chapter, especially those of February 21 and 27, 1581, clearly show her concern about the new constitutions and the coming chapter. Without any methodical order, she makes a number of recommendations, apparently as they enter her mind. What she wanted was one body of law incorporating the Acts of the apostolic visitators into her constitutions, and in addition some other changes she felt necessary.

With Gracián's approval, the Mother Foundress also sought suggestions from her Carmels concerning changes to be made in the constitutions. She intended to send these on to Gracián, but not without first reviewing and revising them herself. As a matter of fact, the only suggestions that seem to have pleased her were those sent by Isabel de Santo Domingo, the prioress in Segovia.[15] As for the memorandum sent by Avila, she was shocked to see what a state the house had got itself into.[16]

The constitutions that resulted and were issued by the chapter are nowadays referred to as the Constitutions of Alcalá, after the city where the chapter was held. They were completed in March of 1581. In the prologue of these new constitutions, Gracián wrote: "Because the laws and the constitutions you have had until now are so holy and religious, drawn up and ordained by such great men having so much authority, those we now give are no different but the same you have had until now, with some few additions, omissions, or changes which seemed suitable for the good of the religious life."[17]

In a letter about these constitutions Gracián lists the founts of this new body of laws: the constitutions of Rubeo and the acts of the visitators, Pedro Fernández and Gracián himself. Rubeo's constitutions were in fact Teresa's approved by Rubeo, but no mention is made of Teresa as the author of the main source of these constitutions of Alcalá. Why? Seemingly it was not feasible in the mind of these men to include a woman among the legislators; with Rubeo's name alone the laws would carry more weight.

The first constitutions drafted for St. Joseph's in Avila would have amounted to about thirteen pages, the later ones came to twenty-nine pages, and those of Alcalá filled forty-nine pages. From a literary point of view, the constitutions of Alcalá, put together from different sources, although Teresa's constitutions were the main fount, are a hybrid.[18] Since they were not drafted by Teresa, editors usually do not include them among her complete works. If they are omitted here, it is with the understanding that the text of the earlier constitutions does not represent Teresa's final word. As for how well the constitutions of Alcalá represent the mind and wishes of Teresa, scholars are not in agreement.[19]

What made the Mother Foundress happy to receive the Alcalá constitutions was that she finally had an established and fully approved text with the signatures she most desired: the pope's representative to the chapter, the apostolic commissary, Juan de las Cuevas, O.P.; the first provincial of the Teresian Carmel, Jerónimo Gracián; his vicar Nicolás Doria; and the provincial counsellors, Antonio de Jesús, St. John of the Cross, Gabriel de la Asunción, and Ambrosio Mariano de San Benito. Teresa's only urgings now were that these constitutions be printed promptly so that there could be no further problem with interpolations. Her pleas were promptly heeded, for the first printed edition, in pocket size, appeared that same year, 1581, in Salamanca.

The constitutions of Alcalá remained in force for no more than a decade. When the first supply of copies was exhausted because of the increasing number of Carmels, Ana de Jesús took the initiative in 1588 to have them reprinted in Madrid. Two years later they were approved by Sixtus V and published in Rome in Latin with some slight retouches. But in 1592, Nicolás Doria, as vicar general of the Spanish congregation of discalced Carmelites, denied that these constitutions of Alcalá were Teresa's constitutions and changed them substantially, receiving approval of his own version from Gregory XIV. The constitutions of Alcalá were never again used as law in the order, though they did continue to remain in use in some autonomous sectors of Carmel. Ana de Jesús had brought them to France, and they continued to be published in French translations.

Not until the second half of the last century were Teresa's earlier constitutions given their place in the editions of her complete works. Don Vicente de la Fuente discovered the copy of these earlier constitutions that was conserved in the Carmel founded by María de Jesús, and he published this text in his edition of Teresa's writings.[20]

Our translation is of this earlier text of Teresa's constitutions but follows the copy chosen by Padre Silverio, that is, the one made for the Portuguese congregation from the autograph now missing. This text is used as well as by both Tomás Alvarez and Fortunato Antolín in their critical editions.

K. K.

THE CONSTITUTIONS

On the Order to Be Observed in Spiritual Matters

1. Matins are to be said after nine, not before, but not so long after nine that the nuns would be unable, when finished, to remain for a quarter of an hour examining their consciences as to how they have spent the day. The bell should be rung for this examen, and the one designated by the Mother prioress should read a short passage from some book in the vernacular on the mystery that will serve as the subject for reflection the following day. The time spent in these exercises should be so arranged that at eleven o'clock the bell may be rung to signal the hour for retirement and sleep. The nuns should spend this time of examen and prayer together in the choir. Once the Office has begun, no Sister should leave the choir without permission.

2. In the summer they should arise at five and remain in prayer until six. In the winter[1] they should rise at six and remain in prayer until seven. Immediately after prayer, they will say the Hours up to None, unless the day is a solemn feast or the feast of a saint to which the nuns have a special devotion. They will in that case postpone None so as to sing it before the Mass. On Sundays and feast days, Mass, Vespers, and Matins are to be sung. On the first days after Easter[2] and on other solemn days they may sing Lauds, especially on the feast of the glorious St. Joseph.

3. The chant should never be sung with musical notation[3] but should be done in a monotone and with uniform voices. Ordinarily, everything should be recited, and also the Mass, for the Lord will be served if some time remains so that the Sisters may earn their livelihood.

4. The Sisters should try not to miss choir for any light reason. When the Hours are finished, they should go about their duties. Mass will be said at eight o'clock in the summer and at nine in the winter. Those who receive Communion should remain a short while in choir.

The Days for Receiving the Lord

5. Communion will be received every Sunday, on feast days, and on days honoring our Lord, our Lady, our Father St. Albert, and St. Joseph, and on other days that the confessor designates in accordance with the devotion and spirit of the Sisters and with the permission of the Mother prioress. Communion will also be received on the titular feast of the house.

6. Shortly before meals, the bell will be rung for the examen of conscience as to what has been done up to that time. Each one should propose to correct the greatest fault she sees in herself and recite an Our Father that God might give her the grace to do so. Each Sister should kneel down wherever she is and make her examen briefly. At two o'clock Vespers should be said, except during Lent when it will be said at eleven.[4] During the times when Vespers is said at two, it should be followed by an hour of reading[5] (during Lent the hour of reading takes place at two o'clock); this means that at two o'clock the bell is rung for Vespers. On the vigil of feast days, this hour of reading will take place after Compline.

7. In summer, Compline is to be said at six o'clock; in the winter, at five. In both winter and summer the bell is rung for silence at eight o'clock, and the silence is kept until after Prime of the following day. This silence should be observed with great care. During the other times, no Sister may speak with another without permission, except about necessary matters if she has duties to fulfill.[6] The Mother prioress may give permission should one Sister desire to speak with another so as to quicken the love each has for her Spouse or to be consoled in a time of some need or temptation. This rule of silence should not be understood to refer to a question and answer or to a few words, for such things can be spoken without permission. An hour before they say Matins, let the bell be rung for prayer. This hour of prayer may be spent in reading if they are drawn in spirit to spend the hour after Vespers in prayer. They may decide in accordance with what helps them most toward recollection.

8. The prioress should see to it that good books are available, especially *The Life of Christ* by the Carthusian, the *Flos Sanctorum, The Imitation of Christ, The Oratory of Religious,* and those books written by Fray Luis de Granada and by Father Fray Pedro de Alcantara.[7] This sustenance for the soul is in some way as necessary as is food for the body. All of that time not taken up with community life and duties should be spent by each Sister in the cell or hermitage designated by the prioress; in sum, in a place where she can be recollected and, on those days that are not feast days, occupied in doing some work. By withdrawing into solitude in this way, we fulfill what the rule commands: that each one should be alone.[8] No Sister, under pain of a grave fault, may enter the cell of another without the prioress's permission. Let there never be a common workroom.[9]

On Temporal Matters

9. Let them live always on alms and without any income,[10] but insofar as possible let there be no begging. Great must be the need that makes them resort to begging. Rather, they should help themselves with the work of their hands, as St. Paul did;[11] the Lord will provide what they need. Provided they want no more than this and are content to live simply, they will have what is necessary to sustain life. If they strive with all their might to please the Lord, His Majesty will keep them from want. Their earnings must not come from work requiring careful attention to fine details but from spinning and sewing or other unrefined labor that does not so occupy the mind as to keep it from the Lord. Nor should they do work with gold or silver. Neither should there be any haggling over what is offered for their work. They should graciously accept what is given. If they see that the amount offered is insufficient, they should not take on the work.

10. In no way should the Sisters have any particular possessions, nor should such permission be granted; nothing in the line of food or clothing; nor should they have any coffer or small chest, or box, or cupboard, unless someone have an office in the

community. But everything must be held in common. This is very important because through small things the devil can bring about a relaxation of the perfection in which poverty is observed. For this reason the prioress should be very careful. If she sees that a Sister is attached to something, be it a book, or a cell, or anything else, she should take it from her.

On Fasting

11. A fast is observed from the feast of the Exaltation of the Cross, which is in September, until Easter, with the exception of Sundays. Meat must never be eaten unless out of necessity as the rule prescribes.[12]

12. The habit should be made of coarse cloth or black, rough wool, and only as much wool as is necessary should be used. The sleeves should be narrow, no wider at the opening than at the shoulder. Circular, without pleats, and no larger in the back than in the front, the habit should extend in length to the feet. The scapular should be made of the same material and four fingers shorter in length than the habit. The choir mantle should be white, of the same coarse cloth, and equal in length to the scapular. They should use as little cloth for this as possible, attending always to the necessary rather than to the superfluous. Let them always wear the scapular over the toque. The toques should be made of fine tow and without pleats; the inner tunics of fine wool, and the sheets of the same. Let sandals made from hemp be worn and, for the sake of modesty, stockings of rough wool or of cloth made from rough tow. The pillowcases may be of fine tow or, when necessary, of linen.

13. Straw-filled sacks will be used for mattresses, for it has been shown that these can be tolerated even by persons with weak health. No hangings should be used except, in cases of necessity, hemp mattings or, to cover a doorway, a blanket or some rough, woolen cloth or something similar that is poor. Each nun should have her own bed. Let there be no carpeting or cushions, except in the church. These are all matters of proper

religious observance. They are mentioned here because with relaxation there comes sometimes a forgetfulness of what pertains to religious life and its obligations. Colored clothing or bedding must never be used, not even something as small as a ribbon. Sheepskins should never be worn. If someone is sick, she may wear an extra garment made of the same rough wool as the habit.

14. The Sisters must keep their hair cut so as not to have to waste time in combing it. Never should a mirror be used or any adornments; there should be complete self-forgetfulness.

On the Enclosure

15. No nun should be seen with her face unveiled[13] unless she is with her father, mother, brothers, or sisters, or has some reason which would make it seem as appropriate as in the cases mentioned. And her dealings should be with persons who are an edification and help for the life of prayer and who provide spiritual consolation rather than recreation. Another nun should always be present unless one is dealing with conscience matters. The prioress must keep the key to both the parlor and the main entrance. When the doctor, barber surgeon, confessor, or other necessary persons enter the enclosure, they should always be accompanied by two nuns. When some sick nun goes to confession, another nun must always be standing there at a distance so that she sees the confessor. She should not speak to him, unless a word or two, but only the sick nun may do so.

16. In houses that have a choir, within the enclosure, where the Blessed Sacrament is reserved, and have chaplains or help for taking care of the church, there should be no door leading into the church.[14] Where this help is not present, and the nuns cannot dispense from having a door, the prioress should keep the key. The door should be opened only when necessary and by two Sisters. When there is help for taking care of the church, the entrance should be closed up if there had been a door there.

17. The novices should be allowed visitors just as are the professed. For if they are in any way unhappy, this should make it

clear that they are expected to remain only if they are very willing to do so.[15] And they should be given the opportunity to say so if they do not want to remain.

18. The Sisters should pay no attention to the affairs of the world, nor should they speak about them. They may do so if the matter concerns something for which they can offer a remedy or help those with whom they are speaking, assist them in finding the truth, or console them in some trial. If no effort is being made to make the conversation a fruitful one, they should bring it to a quick conclusion, as was said. It is very important that those who visit us leave with some benefit, and not after having wasted time, and that we benefit too. The companion should watch carefully whether this rule is observed. She is obliged to inform the prioress if it is not. When she does not do this, she incurs the same penalty as the one who breaks the rule. The punishment is that after having been warned twice by her companion, a nun on the third occasion should be given nine days in the prison cell and, on the third day of the nine, a discipline in the refectory. For the above rule is very important to the religious life.

19. As much as they can, the Sisters should avoid a great deal of conversation with relatives. Aside from the fact that they will become preoccupied with their relatives' affairs, they will find it difficult to avoid talking to them about worldly things.

20. Let them be very careful in speaking with outsiders, even though these may be close relatives. If these persons are not the kind who find their satisfaction in speaking about the things of God, they should be seen seldom, and the visit kept short.

On Accepting Novices

21. Let the nuns consider carefully whether those about to be received are persons of prayer desiring full perfection and contempt for the world. These aspirants should be at least seventeen. And if they are not detached from the world, they will find the way we live here hard to bear. It is better to consider these

things beforehand than to have to turn these persons away afterward. Aspirants should be healthy, intelligent, and able to recite the Divine Office and assist in choir. Profession should not be allowed if during the year of novitiate the novice does not show that she has the temperament and other qualities necessary for the kind of life she would have to live here. If some of these qualities are lacking, she should not be accepted, unless she is a person so taken with the service of the Lord and useful to the house that the deficiencies would give no cause whatsoever for disquiet and our Lord would be served by our consenting to her holy desires. If these latter are not great, for great desires will be the sign that God is calling her to this state, she should by no means be received. An applicant with whom the nuns are pleased should not be turned away because she has no alms to give the house; and this has always been the procedure. Should she desire to give an alms to the house, and holds it for that reason, she should not be refused profession if afterward she does not for some reason give it, nor should the nuns try to get the money through litigation. Let them be careful so as not to be motivated by self-interest. Little by little greed could so enter that they would look more to the alms than to the goodness and quality of the person. This should in no way be done, for doing so would be a great evil. They must ever keep in mind their profession of poverty that they might always in everything give off its fragrance. Let them reflect that it is not money that will sustain them but faith, perfection, and trust in God alone. This law should be considered carefully and be observed; it is appropriate and should be read to the Sisters. When someone is accepted, it should always be done in accordance with the majority opinion of the community, and the same holds for profession. Candidates being considered for admission as lay Sisters should be robust and be persons who show that they want to serve the Lord. They should spend a year before receiving the habit so that it may be seen whether they are fit for the demands of such a life, and so that they themselves may see whether they can bear up with it. They should not cover their faces with a veil, nor should they wear a black one. They may make profession two years after receiving the habit, unless through their great virtue they merit making profession sooner. They should be treated with complete sisterly charity, and food and clothing should be provided for them just as they are for all.

On the Humble Offices

22. The Mother prioress should be the first on the list for sweeping so that she might give good example to all. She should pay careful attention to whether those in charge of the clothes and the food provide charitably for the Sisters in what is needed for subsistence and in everything else. Those having these offices should do no more for the prioress and the older nuns than they do for all the rest, as the rule prescribes,[16] but be attentive to needs and age, and more so to needs, for sometimes those who are older have fewer needs. Since this is a general rule, it merits careful consideration, for it applies in many things. Let no Sister comment on whether the food given to eat is much or little, well or poorly seasoned. Let the prioress and the provider take care so that what is given (depending on what the Lord has given) is well prepared and the nuns will be able to get along with it, for they have nothing else. The Sisters should be obliged to tell the Mother prioress of their needs, and the novices to tell the novice mistress; this with regard to both clothing and food. And if they need something more than the usual things, they should, even though this may not be great, commend the matter to our Lord first. Our human nature often asks for more than what it needs, and sometimes the devil helps so as to cause fear about the practice of penance and fasting.

On the Sick

23. The sick should be cared for with fullness of love, concern for their comfort, and compassion in accordance with the poverty we practice. And they should praise God, our Lord, when they are well provided for. If they lack the things the wealthy possess for bringing relief in their illnesses, let them not

become sad. In joining us one must be very resolved about such matters. This is what it means to be poor: to be in want, perhaps, at times of greater need. The Mother prioress should be very careful that the healthy nuns be deprived of something necessary rather than have the sick ones go without some deeds of kindness. The sick ought to be visited and comforted by the Sisters. Let an infirmarian be appointed who has the ability and charity for this office. The sick nuns should strive, then, to show the perfection they acquired when healthy, being patient and as little a bother as possible if the illness is not serious. They should be obedient to the infirmarian, for her benefit and for the edification of the Sisters, that they themselves might gain through their illness. They should have linens and good beds (I mean, with mattresses) and should be treated with much charity and cleanliness.

24. Work with a time limit should never be given to the Sisters. Each one should strive to work so that the others might have food to eat. They should take into careful account what the rule ordains (that whoever wants to eat must work) and what St. Paul did.[17] If someone should volunteer to take on a fixed daily amount of work, she may do so but ought not be given a penance if she fails to finish it.

25. Each day after supper, or collation, when the Sisters are gathered together, the turnkeeper should announce what was given that day in alms, naming the donors so that all may take care to pray that God will repay them.

26. The time for dinner cannot be fixed since this depends on how the Lord gives. When possible, during the winter, on Church fast days, the bell for dinner should be rung at eleven-thirty and on fast days of the order, at eleven; during the summer, at ten. Should the Lord give a Sister the desire to perform a mortification, she should ask permission. This good, devotional practice should not be lost, for some benefits are drawn from it. Let it be done quickly so as not to interfere with the reading. Outside the time of dinner and supper, no Sister should eat or drink without permission. When they are through with the meal, the Mother prioress may dispense from the silence so that all

may converse together on whatever topic pleases them most as long as it is not one that is inappropriate for a good religious. And they should all have their distaffs with them there.

27. Games should in no way be permitted, for the Lord will give to one the grace to entertain the others. In this way, the time will be well spent. They should strive not to be offensive to one another, but their words and jests must be discreet. When this hour of being together is over, they may in summer sleep for an hour; and whoever might not wish to sleep should observe silence.

28. After Compline and prayer, as was mentioned above,[18] in both winter and summer, the Mother may allow the Sisters to talk together, each one having her work, as was mentioned. The amount of time should be determined by the Mother prioress. Let no Sister embrace another or touch her on the face or hands. The Sisters should not have particular friendships but should include all in their love for one another, as Christ often commanded His disciples.[19] Since they are so few, this will be easy to do. They should strive to imitate their Spouse who gave His life for us. This love for one another that includes all and singles out no one in particular is very important.

29. No nun should reprove another for the faults she sees her commit. If they are serious, she should admonish her privately in a charitable way. And if the nun after being told three times does not amend, the Mother prioress should be told but no other Sister. Since there are Sisters appointed as monitors to attend to the faults, the rest of the Sisters need not bother and may pass over those seen in others and pay attention to their own. Nor should they meddle with faults committed in the fulfilment of offices, unless it's a serious matter which they are obliged to make known, as was mentioned. They should be very careful not to excuse themselves unless in matters where it is necessary to do so, for they will find much benefit in this practice.

30. The monitors should take great care to notice the faults and, when ordered by the prioress, should at times reprimand the Sisters in public, even though this may mean that a younger

Sister is reprimanding an older one. One is thereby exercised in humility. Thus the Sisters should not answer back even if they are without fault. No Sister may give or receive or ask for anything, even from her parents, without permission from the prioress. Everything that is offered as alms, should be shown to the prioress. Never should the prioress or any of the Sisters use the title Doña.[20]

31. The punishment for the faults and failings committed in matters that were mentioned should be those penalties designated at the end of these constitutions, according to the seriousness of the fault, since almost everything is set up in conformity with our rule. In all of the above, the Mother prioress may with discretion and charity dispense in accordance with what may be just, and its observance does not oblige under pain of sin but of corporal punishment.

32. The house, with the exception of the church, should never be adorned, nor should there be anything finely wrought, but the wood should be rough. Let the house be small and the rooms humble: something that fulfills rather than exceeds the need. It should be as strong as possible. The wall should be high, and there should be a field where hermitages can be constructed so that the Sisters may be able to withdraw for prayer as our holy Fathers did.[21]

On the Deceased

33. The sacraments should be administered as ordained in the ordinal.[22] The funeral and burial of a deceased nun should include a vigil and sung Mass; and also on the first anniversary, an office of the dead and a sung Mass. If it is possible the Gregorian Masses should be said for them; and if not, whatever is possible. The whole community should recite an Office of the dead for the nuns of their own monastery; and for other nuns (those of the primitive rule), an Office of the dead should be recited and, if possible, a Mass sung. For nuns of the mitigated observance, an Office of the dead should be recited.

On the Obligations of Each Office

34. It is the duty of the Mother prioress to take great care in everything about the observance of the rule and constitutions, to look after the integrity and enclosure of the house, to observe how the offices are carried out, and to see that both spiritual and temporal needs are provided for; and these things should be done with a mother's love. She should strive to be loved so that she may be obeyed. The prioress should appoint as portress and sacristan persons whom she can trust. So as not to allow for any attachment to an office, she may remove them as she sees fit. She should appoint nuns to all the other offices as well with the exception of those of subprioress and key-bearer which are elected offices. At least two of the key-bearers should know how to write and keep accounts.

35. It is the duty of the Mother subprioress to take care of the choir so that the recitation and chanting be done well, and the pause observed. This should be looked after carefully. When the prioress is absent, the subprioress should preside, be always present in the community, and correct the faults that are committed in the choir and refectory.

36. The key-bearers should receive a monthly report from the treasurer with the prioress present; the prioress should seek the opinion of the key-bearers in serious matters and have a chest, to which there should be three keys, for the community documents and funds. The prioress must have one key, and the oldest key-bearers the other two.

37. It is the duty of the sacristan to take care of all the things pertaining to the church and to see to it that the Lord is served there with much reverence and cleanliness. She should arrange that the hearing of confessions proceed in good order and, under pain of grave fault, she must not allow anyone to approach the confessional without permission unless to confess to an appointed confessor.

38. The duty of the treasurer and elder portress (offices that should be held by the same person) is to take care of providing in due time, if the Lord gives the means, for all that must be

bought for the house. This Sister must speak at the turn with a subdued voice and in an edifying way. She must look after the needs of the Sisters with charity and keep accounts of income and expenses. When she buys something she should not engage in haggling and bargaining over the price, but after discussing the cost twice she should either take the item or leave it. She shouldn't allow any Sister to come to the turn without permission. If a Sister must go to the grate to speak with someone, another Sister should be called to accompany her. The portress should tell no one about what comes to pass at the turn except the prioress, nor should she give anyone a letter without first giving it to the prioress to read. Neither should she, under pain of grave fault, give a message to any Sister or pass one along to someone outside without first giving it to the prioress.

39. The monitors should take great care to notice faults, for this is an important office, and they should tell the prioress about them, as was mentioned.[23]

40. The novice mistress should be very prudent, prayerful, and spiritual. She should take great care to read the constitutions to the novices and teach them all that they have to do with regard to ceremonies and mortification. She should stress the interior life more than exterior things, taking daily account of how the novices are progressing in prayer, how they get along with the mystery on which they must meditate, and of the benefit they are deriving from it. She should teach them how to proceed with this practice and how in times of dryness to break their own will even in small things. Let the one who has this office be careful lest she grow careless in anything, for it is a matter of educating souls so that the Lord might dwell in them. Let her treat them compassionately and lovingly, not being surprised by their faults, for they must advance little by little, and mortify each one according to what her spirit can suffer. She should lay more stress on doing away with the lack of virtue than on rigorous penance. The prioress should send someone to help her teach them to read.

41. All the Sisters should give the prioress a monthly account of how they have done in prayer, of how the Lord is leading

them, for His Majesty will give her light so that if they are not proceeding well she might guide them. Doing this requires humility and mortification and is very beneficial. Should the prioress find that she has no one competent for the office of novice mistress, she should herself take on the office and regard this work as something most important and appoint someone to help her.

42. When those who have an office must spend the hour designated for prayer at their task, they should take another hour for prayer in which they are the most likely to be free. This should be understood to apply when they are not able to give themselves to prayer for the whole, or greater part, of the hour.[24]

57. In each monastery a copy of these constitutions should be kept in the chest of three keys, and there should be other copies so that they may be read once a week to all the Sisters gathered in community at a time fixed by the Mother prioress. Each Sister should keep them very much in mind, for this is what they must do in order, with the help of the Lord, to advance far. They should read them at times, and thus there should be more copies in the monastery than those mentioned so that each one, if she desires, may take a copy to her cell.

58. Alms in the form of money that the Lord might give should always be placed at once in the chest of three keys save when it amounts to less than nine or ten ducats. In this latter case it should be given to the key-bearer designated by the prioress, and she in turn will give the procuratrix what the prioress has told the latter to spend. Each night before the bell is rung for silence, the procuratrix should give a detailed account to either the prioress or the key-bearer. And when the accounting is made, they should together record it in the monastery book so as to render a yearly account to the visitor.

Deo Gratias

59. The ordinal prescribes some of the disciplines that are to be taken when the ferial Office is recited; the discipline is taken

on ferial days in Advent and Lent; outside these times, on Mondays, Wednesdays, and Fridays when the ferial Office is recited. In addition, it should be taken every Friday of the year for the increase of the faith, for benefactors, for souls in purgatory, for captives, and for those in mortal sin. A *Miserere* and prayers for the Church and for those intentions mentioned should be recited. Each one should take these disciplines herself in the choir after Matins. The others are given with twigs as the ordinal prescribes.[25] No one should take any more disciplines without permission, nor do anything penitential without it.

ON MAKING THE VISITATION

INTRODUCTION

A s with the greater part of the Teresian writings, this work represents a response to an obedience and reveals the customary repugnance toward beginning the work. But when finished, Teresa thought the result of her effort would prove beneficial (no. 54), a conclusion that was not unusual for her.

Although nothing is expressly stated concerning the identity of the one who gave her the orders to write this treatise, there is no lack of evidence to the fact that it was Gracián. The visitator for whom she was writing (no. 54) was in fact the one who had ordered her to write her *Foundations,* and this latter was by Teresa's own admission, Gracián (*Foundations,* ch. 27, no. 22).

It is not known with any certitude when Gracián gave Teresa the orders to put her thoughts on paper with regard to a visitation. All we can state definitely is that the work was finished before she began the final part of the *Foundations.* But this "final part of the Foundations" need not refer to the last foundations, which Teresa began in 1581. It refers most probably to those foundations described in chapters 20-27 of that work. After the foundation in Caravaca in 1576, Teresa figured that her task was finished since the prior general had begun to oppose any new Teresian Carmels. What seems certain, then, is that this little treatise would have been written in Toledo during the summer of 1576, since on October 5, 1576, she wrote to Gracián stating that she was going to begin writing about the other foundations.

In the first edition of St. Teresa's works, published in 1588 by Fray Luis de León, this present writing, as was true also of the

Foundations, was omitted. After Luis de León's death, the autograph of this treatise remained in the possession of Dr. Francisco Sobrino, who was a professor at the university of Valladolid. When Philip II sought the manuscripts of Teresa for his library at the Escorial, this autograph was sent there, where it still remains.

Not until 1613 was it published for the first time, and this in compliance with the wishes of the general of the order, Alonso de Jesús María. The printed edition also included a pastoral letter by Padre Alonso. No mention was made of Gracián, who was still alive, and some passages referring to him were retouched; the epilogue (nos. 54–55), addressed to him personally, was suppressed. Since the autograph contains no title, one had to be given: "A Treatise on the Manner of Visiting the Convents of the Discalced Nuns of Our Lady of Mount Carmel. Composed by Mother Teresa of Jesus, their Foundress."

This edition of Padre Alonso served as the model for others until the last century. A faithful rendering of the text of the autograph did not appear until the critical edition of Padre Silverio in 1919.

Speaking frankly in this work with Gracián, who tended to be somewhat soft, Teresa offers to visitators the fruit of her experiences in religious life and of her understanding of the feminine psyche. She presents a series of practical counsels and suggestions so that a visitation might amount to something more than a mere formality. Her short treatise reveals solid common sense and realism as well as some keen powers of observation and insight into human nature.

K. K.

ON MAKING THE VISITATION

1. I confess, first of all, my imperfect obedience at the outset of this writing. Even though I desire the virtue of obedience more than anything else, beginning this work has been the greatest mortification for me, and I have felt a strong repugnance toward doing so. May it please our Lord that I succeed in saying something, for I trust only in His mercy and in the humility of the one who ordered me to write this, so that, through that humility, God, who is powerful, will do the work and not depend on me.

2. It seems an inappropriate thing to begin with temporal matters. Yet I think that these are most important for the promotion of the spiritual good, although in monasteries founded in poverty this doesn't seem to be so. But in all monasteries it is necessary to have good order and attend to matters concerning government and the harmonious organization of everything.

3. First, let it be presupposed as extremely appropriate that the visitator so behave toward the nuns that even though on the one hand he is affable and loving, on the other hand he makes it known that in essential matters he will be strict and by no means lenient. I don't believe there is anything in the world that harms a visitator as much as does being unfeared and allowing subjects to deal with him as with an equal. This is true especially in the case of women. Once they know that the visitator is so soft that he will pass over their faults and change his mind so as not to sadden them, he will have great difficulty in governing them.

4. It is very necessary that they understand there is some one in command, who is not tenderhearted, when it comes to matters that would weaken the religious observance. The judge must be so upright in administering justice that they become convinced he will not turn aside from whatever might be more perfect and for the greater service of God even if the whole world crumbles. And they must understand that he will be affable and

loving toward them as long as he knows there is no fault in the above. Just as it is necessary that he also show compassion and that he love them as a father—and this is very important for their consolation and that he not alienate them—so are these other qualities I mentioned necessary. And if either of these be lacking, it is imcomparably better that the latter be lacking than the former.

5. The official visitation should take place once a year so that with love faults may be gradually corrected and removed. For if the nuns do not understand that at the end of the year those who have committed them will be corrected and punished, year after year goes by and the religious observance becomes so lax that when one wants to provide a remedy it is impossible to do so. Although the fault lies with the prioress, and even though she is changed for another, the nuns grow accustomed to the relaxation in observance. In our human nature custom is a terrible thing, and little by little, through small things, irremediable harm is done to the order. The visitator who does not provide a remedy in time will have to give a terrible accounting to God.

6. It seems to me that by dealing with these matters I'm being offensive to these monasteries of the Virgin, our Lady, since through the Lord's goodness they are far removed from any need for this severity. But it is my fear that makes me say this, a fear stemming from the fact that with time, through a lack of carefulness at the beginning, laxity usually creeps into monasteries. Also I see that each day through the goodness of God the nuns are making more progress. And in some communities there might have been some failure if the visitator had not done what I am saying here about severity in remedying these little things and deposing the prioresses whom they found were not suited for the job.

7. In this latter regard, especially, there must be no pity, because many prioresses will be very holy but not suited for the office of prioress, and it's necessary to remedy the matter quickly. Here, where there is so much concern for mortification and practices of humility, this will not be taken as an offense. If a nun should take it as an offense, it's obvious that she is not suited for the office. Anyone who has so little perfection that she wants

to be prioress should not be governing souls who are so much involved with the pursuit of perfection.

8. The visitator must keep God in mind and the favor the Lord has granted to these houses lest because of him the favor be lessened; and he should cast out all feelings of pity. The devil causes these for the sake of doing great harm. This pity is the greatest cruelty the visitator could show to the nuns.

9. It's impossible that all those elected prioresses will have the talent for the office. When it is realized that they do not, the first year should by no means pass without their being removed from office. In one year not much harm can be done but if three go by she could destroy the monastery by allowing imperfections to become the custom. And removing her from office is so extremely important that even if it kills him, because he thinks she is holy and her intentions good, he should force himself to do so. This is the only thing I ask, for the love of God. And if he should see that the nuns who are electing a prioress solicit or campaign, which God forbid, he should nullify the election and nominate prioresses from other monasteries for them to choose from. For no good can come from an election made in this way.

10. I don't know if what I've said belongs to the temporal or spiritual order.[1] What I wanted to begin with is that the visitator should examine very carefully and attentively the financial records and not pass over them lightly. Especially in houses having an income, it is very important that the expenses not exceed the income even though the community may have to go without something. For if they spend in accordance with their means, those houses founded with an income will have enough and get along very well, glory to God. Otherwise, if the community begins to go into debt, it will gradually be ruined. For in the event of great need, it will seem inhuman to major superiors to forbid individuals to keep money earned from their work or that relatives provide for them or similar things that are the practice now in different monasteries.[2] I would unquestionably prefer to see a monastery dissolved than to see it reach such a state. This is why I said[3] that a lack of care in temporal matters can cause great harm in spiritual matters, and thus this advice is most important. In the monasteries founded in poverty,

the visitator should examine carefully and advise strongly so that the nuns do not go into debt, because if they have faith and serve God, they will not be in want—unless they spend too much.

11. In the monasteries, both those founded in poverty and those with an income, the visitator should learn in detail about the ration of food the nuns are given and about how they are treated, especially the sick, and he should see to it that the needs of the nuns are sufficiently taken care of. The Lord never fails to provide for these needs as long as the prioress has courage and diligence; experience teaches this.

12. In both kinds of monasteries[4] he should take note of the work that is being done and even record what the nuns have earned by the work of their hands. This is useful for two reasons: first, so as to encourage and thank those who have done a great deal; second, so that in those monasteries where there is not so much care taken about work because there is not so much need the nuns may be told about what others earn. This keeping record of the handwork that is done, apart from the temporal advantages, has advantages in every other respect. And it is very consoling to the nuns when they are at work to know that it will be seen by the visitator. Even though this is not an important matter, we women who live so enclosed a life and whose consolation is found in pleasing the visitator should be treated at times with a sensitive understanding of our weaknesses.

13. He should inquire whether there is any excess in gift giving. This is particularly necessary in houses having an income, for prioresses could overdo it and destroy the monasteries through what seems of little importance. Should it happen that a prioress is extravagant, the nuns could be left without food, it having been given away, as has happened in some monasteries. For this reason, it is necessary to reflect on what can be done, on the amount of alms that can be given in accord with the income, and to have a reasonable and fixed amount for everything.

14. He should not easily consent to houses that are too large, or allow the nuns, without great necessity, to go into debt in order to build or add on to them. And for this it would be neces-

sary to give the order that no construction be undertaken without informing the major superior and giving an account of where it is to be done so that he may judge whether or not to give the permission. This should not be taken to refer to little things that cannot do much harm. But it is better that the nuns suffer the trouble of not having a good house than that they be worried, and disedifying to others, because of debts and lack of food.

15. It is very important that he always inspect the whole house to determine how recollection is preserved, for it is good that he remove the occasions and not trust in the sanctity he sees however great; no one knows the future. And thus it is necessary to think of all the evil that could arise, so that, as I say, the occasion may be removed. He should observe especially whether there be two grates at the grille in the parlor, one on the outside and one on the inside, and whether they are such that no hand can reach through. This is very important. He should look at the confessionals and see to it that the curtains are nailed over the confessional window and that the Communion window is small. The door at the entrance should have two bolts and there should be two keys for the door to the enclosure, as the *Acts*[5] ordain, one of which is kept by the portress and the other by the prioress. I know that this is done now, but so that it will not be forgotten, I have put it down here, for it is always necessary that these things be looked into and that the nuns see that the visitator does so, and thus there will be no carelessness about them.

16. It is very important that he inquire about the chaplain, who the confessor is and whether there is more communication with him than necessary. And he should inquire very particularly about this from the nuns and also about the preservation of recollection in the house. And if some nun should be tempted to misjudge, he ought to listen to her very carefully. Even though often what she thinks will not be so, and she will exaggerate it, he can inquire about the truth from the other nuns putting them under the precept of obedience. And having found out the truth, he should afterward reprimand her severely so that this will not happen again.

17. And if some of the nuns are taken up with trifles or exaggerate things without there being any fault on the part of the

prioress, it's necessary to be strict with them and get them to realize their own blindness so that they don't go about disturbed. If they become aware that their conduct is no benefit to them but recognized for what it is, they will be quiet. When there is nothing serious, the prioresses should always be supported, even though the faults may be corrected. For the sake of peace and quiet, the simplicity of perfect obedience is a great help. The devil could tempt some nuns with the notion that they know better than the prioress and should go about always paying attention to things that matter little, and they could do much harm to themselves. The discreet visitator will recognize this and help them improve, although if they are melancholic he will have a great deal to do. He should never be softhearted with these latter, for if they think they're going to get somewhere, they'll never stop being a bother, nor will they themselves be at rest. They must realize always that they will be punished and that they must consequently support the prioress.

18. If some nun should perhaps speak of being transferred to another monastery, he must answer in such a way that neither she nor anyone would think that this is ever something possible. For no one except the one who has seen it happen can know the tremendous troubles that are apt to arise and how the door is open for the devil to tempt the nuns when they think it is possible to transfer from their monastery. They shouldn't think this no matter how great their reasons. And even if a transfer should have to be made, they must not be aware of the reason or think that it was made because they wanted it. Other subterfuges should be used, for she will never settle down anywhere, and much harm will be done to the other nuns. Let the nuns understand that the visitator will never in any way trust the nun who is trying to get a transfer from her house, and that even if he should have to transfer her, I mean because of some need or for some foundation, he will not do so if she is trying for one. This is all right to do because these temptations never come except to melancholics or those of such a temperament that they are not much help for anything. And perhaps it would even be good, before anyone try to do this, that he speak in a conference to the community about how harmful this is and the poor opinion he

will have of the one who considers this temptation, and he should give his reasons and explain how no one any longer can be transferred and that until now there were some occasions in which a transfer was necessary.[6]

19. He should inquire whether the prioress has some particular friendship with a nun, doing more for this one than for the others. As for the rest, he shouldn't bother unless there is some extreme, for prioresses need to deal more with those who have greater intelligence and discretion. And since our human nature doesn't allow us to recognize ourselves for what we are, each nuns thinks she is an expert. Thus, the devil tempts them through trifles coming from inside so that there will always be war; but merit can be gained by resisting. Therefore, it will seem to them that this nun, or these others, are governing the prioress. The visitator should try to get her to moderate any excess that there may be in this friendship because it would occasion a great temptation for the weak nuns. But the friendship should not be taken away entirely, for, as I say, these persons could be the kind for whom it is necessary. However, it is always good to insist that there be no great familiarity with anyone. Soon the true colors will be seen.

20. There are some so extremely perfect, in their opinion, that everything they see seems to be a fault, and these are always the ones who have more faults themselves. But they don't see them and they put all the blame on the poor prioress or on the others. Thus they could fool the visitator into wanting to correct what is being done well. It is, as a result, necessary to avoid believing one nun alone, as I have said,[7] and to inquire about something from the others before correcting it. In a monastery where there is so much rigor, life would become unbearable if each visitator, in each visitation, were to make new decrees. This is very important.[8] Thus he should not make any decrees, unless the matter is serious and, as I say, he has inquired fully of the prioress herself and the other nuns about the correction he wants to make, and about why and how it should be done. For the nuns could become so weighed down with decrees that, unable to observe them, they will also give up what is more important in the rule.

21. What the visitator should insist upon is that the nuns observe the constitutions. A prioress who takes great liberty in breaking the laws of the constitutions and does so for little reason or habitually, thinking that this or that matters little, will do great harm to the house. Let this be understood, and if it doesn't appear so at once, time will prove it. This is the reason monasteries and even religious orders have gone so astray in some places. They pay little attention to small matters and hence come to fall in very great ones. The visitator should insist publicly with the nuns that they inform him of any fault in the monastery with regard to the constitutions and that if he should learn of something afterward he will punish severely the person who should have informed him. With this, the prioresses will be fearful and will proceed carefully.

22. It's necessary to avoid compromising with the prioress whether she becomes sad or not. Let her understand that this method of procedure is to be always followed and that the main reason she was elected to office is that she foster observance of the rule and constitutions and not remove or add according to her own whim and that there will be someone who will watch this and inform the visitator. I hold that it is impossible for any prioress to fulfill her office well if she becomes upset that the visitator learned of something she does. A sign that something is not done fully for the service of God is that I do not want it known by the one who stands in His place. And, thus, the visitator should note whether there is openness and truth in the things the nuns discuss with him, and if there is not, he should reprimand them with great severity and strive by means of warnings to the prioress or officeholders, or by using other procedures, to foster this openness. Even though the nuns may not lie, they can cover up some things. But the head, through whose government one lives, must know everything. It isn't right for the nuns to hide what must be corrected from the visitator, for a good body can do nothing without a head, and he is no less than that.

23. I conclude this matter by saying that if the constitutions are observed everything will run smoothly. If there is no great care for their observance or that of the rule, visitations will be of

little avail—this is the reason for them—unless the prioresses are changed. And even the nuns in the community may be transferred if, God forbid, this has already become a custom, and other nuns who are faithful in keeping the religious observance brought in, as though one were newly founding the monastery. And the former nuns should be divided and each placed in a different monastery, for one or two of them will not be able to do much harm in a well-regulated monastery.

24. It should be noted that there may be prioresses who will ask for some freedom with regard to certain things against the constitutions and will give, perhaps, enough reasons, in their opinion. Either they will perhaps know no better or they will try to make the visitator think this is appropriate. And even though these things may not go against the constitutions, they could be of such kind that it would be harmful to admit them. Since the visitator is not present, he doesn't know what harm there can be—and we know how to exaggerate in order to get what we want. For this reason the best policy is to keep the door closed to anything that is not in conformity with the way things are going now since we see that they are going well and are proven by experience. The certain is better than the doubtful. And in these cases the visitator must be firm and not worry about saying no. Rather, he should act with the freedom and holy authority I mentioned at the beginning[9] so that he is indifferent as to whether he pleases or displeases the prioresses and the nuns in matters that otherwise could cause some trouble in the future. And the fact that something is a novelty is reason enough for not starting it.

25. In regard to the permission to accept nuns, a very important matter, the visitator should not give it without receiving a full account. And he should inquire himself, if he is in a place where it is possible to do so, for there can be prioresses so fond of taking in nuns as to be satisfied with little. And if the prioress wants to admit someone and says that she is well informed, her subjects almost always agree with what she wants. But it could happen that the prioress might be inclined to admit an aspirant because she is a friend or relative or out of some other personal considerations. And she will think she is right and yet be wrong.

26. Any mistake made in admitting nuns can be easily reme-

died. But before allowing them to make profession, it is necessary to be most careful. If there are novices, the visitator at the time of the visitation should inquire about them so that he may make an informed judgment when the time comes to grant the license for profession. Possibly the novice is a friend and protégée of the prioress, and the subjects do not dare speak their mind; but they will to the visitator. And thus, if possible, it would be a good thing to delay the profession, if the time for it is near, until the superior comes to make his visitation. If it seems fitting, he should even tell them to send him the results of the secret balloting as is done for the election. So important is it not to keep anyone in the monastery who will be the cause of trouble and restlessness all her life that every care taken will be well worthwhile.

27. In the receiving of lay Sisters, it is necessary to take careful note because almost all the prioresses are fond of having many lay Sisters, and the houses become filled up, and sometimes with those who can do little work. Thus it's very necessary for him not to yield right away if he sees no notable need. He should inquire about the number of lay Sisters, for since the number has not been established, great harm can be done if there is no prudence about accepting them.

28. An effort should always be made in each house that the number of nuns be less than that allowed so that some vacancies may remain, for it could happen that someone, whom it would be very advantageous for the house to accept, might want to enter, and there will be no room. By no means should one consent to go beyond the fixed number, for this would open the door to no less than the destruction of the monasteries. For this reason it is better to deny what might be advantageous to one monastery than to do harm to them all. It could be, and this would be a remedy, that if in another monastery the number is not complete a nun could transfer to that monastery so that the aspirant might enter. But the nun who is transferring should be given the dowry or alms she brought with her, if she did so, since she will be in the other monastery permanently. But if this should be impossible, let what must be lost be lost, and let not something so harmful to everyone be started. The provincial must neces-

sarily be informed when permission is sought concerning the number of nuns so that he can decide what is fitting; in something so important it's not right to trust the prioresses.

29. It's necessary for the visitator to inquire about whether the prioresses have added more vocal prayers and penances than is obligatory. It could happen that each one, according to her own taste, might add particular things and so burden the nuns that they will lose their health and not be able to do what they are obliged to do. This must not be understood to apply when on some day there is a certain need. But there are usually some prioresses so indiscreet that they do this almost habitually, and the nuns do not dare speak, thinking this would show a lack of devotion. Nor is it right that they do speak except with the visitator.

30. He should look into how the vocal prayer is said in choir, whether chanted or recited, and inquire as to whether it is done slowly, and the chanting should be done in a soft voice which is edifying and in conformity with the life we profess. Chanting with a loud voice is doubly harmful: first, it sounds bad because the vocal prayer is not being sung; second, the reserve and spirit of our way of life are lost. If the above is not greatly insisted upon, they will go to excess and take away the devotion of those who hear them. The voices should be subdued and not manifest any concern on the part of the nuns about sounding nice to those who are listening. This concern has become almost universal, and it seems there will no longer be any remedy for it since it has become fashionable, and thus it is necessary to stress the above a great deal.

31. In regard to important commands, it would be very good for the visitator to order one of the nuns, under obedience, in the presence of the prioress, to write to him if any of the commands is not observed so that the prioress understands that the nun cannot do otherwise. The visitator thereby would in a way be present, for the nuns will proceed more carefully and be on their guard not to go against any of his orders.

32. Before the visitation takes place it would be appropriate for him to stress strongly how wrong it would be for prioresses to

take offense at Sisters who tell the visitator of faults they have
seen. Even though these Sisters may be incorrect in their judgment, they are nonetheless obliged in conscience to do this. And
in a place where mortification is the practice, it is a sure sign
that a prioress is not fit to govern if she takes offense at the nuns
on account of a deed that should please her because it helps her
to serve our Lord and fulfill her office better. The next time
they will not dare speak knowing that the visitator will go away
and that they will be left with trouble; and everything could
gradually grow lax. The visitator should make his remarks however holy the prioresses may be, and should not be trustful in
this matter, for our human nature is weak and the enemy so
skillful that when there are no other things with which to tempt
he will strike hard here and perhaps gain what he loses elsewhere.

33. It is most fitting that the visitator observe great secrecy in
everything and that the prioress be unable to ascertain who the
informer is. For, as I have said,[10] these nuns are still on earth.
And if, for no other reason, he should do so at least for the sake
of removing some temptation, how much more if the temptation is one that could do much harm.

34. If the things they say about the prioresses are not important, the visitator could make them known in a roundabout way
so that it will not be known that the nuns have informed him. It
is most fitting that insofar as possible he let the prioresses think
that the nuns have nothing to say against them. But in important matters it is better that the situation be corrected than that
the prioresses be pleased.

35. It is very important that he inquire whether any money
gets into the hands of the prioresses without the knowledge of
the key-bearers, for this could happen without her adverting to
it, or even whether she possesses anything except in conformity
with the constitutions.[11] This is also necessary in houses founded
in poverty. It seems to me I have said this before,[12] and the same
will happen with other things; but as the days go by I forget and
do not want to take the time to read this over.

36. It will be very bothersome for the visitator to attend to

the many trifling matters referred to here, but it will be more bothersome for him when from his not doing so he sees the back-sliding that will result. As I have said,[13] however holy the nuns may be, it is necessary for him to attend to these matters. And, as I have said at the beginning,[14] the most important thing in the government of women is the necessity of their understanding that they have a head who will not be moved for anything on earth and that he has to observe and comply with all that pertains to religious observance and to punish what is contrary to it. They must perceive that he takes special care about this in each house and that he not only makes a visitation once a year but wants to know what they are doing every day. In this way, they will go on growing in perfection rather than diminishing, for women, in general, are upright and fearful.

37. And what I said is very important so that there be no carelessness. And sometimes, when necessary, action should accompany words; if he punishes one for something, others will avoid it. If out of compassion, or for other motives, he does the opposite at the beginning, when things are small, he will be forced to act more rigorously afterward. And these acts of pity will turn out to be the greatest cruelty, and he will have to render an exact account to God, our Lord.

38. There are some nuns with such great simplicity that they think it is a serious fault on their part to tell the visitator about the faults of the prioresses in matters that have to be corrected. These nuns must be told that even though they may think this an unworthy action they are obliged to do so and also that they should beforehand humbly tell the prioress when they see that she is at fault in observing the constitutions or in matters of importance, for it could be that she doesn't realize this. They should even tell her to correct it, and if afterward she is displeased with them, they should accuse her. There is much ignorance about what to do in these visitations, and thus it is necessary that the visitator discreetly call their attention to this and instruct them.

39. It is very important to inquire about procedures concerning the confessor, and not from one or two nuns but from all of them, and about how much power he is given. Since he is not

the vicar, nor must there ever be one, for this office was taken away so that he might not have such power, it is important that communication with him be only very moderate, and the less there is the better. And the prioress should be very careful with regard to giving gifts and complimentary presents, unless they are very small; although sometimes one cannot avoid giving something. The prioress should rather pay the chaplain more than what is his due from the chaplaincy than have this concern, for it brings with it many troubles.

40. It is also necessary to counsel the prioresses not to be too generous and liberal but to keep in mind that they are obliged to reflect on how they spend money. They are no more than stewards and must not spend as if the money were their own but according to reason and with great care so that their expenditures are not excessive. Apart from the obligation not to disedify, the prioress is obliged in conscience to use this care and to take charge of temporal matters, and not keep especially for herself anything that the others do not have, unless the key to a desk or drawer for keeping papers, I mean letters or similar things, for it is right that these be kept secret, especially if they contain some counsels from the provincial.

41. He should observe whether the habit and toque are made as prescribed in the constitutions. If, God forbid, there should appear at some time something that seems to be an adornment, and not very edifying, he should make the nun burn it in his presence. By his doing something like this, the nuns will be frightened and correct the fault, and the incident will be recounted to those who come in the future.

42. He should also notice their manner of speaking, that it be simple, plain, and religious, more in the style of hermits and solitaries, and that they don't begin to adapt the latest fashionable expressions or the sweet talk, I believe they call it, used in the world, for new things are ever coming into style. In these matters, let them glory in appearing somewhat boorish rather than highly polished.

43. Insofar as possible they should avoid lawsuits, for the Lord will by other means grant them what they might lose by

foregoing a lawsuit. He should always guide them so that they will keep to what is more perfect, and he should order them not to undertake or undergo any lawsuit without informing the provincial and following his special orders.

44. He should warn them, with respect to new members being received into the community, to esteem the personal talents of aspirants more than what they bring with them. No one should be admitted out of self-interest, but in accord with the constitutions, especially if there is some fault in that person's temperament.

45. It is necessary that visitators of the future follow what is done now by the provincial that the Lord has given us.[15] I have taken much of what I've said here from observing his visitations, especially the following point: he shows no more familiarity to one Sister (in such a way that he spends time alone with her or writes to her) than he does to all, but he shows love to all together as a true father. The day in which a visitator in some monastery should have a particular friendship, even though it may be like that between St. Jerome and St. Paula, he will not escape the critical remarks of others, anymore than those two did. And not only will it do harm in that monastery but in all of them, for the devil will at once make it known so as to gain something. Because of our sins the world has gone so astray in this respect that many troubles arise, as is now seen.

46. If the visitator should act in this way, he would be held in less esteem and lose the general love that all the nuns, if he were what he ought to be, would have for him, as they do have now. For they will think that he has set his love on one alone, and it is very advantageous for him to be much loved by all. This does not refer to times in which necessity may require some special attention, but to things that are noticeable and excessive.

47. Let him keep in mind that when he enters the house (I mean the monastery, to visit the enclosure), for it is right that he always do so and that he inspect carefully the whole house, as has already been said,[16] that he should be accompanied by his companion and by the prioress and a few other nuns. By no means, even if this takes place in the morning, should he stay to

eat in the monastery, even if they urge him to do so. But let him carry out his tasks and then leave immediately. If he wants to talk, it is better that he do so at the grille in the parlor. Even though he could do otherwise in complete goodness and simplicity, it would be a beginning. And perhaps with the passing of time someone might come along to whom it would not be fitting to give so much freedom, and he may want to take more. May it please the Lord not to allow this, but may these things, and everything else always be done in an edifying way as they are now, amen, amen.

48. The visitator should never allow them to go to excess in the meals given him during the days of the visitation but consent only to what is appropriate. If he notices otherwise, let him diligently correct this, for it would not be in keeping with the profession of the visitators, which is that of poverty, nor with that of the nuns, nor would it be of benefit to anyone. The visitators should eat no more than what is sufficient, otherwise they would not be giving appropriate edification to the nuns. As for the present, with regard to this excess, I don't think there could be much of a remedy, because the visitator we have doesn't notice whether the food given him is little or much, good or bad, nor do I know if he is capable of recognising the difference unless someone very carefully draws his attention to it.

49. He is most cautious to be alone, without a companion, when he has the official interviews, for he does not want it to be known if there is any fault in the nuns. It's something to be admired when the childish doings of the nuns, if there be any, are kept secret. Now, glory to God, little harm is done because the visitator looks upon things as would a father and thus keeps them secret; and God reveals the seriousness of the task to him, for he stands in God's place. Someone who does not stand in God's place will perhaps think that what amounts to nothing is a great matter. Since such a one does not have the responsibility that the visitator has, he takes little care about not speaking of these things, and the reputation of the monastery is lost for no reason. May it please our Lord that the visitators keep these things in mind so as to behave always in this way.

50. It is not fitting for the visitator to show any great love for the prioress or that he gets along well with her, at least not in the presence of all the nuns. For this will make them lose courage, and they will not dare tell him her faults. He should be very aware that they have to know that he will correct whatever has to be corrected. There is no affliction like the one that comes to a soul zealous for God and the order when she becomes anxious at seeing that the order is failing and hopes that the visitator will correct the matter only to find out that everything remains the same. Seeing the little good that it did her to speak up, she turns to God and decides to be quiet from then on even though everything crumbles.

51. The poor nuns are heard no more than once, that is, when they are called for the official interview, whereas the prioresses have much time for excusing faults and giving reasons and setting their own times for speaking with the visitator, and will perhaps suggest that the poor nun who may have said something is over emotional. Even though he may not be told who this nun is, the visitator will more or less understand to whom these prioresses are referring. He is not himself a witness, but things are told to him in such a way that he cannot help believing them. For these reasons, after the visitation, everything stays as it was. If he could be a witness within the community for many days, he would know the truth. The prioresses do not think they are untruthful, but this self love of ours is such that it's a wonder if we ever blame ourselves, nor do we know ourselves.

52. I myself have experienced this many times, and with prioresses who were very, very great servants of God whom I trusted so much that it seemed to me impossible for the facts to be otherwise. Yet once, after spending some days in a house, I was amazed to see something so contrary to what I had been told, in an important matter, that I came to recognize along with almost half the community the partiality involved, and it was the prioress herself who did not realize this as afterward she came to understand. Since the devil does not have many opportunities to tempt the Sisters, I think he tempts the prioresses so

that they might have opinions in some matters different from those of the Sisters; and to see how these latter suffer everything is something for which to praise our Lord. Thus it is now my practice not to believe anyone until I have gathered all the information so that I can make the one who has been deceived understand that she has. Without proceeding in this way, it would be difficult to correct a wrong. Nothing of this refers to serious faults, but if we do not proceed with care, the faults could grow worse.

53. I am amazed to see the subtlety of the devil and how he makes each one think she is telling the greatest truth in the world. This is why I have said[17] that complete trust should not be given to the prioress or to any nun in particular but that information should be gathered from a greater number, when dealing with something important, so that an effective remedy may be provided. May our Lord provide such a remedy by always giving us a holy and prudent visitator, for if he possesses these qualities, he will be enlightened by His Majesty so as to do the right thing in all and come to know us. In this way the government will be very good, and souls will grow in perfection for the honor and glory of God.[18]

54. I beg your Paternity, in payment for the mortification I underwent in writing this, that you undergo the same by writing yourself some counsels for visitators. If anything useful has been said here, it can be put into better order; and it will be helpful. Now I am going to begin the final part of the Foundations,[19] and this can be added there; for it will prove very beneficial. Yet, I am afraid that there will be no one else so humble, as the one who ordered me to write, that he will want to benefit from it. But if God wants this, such a one will be unable to do otherwise. If these monasteries are visited in the way that is now customary in the order, there will be little fruit;[20] and there could come more harm than good. In fact, it would be necessary to mention many more things than I have here (for either I don't know them or I don't remember them now). Greater care is necessary only at the beginning. If the nuns understand that the

visitation will be carried out in this way, there will be little trouble in governing them.

55. Do your part by writing those counsels I mentioned about the way in which Your Paternity now proceeds in these visitations.[21] Through His mercy and the merits of these Sisters, our Lord will provide the rest since the Sisters' intention is to do what is right for His service in everything and to be taught how to do so.

A SATIRICAL CRITIQUE

INTRODUCTION

ONCE IN PRAYER Teresa heard the words, "seek yourself in me." In awe over the meaning they might contain, she sent them to her brother Don Lorenzo so that he might reflect on them. Lorenzo took the matter so seriously that, unable to penetrate what lay hidden in the words, he decided to consult his spiritual friends. The consultation was a serious and solemn one at which the consultants were gathered in the parlor of the monastery of St. Joseph in Avila at Christmas time in 1576. Those who took part in the discussion, in the presence of the nuns and the bishop of Avila, were Francisco de Salcedo, Julián de Avila, Don Lorenzo de Cepeda, and St. John of the Cross. As the discussion was in progress the circle of friends began to feel keenly the absence of Madre Teresa. At the time she was staying in Toledo, but she was a member of the community of Avila and it was there that she had chosen to reside in obedience to the orders of the prior general. The outcome was a decision by the bishop that those present should write out their reflections on the meaning of the words and that these be sent to Teresa for her judgment. The nuns also sent their reflections.

The style of Teresa's response is shaped by the kind of satirical ceremony that was at that time held in Spanish universities before conferral of the doctor's degree. In these comical sessions the candidate became the subject of some festive bantering by professors and students. Teresa states expressly "I have no intention of saying anything good about what the contestants have written" (no. 3). Her critique, then, of their written reflections sparkles with a kind of playful satire.

With the exception of nos. 8-9, the autograph text is conserved in the monastery of the Carmelite nuns in Guadalajara. The last two numbers are taken from the text found in the edition of Teresa's letters published in Zaragosa in 1658 by Palafox.

None of the contestants' responses has been preserved save Don Lorenzo's. The nuns of St. Joseph's had also sent their reflections, but all that we know of Teresa's judgment of them is contained in her letter to Don Lorenzo, January 2, 1577: "Some of the Sisters' replies made me laugh. Others were extremely good and have given me light on the matter." As for Teresa's own thoughts on the words, they may in part be found in her poem *Seeking God*.

K. K.

A SATIRICAL CRITIQUE

On the Words "Seek Yourself in Me"

1. If obedience had not forced me, I would certainly not have answered, nor, for certain reasons, would I have accepted the role of judge. But none of my reasons is the one the Sisters here give: namely, that my brother is among the contestants and that seemingly affection will distort justice. Indeed, I love all the contestants since each of them has helped me bear my trials. My brother came along at the end of my drinking from the chalice, although he has shared in some part of it and will share in it more with the Lord's help. With the condition my head is in after the many letters and business matters I have been attending to from last night till now, I ask God to give me the grace not to say anything that might merit my being denounced to the Inquisition. But obedience can do all, and thus I will do what Your Excellency commands, whether it turns out good or bad. I have desired to enjoy myself for a while reflecting on the contestants' papers that were sent to me, but I have had no chance to do so.

On Francisco de Salcedo's Reply

2. It seems that the motto, "Seek yourself in Me" is said by the Spouse of our souls. Well, an indication that Señor Francisco de Salcedo errs is that he stresses so much that God is in all things; the Spouse knows that He is in all things.

3. Señor Francisco also says a great deal about the intellect and union. It is well known that in union the intellect does not work. If it does not work, how can it seek? That which he says, quoting David, "I will hear what God speaks within me,"[1] pleased

me very much, for this peace in the faculties (referred to by the word "people") is to be highly esteemed. But I have no intention of saying anything good about what the contestants have written. Thus, I say that the explanation is off the mark because the motto does not say "let us hear," but "let us seek."

4. And worst of all, if he does not retract what he wrote, I will have to denounce him to the Inquisition which is nearby. For after quoting again and again throughout the entire paper words of St. Paul and the Holy Spirit, he refers, in signing his paper, to the things he wrote as stupidities. Let him correct this at once; if he doesn't he will see what happens!

On Julián de Avila's Reply

5. He began well, but ended poorly; thus, the honor should not be given to him. They didn't ask him here to explain how the uncreated and the created light are joined but how we seek ourselves in God. Nor did we ask him what a soul feels when it is united with its Creator. And if it is united with Him, how does it have an opinion about whether there is a difference or not? In this union the intellect is, I think, incapable of entering into these disputes. If it were capable, it could easily understand the difference that lies between the Creator and the creature. The contestant also says, "when it is purified." I believe that neither virtues nor purifications are enough here because the union is a supernatural thing, and God gives it to whom He wants. If there is something that disposes for this union, it is love. But I forgive him his errors because he did not go on at such length as did my Father Fray John of the Cross.

On Father Fray John of the Cross's Reply

6. In his answer he presents very good doctrine for anyone who might want to follow the exercises they make in the Society of Jesus but not for what we have in mind. Seeking God would be very costly if we could not do so until we were dead to the world. The Magdalene was not dead to the world when she found him,

nor was the Samaritan woman or the Canaanite woman.[2] Furthermore, he treats a great deal about becoming one with God in union. But when this union comes about and God grants the soul this favor, one would not say that the soul seeks Him but that it has already found Him.

7. God deliver me from people so spiritual that they want to turn everything into perfect contemplation, no matter what. Nonetheless, we are grateful to him for having explained so well what we did not ask. Thus, it is good to speak always of God, for where we do not expect it, benefit will come to us.

Señor Lorenzo de Cepeda's Reply

8. So, benefit has come to us in Señor Lorenzo de Cepeda's reply. We are very grateful to him for his couplets and response. If he has spoken of more than he understands, we pardon him — because of the recreation he has given us — for his little humility in getting into such sublime matters, as he himself says in his answer. And in regard to the good counsel he gives (without having been asked for it), that they practice the prayer of quiet, as if this were in their power: anyone who does this already knows the affliction to which it obliges her.

Please God that since he is near the honey[3] something good will stick to him, for his answer gave me great consolation — although he was very right in being ashamed of it. In this respect, it is impossible to judge which reply is better, for since without my doing an injustice to any of them by so stating, each of the replies has its faults.

Recommendations to Don Alvaro

9. Your Excellency should order the contestants to make amends. I, myself, will make amends by not being like my brother in his little humility. All these gentlemen are so divine that they have lost by going beyond what was asked by the question. As I have said,[4] one would not tell the soul that attains this favor of union with God to seek Him, for it already possesses Him.

I kiss Your Excellency's hand many times for the favor you granted me with your letter. So as not to tire you further with these silly things, I am not writing now.

Unworthy servant and subject of Your Excellency,

Teresa of Jesus

RESPONSE TO A SPIRITUAL CHALLENGE

INTRODUCTION

THIS WORK TAKES on the form of a tournament and is cast in the model of those jousts of the Middle Ages in which knights participated. Of course, here the contest regards the world of the spirit. While Teresa was prioress at the Incarnation, a spiritual challenge arrived from "the knights and the daughters of the Virgin," probably from the discalced friars and nuns of Pastrana. It was addressed to the nuns at the Incarnation.

In her reply, Teresa gave notice that her nuns would enter the contest only under certain conditions. Though the text of the challenge is unknown, one can suppose, considering its source, that it included some eccentric and extreme forms of penance and austerity, things that were foreign to Teresa's feel for balance and humility. Thus the responses from the Incarnation lean toward the unexceptional and emphasize what is more authentic.

Out of the twenty-four extant answers, one of them is most probably from St. John of the Cross, who was then confessor at the Incarnation. And at the end, the serious tone of them all is suddenly broken by an amusing touch of wit in the response of the prioress, Teresa of Jesus. The time of the writing is not certain, possibly sometime at the end of 1572 or the beginning of 1573.

Up to the eighteenth century the autograph was conserved in the monastery of the Carmelite nuns in Burgos except for the last page, which is still conserved by the Carmelite nuns in Guadalajara. But a copy of the autograph is preserved at the Biblioteca Nacional in Madrid in volume 4 (Ms. 6.615) of the Teresian letters edited by Antonio de San José. That copy has provided the text for editors of Spanish editions. But, skipping from folio 2 to folio 8, the autograph from which it was made did not provide the complete text. In this translation we have followed the text of that copy, which is as close as one can come to the original.

K. K.

RESPONSE TO A SPIRITUAL CHALLENGE

1. After reading the cartel, it seemed that our forces would be incapable of taking to the field against such valiant and strong knights, for these latter would certainly win the victory and leave us totally despoiled of our provisions and even, perhaps, intimidated so that we'd be unable to do what little we could. With this in view, no one—Teresa of Jesus least of all—wanted to sign the challenge. Such is the unfeigned and absolute truth.

2. We resolve to do what lies within our strength, and after spending some days in the exchange of these courtesies, it could be that, with the favor and help of those who might want to take part, we'd be able to sign the cartel within a few days.

3. We will sign under the condition that the defender not turn his back by entering those caves, but he must take to the field of this world where we are. It might happen that in seeing himself always at war where it is necessary not to lay down one's arms, or grow careless, or have a moment of safe rest, he will not be so filled with fury. For there is a great difference between the two and between speaking and acting, for we shall shortly understand the difference that lies between them.

4. Come out, come out from that pleasant life, we say to him and his companions. It may happen that they will so quickly begin stumbling and falling that it will be necessary to help them get up. For it is a terrible thing to be always in danger and loaded down with arms and without food. Well, the defender provided so amply that he quickly sends the sustenance he promises. Should he win by starving us, he would gain little honor or benefit.

5. Any knight or daughter of the Virgin who asks the Lord each day to keep Beatriz Juarez in His grace and makes the effort never to speak inadvertently and to direct all things to the

365

Lord's glory will be given the merit she has gained in two years while caring for Sisters with very painful illnesses.

6. Sister Ana de Vergas says that if the said knights or brothers ask the Lord to remove the opposition she is undergoing and give her humility she will give them all the merit she will thereby gain if the Lord should grant it.

7. Mother Subprioress asks that those mentioned beg the Lord to take away her self-will and says that she will give them what she may have merited in two years. Her name is Isabel de la Cruz.

8. Sister Sebastiana Gómez says that to any of those mentioned who will look at the crucifix three times a day in memory of the three hours the Lord hung on the cross and thereby obtain for her the grace to conquer a strong passion which torments her, she will apply the merit she gains (if the Lord grant it) in the conquering of that passion.

9. Mother María de Tamayo will give a third part of what she suffers to any of those mentioned who recites every day an Our Father and a Hail Mary that the Lord might give her patience and conformity to His will in the endurance of her illness; this she will give each day. And her illness is very serious; for more than a year she has been unable to speak.[1]

10. Sister Ana de la Miseria says that to any of the knights or daughters of the Virgin who should ask Jesus Christ, while considering the poverty in which He was born and died, that spiritually she might give what she promised to His Majesty she will give all the merit she might have before the Lord despite the faults she commits in His service.

11. Sister Isabel de Santángelo will give a share in what she has gained from the trials of soul she has undergone to any of the knights and daughters of the Virgin who accompanies the Lord during the three hours He remained alive on the cross and obtains from His Majesty the grace for her to keep her three vows with perfection.

12. Sister Beatriz Remón says that she will give a year of her merits to any brother or daughter of the Virgin who asks our Lady each day to grant her humility and obedience.

13. Sister María de la Cueva gives three years of her merits to any knight or daughter of the Virgin who prays to our Lady for her each day in faith and light and grace. (I know that Sister's merits are many, for she suffers great interior trials.)

14. Sister María de San José says that she will give one year of her merits to anyone of those mentioned who asks of the Lord humility and obedience for her.

15. Sister Catalina Alvarez says that she gives to anyone who asks the Lord to grant her self-knowledge one year of her sufferings, which is a great deal.

16. For any knight or Sister who prays to our Lady to obtain the grace from her Son so that Sister Leonor de Contreras might serve Him and persevere, this latter Sister will recite three *Salves* each day as long as she lives, and thus they must pray for her each day.

17. Sister Ana Sánchez says that for any knight or daughter of the Virgin who daily asks the Lord to give her His love she will recite daily three Hail Marys in honor of the purity of our Lady.

18. Sister María Gutiérrez says that she will give a part of all her merits with the Lord to any of those mentioned who pray that she be granted perseverance and perfect love of God.

19. Sister María Cimbrón says that those mentioned who pray each day for a happy death for her will have a part in all she merits through her suffering; it has been a long time since she has been able to stir from her bed, and she is close to the end.[2]

20. Sister Inés Díaz says that for anyone of those mentioned who prays that she might share in the Blessed Virgin's feelings at the foot of the cross she will recite, each day that they do so, five Our Fathers and Hail Marys.

21. Sister Juana de Jesús says that to any of the knights and Sisters mentioned who ask the Lord each day to give her contrition for her sins she will give a share in what she merits from her many trials, which are certainly many, and the affronts she has suffered because of them.

22. Sister Ana de Torres says that to those mentioned she will

give what she merits this year if they pray each day that through the torment the Lord suffered when He was nailed to the cross she might be given the grace to succeed in serving Him and to obey.

23. Sister Catalina de Velasco says that to anyone of those mentioned who asks the Lord, through the pain He suffered when He was nailed to the cross, to give her the grace not to offend Him and that our order continue to grow she will give those times that she spends with our Lady each day; they are indeed many.

24. Sister Jerónima de la Cruz says that to anyone of those mentioned who prays that she be given humility, patience, and light to serve the Lord she will recite three Creeds each day and offer a year of the trials she has suffered. This petition must be made for her each day.

25. A knight-errant[3] says that if the Grand Master of the field obtains for him the grace he needs to serve the Lord perfectly in all that which obedience asks of him, he will give in return all the merit he gains this year in serving the Lord through obedience.

26. Sister Estefanía Samaniego says that for any knight or daughter of the Virgin who prays to our Lord that she might serve Him and not offend Him and be given living faith and meekness she will recite each day the prayer in honor of the name of Jesus and offer the merits gained from a year of illnesses and temptations that she has suffered.

27. Sister Antonia del Aguila says that to any knight or daughter of the Virgin who recalls our Lady's sorrows for a time each day and prays that she might be helped in a matter of great need for her soul and that our Mother prioress, Teresa of Jesus, live long for the increase of our order, she will give a third part of her trials and illnesses for the rest of her life.

28. Teresa of Jesus says that to any knight of the Virgin who makes each day a very resolute act of willingness to suffer all his life from a superior who is very wicked, vicious, gluttonous, and badly disposed to him she will give, each day that he does so, half of what she merits that day both in her Communion and

the many sufferings she bears; in sum, her merits in everything, which will be very little. He must consider the humility with which the Lord stood before the judges and how this Lord was obedient even to the death of the cross. This contract is valid for a month and a half.

POETRY

INTRODUCTION

Whoever reads the spiritual treatises of St. John of the Cross must read his poetry as well since his prose works are closely linked to his poetry. St. Teresa, on the other hand, kept her spiritual treatises separate from her poetry, and as a result the latter has suffered a kind of neglect.

As for her impulse to write poetry, Teresa has left an important statement in her *Life*: "Oh, help me God! What is the soul like when it is in this state! It would want to be all tongues so as to praise the Lord.... I know a person who though not a poet suddenly composed some deeply-felt verses well expressing her pain. They were not composed by the use of her intellect; rather, in order that she enjoy the glory so delightful a distress gave to her, she complained of it in this way to God" (ch. 16, no. 4). The impulses of love, pain over the absence of the beloved, joy in his presence, longings for death, and even a certain hatred of life, these are the common themes of lovers, and especially of mystics, the great lovers of God. In her ardent moments of love, Teresa was not interested in writing poems for their own sake; she wrote them as a release for the mystical fire she could no longer contain in her heart.

But this was not the only circumstance under which she felt urged to express herself in verse. Besides her lyric-mystical poetry, she composed many didactic and devotional poems. In a word, she also made use of poetry as an instrument of spiritual formation for her daughters. Keenly sensitive to the thousand happenings around her, she enjoyed speaking in verse of her perceptions. She understood the captivating and suggestive power of poetry with its rhythms and sounds and used it to impress on the hearts of her daughters profound teachings about the religious and spiritual life. At the same time she was delighting them with rhymes and cadences. Teresa, then, also thought of poetry as something to be enjoyed. She once thanked her brother Lorenzo for the verses he had sent her and for the "recreation" she found in reading his couplets. She was especially happy when the nuns put her verses to music and devoutly sang them.

In the minds of her acquaintances Teresa was a good poet. Padre Julián de Avila, who accompanied her on so many of her journeys through Spain, wrote of how she frequently entertained the other travelers by composing poems and that these poems were very good ones. In seeking a critical judgment of the merits of her poetry, one finds at present a difference of opinion. Two critics who have recently approached the question have come to different conclusions. Angel Custodio Vega thinks that in her mystical poetry Teresa has reached sublime heights; whereas Victor de la Concha thinks that as a poet Teresa is at most mediocre.[1] Whatever one may think of the merits of Teresa's poetry, it is definitely written in a popular vein, notably simple and spontaneous.

When asked about the number of poems written by Madre Teresa, one can only speculate. Certainly, not all have been preserved, nor do we even know if we have a record of each of those that has been preserved. The poems we do have in our possession come to a number proportionately small when compared to what the number would be were we to have them all. According to María de San José, Teresa composed many romances about the variety of events that took place on her journeys to make foundations. And Ana de la Encarnación testifies that Madre Teresa was devoted to the saints and composed verses to sing on their feastdays. Ana de Jesús declares that during the Christmas season Teresa would compose words for carols to be sung by the nuns. Probably, in addition, a number of Teresa's poems were not written down at all but were composed on the spot and recited orally so as to contribute to the celebration of some special occasion.

The pieces of paper on which her poems were written were easy to pass around and easy to lose. Thus we do not have the autographs of Teresa's poetry. Recently, however, the Teresian scholar Tomás Alvarez did find in some Italian monasteries the first autograph fragments of Teresa's poems.[2] This discovery leaves scholars with the hopes that more may be found.

As for copies, the most important are those made by Padre Andrés de la Encarnación and preserved in manuscript 1400 in the Biblioteca Nacional de Madrid. Padre Andrés was given the task in 1754 of seeking out all of Teresa's writings in the archives and libraries of Spain. Modern editors base their editions of the poetry on the copy made by Padre Andrés. But both the lack of autographs and the mixture of Teresa's poetry with that of other Carmelites give rise to the problem of authenticity, particularly the authenticity of some of the poems. Further critical study needs to be done. We selected for this translation those poems that Tomás Alvarez included in his Spanish edition[3] and are grateful to Father Adrian J. Cooney for contributing to this volume by his English rendering of them. Rather than sacrifice the meaning of each verse for the sake of a metre and rhyme scheme as found in the original poems, the translator sought to provide a rendering that is both accurate and lyrical.

K.K.

POETRY

Translated by
Adrian J. Cooney, O.C.D.

1.

Vivo Sin Vivir En Mí	Aspirations toward Eternal Life
Vivo sin vivir en mí,	*I live without living in myself,*
Y de tal manera espero,	*And in such a way I hope,*
Que muero porque no muero.	*I die because I do not die.*
Vivo ya fuera de mí,	Since I die of love,
Después que muero de amor,	Living apart from love,
Porque vivo en el Señor,	I live now in the Lord,
Que me quiso para sí.	Who has desired me for Himself.
Cuando el corazón le di	He inscribed on my heart
Puso en él este letrero:	When I gave it to Him:
Que muero porque no muero.	*I die because I do not die.*
Esta divina prisión,	Within this divine prison,
Del amor con que yo vivo,	Of love in which I live,
Ha hecho a Dios me cautivo.	My God my captive is.
Y libre mi corazón	My heart is free
Y causa en mí tal pasión,	To behold my prisoner-God,
Ver a Dios mi prisionero,	Passion welling in my heart,
Que muero porque no muero.	*I die because I do not die.*
¡Ay, que larga es esta vida!	Ah, how weary this life!
¡Que duros estos destierros!	These exiles so hard!
Esta cárcel y estos hierros	This jail and these shackles
En que el alma está metida!	By which the soul is fettered!
Sólo esperar la salida	Longing only to go forth
Me causa un dolor tan fiero,	Brings such terrible sorrow,
Que muero porque no muero.	*I die because I do not die.*

¡Ay, qué vida tan amarga
Do no se goza el Señor!
Porque si es dulce el amor,
No lo es la esperanza larga.
Quíteme Dios esta carga,
Más pesada que el acero,
Que muero porque no muero.

Sólo con la confianza
Vivo de que he de morir,
Porque muriendo el vivir
Me asegura mi esperanza.
Muerte do el vivir se alcanza,
No te tardes, que te espero,
Que muero porque no muero.

Mira que el amor es fuerte.
Vida, no me seas molesta.
Mira que sólo me resta
Para ganarte perderte.
Venga ya la dulce muerte,
El morir venga ligero.
Que muero porque no muero.

Aquella vida de arriba,
Que es la vida verdadera,
Hasta que esta vida muera,
No se goza estando viva.
Muerte, no me seas esquiva;
Viva muriendo primero,
Que muero porque no muero.

Vida, ¿que puedo yo darte
A mi Dios, que vive en mí,
Si no es el perderte a ti,
Para merecer ganarte?
Quiero muriendo alcanzarte,
Pues tanto a mi amado quiero:
Que muero porque no muero.

Ah, how bitter a life
When the Lord is not enjoyed!
While love is sweet,
Long awaiting is not.
O God, take away this burden
Heavier than steel,
I die because I do not die.

Only with that surety
I will die do I live,
Because in dying
My hope in living is assured.
Death, bringing life,
Do not tarry; I await you,
I die because I do not die.

See how love is strong.
Life, do not trouble me.
See how all that remains
Is in losing you to gain.
Come now, sweet death,
Come, dying, swiftly.
I die because I do not die.

That life from above,
That is true life,
Until this life dies,
Life is not enjoyed.
Death, be not aloof;
In dying first, may life be,
I die because I do not die.

Life, what can I give
To my God living in me,
If not to lose you,
Thus to merit Him?
In dying I want to reach
Him alone whom I seek:
I die because I do not die.

2.

En Las Manos De Dios	In the Hands of God

Vuestra soy, para Vos nací,
¿Qué mandáis hacer de mí?

I am Yours and born for you,
What do You want of me?

Soberana Majestad,
Eterna sabiduría,
Bondad buena al alma mía;
La gran vileza mirad
Dios, alteza, un ser, bondad.
Que hoy os canta amor así:
¿Qué mandáis hacer de mí?

Majestic Sovereign,
Unending wisdom,
Kindness pleasing to my soul;
God sublime, one Being Good,
Behold this one so vile.
Singing of her love to you:
What do You want of me?

Vuestra soy, pues me criastes,
Vuestra, pues me redimistes,
Vuestra, pues que me sufristes,
Vuestra, pues que me llamastes,
Vuestra, pues que me esperastes,
Vuestra, pues no me perdí.
¿Qué mandáis hacer de mí?

Yours, you made me,
Yours, you saved me,
Yours, you endured me,
Yours, you called me,
Yours, you awaited me,
Yours, I did not stray.
What do You want of me?

¿Que mandais, pues, buen
    Señor,
Que haga tan vil criado?
¿Cual oficio le habéis dado
A este esclavo pecador?
Veisme aqui, mi dulce Amor,
Amor dulce, veisme aquí,
¿Qué mandáis hacer de mí?

Good Lord, what do you want
    of me,
What is this wretch to do?
What work is this,
This sinful slave, to do?
Look at me, Sweet Love,
Sweet Love, look at me,
What do You want of me?

Veis aquí mi corazón,
Yo le pongo en vuestra palma,
Mi cuerpo, mi vida y alma,
Mis entrañas y afición,
Dulce Esposo y redención,
Pues por vuestra me ofrecí,
¿Qué mandáis hacer de mí?

In Your hand
I place my heart,
Body, life and soul,
Deep feelings and affections mine,
Spouse—Redeemer sweet,
Myself offered now to you,
What do You want of me?

Dadme muerte, dadme vida,
Dad salud o enfermedad,
Honra o deshonra me dad,

Give me death, give me life,
Health or sickness,
Honor or shame,

Dadme guerra o paz crecida,
Flaqueza o fuerza cumplida,
Que a todo digo que sí,
¿Qué mandáis hacer de mí?

Dadme riqueza o pobreza,
Dad consuelo o desconsuelo,
Dadme alegría o tristeza,
Dadme infierno o dadme cielo,
Vida dulce, sol sin velo,
Pues del todo me rendí.
¿Qué mandáis hacer de mí?

Si queréis, dadme oración,
Si no, dadme sequedad,
Si abundancia y devoción,
Y si no esterilidad,
Soberana Majestad,
Sólo hallo paz aquí,
¿Qué mandáis hacer de mí?

Dadme, pues, sabiduría,
O por amor, ignorancia,
Dadme años de abundancia,
O de hambre y carestía
Dad tiniebla o claro día,
Revolvedme aquí o allí.
¿Qué mandáis hacer de mí?

Si queréis que esté holgando,
Quiero por amor holgar;
Si me mandáis trabajar,
Morir quiero trabajando.
Decid, ¿dónde, cómo y cuándo?
Decid, dulce Amor, decid.
¿Qué mandáis hacer de mí?

Dadme Calvario o Tabor,
Desierto o tierra abundosa,
Sea Job en el dolor,
O Juan que al pecho reposa;

War or swelling peace,
Weakness or full strength,
Yes, to these I say,
What do You want of me?

Give me wealth or want,
Delight or distress,
Happiness or gloominess,
Heaven or hell,
Sweet life, sun unveiled,
To you I give all.
What do You want of me?

Give me, if You will, prayer;
Or let me know dryness,
An abundance of devotion,
Or if not, then barrenness.
In you alone, Sovereign Majesty,
I find my peace,
What do You want of me?

Give me then wisdom.
Or for love, ignorance,
Years of abundance,
Or hunger and famine.
Darkness or sunlight,
Move me here or there:
What do You want of me?

If You want me to rest,
I desire it for love;
If to labor,
I will die working:
Sweet Love say
Where, how and when.
What do You want of me?

Calvary or Tabor give me,
Desert or fruitful land;
As Job in suffering
Or John at Your breast;

Sea viña fructuosa
O estéril, si cumple así.
¿Qué mandáis hacer de mí?

Barren or fruited vine,
Whatever be Your will:
What do You want of me?

Sea José puesto en cadenas,
O de Egipto Adelantado
O David sufriendo penas,
O ya David encumbrado,
Sea Jonás anegado,
O libertado de allí,
¿Qué mandáis hacer de mí?

Be I Joseph chained
Or as Egypt's governor,
David pained
Or exalted high,
Jonas drowned,
Or Jonas freed:
What do You want of me?

Esté callando o hablando,
Haga fruto o no le haga,
Muéstrame la ley mi llaga,
Goce de Evangelio blando;
Esté penando o gozando,
Sólo Vos en mi vivid,
¿Qué mandáis hacer de mí?

Silent or speaking,
Fruitbearing or barren,
My wounds shown by the Law,
Rejoicing in the tender Gospel;
Sorrowing or exulting,
You alone live in me:
What do You want of me?

Vuestra soy, para Vos nací,
¿Qué mandáis hacer de mí?

Yours I am, for You I was born:
What do You want of me?

3.

Sobre Aquellas Palabras "Dilectus Meus Mihi"

On Those Words "Dilectus Meus Mihi"

Yo toda me entregué y di,
Y de tal suerte he trocado,
Que mi Amado para mí,
Y yo soy para mí Amado.

Myself surrendered and given,
The exchange is this:
My Beloved is for me,
And I am for my Beloved.

Cuando el dulce Cazador
Me tiró y dejó rendida,
En los brazos del amor,
Mi alma quedó caída;
Y cobrando nueva vida,
De tal manera he trocado
Que mi Amado para mí,
Y yo soy para me Amado.

When the Gentle hunter
Wounded and subdued me,
In love's arms,
My soul fallen;
New life receiving,
Thus did I exchange
My Beloved is for me,
And I am for my Beloved.

Tiróme con una flecha
Enerbolada de amor,
Y mi alma quedó hecha
Una con su Criador.
Ya yo no quiero otro amor,
Pues a mi Dios me he entregado,
Y mi Amado para mí,
Y yo soy para mí Amado.

The arrow he drew
Full of love,
My soul was oned
With her Creator.
Other love I want not,
Surrendered now to my God,
That my Beloved is for me,
And I am for my Beloved.

4.

Coloquio Amoroso

Loving Colloquy

Si el amor que me tenéis,
Dios mío, es como el que os
   tengo,
Decidme ¿en qué me detengo?
O Vos ¿en qué os detenéis?
—Alma ¿qué quieres de
   mí?
—Dios mío, no más que
   verte.
—Y ¿qué temes más de
   ti?
—Lo que más temo es
   perderte.
Un alma en Dios escondida
¿Qué tiene que desear,
Sino amar y más amar,
Y en amor toda escondida
Tornarte de nuevo a amar?

Un amor que ocupe os pido,
Dios mío, mi alma os tenga,
Para hacer un dulce nido
Adonde más la convenga.

If the love You have for me,
Is like the love I have for
   You,
My God, what detains me?
Oh, what is delaying You?
—Soul, what is it you desire
   of me?
—My God, nothing other than to
   see You.
—What is it that you fear more
   than self?
—What I fear most is the loss
   of You.
A soul hidden in God,
What has it to desire
Save to love more and more,
And, in love all hidden
Again and again to love You?

One all possessing love I ask
My God, my soul centered in You,
Making a delightful nest,
A resting place most pleasing.

5.

Feliz El Que Ama a Dios	Happy the Enamored Heart

Dichoso el corazón enamorado
Que en solo Dios ha puesto el
pensamiento
Por él renuncia todo lo criado,

Y en él halla su gloria y su
contento.
Aun de sí mismo vive
descuidado,
Porque en Dios está todo su
intento,
Y así alegre pasa y muy gozoso
Las hondas de este mar
tempestuoso.

Happy the enamored heart,
Thought centered on God
alone,
Renouncing every creature for
Him,
Finding in Him glory and
contentment.
Living forgetful of
self,
In God is all its intention,

Happy and so joyfully it journeys
Through waves of this stormy
sea.

6.

Ante La Hermosura De Dios*	Oh Exceeding Beauty

¡Oh, Hermosura que excedéis
A todas las hermosuras!
Sin herir dolor hacéis,
Y sin dolor deshacéis,
El amor de las criaturas.

Oh, ñudo que así juntáis
Dos cosas tan desiguales,
No sé por que os desatáis,
Pues atado fuerza dais
A tener por buen los males.

Juntáis quien no tiene ser
Con el Ser que no se acaba;
Sin acabar acabáis,

Oh Beauty exceeding
All other beauties!
Paining, but You wound not
Free of pain You destroy
The love of creatures.

Oh, knot that binds
Two so different,
Why do You become unbound
For when held fast You strengthen
Making injuries seem good.

Bind the one without being
With being unending;
Finish, without finishing,

*For the origin of this poem, see the postscript in her letter to Don Lorenzo, Jan. 2,
1577; and also her letter to him on Jan. 17, 1577.

Sin tener que amar amáis,
Engrandecéis nuestra nada.

Love, without having to love,
Magnify our nothingness.

7.

Ayes Del Destierro

Sighs in Exile

¡Cuan triste es, Dios mío,
La vida sin ti!
Ansiosa de verte,
Deseo morir.

My God, how sad is
Life without You!
Longing to see You,
Death I desire.

Carrera muy larga
Es la de este suelo,
Morada penosa,
Muy duro destierro.
¡Oh Dueño adorado!
Sácame de aquí.
Ansiosa de verte,
Deseo morir.

This earth's journey
How long it is;
A painful dwelling,
An exile drear.
Oh, Master adored,
Take me away!
Longing to see You,
Death I desire.

Lúgubre es la vida,
Amarga en extremo;
Que no vive el alma
Que está de ti lejos.
¡Oh dulce bien mío,
Que soy infeliz!
Ansiosa de verte,
Deseo morir.

Dismal is life,
Bitter as can be:
The soul lifeless,
Apart from You.
O my sweet Goodness,
How sad am I!
Longing to see You,
Death I desire.

¡Oh muerte benigna,
Socorre mis penas!
Tus golpes son dulces,
Que el alma libertan.
¡Que dicha, oh mi amado,
Estar junto a Ti!
Ansiosa de verte,
Deseo morir.

O kind death
Free me from trials!
Gentle are your blows,
Freeing the soul.
Oh, my Beloved, what joy
To be oned to You!
Longing to see You,
Death I desire.

El amor mundano	To this life
Apega a esta vida;	Worldly love adheres;
El amor divino	Love divine
Por la otra suspira.	For the other sighs.
Sin ti, Dios eterno,	Eternal God, without You,
¿Quien puede vivir?	Who can live?
Ansiosa de verte,	*Longing to see You,*
Deseo morir.	*Death I desire.*
La vida terrena	Unending sorrow
Es continuo duelo:	Is this earthly life;
Vida verdadera	Life that is true
La hay sólo en el cielo.	In heaven alone is found.
Permite, Dios mío,	My God, allow
Que viva yo allí,	That there I may dwell.
Ansiosa de verte,	*Longing to see You,*
Deseo morir.	*Death I desire.*
¿Quien es el que teme	Who fears
La muerte del cuerpo,	The body's death
Si con ella logra	If one then gains
Un placer inmenso?	Pleasure so great?
¡Oh! si, el de amarte,	Oh, yes, in loving You,
Dios mío, sin fin.	Forever, my God!
Ansiosa de verte,	*Longing to see You,*
Deseo morir.	*Death I desire.*
Mi alma afligida	Afflicted, my soul
Gime y desfallece.	Sighs and faints.
¡Ay! ¿Quien de su amado	Ah, who can stay apart
Puede estar ausente?	From her Beloved?
Acabe ya, acabe	Oh! end now,
Aqueste sufrir,	This my suffering.
Ansiosa de verte,	*Longing to see You,*
Deseo morir.	*Death I desire.*
El barbo cogido	The fish caught
En doloso anzuelo,	On the painful hook,
Encuentra en la muerte	In death's embrace
El fin del tormento.	Its torment ending.

¡Ay! tambien yo sufro,
Bien mío, sin ti:
Ansiosa de verte,
Deseo morir.

Ah, how I suffer,
Without You, my Love.
Longing to see You,
Death I desire.

En vano mi alma
Te busca, oh mi dueño;
Tu siempre invisible
No alivias su anhelo
¡Ay! esto la inflama
Hasta prorrumpir:
Ansiosa de verte,
Deseo morir.

Master, my soul
In vain seeks You!
Always unseen
You leave me anxiously longing.
Ah! the very longing inflames
Until I cry out:
Longing to see You,
Death I desire.

¡Ay! cuando te dignas
Entrar en mi pecho,
Dios mío, al instante
El perderte temo.
Tal pena me aflige,
Y me hace decir:
Ansiosa de verte,
Deseo morir.

When at last
You enter my heart,
My God, then at once
I fear your leaving.
The pain that touches me
Makes me say,
Longing to see You,
Death I desire.

Haz, Senor, que acabe
Tan larga agonía;
Socorre a tu sierva
Que por ti suspira.
Rompe aquestos hierros
Y sea feliz.
Ansiosa de verte,
Deseo morir.

Lord, end now
This long agony.
Comfort your servant
Sighing for You.
Shatter the fetters
Let her rejoice.
Longing to see You,
Death I desire.

Mas no, dueño amado,
Que es justo padezca;
Que expíe mis yerros,
Mis culpas inmensas.
¡Ay! logren mis lágrimas
Te dignes oír
Ansiosa de verte,
Deseo morir.

Ah, no, Beloved Master,
It is only that I suffer
My sins to atone
My guilt unbounded
Ah! may my tears gain
Your listening to me:
Longing to see You,
Death I desire.

8.

Buscando A Dios	Seeking God

Alma, buscarte has en Mí,
Y a Mí buscarme has en ti.

De tal suerte pudo amor,
Alma, en mí te retratar,
Que ningún sabio pintor
Supiera con tal primor
Tal imagen estampar.

Fuiste por amor criada
Hermosa, bella, y así
En mis entrañas pintada,
Si te perdieres, mi amada,
Alma, buscarte has en Mí.

Que yo sé que te hallaras
En mi pecho retratada
Y tan al vivo sacada
Que si te ves te holgaras
Viéndote tan bien pintada.

Y si acaso no supieres

Donde me hallarás a Mí,
No andes de aquí para allí,
Sino, si hallarme quisieres
A Mí buscarme has en ti.

Porque tú eres mi aposento,
Eres mi casa y morada,
Y así llamo en cualquier tiempo,
Si hallo en tu pensamiento
Estar la puerta cerrada.

Fuera de ti no hay buscarme,
Porque para hallarme a Mí,
Bastará solo llamarme,
Que a ti iré sin tardarme
Y a Mí buscarme has en ti.

Soul, you must seek yourself in Me
And in yourself seek Me.

With such skill, soul,
Love could portray you in Me
That a painter well gifted
Could never show
So finely that image.

For love you were fashioned
Deep within me
Painted so beautiful, so fair;
If, my beloved, I should lose you,
Soul, in yourself seek Me.

Well I know that you will discover
Yourself portrayed in my heart
So lifelike drawn
It will be a delight to behold
Yourself so well painted.

And should by chance you do
  not know
Where to find Me,
Do not go here and there;
But if you wish to find Me,
In yourself seek Me.

Soul, since you are My room,
My house and dwelling,
If at any time,
Through your distracted ways
I find the door tightly closed,

Outside yourself seek Me not,
To find Me it will be
Enough only to call Me,
Then quickly will I come,
And in yourself seek Me.

9.

Eficacia De La Paciencia	Efficacy of Patience

Nada te turbe,
Nada te espante,
Todo se pasa,
Dios no se muda,
La Paciencia
Todo lo alcanza;
Quien a Dios tiene
Nada le falta.
Sólo Dios basta.

Let nothing trouble you,
Let nothing scare you,
All is fleeting,
God alone is unchanging.
Patience
Everything obtains.
Who possesses God
Nothing wants.
God alone suffices.

10.

Hacia La Patria	On the Way to Heaven

Caminemos para el cielo,
Monjas del Carmelo.

Toward heaven let us journey,
Nuns of Carmel.

Vamos muy mortificadas,
Humildes y despreciadas,
Dejando el consuelo,
Monjas del Carmelo.

Mortified, humble, and despised,
Let us walk,
Consolations left aside,
Nuns of Carmel.

Al voto de la obediencia
Vamos, no haya resistencia,
Que es nuestro blanco y
      consuelo,
Monjas del Carmelo.

Unresisting let us go
To vowed obedience,
Our consoling aim,

Nuns of Carmel.

La pobreza es el camino,
El mismo por donde vino
Nuestro Emperador del cielo,
Monjas del Carmelo.

Poverty is the way,
The very road He came,
Our heavenly Emperor,
Nuns of Carmel.

No deja de nos amar
Nuestro Dios y nos llamar
Sigámosle sin recelo,
Monjas del Carmelo.

Untiring in loving,
Our God is calling;
Trusting Him, let us follow,
Nuns of Carmel.

An amor se está abrasando
Aquel que nació temblando
Envuelto en humano velo
Monjas del Carmelo.

Vámonos a enriquecer,
A donde nunca ha de haber
Pobreza ni desconsuelo,
Monjas del Carmelo.

Al Padre Elías siguiendo
Nos vamos contradiciendo
Con su fortaleza y celo,
Monjas del Carmelo.

Nuestro querer renunciando,
Procuremos el doblado
Espíritu de Eliseo,
Monjas del Carmelo.

Afire in love's burning,
He, once born trembling,
Veiled in our humanity,
Nuns of Carmel.

Hasten to this enrichment
Where poverty and grief
Will never be,
Nuns of Carmel.

Elijah, our Father, leads,
In our self-denying we follow him
Strongly and zealously,
Nuns of Carmel.

Renouncing our will,
We long to attain
Elisha's double spirit,
Nuns of Carmel.

11.

Al Nacimiento De Jesús

To the Birth of Jesus

¡Ah, pastores que veláis,
Por guardar vuestros rebaños,
Mirad que os nace un Cordero,
Hijo de Dios Soberano!

Viene pobre y despreciado,
Comenzadle ya a guardar,
Que a lobo os le ha de llevar
Sin que le hayamos gozado.
—Gil, dame acá aquel cayado
Que no me saldrá de mano,
No nos lleven al Cordero:
—*¿No ves que es Dios Soberano?*

¡Sonzas! que estoy aturdido
De gozo y de penas junto.
—¿Si es Dios el que hoy ha
nacido,

Ah, shepherds watching,
Guarding your flocks!
Behold, a Lamb born for you,
Son of our Sovereign God.

Poor and despised He comes,
Begin now guarding Him,
Lest the wolf carry Him off.
Before rejoicing in Him,
Bring me your crook, Giles.
Firmly will I grasp it,
Preventing theft of the Lamb:
See you not He is Sovereign God?

Come now, bewildered am I
By joy and sorrow joined.
If today God be born,

Cómo puede ser difunto?
¡Oh, que es hombre también
   junto!
La vida estará en su mano;
Mirad, que es este el Cordero,
Hijo de Dios Soberano.

How can He then die?
Oh, since He is man as well,

Life in His hands will be!
In this Lamb behold,
The Son of our Sovereign God.

No sé para qué le piden,
Pues le dan después tal guerra;
—Mía fe, Gil, mejor será
Que se nos torne a su tierra,
Si el pecado nos destierra,
Y está el bien todo en su mano.
Ya que ha venido padezca
Este Dios tan Soberano.

Why do they ask for Him
And then against Him war.
Giles, in faith it would be better
For Him to return to His land.
If by sin we are banished,
In His hand all good lies
Since to suffer He came,
This God truly sovereign.

Poco te duele su pena;
¡Oh, como es cierto, del hombre
Cuando nos viene provecho,
El mal ajeno se esconde!
¿No ves que gana renombre
De pastor de gran rebaño?

His suffering so little troubles you:
Oh, how true of men.
When profit comes,
Evil we ignore!
Do you see He gains renown
As the Shepherd of the great
   flock?

Con todo, es cosa muy fuerte
Que muera Dios Soberano. *

Terrible it is nonetheless
*That the Sovereign God should
   die.*

12.

Al Nacimiento De Jesús   At the Birth of Jesus

Hoy nos viene a redimir

Un Zagal, nuestro pariente,
Gil, que es Dios omnipotente.

Por eso nos ha sacado
De prisión a Satanás;

Giles, today there comes to
   redeem us

A shepherd boy, our kinsman,
God Omnipotent!

He frees us from
Satan's prison;

---

*The autograph of the two last stanzas is conserved in the monastery of the Discalced Carmelite nuns in Florence.

Mas es pariente de Bras,	But He is kin of Bras,
Y de Menga, y de Llorente.	Menga, and Llorente,
¡Oh, que es Dios omnipotente!	*Oh, He is God Omnipotent!*

Pues si es Dios, ¿como es vendido	If He be God, why sold
Y muere crucificado?	And crucified dies?
—¿No ves que mató el pecado,	Giles, in His suffering innocently,
Padeciendo el inocente?	Do you see, He vanquished sin?
Gil, que es Dios omnipotente.	*He is God Omnipotent.*

Mi fe, yo lo vi nacido	Oh, I saw Him being born
De una muy linda Zagala.	Of a shepherdess most fair.
—Pues si es Dios ¿como ha querido	If He is God, why did He desire
Estar con tan pobre gente?	Among such poor folk to be?
—¿No ves, que es omnipotente?	*See you not that He is Omnipotent?*

Déjate de esas preguntas,	No more questioning,
Muramos por le servir,	Let us serve Him.
Y pues El viene a morir	Llorente, since He comes to die,
Muramos con El, Llorente,	Let us die with Him.
*Pues es Dios omnipotente.**	*He is God Omnipotent.*

13.

Para Navidad	For Christmas

Pues el amor	Since love
Nos ha dado Dios,	Has given us God
Ya no hay que temer,	*No reason is there to fear,*
Muramos los dos.	*Let us both die.*

Danos el Padre	The Father gives us
A su único Hijo:	His only Son,
Hoy viene al mundo	Born this day in a stable poor,

---

*The autograph of the thirteen first verses is conserved in the same Carmel of Florence. The autograph of the last two stanzas is conserved in the Carmel of Savona, also in Italy.

En un pobre cortijo.
¡Oh, gran regocijo,
Que ya el hombre es Dios!
No hay que temer,
Muramos los dos.

Mira, Llorente
Qué fuerte amorío,
Viene el inocente
A padecer frío;
Deja un señorío
En fin, como Dios,
No hay que temer,
Muramos los dos.

Pues, ¿como, Pascual,
Hizo esa franqueza,
Que toma un sayal
Dejando riqueza?
Mas quiere pobreza,
Sigámosle nos;
Pues ya viene hombre,
Muramos los dos.

Pues, ¿que le daran
Por esta grandeza?
Grandes azotes
Con mucha crudeza.
Oh, qué gran tristeza
Será para nos:
Si esto es verdad,
Muramos los dos.

Pues ¿cómo se atreven
Siendo Omnipotente?
Ha de ser muerto
De una mala gente.
Pues si eso es, Llorente;
Hurtémosle nos,
No ves que El lo quiere,
Muramos los dos.

To the world He comes.
Oh, great rejoicing,
Now man is God!
No reason is there to fear,
Let us both die.

Llorente, look,
With what great love,
The Innocent comes
To suffer in the cold.
He leaves His lordship,
For He is God:
No reason is there to fear,
Let us both die.

Pascual, why did He
So graciously take
Garments so coarse
Forsaking such richness?
Let us follow Him,
In seeking poverty;
He became man for this.
Let us both die.

For a deed so great
What can we give Him?
Lashes severe
Given so cruelly.
Sorrow so deep
Will be for us!
Should this be true,
Let us both die.

Oh, how bold they are
Daring the All Powerful!
He will know death
By an evil people.
Llorente, if this be true,
We must steal Him.
Can you not see He wishes this?
Let us both die.

14.

Al Nacimiento Del Niño Dios	At the Birth of the Infant God

Mi gallejo, mira quién llama.
Angeles son, que ya viene
el alba.

My Gallejo, look who is coming.
Angels they are, the dawn
is nigh.

Hame dad un gran zumbido
Que parece cantillana,
Mira Bras, que ya es de día,
Vamos a ver la zagala.
Mi gallejo, mira quién llama.
Angeles son, que ya viene
el alba.

My ears are ringing
With what seems an old song
Look, Bras, daylight is here.
Let us go to the shepherdess.
My Gallejo, look who is coming.
Angels they are, the dawn
is nigh.

¿Es parienta del alcalde,
U quién es esta doncella?
Ella es hija de Dios Padre,
Relumbra, como una estrella.
Mi gallejo, mira quién llama.
Angeles son, que ya viene
el alba.

Is she a relative of the Mayor,
Or who is this maiden?
God the Father's daughter,
Glowing starlike.
My Gallejo, look who is coming.
Angels they are, the dawn
is nigh.

15.

A La Circuncisión	The Circumcision

Vertiendo está sangre,
¡*Dominguillo, eh*!
Yo no sé por qué.

He is shedding blood,
Dominguillo, eh!
Why I know not!

¿Por qué, te pregunto,
Hacen dél justicia,
Pues es inocente
Y no tiene malicia?
Tuvo gran codicia,
Yo no sé por qué,
De mucho amarme,
¡*Dominguillo, eh*!

I ask you why,
Him they condemn,
Innocent He is,
And without evil?
How ardent His desire,
I know not why,
To love me so ardently:
Oh, Dominguillo!

¿Pues luego en naciendo,
Le han de atormentar?

Then after He was born,
Why did they torment Him?

—Sí, que está muriendo
Por quitar el mal;
¡Oh, que gran Zagal
Será, por mi fe!
¡*Dominguillo, eh*!

—Yes, for He is dying
To cast out evil.
Oh, what a great Shepherd
He will surely be!
Oh, Dominguillo!

¿Tú no lo has mirado,
Que es niño inocente?
—Ya me lo han contado
Brasillo y Llorente;
Gran inconveniente
Será no amalle,
¡*Dominguillo, eh*!

Certainly you have seen
He is but a sinless child?
—They have told me,
Brasillo and Llorente;
Great will be the loss
Not to love Him
Oh, Dominguillo!

16.

Otra A La Circuncisión

Another on the Circumcision

Este Niño viene llorando;
Mírale, Gil, que te está
   llamando.

This little Child comes crying,
Look, Giles, He calls you.

Vino del cielo a la tierra
Para quitar nuestra guerra;
Ya comienza la pelea,
Su sangre está derramando,
Mírale, Gil, que te está
   llamando.

To earth from heaven He came
Our warring to end.
Already the battle rages,
His blood is flowing:
Look, Giles, He calls you.

Fue tan grande, el amorío,
Que no es mucho estar llorando,
Que comienza a tener brío,
Habiendo de estar mandando.
Mírale, Gil, que te está
   llamando.

So strong is his loving,
His crying is without surprise.
Courage grows within Him,
For He is to lead.
Look, Giles, He calls you.

Caro nos ha de costar,
Pues comienza tan temprano,
A su sangre derramar,
Habremos de estar llorando
Mírale, Gil, que te está
   llamando.

How great the price will be
Since He begins so young
Bleeding for us.
Oh, weeping we should be.
Look, Giles, He calls you.

No viniera El a morir
Pues podía estarse en su nido,
¿No ves, Gil, que si ha venido
Es como león bramando?
Mírale, Gil, que te está
llamando.

Dime Pascual, ¿que me quieres,
Que tantos gritos me das?
Que le ames, pues to quiere,
Y por ti está tiritando;
Mírale, Gil, que te está
llamando.

Has He not come to die,
For in His dwelling He could stay.
Giles, do you see He has come
As a roaring lion?
Look, Giles, He calls you.

Pascual, why do you shout?
What do you want?
Love Him for He loves you
And shivers here for you.
Look, Giles, He calls you.

17.

En La Festividad De Los Santos Reyes

On the Feast of the Holy Kings

Pues la estrella
Es ya llegada,
Vaya con los Reyes
La mi manada.

Vamos todos juntos
A ver el Mesías,
Pues vemos cumplidas
Ya las profecías;
Pues en nuestros días,
Es ya llegada,
Vaya con los Reyes
La mi manada. *

Llevémosle dones
De grande valor,
Pues vienen los Reyes
Con tan gran hervor.
Alégrese hoy

Now that the star
Has come,
Accompany the Kings,
Go, my flock.

Together let us go
The Messiah to behold.
We see fulfilled now
The prophet's words:
In these our days,
At last He has come.
Accompany the Kings,
Go, my flock.

Our gifts so dear
Let us bring Him.
With fervor so full,
The Kings are coming.
Today may she rejoice,

*The autograph of the first twelve verses is conserved in the Carmel of Savona, Italy.

Nuestra gran Zagala,
Vaya con los Reyes
La mi manada.

No cures, Llorente,
De buscar razón,
Para ver que es Dios
Aqueste garzón;
Dale el corazon,
Y yo esté empeñada,
Vaya con los Reyes
La mi manada.

Our shepherdess so grand.
Accompany the Kings,
Go, my flock.

Llorente, trouble not
In seeking a reason,
For He is God,
This young Boy.
While I in debt fall,
Give Him your heart.
Accompany the Kings,
Go, my flock.

18.

A La Cruz

To the Cross

Cruz, descanso sabroso de mi
*   vida*
Vos seáis la bienvenida.

O Cross, my life's delightful
*   rest,*
My welcome be.

Oh, bandera, en cuyo amparo
El más flaco será
    fuerte;
Oh, vida de nuestra muerte,
Qué bien la has resucitado
Al león has amansado.
Pues por ti perdió la vida,
Vos seáis la bienvenida.

Beneath your protecting banner
Even the weakest are made
    strong!
O life of our death,
Reviving it so well.
Having tamed the lion,
By you he was slain:
My welcome be.

Quien no os ama está cautivo
Y ajeno de libertad;
Quien a vos quiere allegar
No tendrá en nada desvío.
Oh dichoso poderío,
Donde el mal no halla cabida,
Vos seáis la bienvenida.

Captive is he that loves you not,
No freedom does he know;
Those who approach you
From bad paths are saved.
Oh, in this Kingdom blessed
Evil finds no rest:
My welcome be.

Vos fuisteis la libertad
De nuestro gran cautiverio;
Por vos se reparó mi mal

You are the freedom
From our dread captivity;
With so precious remedy,

Con tan costoso remedio
Para con Dios fuiste medio
De alegría conseguida,
Vos seáis la bienvenida.

From evilness You restored me.
In God the means
Of this joy obtained:
My welcome be.

19.

El Camino De La Cruz

The Way of the Cross

En la cruz está la vida
Y el consuelo,
Y ella sola es el camino
Para el cielo.

Within the cross is life
And consolation.
It alone is the road
Leading to heaven.

En la cruz está el Señor
De cielo y tierra,
Y el gozar de mucha paz,
Aunque haya guerra.
Todos los males destierra
En este suelo,
Y ella sola es el camino
Para el cielo.

The Lord of heaven and earth
Is on the cross.
On it, too, delight in peace.
Though war may rage,
It banishes all evil
Dwelling here on earth.
It alone is the road
Leading to heaven.

De la cruz dice la Esposa
A su Querido
Que es una palma preciosa
Donde ha subido
Y su fruto le ha sabido
A Dios del cielo,
Y ella sola es el camino
Para el cielo.

From the cross the bride
To her Beloved says
This is a precious palm
Upon which she has climbed,
Its fruit tasting
Like the God of paradise:
It alone is the road
Leading to heaven.

Es una oliva preciosa
La santa cruz,
Que con su aceite nos unta
Y nos da luz.
Alma mía, toma la cruz
Con gran consuelo,
Y ella sola es el camino
Para el cielo.

This sacred cross,
An olive tree so dear,
With its oil anoints us
Giving us light.
My soul, take up this cross
Rich with consolations great.
It alone is the road
Leading to heaven.

Es la cruz el árbol verde	This cross is the verdant tree
Y deseado	Desired by the bride.
De la Esposa, que a su sombra	In its cool shade
Se ha sentado.	Now she is resting,
Para gozar de su Amado	Delighting in her Beloved,
El Rey del cielo,	Heaven's King:
Y ella sola es el camino	*It alone is the road*
Para el cielo.	*Leading to heaven.*
El alma que a Dios está	The soul to God
Toda rendida,	Is wholly surrendered,
Y muy de veras del mundo	From all the world
Desasida,	Now truly free,
La cruz le es árbol de vida	The cross is at last
Y de consuelo,	Her "Tree of Life" and
	consolation:
Y ella sola es el camino	*It alone is the road*
Para el cielo.	*Leading to heaven.*
Después que se puso en cruz	After our Saviour
El Salvador,	Upon the cross placed Himself,
En la cruz está la gloria	Now in this cross is
Y el honor,	Both glory and honor.
Y en el padecer dolor	In suffering pain
Vida y consuelo,	There is life and comfort,
Y el camino más seguro	*And the safest road*
Para el cielo.	*Leading to heaven.*

20.

Abrazadas A La Cruz	Embracing the Cross
Caminemos para el cielo	*To heaven let us walk,*
Monjas del Carmelo.	*Nuns of Carmel.*
Abracemos bien la Cruz	Embracing the cross,
Y sigamos a Jesús,	Let us follow Jesus,
Que es nuestro camino y luz	He is our way and light
Lleno de todo consuelo,	Abounding in consolations,
Monjas del Carmelo.	*Nuns of Carmel.*

Si guardáis más que los ojos	Guard more than your eyes,
La profesión de tres votos,	Your three vows professed
Libraros de mil enojos,	From a thousand vexations
De tristeza y desconsuelo,	Of sadness and distress,
Monjas del Carmelo.	*Nuns of Carmel.*

El voto de la obediencia,	The vow of obedience,
Aunque es de muy alta ciencia,	Is of great wisdom,
Jamás se la hace ofensa	Only in resisting it
Sino cuando hay resistencia.	Does harm come.
De ésta os libre Dios del cielo,	Heaven deliver you,
Monjas del Carmelo.	*Nuns of Carmel.*

El voto de castidad	Keep with great care
Con gran cuidado guardad.	Chastity's vow;
A solo Dios desead,	Seek God alone,
Y en El mismo os encerrad,	Be cloistered in Him,
Sin mirar cosa del suelo,	Look at nothing earthly,
Monjas del Carmelo.	*Nuns of Carmel.*

El que llaman de pobreza,	What is named poverty
Si se guarda con pureza,	If with purity kept
Está lleno de riqueza	Is with riches overflowing
Y abre las puertas del cielo,	Opening Heaven's Gates,
Monjas del Carmelo.	*Nuns of Carmel.*

Y si así lo hacemos	Opponents we conquer
Los contrarios venceremos	In following this way,
Y a la fin descansaremos	At last we will rest in
Con el que hizo tierra y cielo,	The Maker of Heaven and Earth,
Monjas del Carmelo.	*Nuns of Carmel.*

21.

A San Andrés	To Saint Andrew
¿Si el padecer con amor	*If suffering for love's sake*
Puede dar tan gran deleite?	*Can give such wondrous delight?*
¡Que gozo nos dara el verte!	*What joy will gazing on You be?*

¿Qué será cuando veamos
A la eterna Majestad,
Pues de ver Andrés la cruz
Se pudo tanto alegrar?
¡Oh, que no puede faltar
En el padecer deleite!
¡Qué gozo nos dará el verte!

What will it be beholding
The Majesty eternal
Since Andrew seeing the cross
Was so filled with rejoicing?
Oh, how can it be wanting,
Delight in suffering's midst!
What joy will gazing on You be?

El amor cuando es crecido
No puede estar sin obrar,
Ni el fuerte sin pelear,
Por amor de su Querido.
Con esto le habrá vencido,
Y querrá que en todo acierte,
¡Que gozo nos dara el verte!

Love, when it has grown,
Save in laboring cannot live,
Nor the hearty without fighting
Because of love for his Beloved.
By this love is victory won
And the desire to be right in all.
What joy will gazing on You be.

Pues todos temen la muerte
¿Como te es dulce el morir?
¡O, que voy para vivir
En más encumbrada suerte!
¡Oh mi Dios! que con tu muerte
Al más flaco hiciste fuerte:
¡Qué gozo nos dará el verte!

Since all people dread dying,
Why is it sweetness to You?
Oh, I will live
In a loftier way.
By Your death, O my God,
The weakest knows strength.
What joy will gazing on You be?

¡Oh Cruz! madero, precioso
Lleno de gran majestad,
Pues siendo de despreciar
Tomaste a Dios por esposo.
A ti vengo muy gozoso,
Sin merecer el quererte.
Esme muy gran gozo el verte.

O cross, wood so precious
Majestic and grand!
Once greatly despised,
Now espoused to God,
With rejoicing I come,
Unworthy to love you.
What joy will gazing on You be?

22.

A San Hilarion

To Saint Hilarion

Hoy vencido un guerrero
Al mundo y a sus valedores.
Vuelta, vuelta, pecadores,
Sigamos este sendero.

Today a warrior has conquered
The world and its defenders.
Return, return, sinners,
Let us follow this path.

Sigamos la soledad
Y no queramos morir,
Hasta ganar el vivir
En tan subida pobreza.
¡Oh, qué grande es la destreza
De aquéste nuestro guerrero!
Vuelta, vuelta, pecadores,
Sigamos este sendero.

Con armas de penitencia
Ha vencido a Lucifer,
Combate con la paciencia,
Ya no tiene que temer.
Todos podemos valer
Siguiendo este caballero,
Vuelta, vuelta, pecadores,
Sigamos este sendero.

No ha tenido valedores,
Abrazóse con la cruz:
Siempre en ella hallamos luz

Pues la dio a los pecadores.
¡Oh, qué dichosos amores
Tuvo este nuestro guerrero!
Vuelta, vuelta, pecadores,
Sigamos este sendero.

Ya ha ganado la corona,
Y se acabó el padecer,
Gozando ya el merecer,
Con muy encumbrada gloria.
¡Oh venturosa victoria
De nuestro fuerte guerrero!
Vuelta, vuelta, pecadores,
Sigamos este sendero.

In solitude let us be
And cease longing for death
Until gaining life
Through poverty sublime.
Oh, great is the skilfulness
Our Warrior has!
Return, return, sinners,
Let us follow this path.

With penance as His arms,
Lucifer He vanquished,
In patience He fights,
Nothing frightens Him.
We, too, can conquer
In following this Knight!
Return, return, sinners,
Let us follow this path.

Without any defenders,
The cross He embraced
In this our source of unwavering
    light,
Given to us sinners.
Ah, what blessed love
Our Warrior possessed!
Return, return, sinners,
Let us follow this path.

Now the crown he has won,
Suffering has passed,
Rejoicing in His triumph
In glory exalting.
Oh, victory, most fortunate
Won by our Warrior strong!
Return, return, sinners,
Let us follow this path.

23.

A Santa Catalina Martir	To Saint Catalina, Martyr
¡Oh gran amadora	O great lover
Del Eterno Dios	Of God eternal!
Estrella luciente,	Shining star
Amparadnos vos!	Protect us!
Desde tierna edad	In years so tender
Tomaste Esposo	A Spouse you took,
Fue tanto el amor,	So ardent the love,
Que no os dio reposo.	You knew no rest.
Quien es temeroso,	He that is fearful
No se llegue a Vos,	Away from You should stay.
Si estima la vida	If life he values
Y el morir por Vos.	And from death would run.
Mirad los cobardes	Oh, you cowards, see
Aquesta doncella,	This little maid
Que no estima el oro	Who values not gold
Ni verse tan bella.	Nor her beauty admires.
Metida en la guerra	She embraces the war
De persecución,	And persecution endures
Para padecer	To suffer bravely
Con gran corazón.	With heart truly great.
Mas pena le da	Greater suffering would it be
Vivir sin su Esposo	Without her Spouse to live;
Y así en los tormentos	In torments' midst
Hallaba reposo:	Rest she found.
Todo le es gozoso,	Joy comes abounding.
Querría ya morir,	Now she longs to die,
Pues que con la vida	For in living
No puede vivir.	She cannot live.
Las que pretendemos	Those of us seeking
Gozar de su gozo,	Her joy to possess
Nunca nos cansemos,	Never may we weary,
Por hallar reposo,	Seeking our rest.
¡Oh engaño engañoso,	Oh, mistake deceiving,

Y que sin amor,	Free of all love,
Es querer sanar,	Desiring to be healed
Viviendo el dolor!	While pain is living.

24.

A La Vestición De La Hermana Jerónima De La Encarnación	For the Clothing of Sister Jerónima De La Encarnación

¿Quién os trajo acá doncella,	Who has brought you here young lady
Del valle de la tristura?	From the valley of grieving?
—Dios y mi buena ventura.	—God and my good fortune.

25.

Al Velo De La Hermana Isabel De Los Angeles	For the Veiling of Sister Isabel De Los Angeles

Hermana, porque veléis,	*So that you will be watchful, Sister,*
Os han dado hoy este velo,	*Today they have veiled you;*
Y no os va menos que el cielo;	*On that your Heaven depends;*
Por eso, no os descuidéis.	*Do not be careless.*
Aqueste velo gracioso	This veil so graceful
Os dice que estéis en vela,	Proclaims you keep vigil,
Guardando la centinela	The watchful sentinel
Hasta que venga el Esposo,	Awaiting her Bridegroom,
Que, como ladron famoso,	Who as the famed thief
Vendrá cuando no penséis;	Will come with surprise;
Por eso, no os descuidéis.	*Do not be careless.*
No sabe nadie a cuál hora,	That hour is unknown,
Si en la vigilia primera	What watch it will be,
O en la segunda o tercera,	First, second, or third;
Todo cristiano lo ignora.	All Christians know not,
Pues velad, velad, hermana,	So watch, watch, sister,
No os roben lo que tenéis;	Lest your treasure be stolen.
Por eso, no os descuidéis.	*Do not be careless.*

En vuestra mano encendida
Tened siempre una candela,
Y estad con el velo en vela,
Las renes muy bien ceñidas.
No estéis siempre amodorrida,
Catad que peligraréis.
Por eso, no os descuidéis.

Tened olio en la aceitera
De obras y merecer,
Para poder proveer
La lámpara, que no se muera;
Porque quedaréis de fuera
Si entonces no lo tenéis;
Por eso, no os descuidéis.

Nadie os le dará prestado;
Y si lo vais a comprar,
Podríaseos tardar,
Y el Esposo haber entrado,
Y desque una vez cerrado,
No hay entrar aunque llaméis;
Por eso, no os descuidéis.

Tened continuo cuidado
De cumplir con alma fuerte,
Hasta el día de la muerte,
Lo que habéis hoy profesado;
Porque habiendo así velado
Con el Esposo entraréis.

Por eso, no os descuidéis.

Hold always in your hand
A candle bright;
Veiled, keep the watch
With loins girded well.
Be free of deep sleep,
Mindful of the danger near.
Do not be careless.

Keep ready your oil jar
Of merit and deeds,
Ample to keep
Your lamp aflame
Lest outside you be kept
When He comes.
Do not be careless.

No one will lend you oil
If you hasten to buy it;
Late you could be,
Once the Bridegroom is within,
The door then is closed;
Your cries will avail you not.
Do not be careless.

Be constant in care,
Fulfilling all bravely,
What you vowed today
Until death comes.
In keeping well your watch,
With the Bridegroom you will
          enter.
Do not be careless.

26.

A La Profesión De
Isabel De Los Angeles

For the Profession of
Isabel De Los Angeles

Sea mi gozo en el llanto,
Sobresalto mi reposo,

In weeping be my joy,
My rest in fright,

Mi sosiego doloroso,	In sorrowing my serenity,
Y mi bonanza el quebranto.	My wealth in losing all.
Entre borrascas mi amor,	Amid storms be my love,
Y mi regalo en la herida,	In the wound my delight.
Esté en la muerte mi vida,	My life in death,
Y en desprecios mi favor.	In rejection my favor.
Mis tesoros en pobreza,	In poverty be my riches,
Y mi triunfo en pelear,	My triumph in struggling,
Mi descanso en trabajar,	Rest in laboring,
Y mi contento en tristeza.	In sadness my contentment.
En la oscuridad mi luz,	In darkness be my light,
Mi grandeza en puesto bajo.	My greatness in the lowly place,
De mi camino el atajo	My way on the short road,
Y mi gloria sea la cruz.	In the cross my glory.
Mi honra sea el abatimiento,	In humiliation be my honor,
Y mi palma padecer,	My palm in suffering
En las menguas mi crecer,	Increase in my wanting
Y en menoscabo mi aumento.	In losing my gain.
En el hambre mi hartura,	My fullness be in hunger,
Mi esperanza en el temor,	In fearing my hope,
Mis regalos en pavor,	My rejoicing in fear,
Mis gustos en amargura.	In grieving my delight.
En olvido mi memoria,	In forgetting be my memory,
Mi alteza en humillación,	Humiliation my exalting,
En bajeza mi opinión,	In lowliness my repute,
En afrenta mi vitoria.	Affronts my victory.
Mi lauro esté en el desprecio,	My laurels be in contempt,
En las penas mi afición,	In afflictions my fondness,
Mi dignidad sea el rincón,	My dignity a lowly nook,
Y la soledad mi aprecio.	In solitude my esteem.
En Cristo mi confianza	In Christ be my trust,
Y de El sólo mi asimiento,	My affection in Him alone,
En sus consancios mi aliento,	In His weariness my vigor,
Y en su imitación mi holganza.	My repose in His imitation.

Aquí estriba mi firmeza,	My strength is founded here,
Aquí mi seguridad,	In Him alone my surety,
La prueba de mi verdad,	My integrity's proof,
La muestra de mi fineza.	In His likeness my purity.

27.

A Una Profesa	To a Professed Nun

¡Oh! *dichosa tal zagala*	*Oh, blessed this shepherdess*
Que hoy se ha dado a un tal Zagal	*Given today to this Shepherd*
Que reina y ha de reinar.	*Who rules and will rule.*

Venturosa fue su suerte	Good fortune was hers
Pues mereció tal Esposo.	Meriting such a Spouse.
Ya yo, Gil, estoy medroso,	Giles, now I am fearful:
No la osaré más mirar,	No more will I gaze on her
Pues ha tomado marido	For a husband she has taken
Que reina y ha de reinar.	*Who rules and will rule.*

Pregúntale qué le ha dado	Ask her what she gave Him
Para que lleve a su aldea	To carry to His farm.
El corazón le ha entregado	With such delight
Muy de buena voluntad.	She gave her heart.
Mi fe, poco le ha pagado	Oh, what a trifle she paid,
Que es muy hermoso el Zagal,	So handsome is the Shepherd
Que reina y ha de reinar.	*Who rules and will rule.*

Si más tuviera más diera.	Much greater present would she give.

¿Por qué le avisas, carillo?	Dear, why chide her?
Tomemos el cobanillo,	We will accept this dowry small
Sirva nos deja sacar,	She brings us now,
Pues ha tomado marido,	For a husband she has
Que reina y ha de reinar.	*Who rules and will rule.*

Pues vemos lo que dio ella,	Now knowing what she gave,
¿Que le ha de dar el Zagal?	What is the shepherd's gift?
Con su sangre le ha comprado;	He purchased her with His blood.

¡Oh que precioso caudal,	Oh fortune so precious,
Y dichosa tal zagala	Happy this shepherdess
Que contentó a este Zagal!	*Who delights this Shepherd!*
Mucho le debía amar,	With what great love He should give
Pues le dio tan gran tesoro,	For his gift was such a treasure.
¿No ves que se lo da todo	He gave all, do you not see her
Hasta el vestir y calzar?	Fully clothed by Him?
Mira que es ya su marido	See, now He is her Husband
Que reina y ha de reinar.	*Who rules and will rule.*
Bien será que la tomemos,	Good it is that we take her
Para este nuestro rebaño,	As a member of our flock.
Y que la regocijemos	Let us entertain her,
Para ganar su amistad,	Her friendship to gain,
Pues ha tomado marido,	For a husband she has taken
Que reina y ha de reinar.	*Who rules and will rule.*

28.

En Una Profesión	For a Profession
¡Oh que bien tan sin segundo!	*Oh, what good unequalled!*
¡Oh casamiento sagrado!	*Oh, marriage most sacred!*
Que el Rey de la Majestad,	*That the King of Majesty,*
Haya sido el desposado.	*Should be Betrothed.*
¡Oh que venturosa suerte,	Ah, wondrous happening
Os estaba aparejada,	Ready now for you!
Que os quiere Dios por amada,	God wants His bride
Y haos ganado con su muerte!	Having won you by His death!
En servirle estad muy fuerte,	In serving Him be strong
Pues que lo habéis profesado,	For you are vowed to this.
Que el Rey de la Majestad,	*Already the King of Majesty*
Es ya vuestro desposado.	*Is your Betrothed.*
Ricas joyas os dará	Bright jewels will He give
Este Esposo, Rey del cielo	This heavenly Spouse—King;
Daros ha mucho consuelo,	He comforts you greatly

Que nadie os lo quitará,
Y sobre todo os dará
Un espíritu humillado.
Es Rey y bien lo podrá,

Pues quiere hoy ser desposado.

No one can deprive you of this.
Of all that He blesses you,
A humble spirit is the best,
*For the King all this is given
    easily,*
He longs this day to be betrothed.

Mas os dará este Señor,
Un amor tan santo y puro,
Que podréis, yo os lo asiguro,
Perder al mundo el temor,
Y al demonio muy mejor
Porque hoy queda maniatado;

The Lord will grant you
Love holy and pure.
You will forget
The world's fears,
Ah, much more, the devil, too.
Now the demon is manacled today

Que el Rey de la Majestad,
Ha sido hoy el desposado.

The King of Majesty
Is now betrothed.

29.

Para Una Profesión

For a Profession

Todos los que militáis
Debajo desta bandera,
Ya no durmáis, ya no durmáis,
Pues ya no hay paz en la tierra.

All who serve in the army
Beneath this banner,
Sleep no longer, sleep no more,
For now there is no earthly peace.

Si como capitán fuerte
Quiso nuestro Dios morir,
Comencémosle a seguir
Pues que le dimos la muerte,
Oh qué venturosa suerte
Se le siguió desta guerra;
Ya no durmáis, ya no durmáis,
Pues Dios falta de la tierra.

As the captain strong
Our God wished to die,
Let us follow Him now
For we caused His death.
Oh what a happy lot
He won from this strife!
Sleep no longer, sleep no more,
For God is wanting from the earth.

Con grande contentamiento
Se ofrece a morir en cruz,
Por darnos a todos luz
Con su grande sufrimiento.

With contentment great
On the cross He longs to die
His light to give us all
In His sufferings severe.

¡Oh, glorioso vencimiento!*	Oh victory so glorious!
¡Oh, dichosa aquesta guerra!	Oh fortunate this war!
Ya no durmáis, ya no durmáis,	*Sleep no longer, sleep no more,*
Pues Dios falta de la tierra.	*For God is wanting from the earth.*
No haya ningún cobarde,	Not one coward will there be!
Aventuremos la vida,	Let us risk our lives!
Pues no hay quien mejor la guarde	None better guards it
Que el que la da por perdida.	Than he who loses it.
Pues Jesús es nuestra guía,	Our guide is Jesus,
Y el premio de aquesta guerra;	The reward of this warring.
Ya no durmáis, ya no durmáis,	*Sleep no longer, sleep no more,*
Porque no hay paz en la tierra.	*For there is no peace on earth.*
Ofrezcámonos de veras	Let us truly offer ourselves
A morir por Cristo todas,	All to die for Christ,
Y en las celestiales bodas,	In the wedding in heaven
Estaremos placenteras;	Joyful we will be.
Sigamos estas banderas	Follow these banners
Pues Cristo va en delantera,	Christ leads us on.
No hay que temer, no durmáis,	*Fear nothing, do not sleep,*
Pues que no hay paz en la tierra.	*For there is no peace on earth.*

30.

En Una Profesión	For a Profession
Pues que nuestro Esposo	*Since our Spouse*
Nos quiere en prisión,	*Wants us in prison,*
A la gala gala	*Let us glory,*
De la Religión.	*Glory in religion.*
Oh qué ricas bodas	Oh what a splendid wedding
Ordenó Jesús;	Jesus arranged!
Quiérenos a todas,	All of us He loves
Y danos la luz;	And gives us His light.
Sigamos la Cruz,	The cross let us follow

*The autograph of the three preceding verses is preserved in the Carmel of Savona, Italy.

Con gran perfección;
A la gala gala
De la Religión.

With perfection great.
Let us glory,
Glory in religion.

Este es el estado
De Dios escogido
Con que del pecado
Nos ha defendido;
Hanos prometido
La consolación,
Si nos alegramos
En esta prisión.
A la gala gala
De la Religión.

This is our state
God chose for us,
From sinful ways
He has protected us,
He has promised us
Consolations great
If in this prison
We rejoice.
Let us glory,
Glory in religion.

Darnos ha grandezas
En la eterna gloria
Si por sus riquezas
Dejamos la escoria,
Que hay en este mundo,
Y su perdición,
A la gala gala
De la Religión.

Greatness He will give us
In glory everlasting
If for his riches
We give up the dross
Found in this world
With all its ruin.
Let us glory,
Glory in religion.

Oh qué cautiverio
De gran libertad,
Venturosa vida
Para eternidad;
No quiero librar
Ya mi corazón.
A la gala gala
De la Religión.

Oh what captivity
Of such great liberty!
Life so fortunate
For time unending.
I desire not to free
My heart now.
Let us glory,
Glory in religion.

31.

Contra Un Ganadillo Impertinente	Against an Impertinent Little Flock
Pues nos dais vestido nuevo	*Now that you give us clothing new,*
Rey celestial,	*Heavenly King,*
Librad de la mala gente	*From all nasty creatures*
Este sayal.	*Free this cloth of wool.*

La Santa:
Hijas, pues tomáis la cruz,

Tened valor,
Y a Jesús, que es vuestra luz,
Pedid favor.
El os será defensor
En trance tal.

St. Teresa:
Daughters, since you have taken the cross,
Take courage.
Ask a favor
Of Jesus, your light.
Your defender He will be
In such peril.

Todas:
Librad de la mala gente
Este sayal.

All:
From all nasty creatures
Free this cloth of wool.

La Santa:
Inquieta este mal ganado
En oración,
El ánimo mal fundado,
En devoción;
Mas en Dios el corazón
Tened igual.

St. Teresa:
These nasty creatures
The prayer disturbs
Of the spirit
In devotion weak;
Yet strongly kept
Is that heart in God.

Todas:
Librad de la mala gente
Este sayal.

All:
From all nasty creatures
Free this cloth of wool.

La Santa:
Pues vinisteis a morir
No desmayéis,
Y de gente tan cevil
No temeréis.
Remedio en Dios hallaréis
En tanto mal.

St. Teresa:
Since you came here to die,
Do not become confused;
And of such evil creatures
You will have no fear.
In God is found
Your remedy for this evil.

Todas:
Pues nos dais vestido nuevo

Rey celestial,
Librad de la mala gente
Este sayal.

All:
*Now that you give us clothing
new,*
Heavenly King,
From all nasty creatures
Free this cloth of wool.

NOTES

THE FOUNDATIONS

INTRODUCTION

1. See *The Collected Works of St. Teresa of Avila,* trans. Kieran Kavanaugh and Otilio Rodriguez, vol. 1 (Washington: ICS Publications, 1976).
2. See *The Collected Works of St. Teresa of Avila,* vol. 2 (Washington: ICS Publications, 1980).
3. All references incorporated into the text are to the *Foundations* and give the chapter number followed by the paragraph number or numbers; in those cases where more than one chapter is referred to, the new chapter will be introduced by a semicolon placed after the preceding paragraph number.
4. See *Spir. Testimonies* 6, in vol. 1.
5. The letters of St. Teresa have been translated into English by E. Allison Peers, 2 vols. (Westminster, Maryland: Newman Press, 1950). The letters will be identified by the date and person to whom written.
6. See *Interior Castle,* Prol., 2, in vol. 2.
7. See also the final section of this introduction, *The Autograph.*
8. See also ch. 18, no. 2.
9. Cf. also ch. 17, no. 3; ch. 28, nos. 15-16.
10. See ch. 5, nos. 6, 10-17; ch. 8, nos. 2-4; ch. 27, no.5; ch. 29, no. 20.
11. Cf. also ch. 25, no. 14; ch. 28, nos. 2, 5.
12. Ephesians 6:12.
13. Cf. also ch. 27, nos. 11-12.
14. *Constitutions,* no. 27.
15. See *Biblioteca Mística Carmelitana,* ed., Silverio de Santa Teresa, 20 vols (Burgos: El Monte Carmelo, 1915-35), 18:433.
16. See *Analecta Ordinis Carmelitarum,* vol. 3 (Rome, 1934), p. 166.

17. See Elias Friedman, *The Latin Hermits of Mount Carmel: A Study in Carmelite Origins* (Rome: Teresianum, 1979).
18. 1 Kings 17:2-4. See "The Institution of the First Monks" in *Ancient Carmelite Texts*, translated and edited by Roots Committee (privately printed by Carmelite Communities Associated, 1982), pp. 41-56.
19. See *Rule of Saint Albert*, Eds. H. Clarke and B. Edwards (Aylesford: Carmelite Priory, 1973).
20. See Otger Steggink, *La Reforma del Carmelo Español* (Roma: Institutum Carmelitanum, 1965).
21. *Life*, ch. 7, no. 3. For the early history of the Carmelite Order, see: Gabriel Barry, *Historical Notes on the Carmelite Order* (privately printed by Darlington, England); Joachim Smet, *The Carmelites: A History of the Brothers of Our Lady of Mount Carmel*, vols. 1 and 2 (Darien, Illinois: Carmelite Spiritual Center, 1975-76).
22. See J. H. Elliott, *Imperial Spain* (New York: Mentor Books, 1966); J. García Oro, "Reformas y Observancias" in *Perfil Histórico De Santa Teresa* (Madrid: Editorial de Espiritualidad, 1981), pp. 33-54; Steggink, *La Reforma del Carmelo Español*.
23. *Life*, ch. 8, no. 2, in vol. 1.
24. *Ibid.*, ch. 32, no. 10, note 5.
25. *Ibid.*, ch. 35, nos. 1-7.
26. See Juan Bosco, "A la recuperación de un nombre perdido: Teresa de Jesús," in *Monte Carmelo* 90 (1982), pp. 266-304.
27. See *Francis and Clare: The Complete Works*, trans. Regis J. Armstrong and Ignatius C. Brady (New York: Paulist Press, 1982), pp. 209-25
28. In vol. 2, ch. 2, no. 9.
29. See ch. 10, no. 3; letters to María de San José, April 3, 1580, and to Gracián, Feb. 17, 1581.
30. See letter to Gracián, Dec. 12, 1579.
31. See 1 Cor. 11:3-6.
32. See F. Suarez, *De religione*, tr. 6, tit. 1, col. 2.
33. See *Life*, ch. 32, no. 13.
34. See letter to Doña Luisa de la Cerda, Nov. 7, 1571.
35. On these points, see Efrén J. Montalva, *La Herencia Teresiana* (Madrid: Editorial de Espiritualidad, 1975), pp. 15-70; also my introduction to the *Way of Perfection* in vol. 2.
36. See *Life*, ch. 27, nos. 16-20.
37. See Melquiades Andres, *La Teología Española en El Siglo XVI*, vol. 2 (Madrid: B.A.C., 1977), pp. 172-73.

38. Francisco de Osuna, *The Third Spiritual Alphabet,* trans. Mary E. Giles (New York: Paulist Press, 1981), p. 97.
39. *Spir. Testimonies* 19, in vol. 1.
40. *Life,* ch. 35, nos. 1-2; ch. 36, no. 28.
41. See *On Making The Visitation,* nos. 22, 24, 29.
42. See *Monumenta Historica Carmel Teresiani,* ed., Institutum Historicum Teresianum (Rome: Teresianum, 1973-), 1:17-19.
43. See ch. 3, no. 1; ch. 27, no. 1; ch. 28, no. 37; ch. 31, no. 45.
44. See ch. 14, no. 12; ch. 23, nos. 1-10; P. H. Gracián, "Historia Fundationum" in *Monumenta,* 3:548-53.
45. For a summary of many of these events and further bibliography, see Ildefonso Moriones, *El Carmelo Teresiano* (Vitoria: Ediciones El Carmen, 1978).
46. See *Monumenta,* 3: 549.
47. *Life,* ch. 20, no. 27.
48. *Ibid,* ch. 40, no. 1.
49. See also ch. 22, nos. 5, 10; ch. 26, nos. 7-8.
50. *Life,* ch. 35, no. 2.
51. Jan. 17, 1570.
52. May 9, 1576.
53. For more details about these economic matters, see Teófanes Egido, "Ambiente Historico" in *Introducción A La Lectura De Santa Teresa* (Madrid: Editorial de Espiritualidad, 1978), pp. 88-103.
54. See also *Spir. Testimonies,* 65, no. 4, in vol. 1.
55. See *Monumenta,* vol. 3, p. 574.
56. See also ch. 3, no. 10.
57. Julián de Avila, *Vida de Santa Teresa de Jesús,* obra inedita, anotada y adicionada por Don Vicente de la Fuente (Madrid: Antonio Perez Dubrull, 1881).
58. Letter to Don Antonio Gaytán, July 10, 1575; see *Way of Perfection,* ch. 40, no. 9.
59. For a pictorial account of Teresa's travels, see Tomás Alvarez and Fernando Domingo, *Saint Teresa of Avila: A Spiritual Adventure* (Washington, D.C.: ICS Publications, 1981).
60. This is the carefully demonstrated conclusion of Dr. Avelino Senra Varela, a pathologist and professor at the University of Cádiz, in a paper given at the Teresian Institute in Avila, March 22, 1982. See A. Senra Varela, "La Enfermedad de Santa Teresa de Jesús," *Revista de Espritualidad* 41 (1982), pp. 601-612.
61. Letter to María de San José, June 4, 1578.

62. Letter to Don Lorenzo, Feb. 10, 1577.
63. April 29, 1579.
64. See *Constitutions*, nos. 21 and 23; letter to María de San José, Feb. 1, 1580.
65. See Dr. César Fernández-Ruiz, "Medicina y Médicos en la Vida y Obra de Santa Teresa de Jesús," in *Revista de Espiritualidad*, 23, (1964), pp. 186-209.
66. See *Life*, ch. 33, no.5.
67. See *Monumenta*, 3:584-85.
68. See *Spir. Testimonies*, 58, 59, in vol. 1.
69. *Monumenta*, 1:67-71.
70. See Joachim Smet, *The Carmelites*, 2:52-53.
71. See *Monumenta*, 3:560.
72. See *Spir. Testimonies*, 16, in vol. 1.
73. See I. Moriones, *El Carmelo Teresiano*, p. 101.
74. See *Monumenta*, 3:557-58; 560-61; 578.
75. Letter to Don Roque de Huerta, October, 1578.
76. October 15, 1578.
77. See *Monumenta*, 3:613-15.
78. *Ibid.*, p. 615.
79. See *Monumenta*, 3:617.
80. See Juan Luis Astigarraga, "Ultimos Dias y Muerte de Santa Teresa," *Teresianum Ephemerides Carmeliticae* 33 (1982), pp. 7-69.
81. Sept. 1, 1582.
82. See "Autobiografia A," *Obras Completas de la Beata Ana de San Bartolomé*, ed. Julián Urkiza, vol. 1 (Roma: Teresianum, 1981), p. 306.
83. See Astigarraga, "Ultimos Dias y Muerte de Santa Teresa," pp. 42-43.
84. See *Interior Castle*, III, ch. 1, note 2, in vol. 2, p. 486.
85. See Teófanes Egido, "Libro de las Fundaciones," *Introducción a la Lectura de Santa Teresa*, ed. Alberto Barrientos (Madrid: Editorial de Espiritualidad), pp. 241-68.

PROLOGUE

1. Teresa wrote the history of the first foundation, St. Joseph's in Avila, in her *Life*, chs. 32-36. Fr. García de Toledo was the confessor for whom Teresa wrote the *Life*, especially the account of the foundation of St. Joseph's. See introduction to the *Life*, vol. I, pp. 17-19; also *Life*, ch. 34, no. 6, note 5.
2. Fr. Jerónimo Ripalda (1535-1618) joined the Society of Jesus in 1551. While rector of the Jesuit college in Salamanca in 1573, he

became Teresa's confessor. He was rector also of Villagarcía, Burgos, and Valladolid. He died in Toledo. See *Spir. Test.*, 58, no. 3, note 8.

3. The other seven monasteries were: Medina del Campo (1567); Malagón (1568); Valladolid (1568); Toledo (1569); Pastrana (1569); Salamanca (1570); and Alba de Tormes (1571).

4. The foundation in Duruelo (1568), which transferred to Mancera in 1570.

5. The monastery in Salamanca.

6. The date, in fact, was August 25.

CHAPTER 1

1. The foundation was made August 24, 1562.

2. In regard to the number of nuns in each monastery, Teresa later allowed for an increase to twenty. See *Way of Perfection*, ch. 2, no. 9, note 5; *Life*, ch. 32, no. 13; ch. 36, no. 19.

3. This Sister, María Bautista (de Ocampo) (1543-1603), later became prioress of Valladolid. She was one of Teresa's most frequent correspondents. See ch. 29, note 5; *Life*, ch. 32, no. 10, note 5.

4. This well still exists. The Sister alluded to is again María Bautista. Teresa called the well "the Samaritan woman's well."

5. Alonso Maldonado (c.1510-c.1600) had been a Franciscan missionary in Mexico (1551-1561). He became a defender of the rights of the indigenous people and pleaded their cause in Madrid and Rome before the king and the pope. A man of extreme zeal, he was at the end of his life tried by the Inquisition.

6. One of the hermitages she arranged to have constructed in the garden of St. Joseph's in Avila.

CHAPTER 2

1. No general had ever been to Castile. A general, Fr. John Alerio, had presided at the general chapter held in Barcelona in 1324.

2. See *Life*, ch. 32, nos. 13-15; ch. 33, no. 16. In the final chapter of this book of *Foundations*, she tells how her monastery at Avila returned to the jurisdiction of the Carmelite order.

3. The historian of the monastery of the Incarnation, María Pinel, wrote that the number reached 180 nuns. See *Biblioteca Mística Carmelitana*, 2:140. (Henceforth cited as BMC.)

4. The general, Fr. John Baptist Rossi (1507-1578), whose last name was Latinized in Spain to Rubeo, was elected general in 1564 and visited Avila, February 16-18, 1567.

5. Don Alvaro de Mendoza (d. 1586) was appointed bishop of Avila in 1560 and under his jurisdiction St. Joseph's was placed when Teresa's provincial refused to accept it. Always a staunch supporter of Teresa's work, he was buried, at his request, in the monastery church of St. Joseph in Avila.

6. This is true of Spain. In Italy, the primitive rule was being observed at Monte Oliveto, near Genoa. In regard to the primitive rule, see *Life*, ch. 36, no. 26, note 27.

7. For these patent letters of Rubeo to Teresa, one dated April 27, 1567, and the other May 16, 1567, see *Monumenta Historica Carmeli Teresiani*, ed., Institutum Historicum Teresianum (Rome: Teresianum, 1973-), 1:67-71. (Henceforth cited as MHCT.)

8. See ch. 1, no. 8.

9. The patent letter granting permission for the foundation in Castile of two monasteries of the Teresian Carmel for friars was signed by Rubeo in Barcelona, not Valencia, August 10, 1567. See MHCT, 1:67-71.

10. The provincial at the time, as of April 12, 1567, was Alonso Gonzáles, and the former provincial was Angel de Salazar.

CHAPTER 3

1. See, for example, *Life*, ch. 23, nos. 3, 9; ch. 33, no. 7.

2. Fr. Baltasar Alvarez (1533-1580) was not provincial at that time, 1573, but was substituting for the provincial, Gil González Dávila, who was in Rome.

3. Don Pedro González, bishop of Salamanca, to which diocese Medina belonged.

4. Julián de Avila (1527-1605) was ordained in 1558 and appointed chaplain of St. Joseph's in 1563, remaining so until the year before his death. His sister, María de San José (Dávila) was among the first four nuns to take the habit at St. Joseph's.

5. This young lady was Isabel Fontecha. She received the habit in Medina in 1567 and took the name Isabel de Jesús.

6. From St. Joseph's she took María Bautista and Ana de los Angeles. From the Incarnation came: Inés de Jesús, Ana de la Encarnación (Tapia), Teresa de la Columna (Quesada), and Isabel de la Cruz (Arias).

7. Antonio de Heredia (1510-1601) made the first foundation of Teresian Carmelites in 1568 with St. John of the Cross. He changed his name to Antonio de Jesús, held important offices in the order, and assisted at the deaths of both Teresa and John of the Cross. See nos. 16-17.

8. Doña María Suárez.

9. The monastery was Our Lady of Grace; the priest friend, Alonso Esteban.

10. These two out of the four from the Incarnation were Isabel Arias, the subprioress, and Teresa de Quesada.

11. Domingo Báñez (1528-1604) was one of the most distinguished theologians of the sixteenth century. See *Life*, ch. 36, no. 15; see also ch. 34, no. 14; ch. 39, no. 3.

12. Teresa thought that a foundation could not exist without the reservation of the Blessed Sacrament. She discovered her error later. See ch. 19, no. 3.

13. For clarification on Teresa's understanding of "Lutherans" see the introduction to *The Way of Perfection* in *The Collected Works of St. Teresa of Avila*, vol. 2 (I.C.S. Publications: Washington, D.C. 1980) pp. 19-20.

14. This merchant was Blas de Medina.

15. She was a niece of Cardinal Quiroga, the general inquisitor. In 1581 she entered the Carmel in Medina, taking the name Elena de Jesús. Her daughter, Jerónima de la Encarnación, was already a member of that community.

16. In ch. 2, nos. 5-6.

17. See no. 3.

18. This was St. John of the Cross (1542-1591), then a Carmelite with the name Juan de Santo Matía.

CHAPTER 4

1. In chs. 4-8 Teresa inserts a short treatise concerning the life of prayer in her communities, useful not only for her daughters but for confessors and spiritual directors as well.

2. The story of the foundation of St. Joseph's in Avila (*Life*, chs. 32-36) was written in 1565. Teresa wrote this chapter of the *Foundations* in the later months of 1573 at Salamanca. The reason she had not founded more was that the apostolic visitator Pedro Fernández, O.P., had appointed her prioress at the Incarnation (1571-1573). For the seven monasteries, in addition to Avila, see prol., note 3.

3. See for example *Way of Perfection*, ch. 21, no. 7.

4. See *Way of Perfection*, ch. 21, no. 7; *Life*, ch. 20, no. 16.

5. Teresa wrote carefully in the margin: "I am not dealing here with founders of Religious orders, for since God chose them for a great work, He gave them more grace." This annotation may have been motivated by the same scruple that occasioned a cancellation in

the previous number for which she substituted "and this is true."
In the autograph, paragraph no. 7 is highlighted by vertical lines in
the margin. See parallel passage in *Interior Castle*, V, ch. 4, no. 6.
6. In no. 5.

CHAPTER 5
1. For example, see *Life*, ch. 17, nos. 5-7; *Way of Perfection*,
ch. 31, no. 8; *Interior Castle*, IV, ch. 1, no. 8.
2. Mt. 25:40.
3. Ph. 2:8: "obedient unto death."
4. For the second reason, see no. 14.
5. Allusion to Ps. 34:9.
6. In no. 1.
7. Lk. 10:16.
8. IK. 18:38.
9. The first reason is stated in no. 4.
10. For the Teresian proverb in this respect, see *Interior Castle*, VII,
ch. 4, no. 7, note 8.
11. Allusion to Mt. 26:31-35, 67-75.
12. On this subject, see *Interior Castle*, VII, ch. 4, no. 5, note 6.

CHAPTER 6
1. In this chapter Teresa exposes a kind of psychological anomaly
that only appears to be mystical in nature. She creates her own
terminology, a number of expressions, in order to speak of it: *em-
bebecimiento* (nos. 1, 2, 6, 7): absorption; *embobamiento* (no.
3): stupefaction; *pasmos* (no. 5): states of daze; *pausada* (no. 5):
listless; *amortecimientos* (no. 6): swoons.
2. See *Life*, ch. 20.
3. This kind of self-abandonment (*dejarse*) to these absorptions was
practiced by the group within the illuminist movement known as
dejados. Their spirituality developed along unorthodox lines. See
Collected Works of St. Teresa, 1:7.
4. In ch. 7.
5. In no. 2.
6. In ch. 5, nos. 2, 10-11.
7. In no. 6.
8. Teresa is purposely vague about their identities, and it is not easy
to pinpoint either the place or the names. Fr. Silverio believed she
was referring to Alberta Bautista who died a saintly death at the
age of 35, and to Inés de la Concepción, the lay Sister, both of the
monastery in Medino del Campo. See BMC, 6:51.

9. Inés de Jesús (Tapia).
10. In no. 4.
11. She is speaking of herself; see *Life*, ch. 25, no. 14.
12. Allusion to 1S. 15:22.
13. Allusion to what was said in chs. 4 and 5.
14. Allusion to Mt. 16:19.

CHAPTER 7

1. Under the term "melancholy," Teresa includes a whole series of emotional and mental disorders difficult to reduce to a definite category. The humor called melancholy (black bile) was in the past looked upon as one of the four chief bodily fluids. Mental disorder was supposed to be caused by an excess of this humor.
2. See *Way of Perfection*, ch. 24, nos. 4-5.
3. In nos. 2-3.
4. In no. 3.
5. The danger to one's salvation; see nos. 3-4.
6. In no. 5.
7. In nos. 3-4.
8. Here Teresa is suggesting that these nuns, lest they suffer physical weakness, be dispensed from the perpetual abstinence from meat (see *Constitutions*, no. 11); fish was a customary substitute for meat in her Carmels.
9. In nos. 8-9.

CHAPTER 8

1. This statement is a marginal gloss in Teresa's hand.
2. Teresa is referring to herself. See *Life*, ch. 29, nos. 5-7; *Interior Castle*, VI, ch. 9, nos. 12-13.
3. Teresa noted in the margin: "Fray Maestro Domingo Báñez."
4. In no. 3.
5. Allusion to Mt. 15:27.
6. Teresa is referring to her own experience. As for the man of whom she speaks, some think it was Juan Manteca, a peasant from Avila famous for his extraordinary mystical experiences. After speaking with him, Teresa was left dissatisfied with his spirit. He was later brought to justice for his fraud. See BMC, 19:81.

CHAPTER 9

1. Doña Luisa de la Cerda. See *Life*, ch. 34, note 1.
2. Malagón is a small town, still today, in the province of Ciudad Real. In feudal times it belonged to the duchy of Medinaceli.

3. Her confessor at the time was Domingo Báñez, O.P. See ch. 3, note 11; *Spiritual Testimonies*, 58, note 17. Báñez was opposed to Teresa's desires for absolute poverty (see *Life,* ch. 36, no. 15). His opposition was based on the mind of the Council of Trent (1545-1563), Session 25, *De reformatione regularium,* ch. 3.

4. April 11. Teresa urged Doña Luisa to build her nuns in Malagón a new monastery, the construction of which she supervised carefully. Inaugurated December 8, 1579, this building remains today, an exceptional relic still housing Teresa's daughters.

CHAPTER 10

1. Because of the kind of life this young man lived, Teresa does not give his name. He was, in fact, Don Bernardino de Mendoza, brother of the bishop of Avila, Don Alvaro de Mendoza, and of Doña María de Mendoza, who is also spoken of in this chapter.

2. The estate was called Rio de Olmos and was close to the river Pisuerga toward the south of the city. It had been previously occupied by a community of Carmelite friars who moved into the city February 1, 1563. Besides being unhealthy, the place was impractically located in view of the nuns' dependence on alms, for Teresa had founded the monastery in poverty.

3. He died in Ubeda in February of 1568 while Teresa was in Alcalá de Henares.

4. She arrived in Valladolid August 10, 1568, and on August 15 inaugurated the foundation at Rio de Olmos.

5. The monastery of the Carmelite friars. See note 2.

6. They were Isabel de la Cruz, Antonia del Espíritu Santo, and María de la Cruz.

7. See ch. 3, no. 2.

8. St. John of the Cross who in Valladolid underwent a kind of apprenticeship in the new form of Carmelite life under the guidance of Teresa. See ch. 3, nos. 16-17.

9. See no. 2.

10. The priest was Julián de Avila who later wrote of this event: " . . . and when I gave the Blessed Sacrament to the Mother, I saw her in a great rapture, which she often experienced before or after receiving Communion" (BMC, 18:221). The painter Rubens immortalized this scene.

11. From August 15 until October of the same year when they moved to a temporary location.

12. Don Francisco de los Cobos had been a secretary and confidant of Charles V and a counselor of Philip II. He died in 1547.

13. The bishop of Avila was Don Alvaro de Mendoza. See *Life,*ch. 36, nos. 1-2.
14. February 3, 1569, they moved to the place inside Valladolid known today as the *Rondilla de Santa Teresa.*
15. She speaks of the third, youngest daughter in no. 13.
16. Antonio Manrique de Padilla entered the Jesuits March 8, 1572, and was a novice under the direction of Baltasar Alvarez, the former confessor of Teresa's.
17. This confessor was Fr. Jerónimo de Ripalda, S.J.

CHAPTER 11
1. She was Estefanía de los Apóstoles who received the habit in Valladolid July 2, 1572. The fame of her simple and saintly life spread even to the king, Philip II, and many edifying stories were told about her. A manuscript biography of her was written by María de San José. Despite this mention, Teresa then neglects to tell us about her.
2. Doña Luisa de Padilla, widow of Don Antonio Manrique and mother of Don Martín de Padilla.
3. Ch. 10, no.15.
4. The prioress of Valladolid was María Bautista.
5. Domingo Báñez. See ch. 3, no. 5, note 11.
6. At the time (July 1573), Teresa was probably in Salamanca.
7. That is, December 8-28, 1573.
8. A monastery of Dominican nuns in Valladolid.
9. Doña Casilda was professed a week after her fifteenth birthday, January 13, 1577. But this story has a further ending, a surprise and disappointing one for Teresa. In a letter to Gracián, September 17, 1581, she speaks of the news, "shocking" to her, that Doña Casilda, then about twenty, had left the Carmelite monastery in Valladolid. It seems both Casilda's mother and the Jesuit confessor, neither of whom got along with the subprioress, had some influence on the decision. Casilda joined the Franciscan nuns of Santa Gadea del Cid, where she became abbess.

CHAPTER 12
1. This chapter heading is not in Teresa's hand. The account of this nun's life and virtues is an example of the kind of necrological literature later imitated by Teresa's friars and nuns alike. The monastery referred to is Valladolid (see ch. 10).

2. Beatriz de la Encarnación (Oñez) (d. 1573) was born in Arroyo, in the province of Valladolid, received the habit of Carmel September 8, 1569, and made profession in 1570.
3. See *Constitutions*, nos. 29, 30, 39, and 43.
4. In nos. 4-9.

CHAPTER 13

1. In chap. 3, nos. 16-17.
2. In fact, she was satisfied only with Fray John of the Cross. See ch. 3, nos. 16-17.
3. To distinguish the two groups in Carmel, Teresa uses the terms "calced" and "discalced," which stem from a difference in footwear. In these *Foundations* and in her *Letters* she refers to them as well by the stuff of their habits: cloth or frieze (rough wool).
4. Don Rafael Mejía Velázquez. See MHCT, 1:74-75.
5. The official name was and still is today Duruelo. But the place looks more like a small farm or pasture land than a town and gives the impression of being even more insignificant than it was formerly.
6. The Sister companion was Antonia del Espíritu Santo, one of the four first nuns who formed the little community of St. Joseph's in Avila. The priest was Julián de Avila, the first chaplain of that monastery in Avila.
7. The foundations were: Duruelo (1568), which was transferred to Mancera (1570), Pastrana (1569), Alcalá (1570), Altomira (1571), La Roda (1572), Granada (1573), La Peñuela (1573), Los Remedios in Seville (1574), Almodóvar del Campo (1575). Since Duruelo had been abandoned, there were only nine.
8. See ch. 2, no. 5. The previous provincial was Angel de Salazar and the present one was Alonso González.
9. See *Litterae Patentes P. Joannis Baptista Rossi* in MHCT, 1:68-71.
10. In ch. 10.
11. This important paragraph shows how St. John of the Cross received special, personal instructions from St. Teresa about the spirit and way of life of the new Carmels she was founding.

CHAPTER 14

1. It was the First Sunday of Advent, November 28, 1568. See MHCT, 1:74-75.
2. In 1569, the First Sunday of Lent fell on February 27. Teresa had written "the first week of" the following Lent, but later crossed out "the first week of." Nonetheless, the visit did occur around the

first week of Lent. She left Valladolid February 22 for Toledo passing through Medina, Duruelo, and Avila.

3. These two were Father Lucas de Celis and Brother José de Cristo, a deacon. Neither of them persevered for long. See Silverio de Santa Teresa, *Historia del Carmen Descalzo en España, Portugal y América*, 15 vols. (Burgos: El Monte Carmelo), 3:206-07. (Henceforth cited HCD)

4. Don Luis de Toledo was both a relative of the duke of Alba and lord of Mancera, the town to which the foundation of Duruelo was transferred, as well as of five other towns. See HCD, 3:234.

5. Its full name is Mancera de Abajo to distinguish it from Mancera de Arriba. The first foundation in Duruelo was transferred to Mancera June 11, 1570 and remained there until 1600 when it was transferred to Avila. See HCD, 3:234-40.

6. After the digression on Mancera, Teresa returns to her account of Duruelo.

CHAPTER 15

1. Martín Ramírez (d.1568), a wealthy merchant from Toledo, provided for the foundation in Toledo.

2. A Galician, from Santiago de Compostela, Pablo Hernández (b.1528) was one of the many Jesuits who helped Teresa in carrying out her mission. Her letters reveal her trust in him, and at this time she responded by giving him power to proceed in her name.

3. The chaplaincy is a fund established for the celebration of daily Mass in a particular church by chosen chaplains.

4. Today this feast is known as the Annunciation. Teresa left Valladolid Feb. 21, 1569, stayed in Avila for about two weeks and arrived in Toledo March 24, 1569.

5. They were Isabel de San Pablo (1547-82) and Isabel de Santo Domingo (1537-1623). The latter was a nun in whom Teresa placed special trust. She was made prioress in Toledo and later sent as prioress to Pastrana where she had to deal tactfully with the difficult situations caused by the Princess of Eboli (see ch. 17, no. 17).

6. The archbishop of Toledo was the noted Bartolomé de Carranza (1503-76), who was then involved in a struggle because of the proceedings instituted against him by the Spanish Inquisition. The diocese was being governed by an administrator.

7. Pedro Manrique de Padilla (d.1577) was the uncle of Casilda de Padilla, whose vocation is described in chs. 10-11.

8. These are still preserved and venerated by the Carmelite nuns in

Toledo. One represents Jesus having fallen with the cross, and the other represents Him seated during His Passion in deep suffering and meditation.

9. Alonso de Avila (d.1586) was one of the many merchants of judeo-converso origin from Toledo. A short biography of him in manuscript form exists in the conventual archives of the Carmelite nuns in Toledo and was written by P. Hernando Dávila.
10. Alonso de Andrada was a young twenty-two year old student.
11. In no. 10.
12. From May 14, 1569 to the end of May, 1570.
13. In nos. 4 and 11.
14. Doña Luisa de la Cerda.
15. In nos. 1-2.

CHAPTER 16

1. Ana de la Madre de Dios (Palma) (1529-1610) was married and became a widow at age 21. She met Teresa in the palace of Doña Luisa de la Cerda and generously offered her wealth for the foundation in Toledo. She made her profession there November 15, 1570, and governed as prioress several times. She died in the Carmel of Cuerva.
2. At first Teresa wrote: "I had to be careful about what I said." She then added between the lines, "the prioress ... what she said," so as to make the account sound more impersonal.
3. Teresa had first written, "she came to speak to me. I asked her, etc." She obviously wanted to withhold the part she played in these incidents, as is indicated at the end of this number.
4. She is speaking of Petronila de San Andrés (Robles del Aguila) (1545-1576) born in Toledo and professed there in 1571. See BMC, 5:444-446.

CHAPTER 17

1. In 1569, the months of May, June, and July kept Teresa busy with activities and travels, which may be summarized as follows: May 14, the foundation day of the Carmel in Toledo; May 30, leaves for Pastrana and arrives the same day in Madrid; June 8, arrives in Pastrana; June 23, foundation day for the Carmel of nuns in Pastrana; July 13, foundation for the friars in Pastrana; July 21, returns to Toledo.
2. They were six in all, four from the Incarnation and two from the Carmel in Malagón.
3. Ruy Gómez de Silva, a Portuguese by birth, was brought up with

Philip II, who liked and favored him. His wife, Doña Ana de Mendoza, better known by her title, the princess of Eboli, was a capricious, willful woman who later became a source of much trouble for Teresa and her nuns.

4. Her confessor at that time was Father Vicente Barrón. See *Life*, ch. 7, no. 16-17; *Spir. Test.*, 58, note 16.

5. Doña Leonor de Mascareñas (1503-1584), Portuguese by birth, had become Philip II's governess and was later dissuaded by him from entering a monastery. In 1564 she founded in Madrid a monastery of Franciscan nuns called "Descalzas Reales," which was close to her mansion where Teresa occasionally stayed.

6. Mariano Azzaro (Fr. Ambrosio Mariano de San Benito) (1510-1594), was born in Bitonto, Italy, in the province of Bari. Having studied theology and law to such effect that he attended the Council of Trent, he was also skilled in mathematics and engineering. As an engineer in the service of Philip II, he was examining the possibility of making the Guadalquivir navigable from Seville to Cordoba and of using it for irrigation purposes when he experienced the call to become a hermit. Later, as a Carmelite friar, he continued to be esteemed by the king and consulted on various engineering projects. Hasty and impulsive, he was at times difficult to deal with as is evident in Teresa's correspondence.

7. Juan de la Miseria (Giovanni Narduch) (c. 1526-1616), was born in Boggiano, Italy, in the province of Naples. A painter, disciple of Sánchez Coello, he is remembered especially for the portrait he did of Teresa in Seville in 1576. After joining Teresa's friars, he later transferred to the Carmelites of the observance and then to the Franciscans, but finally returned to the Teresian Carmelites and went on the foundation to Genoa. In his old age he suffered from paralysis and blindness. He died in Madrid where his body is preserved incorrupt.

8. In Dn. 13.

9. Mateo de la Fuente (1524-1575), born in Alminuete, near Toledo, later placed his hermits under the rule of St. Basil because of the demands of the Council of Trent.

10. When she speaks of the Council as coming, she is referring to the introduction of the decrees of the Council of Trent into Spain. In the constitution *Lubricum genus,* November 17, 1568, Pius V granted a year within which to comply. See Council of Trent, Sess. 25, ch. 5, *De reformation religiosorum.*

11. See no. 3.

12. At the time she was writing this chapter (1574-1576), the opposition to her had begun.
13. Duruelo, which at the time of this writing had been transferred to Mancera, as is indicated further on in no. 14.
14. Alonso González and Angel de Salazar respectively.
15. In fact, about two months. She left Toledo May 30 and returned July 21.
16. In no. 6.
17. Baltasar de Jesús (Nieto) (1524-1589), a restless and inglorious figure in the history of Carmel, became the first superior of Pastrana. Omitting her customary accolade about the person being a great servant of God, Teresa refers to him as neither young nor old and a very good preacher. Nor did Teresa want the foundation established until Fr. Antonio arrived July 13.
18. During Lent 1574.
19. Ruy Gómez died July 29, 1573. His widow, the princess, thirty-three at the time, distressed over her loss, insisted on becoming a nun in the Carmel at once.
20. In ch. 21.
21. In no. 16.

CHAPTER 18

1. The two foundations were those in Pastrana, one for the nuns and one for the friars. Teresa returned to Toledo July 22, 1569, where she bought the house mentioned in ch. 15, no. 17.
2. The rector was Martín Gutiérrez (1504-1573). On a trip to Rome for the election of a general to succeed St. Francis Borgia, he was taken prisoner by the Huguenots and died in captivity.
3. Teresa's monasteries were now of two kinds: those founded in poverty, dependent on alms, and those founded with the endowment of a fixed income. See ch. 9, nos. 2-4.
4. Probably not remembering the name of the bishop, Teresa left the space blank; she never did remember to fill it in. The bishop's name was Don Pedro González de Mendoza.
5. This lady was probably Doña Beatriz Yáñez de Ovalle, a relative of Teresa's brother-in-law.
6. This chapter was being written sometime between 1574-1576.
7. María del Sacramento (Suárez) (d.1589), originally from the monastery of the Incarnation and later the prioress of Alba de Tormes.
8. See ch. 3, nos. 11-14.
9. October 31, 1570.

10. The chapter is a community meeting at which faults in the observance of the constitutions are corrected. See *Constitutions,* no. 43 in note 24.

11. Teresa is here referring to the legend in the Roman Martyrology (October 21) concerning the eleven thousand virgins martyred near Cologne by the Huns; one of them named Cordula fled at first and hid, but later, moved by the grace of God, offered herself to the persecutors and was beheaded.

CHAPTER 19

1. See ch. 18, no. 3.
2. Nicolás Gutiérrez, a Salamancan businessman, had six daughters in the monastery of the Incarnation, all of whom later entered the Teresian Carmel.
3. In ch. 18, no. 2.
4. In fact, two nuns came from Medina and one from Valladolid; later three others joined them from Avila.
5. See ch. 18, no. 3.
6. They were Poor Clare Franciscan nuns.
7. It was the custom to toll the church bells on the vigil and the day itself of All Souls. See no. 2.
8. She was appointed prioress of the monastery of the Incarnation in Avila by the apostolic visitator, Pedro Fernández, O.P., in July of 1571 and took possession of the office in October. Fernández had been named to the office by Pius V, August 20, 1569.
9. The apostolic visitator, Pedro Fernández.
10. The gentleman's name was Pedro de la Banda.
11. See ch. 3, no. 2; ch. 10, no. 4.
12. September 28, 1573. The sermon was preached by the noted Diego de Estella.
13. Doña María Pimentel was a daughter of the fifth count of Benevente and wife of Don Alonso Zúñiga, the third count of Monterrey.
14. In fact, in 1579, Teresa had to obtain permission from the bishop to move the community to another house, and after her death in 1582, the nuns moved.

CHAPTER 20

1. Domingo Báñez, the noted Dominican theologian, had been Teresa's confessor during the years 1561-1567. For other instances of his opinion in this regard, see ch. 9, no. 3; *Life,* ch. 36, no. 15. In regard to the Council of Trent, see ch. 9, note 3.

2. Teresa de Layz was a daughter of Don Diego Layz and Doña Beatriz de Aponte. "Pure blood" was the term used to exclude Jewish or Moorish background and illustrates a prejudice of the time.
3. He was, in fact, administrator of the University of Salamanca from May 17, 1541 to February 1, 1566.
4. It was the office of administrator for the duke. See no. 1.
5. See Jon. 1–2.
6. January 25.
7. She feared giving this impression if she had a part to play in the account she was giving. See ch. 16, no. 3.
8. Teresa's difficulties in remembering the dates are manifest in the titles of the following three chapters.

CHAPTER 21

1. See chapter 19, no. 6. Pedro Fernández (d. 1580) was a great help to Teresa and her foundations especially during the years 1571–1574.
2. She arrived in Salamanca July 31, 1573.
3. They were received into the order by Teresa. The mother took the name Ana de Jesús and the daughter, María de la Encarnación. They made their profession July 2, 1575. Both of them later exercised the office of prioress.
4. The apostolic commissary and visitator, Fr. Pedro Fernández, invested with pontifical authority.
5. The discalced friar was St. John of the Cross, though it seems the first Mass was said by Julián de Avila. Antonio Gaytán from Alba de Tormes was converted, through Teresa's influence, to a more spiritual life. Assisting the Saint on her foundations of Segovia, Beas, Caravaca, and Seville, he became the recipient of her great confidence, especially in the foundation of Caravaca in which Teresa authorized him to act in her name. His daughter Mariana de Jesús (1570–1615) was admitted by Teresa into the monastery of Alba de Tormes at the exceptional age of seven as an act of gratitude for the services rendered by her father.
6. Isabel de Jesús, sister of Andrés Jimena (see no. 5), best known for the incident at Salamanca (Easter 1571) when, as a novice, she sang a song that sent Teresa into a rapture. She was later a prioress both in Palencia and Salamanca.
7. That is, from March 19 to September 24 when Teresa took possession of the houses for the new monastery.

8. Don Juan de Orozco y Covarrubias de Leiva, prior of the cathedral chapter and later bishop of Guadix and Baza.
9. They moved on September 24, 1574.
10. See no. 1. Teresa left Segovia September 30, 1574. She concluded her three year office of prioress October 6. It might be remembered that shortly after she took possession of the house in Segovia, Teresa sent Fr. Julián de Avila and Gaytán to bring the fourteen nuns in Pastrana to Segovia where they would be free of the disturbances caused by the princess of Eboli. They arrived in Segovia in five wagons April 7, 1574. See chapter 17, no. 17.

CHAPTER 22
1. February 24. Teresa had written 1574. She erred on the date also in nos. 4 and 19. But in the three instances the final 4 was corrected to 5.
2. In ch. 21, no. 1.
3. In ch. 21, no. 1.
4. See ch. 2, nos. 3-4.
5. She is referring to one of the military orders of knights of that time called the Order of Santiago (St. James). In a military order, the knights combined the principles of monasticism and chivalry, pledging themselves to the practice of asceticism and the recitation of the canonical hours as well as to the defense of Christendom against the infidel. Certain territories were governed by the order and were under its jurisdiction rather than the ecclesiastical. See no. 13.
6. Here she begins an account of the conversion and vocation of Catalina Sandoval y Godínez (de Jesús) (1540-1586) which led to the foundation in Beas. Catalina succeeded Ana de Jesús as prioress in 1582. St. John of the Cross was her spiritual director until her death.
7. Allusion to Jn. 9:2.
8. In no. 5.
9. March 19, 1558.
10. In 1560; her mother (see no. 13), in 1565.
11. January 19, 1574.
12. Allusion to what was referred to in no. 14.
13. February 24. Accompanying Teresa on the journey were Fr.Julián de Avila, Antonio Gaytán, and Fr. Gregorio Martínez (1548-1599), who received the habit of the discalced Carmelites in Beas from Fr. Gracián and the name Gregorio Nacianceno. Venerable Ana de Jesús (1545-1621), at whose request St. John of the Cross wrote his commentary on the Spiritual Canticle, was appointed the first prioress.

14. They took the names Catalina de Jesús and María de Jesús. Like her sister, María de Jesús (1549-1604) also had St. John of the Cross as her spiritual director, and three of his letters to her have come down to us. In 1589 she went to Córdoba as Prioress.
15. What follows is a kind of appendix to the chapter.
16. Cf. ch. 17, nos. 7, 14, 15.
17. Bartolomé Bustamente. Before entering the Society, he had been a secretary to Cardinal Pardo de Tavera and was acquainted with the cardinal's nephew, the husband of Doña Luisa de la Cerda.
18. In no. 1.
19. In no. 6.
20. Her provincial at that time was Jerónimo Gracián.

CHAPTER 23
1. Here too she wrote 1574; the date was corrected to read 1575.
2. She deals with the Caravaca foundation in ch. 27. Fr. Jerónimo Gracián (1545-1614), an important figure in Teresian history, was born in Valladolid, studied at the university of Alcalá, and was ordained a priest in 1570. Exceptionally gifted, he entered the novitiate in Pastrana in 1572. After meeting Teresa in 1575, he worked closely with her until her death. Later, falling into disfavor with Doria, he was expelled from the order. He died in Brussels.
3. Gracián's father, Diego Gracián, was a secretary in one of the offices of Philip II.
4. Juan de Jesús (Roca) (c. 1540-1614) was born in Sanahuja in Catalonia. A fellow student with Gracián at Alcalá, he entered the novitiate in Pastrana a few months before his companion.
5. The prioress was Isabel de Santo Domingo (1537-1623), one of Teresa's outstanding daughters, who went with the foundress from St. Joseph's in Avila to Toledo, became prioress there, and after a few months was sent to Pastrana as prioress, where she had to deal with many difficult situations because of the princess of Eboli's meddling in community affairs. The nun about whom Gracián spoke to the prioress was Bárbara del Espíritu Santo.
6. See Gracián's *Historia Fundationum* in MHCT, 3: 539-541.
7. The words, "or almost none like him," were added between the lines and strengthen Teresa's glowing evaluation of Gracián.
8. They had twenty children, thirteen reaching adulthood.
9. The friar to whom she is referring was Angel de San Gabriel. Going to extremes in austerities and ascetical testings, he had to be corrected by Domingo Báñez, O.P., and replaced by St. John of

the Cross; cf. MHCT, 1:128-131. The absent prior was Baltasar de Jesús (Nieto); cf. ch. 17, no. 15, note 17.

10. She began to write "I was about to regret," but then changed.

11. Cf. ch. 3, nos. 16-17; ch. 13, no. 1.

12. Teresa seems to deny that the discalced had constitutions from the Father General, Rubeo, and she seems to do so again in no. 13. Nonetheless, around 1568 he did approve constitutions for the friars which were an adaptation of those written by Teresa for her daughters, but apparently they were not used for long. Cf. B. Zimmerman, *Regesta Rubei* (Rome, 1936), pp. 58-65; BMC, 6:399-406; PP. Tomás-Simeón, *La Reforma Teresiana* (Rome, 1962), pp. 97-100.

13. The apostolic visitator, Fr. Francisco Vargas, appointed Gracián a delegate apostolic visitator in September of 1573. In 1574, Gracián was appointed vicar provincial of the Carmelites of the Observance in Andalusia, and in 1575 his authority was extended to the Teresian Carmel. Cf. MHCT, 1:184-185.

CHAPTER 24

1. In ch. 23, no. 1.

2. The meeting between Gracián and Teresa took place in April 1575. Not until August 3 did the nuncio Ormaneto extend Gracián's authority to all the discalced Carmelites. See MHCT, 1:221-223.

3. See ch. 27, no. 6.

4. This should read Andalusia and not Castile. In no. 2 she states that Gracián was apostolic commissary in Andalusia. Beas was in the ecclesiastical province of Andalusia; see no. 4.

5. Don Cristóbal de Rojas y Sandobal (1502-1580), son of the marquis of Denia, had been bishop of Oviedo, Badajoz, and Cordoba, as well as an active member of the Council of Trent.

6. In the division of Spain into provinces, Beas came under the civil jurisdiction of Castile; but ecclesiastically it belonged to the diocese of Cartagena in Andalusia.

7. Cf.no. 2.

8. Fr. Gregorio Nacianceno who had already accompanied Teresa on the foundation to Beas. See ch. 22, no. 19, note 13.

9. May 26, 1575.

10. Their names were: María de San José; Isabel de San Francisco; Leonor de San Gabriel; Ana de San Alberto; María del Espíritu Santo; and Isabel de San Jerónimo.

11. She mentioned only one discalced friar in the group; the other men mentioned were Julián de Avila and Antonio Gaytán. See no. 5.
12. See no. 4.
13. See Council of Trent, Session 25, *De Reformatione regularium*, ch. 3.
14. According to María de San José, the archbishop's opposition came from his desire that Teresa and her daughters reform the existing monasteries of nuns in Seville rather than found a new one. See her *Libro de Recreaciones* (Burgos: El Monte Carmelo, 1913), *Recr.* 9.
15. May 29, 1575. The "said Father" was Fr. Mariano.
16. She had two patent letters from Fr. Rubeo, the general of the Carmelites: one of April 27, 1567; another of April 6, 1571. See MHCT, 1:62-65; 110-112.

CHAPTER 25

1. That is, from May 26, 1575, until February of the next year, a period of nine months.
2. Fr. Gracián.
3. Beatriz de la Madre de Dios. See ch. 26, nos. 2-16.
4. See ch. 27, no. 20.
5. Lorenzo de Cepeda (1519-1580) had departed for America in 1540, and now returned to Spain, a widower, accompanied by three of his children (Francisco, Lorenzo, and Teresita) and his brother Don Pedro. A wealthy man, he disembarked in Sanlúcar de Barrameda and began to help Teresa with her foundation in Seville. Soon, he turned to Teresa for direction in his own spiritual life, and a number of her letters of spiritual direction to him have come down to us. See *Spiritual Testimonies*, no. 41.
6. Garciálvarez (or García Alvarez) continued to help the nuns afterward in the capacity of confessor to the community. From the letters of Teresa to María de San José, one deduces that he was a generous man but lacking in learning and discretion. His interference in community affairs led to his dismissal as confessor of the community.
7. This took place April 5, 1576. The house cost 6,000 ducats, but in a letter to Fr. Mariano, May 9, 1576, Teresa speaks of the great bargain they got and of how the house could not be bought now for 20,000.
8. María de San José (Salazar) (1548-1603). Born in Toledo, she became a servant in the household of Doña Luisa de la Cerda where in 1562 she met Teresa. In 1570 she took the habit in Malagón and in 1575 accompanied Teresa to Beas and then Seville becoming

prioress there. Through correspondence she kept up a warm friendship with Teresa. In 1584 she founded the Carmel in Lisbon. But later, falling into disfavor with Doria, she was imprisoned there. In 1603 she was sent to Cuerva where she died.

9. An irregularity in the contract which had apparently gone unnoticed, made the purchaser liable for a sales tax called the *alcabala*. Since the community could not pay the tax, the guarantor was held responsible. To avoid arrest, Don Lorenzo went into sanctuary.

10. Fernando de Pantoja (d. 1582) was prior of the Carthusian monastery of Santa María de las Cuevas in Seville from 1567 to 1580. He was as well a native of Avila. See BMC, 6:250-251.

11. This took place June 3, 1576. When the procession was over Teresa knelt before the archbishop and received his blessing, but then, to her embarrassment, the archbishop knelt before her and asked for her blessing in the presence of all the people. See BMC. 18:469.

CHAPTER 26

1. June 4, 1576 at 2 a.m.

2. To temper the sadness of the nuns in Seville over Teresa's approaching departure, Fr. Gracián ordered Teresa to pose for a portrait which was painted by Fray Juan de la Miseria. Still preserved by the nuns in Seville, it is the only definitely authentic portrait we possess of the Saint. When Teresa saw the finished product, she remarked in good humor, "May God forgive you, Fray Juan, for now that you have painted me, you have made me look ugly and bleary-eyed." See J. Gracián, *Peregrinación de Anastasio* in BMC, 17:201-202.

3. In ch. 18, nos. 4-5; 24, no. 6.

4. Beatriz de la Madre de Dios (Chaves) (1538-1624), this daughter of Alfonso Gómez Ibero and Juana Gómez de Chaves, made her profession September 29, 1576. In the next year her mother was professed as Juana de la Cruz (see no. 15). Her unfortunate childhood may account for the malice she later showed toward the prioress, María de San José, who as a result was deposed. Beatriz then was appointed prioress by Cardenas, the Carmelite provincial of the observance. In less than a year, new superiors, appointed through the intervention of the king, deprived her of office because of both her imprudent leadership and the debts the monastery had accumulated. María de San José was once again elected. Beatriz eventually repented and lived a long and useful life.

5. In nos. 3–5.
6. In no. 9.
7. This monastery was founded January 6, 1574.
8. Gracián was twenty-nine. But Teresa was mistaken about the age of Beatriz who at the time was not twenty-seven but thirty-six.
9. May 29, 1575, the same day on which the first Mass was said. Cf. ch. 24, no. 18.
10. She made her profession Sept. 29, 1576. See Teresa's letter to María de San José, June 18, 1576.
11. She made her profession Nov. 10, 1577.

CHAPTER 27

1. In ch. 22.
2. After Catalina, she left a blank space with the intention of filling in the surname which was de Otalora. Doña Catalina was the widow of Alonso Muñoz, a wealthy and influential gentleman of Caravaca, who had been a member of the councils of Castile and of the Indies.
3. The Jesuit was Father Leiva. The three young ladies were: Francisca de Saojosa, Francisca de Cuéllar, and Francisca de Tauste.
4. Rodrigo de Moya, widower of Doña Luisa de Avila was the father of Francisca de Cuéllar.
5. In making the foundation in Beas, Teresa brought with her enough nuns for two foundations (see ch. 24, no.4). But since Caravaca was under the jurisdiction of the Order of the Knights of Santiago, the license for the foundation had the condition that the foundation render obedience to the council of the Order of Knights, which was something unacceptable to Teresa (see ch. 23, no. 1; ch. 24, no. 3). For this and other reasons the nuns destined for Caravaca were brought to the Seville foundation.
6. On March 10, 1575.
7. In no. 1.
8. Teresa's letter to Philip II has been lost, but the royal dispatch bearing the date June 9, 1575, is still conserved (see BMC, 6: 257–262), as is also Teresa's grateful reply in a letter dated July 19, 1575.
9. In ch. 24, nos. 3–4. She left on May 18.
10. Ana de Alberto (Salcedo) (d. 1624), a native of Malagón, who was one of the first to be professed there. She accompanied Teresa from Malagón to Beas and Seville and from the latter went to Caravaca. At Caravaca she met St. John of the Cross and became one of his spiritual daughters.

11. Ambrosio de San Pedro (d.c. 1593), a native of Pastrana who was at the time vicar of Almodóvar del Campo, and Miguel de la Columna, not a Father but a lay Brother who was later to cause some trouble by signing a slanderous statement claiming that Gracián was living a depraved life. He later declared that he had not read a word of the statement and had been pressured into signing it by Fray Baltasar de Jesús (Nieto), Jerónimo Tostado, and others.
12. They arrived in Caravaca December 18, 1575. The Blessed Sacrament was reserved January 1, 1576 (see chapter heading).
13. This was Francisca de Saojosa, who later, though, was accepted through the intervention of Fr. Gracián and made profession June 1, 1578.
14. Lorenzo de Cepeda (see ch. 25, no. 3).
15. Thinking this would be the end of her book, Teresa left some blank spaces as though what was to follow would serve as an epilogue to what she had written.
16. 1 K. 19:2-5.
17. Gregorio Martínez y López who took the name Gregorio Nacianceno (see ch. 24, no. 5).
18. See ch. 21, no. 2; ch. 22, no. 2, and ch. 24, no. 20. She is referring probably to the patent of April 6, 1571 (See MHCT, 1:110-112).
19. She is referring to the general chapter at Piacenza in Italy, celebrated under the presidency of Father Rubeo in May and June of 1575. The definitory of the chapter imposed on Teresa the command to retire definitively to a monastery in Castile and not go out to make any new foundations. Teresa wanted to submit to this order immediately, but Father Gracián prevented this. As apostolic visitator, he held jurisdiction independent of the superior general. In the acts of the chapter there is no record of this order imposed on the Saint.
20. Teresa uses this term "accidental joy" in the theological sense of her time, but with a very original application. Accidental joy was that joy experienced by the blessed in heaven that did not flow directly from their vision of God.
21. Allusion to 2 Sm: 14-15.
22. She leaves another space of one or two lines and then concludes with the following colophon.
23. In the prologue, no. 2.
24. In view of the circumstances, Teresa thought that her work of founding new monasteries had come to an end.

CHAPTER 28

1. Neither this chapter nor those that follow were numbered by Teresa. At the close of the preceding chapter she inserted the four counsels given her by the Lord for her Carmelite Fathers. Editors usually omit them because they are not a part of this work. See *Spiritual Testimonies*, 64.

2. The foundation in Seville was made in 1575–1576; the present foundation was made in 1580.

3. The word "almost" was inserted by Teresa between the lines.

4. Father Juan Bautista Rubeo; see ch. 2.

5. She is alluding to Frs. Pedro Fernández and Francisco Vargas, O.P., named visitators by Pius V in 1569, and to Fr. Gracián, delegate of the latter (1573) and confirmed in his office by the nuncio Ormaneto (1574).

6. The "holy nuncio" was Nicolás Ormaneto who died in Madrid June 18, 1577. His successor, Felipe Sega (c. 1537–1596) came to Spain (Aug. 30, 1577) badly disposed toward Teresa and her work because of misinformation he had received in Rome prior to his departure. He was in fact a relative of Cardinal Filippo Buoncompagni, Cardinal protector of the Carmelites and nephew of Pope Gregory XIII. Thus, Teresa says the new nuncio was a distant relative of the pope.

7. One of Teresa's ways of referring to the Carmelites of the Observance; cf. ch. 13, no. 1.

8. In a brief dated October 18, 1578, Sega placed the discalced friars and nuns under the authority of the Carmelite provincials of Castile and Andalusia.

9. Allusion to Jon. 1:4–15.

10. The four counselors were: Don Luis Manrique, the king's chaplain and major almoner; Fray Lorenzo de Villavicencio, an Augustinian; and the Dominicans, Hernando del Castillo and Pedro Fernández. On April 1, 1579, they nullified the authority of the provincials over the discalced friars and nuns and appointed in their place as vicar general Teresa's former provincial, Fr. Angel de Salazar.

11. Agustín de Ervías was a learned canon of Cuenco, who exchanged his office for parish priest of Villanueva de la Jara because of his desire for the care of souls.

12. Alonso Velázquez (d. 1587), after spending some years as professor at the University of Alcalá, was made a canon of Toledo, where he became Teresa's confessor and advisor. He was later appointed bishop of Osma, and then, archbishop of Santiago. See *Spir. Test.*, 65.

13. She is alluding to the punishment imposed by Sega; see no. 4. This monastery near La Roda was founded in 1572.
14. Gabriel de la Asunción (1544-1584) was a native of Pastrana and much esteemed by the prince and princess of Eboli. As prior he governed the monastery at la Roda from 1576-1580 and there acted as spiritual director of Catalina de Cardona.
15. She arrived in Malagón Nov. 25, 1579.
16. From Toledo she chose María de los Mártires (for prioress) and Constanza de la Cruz; from Malagón, Elvira de San Angelo (for subprioress) and Ana de San Agustín.
17. In no. 11.
18. Allusion to 1K. 19:9-13.
19. Catalina de Cardona (1519-1577) who arranged for the foundation of this monastery died May 11, 1577.
20. Catalina de Cardona had been governess to Don Juan de Austria, son of Charles V, and to Don Carlos, son of Philip II. In 1563 she withdrew to the solitude of La Roda, and in 1571 began to wear the Carmelite habit, but with the friar's cowl.
21. The hermit's name was Fr. Piña, and he had his hermitage on the mount of La Vera Cruz.
22. "or other things" was added between the lines by Teresa.
23. "a woman" was added in the margin by Teresa.
24. The Carmelite nuns in Toledo; see no. 26.
25. Teresa wrote "Mercenarians." They were, in fact, the Trinitarians at Fuensanta.
26. The part about the tunic was added between the lines by Teresa.
27. This took place May 6, 1571. The habit was given by the prior, Fr. Baltasar de Jesús, in the presence of the prince and princess of Eboli.
28. In ch. 17, nos. 6-15.
29. The tomb (sepulcher) included a carved representation of the dead Christ surrounded by His Mother and others.
30. Gracián crossed out the "Fray" and wrote "Don."
31. In no. 20.
32. Gabriel de la Asunción; see no. 11.
33. February 21.
34. See no. 8.
35. A *beata* was a woman who wore a religious habit and lived a pious Christian life without belonging to any religious order.

CHAPTER 29
1. The monogram IHS precedes the chapter title. The chapter number was omitted. The feast of King David was celebrated December 29.

2. The major superior (vicar general) was Fr. Angel de Salazar. See ch. 28, no. 6.
3. See *Life*, ch. 36 no. 2. Don Alvaro de Mendoza had been appointed bishop of Palencia June 28, 1577.
4. August 8, 1580. The previous March, Teresa became a victim of what was called the "universal influenza," a virus that swept through and leveled Spain that year.
5. The prioress was María Bautista de Ocampo (see ch. 1 note 3). A native of Toledo, she was the daughter of Teresa'a cousin. At the age of eighteen, she was taken by Teresa to live at the Incarnation and was the first to suggest the founding of a new monastery (see *Life*, ch. 32, no. 10). She became a discalced nun at St. Joseph's and was one of the two from St. Joseph's to accompany Teresa on the second foundation of Medina. In 1568, she transferred to Valladolid and in 1571 became prioress there. She was one of Teresa's most frequent correspondents. But in her last days she sided with the mother-in-law of Teresa's nephew Don Francisco de Cepeda who was contesting the inheritance left to St. Joseph's in Avila by Teresa's brother Lorenzo. According to Blessed Anne of St. Bartholomew, Teresa in her last visit to Valladolid shortly before her death was treated rudely by the prioress María Bautista on account of this family dispute over the inheritance.
6. It was he who encouraged Teresa to write about her foundations; see prologue, no. 2.
7. See ch. 3, no. 1 and note 3.
8. In no. 1.
9. December 28, 1580.
10. Jerónimo Reinoso (1546–1600), from then on a close friend of Teresa's.
11. The first, Porras, was confessor to the Carmelite nuns in Valladolid. The second, Agustín de Victoria, was a benefactor of the nuns in Valladolid and had a daughter who was a member of the community, María de San Agustín. Also accompanying Teresa from Valladolid to Palencia was Fr. Gracián.
12. This lay Sister was Blessed Anne of St. Bartholomew (1549–1626). Having entered St. Joseph's in Avila, she learned to write in order to serve as secretary to Teresa. After Teresa broke her arm on Christmas Eve, 1577, Blessed Anne accompanied her on her journeys, nursed her in her illnesses and was with her when she died. Eventually Blessed Anne went to France with a group of Sisters to make foundations there. She became a choir Sister and later prioress. She founded convents at Tours (1608) and at Antwerp

(1612) where she remained till her death. Her autobiography and numerous letters have been published. The other four nuns were: Inés de Jesús (Tapia), a cousin of Teresa's; Catalina del Espíritu Santo; María de San Bernardo; and Juana de San Francisco.

13. Martín Alonso Salinas (d. 1592).
14. In no. 11.
15. Suero de Vega was the son of Juan de Vega, who had been viceroy of Navarra and Sicily and president of the royal council. One of his sons became a discalced Carmelite, Juan de la Madre de Dios.
16. In no. 14.
17. In nos. 15-16.
18. He was thirty-five at the time.
19. The messenger who would be sent by the owner to negotiate the contract (see no. 16).
20. Allusion to Jn. 9:6-7.
21. In nos. 14, 15, 23.
22. The administrator for the bishop was Don Prudencio Armentia; he was also a canon of the Palencia cathedral.
23. May 26, 1581.
24. The brief, *Pia consideratione*, given by Gregory XIII June 22, 1580. See MHCT, 2:191-207.
25. This chapter took place in March of 1581. St. John of the Cross was elected a provincial counselor. For the full documents, see MHCT, 2:236-316.

CHAPTER 30

1. June 14, 1581. In Teresa's time it was generally believed among Carmelites that the prophets Elijah and Elisha often dwelt on Mt. Carmel and that saintly men continued to live there in solitude. These hermits, living in the spirit of the prophets, were later converted by the preaching of the apostles. On one side of the mountain, they then built a church or oratory in honor of our Lady. Thus, according to this tradition, they were the first among all religious orders to be called children of the Blessed Mary of Mount Carmel. Following this version of the order's beginnings which was the accepted one in her time, Teresa as with Elijah refers to Elisha as our Father St. Elisha. Cf. ch. 27, no. 17; ch. 28, no. 20.
2. See ch. 28, no. 10.
3. Beatriz de Beamonte y Navarra (d. 1600) also contributed generously to the foundation of a Carmel in Pamplona in 1583. There she entered as a nun and took the name Beatriz de Cristo.
4. This endowment was a generous one. Twenty-five per thousand

would be the equivalent of 2.5% since sums were expressed in proportions of one thousand rather than one hundred (per cent) so as to avoid decimal percentages.

5. The church was originally named Our Lady of the Villas, but Doña Beatriz had the name changed to Blessed Trinity.

6. Fr. Gracián who was then in the city of Palencia.

7. In no. 2.

8. The seven nuns were: Catalina de Cristo (elected prioress on June 15), Beatriz de Jesús, María de Cristo, Juana Bautista, María de Jesús, María de San José, and Catalina del Espíritu Santo. The lay Sister was María Bautista. Teresa's companion was her nurse and secretary, Blessed Anne of St. Bartholomew. Accompanying this group of nuns were: Fr. Nicolás Doria and Brother Eliseo de la Madre de Dios; Pedro de Ribera (of whom Teresa speaks in nos. 12-13) sent by Don Alvaro de Mendoza; a chaplain by the name of Chacón and a police officer for security, both provided by the bishop of Burgo de Osma; and finally Francisco de Cetina, a chaplain sent by Doña Beatriz.

9. Nicolás de Jesús María (Doria) (1539-1594), born in Genoa, spent his early life as a banker. Arriving in Spain in 1570, he settled in Seville, but then sacrificed his future in finance for the religious life, taking the discalced Carmelite habit in 1577. In 1585, he was elected provincial at the chapter in Lisbon. His interference in the governing of the discalced nuns put him in opposition with Fr. Gracián and St. John of the Cross. He secured the expulsion of Gracián from the order in 1592. In 1593 he attended the general chapter in Cremona in which the separation of the two branches of Carmelites was approved. He died in Alcalá de Henares while holding the office of General.

10. She is alluding to the adage, "For want of good men, my husband was mayor."

11. May 31, 1581.

12. Not only did he give her his blessing, but, as did the archbishop of Seville, he afterward made the Saint give him her blessing.

13. Teresa herself supervised this work.

14. See note 1.

15. August 6.

16. The Jesuit Father was Francisco de la Carrera.

17. In no. 2.

18. In the autograph the word "penitential" is followed by the word "and" and then a long, blank space is left as though Teresa had intended to add something.

19. She left Soria on August 16.
20. See note 8.
21. Blessed Anne of St. Bartholomew.
22. August 23.

CHAPTER 31

1. This chapter (without a number in the orginal manuscript) was written in Burgos the last days of June (cf. no. 17) at a time in which Teresa's health was very poor. The more than average number of misspellings, repetitions, and obscure or ambiguous constructions point to Teresa's weakened and exhausted condition, although the account itself is a very lively one.
2. An Avilan, his name was Don Cristóbal Vela (d. 1599). His father Blasco Nuñez Vela, was the viceroy of Peru under whose orders two of Teresa's brothers fought against Pizarro. Both the viceroy and Teresa's brother Antonio died in the battle of Iñaquito in 1546. Francisco Nuñez Vela, the viceroy's brother, was Teresa's godfather. Don Cristobal was bishop in the Canary Islands from 1575 to 1580 when he was appointed archbishop of Burgos. There he remained until his death.
3. See ch. 29, nos. 1,11,27; ch. 2, note 5; cf. ch. 10, no. 6; 13, no. 6; 17, no. 11.
4. The monastery, today in ruins, was better known as Our Lady del Prado and located outside the city.
5. He received the pallium, which is worn at certain times by archbishops.
6. She is referring to the Council of Trent. See Session 25, *De reformatione regularium*, ch. 3.
7. See ch. 29, no. 1. She is referring to the influenza she contracted in Toledo and from which she suffered a relapse in Valladolid.
8. In ch. 29, no. 6.
9. In ch. 29, no. 6.
10. In the orginal she mistakenly wrote Soria instead of Burgos.
11. See *Life*, ch. 36, nos. 15-17.
12. Teresa had to return to Avila because of some difficulties in the community with regard to certain minor abuses in the observance of poverty and abstinence and also because of the community's financial problems. The prioress, María de Cristo, renounced her office, and Teresa was elected prioress. In her letter of Nov. 8, 1581, she wrote to María de San José, "they have now made me prioress out of pure hunger."

13. Catalina de Tolosa (1538-1608), the widow of Sebastián Muncharez, had seven children who entered Teresa's Carmel. Two daughters were professed in Valladolid, Catalina de la Asunción and Casilda de San Angelo; two in Palencia, María de San José and Isabel de la Trinidad; and one in Burgos, Elena de Jesús. Her two sons became discalced Carmelite priests, Sebastián de Jesús, provincial of Castile 1603-1606, and Juan Crisóstomo, later a professor at Salamanca college. In her fiftieth year, Catalina herself entered the Carmel in Palencia.

14. In no. 7.

15. In ch. 30, nos. 13-14.

16. Inés de Jesús (d. 1601), a cousin of Teresa's, had been professed at the Incarnation in Avila and became the first prioress at Medina del Campo. In 1580, she went with Teresa to the new foundation in Palencia where she became prioress.

17. The words of our Lord in the autograph are enclosed within variously shaped strokes of the pen and thereby highlighted.

18. Catalina Manrique (see no. 10). These letters were received by Teresa in Avila on November 29.

19. The Minims of St. Francis de Paula.

20. In Alcalá on April 9, 1581, Fr. Gracián had already given the license for the foundation.

21. This wagon was the one in which Teresa was riding.

22. They were: Tomasina Bautista (prioress), Inés de la Cruz, Catalina de Jesús, Catalina de la Asunción (daughter of Doña Catalina de Tolosa), and María Bautista, a white veiled nun. The two who were to return with Teresa were Blessed Anne of St. Bartholomew and Teresa's niece Teresita.

23. She mentioned this in ch. 29, no. 30.

24. Cf. ch. 29, no.1.

25. The holy crucifix was venerated at the time in the monastery of the Augustinians and is now in the Cathedral of Burgos.

26. In ch. 29, no. 12.

27. Cf. no. 15.

28. In nos. 18-19.

29. Pedro Manso had been a classmate of Gracián's at the University of Alcalá. He served as Teresa's confessor when Gracián left Burgos. He was later appointed bishop of Calahorra (1594) where he brought the discalced Carmelite nuns (1598) and friars (1603).

30. The church of San Gil.

31. To Valladolid; see no. 31.

32. Hernando de Matanza was the city magistrate and the mayor's

brother, Francisco de Cuevas had been a member of the court of Charles V and was married to the Toledan writer Luisa Sigea de Valasco.

33. In nos. 26-27.
34. In no. 26.
35. Pedro Manso (cf. no. 24) and Antonio Aguiar (cf. no. 33).
36. That is, from Feb. 23 to March 18.
37. Doctor Antonio Aguiar, a physician, had been a classmate of Gracián's at the University of Alcalá. Teresa had not yet mentioned him specifically (cf. nos. 23, 25, 33).
38. The owner was Don Manuel Franco. There were two priests given the authorization to sell: Diego Ruiz de Ayala and Martín Pérez de Rozas.
39. That is, one of those authorized to sell.
40. Juan Ortega de la Torre y Frias.
41. The sale was finalized March 16, 1582. The nuns moved in March 18.
42. The price was 1,290 ducats.
43. In nos. 32 and 34.
44. Jerónimo del Pino and his wife Magdalena Solórzano.
45. In no. 24.
46. The church and hospital of San Lucas, a few yards from the houses bought by Teresa.
47. The license is dated April 18, 1582.
48. See Jn. 4: 7-15.
49. Fr. Gracián had returned from Valladolid.
50. Elena de Jesús who because of her young age did not make profession until June 5, 1586 (cf. note 12).
51. Elena de Jesús received the habit from him April 20. Not only did the archbishop preside at the ceremony but he also preached and publicly accused himself for not having given the license earlier and asked pardon for what he had made Teresa and her nuns go through. See BMC, 2:328.

EPILOGUE

1. In *Life*, chs. 32-36.
2. See *Life*, ch. 33, no. 16.
3. Actually, it lasted fifteen years, from 1562 to 1577.
4. He was appointed bishop of Palencia June 28, 1577. Before mid-July, Teresa had left Toledo for Avila. On August 2, Don Alvaro made the transfer of jurisdiction legal. See MHCT, 1:365.
5. Cf. *Life*, ch. 33, no. 16.
6. Alonso Velázquez. Cf. ch. 28, no. 10 and note 12.

THE CONSTITUTIONS

INTRODUCTION

1. See MHCT, 1:11.
2. See *Life,* ch. 36, no. 27, in *The Collected Works of St. Teresa of Avila,* vol. 1.
3. See María de San José, "Ramillete de mirra" in *Humor Y Espiritualidad* (Burgos: El Monte Carmelo, 1966), p. 423.
4. See BMC, 18:158.
5. In vol. 2 of *The Collected Works,* ch. 4, nos. 1 and 4.
6. See BMC, 19:1-2.
7. Cf. *The Foundations,* ch. 1, no. 1.
8. Cf. *Life,* ch. 35, nos. 1-2; ch. 36, no. 28; in vol. 1 of *The Collected Works.*
9. See *Escritos de Santa Teresa,* ed. D. Vicente de la Fuente, 2 vols. (Madrid: M. Rivadeneyra, 1861-2).
10. See *Obras de Santa Teresa de Jesús,* ed. P. Silverio de Santa Teresa, vol. 5 (Burgos: El Monte Carmelo, 1915-1925); *Santa Teresa de Jesús Obras Completas,* ed. Efrén de la Madre de Dios and Otger Steggink (Madrid: BAC, 1967).
11. See letter to Gracián, February 21, 1581, in *The Letters of St. Teresa,* trans. E. Allison Peers (Westminster, Maryland: Newman Press, 1950).
12. See *On Making the Visitation,* no. 15.
13. Feb. 21, 1581.
14. Nov. 19, 1576.
15. See *Letters,* Feb. 21, 1581.
16. See ibid., Feb. 27, 1581.
17. See BMC, 6:422.
18. See *Santa Teresa de Jesús, Camino de Perfección, Constituciones, Modo de Visitar Los Conventos,* ed. Tomás de la Cruz Alvarez (Burgos: El Monte Carmelo, 1966), pp. 280-281.
19. Tomás Alvarez (ibid.) holds that the ideological and normative content of the work continues to be authentically Teresian. Otilio Rodriguez in a detailed study concludes that the constitutions of Alcalá represent the final wish of the Mother Foundress. See "El Testamento Teresiano" in *El Monte Carmelo* 78(1970), p. 73. Fortunato Antolín in another detailed analysis of the constitutions of Alcalá doubts whether we can speak of a work in collaboration and concludes that it may not be very far from the truth to

think that the impression made on Teresa and her nuns by these new constitutions was a somewhat unfavorable one. See "Observaciones sobre las Constituciones de las Carmelitas Descalzas, promulgadas en Alcalá de Henares 1581" in *Ephemerides Carmeliticae* 24 (1973), p. 373.

20. *Escritos de Santa Teresa*, vol. 1, pp. 251–267.

THE CONSTITUTIONS

1. Winter and summer are considered the equivalents of the times of fasting and non-fasting. Cf. no. 11.
2. The Spanish word *Pascua* would also refer to Christmas and Pentecost.
3. This form of chanting in unison rather than in Gregorian chant was in use also by other religious orders at the time.
4. The practice of reciting Vespers before the noonday meal during Lent lasted until the reform of the Breviary and Missal that went into effect July 25, 1960, and in which it was prescribed that Vespers be said later.
5. Fr. Gracián gave the following explanation: "This means that one hour in all is spent on Vespers and the reading, even when Vespers is chanted. See MHCT, 1:316.
6. See *Rule of St. Albert*, eds. H. Clarke, O. Carm. and Bede Edwards, O.C.D. (Aylesford: Carmelite Priory, 1973), p.91: "For this reason I lay down that you are to keep silence from after Compline until after Prime the next day. At other times, although you need not keep silence so strictly, be careful not to indulge in a great deal of talk."
7. These are but examples of the good books to which she is referring. The Carthusian is Ludolf of Saxony (d. 1370) whose four-volume life of Christ was translated into Spanish by the Franciscan Ambrosio Montesinos (Alcalá 1502–1503). The *Flos Sanctorum* is a collection of lives of the saints. One collection was printed in Zaragosa in 1556, and another, by Martín de Lilio, in Alcalá in 1566. *The Imitation of Christ*, referred to by Teresa as the *Contemptus Mundi*, is attributed to Thomas A'Kempis and existed in Spanish translations from 1491. *The Oratory of Religious* by the Franciscan Antonio Guevara was printed for the first time in Valladolid in 1542. Various works by the Dominican Luis de Granada had been published when Teresa wrote her constitutions. Those she probably has in mind are: *The Book of Prayer and Meditation* (Salamanca 1554); *The Sinners' Guide* (Lisbon 1556); and *The Memorial of The Christian Life* (Lisbon 1565). The

books by St. Peter of Alcantara of whom she speaks in her *Life* (ch. 30, no.2) as the author of some small books on prayer would probably include *The Treatise on Prayer and Meditation* (Lisbon 1556).

8. "Each one of you is to stay in his own cell or nearby, pondering the Lord's law day and night and keeping watch at his prayers unless attending to some other duty." See *Rule of St. Albert*, p. 83.

9. In some monasteries of the order the nuns gathered together in a specified room for their manual work. Teresa preferred that the nuns work in solitude. See *Way of Perfection*, ch. 4, no. 9

10. In 1568, Teresa founded a monastery in Malagón that was endowed with an income. And in 1576, Gracián ordained that in towns where the nuns could not be sustained through alms an income would be permissible. See MHCT, 1:316.

11. Cf. Ac. 20:34.

12. With this constitution, Teresa rendered ineffective for her discalced nuns the briefs that authorized for the order a mitigation of the fast and abstinence. The *Rule of St. Albert* (p. 87) reads: "You are to fast every day, except Sundays, from the feast of the Exaltation of the Holy Cross until Easter Day, unless bodily sickness or feebleness, or some other good reason, demand a dispensation from the fast; for necessity overrides every law." In 1432 Pope Eugene IV mitigated the abstinence by allowing meat to be eaten three days a week, except in Advent and Lent.

13. This was a custom in a number of religious orders at the time.

14. Before the Council of Trent, nuns sometimes had the Blessed Sacrament reserved in the choir or inside the enclosure, and they themselves took care of cleaning and decorating. At other times, the Blessed Sacrament was reserved in the church, or chapel, and the Sisters went out into the church to care for it. This is what Teresa is referring to here. In *De Sacris Virginibus,* December 30, 1572, Gregory XIII, forbade the Religious to go outside the enclosure to enter the church. And the Council of Trent had prohibited the reservation of the Blessed Sacrament in the choir or inside the enclosure (Session 25, De Reformatione, ch. 10).

15. Here Teresa reacts against the prevailing practice of limiting visits for novices.

16. "None of the brothers must lay claim to anything as his own, but you are to possess everything in common; and each is to receive from the Prior—that is from the brother he appoints for the purpose—whatever befits his age and needs." See *Rule of St. Albert*, p. 85.

17. Cf. *Rule of St. Albert*, pp. 89-90 and 2Th. 3:8-12.
18. In no. 7.
19. See Jn. 15:12,17.
20. A title for nobility.
21. These were the hermits on Mt. Carmel to whom she alludes in other works. See *Way of Perfection*, ch. 4, no. 4; *Interior Castle*, V, ch.1, no. 2; *Foundations*, ch. 14, nos. 4,5.
22. A book of rubrics for the divine service that was in use in the Carmelite Order.
23. In no. 30.
24. Teresa did not compose the next part of her constitutions, included in this note (with the standard numbering), but took it all from the constitutions of the monastery of the Incarnation. Such penal codes were characteristic of monastic constitutions in those times. Since vows were considered solemn and final and many were in Religious life without the desire to be there, greater provision had to be made in the law for both preserving the community peace and dealing with troublemakers—sometimes even with crime:

On The Chapter of Grave Faults

43. The chapter of grave faults, in which according to the rule the faults of the Sisters must be corrected with charity, should take place once a week. It should always be held while the nuns are fasting. Thus when the signal is given and all have come together in the chapter room, the Sister who has the office of reader, when given a sign by the prioress or presider, should read from these constitutions and the rule. The reader should say: Jube Domne benedicere, *and the presider respond:* Regularibus disciplinis nos instruere digneris Magister Celestis. *They will answer:* amen. *Then, if it should seem opportune to the Mother prioress to mention some things briefly about the reading or the correction of the Sisters before beginning with the latter, she should say:* Benedicite, *and the Sisters should respond:* Dominus, *and prostrate until they are told to rise. When they have risen they should return to their seats. Beginning with the novices and lay Sisters, followed by the older nuns, the Sisters should come to the middle of the choir, two by two, and tell their manifest faults and negligences to the presider. First the lay Sisters and novices may be dismissed, as well as those who do not have a place or voice in the chapter. The Sisters should not speak in chapter except for two reasons: to tell simply their own faults and those of their Sisters and to respond to the questions of the presider. And anyone who is accused should be on her guard lest she accuse another solely out of suspicion. If anyone does this, she should receive the very punishment that goes with the crime about which she made the accusation. And the same goes for anyone making an accusation about a fault for which satisfaction has already been made. But so that vices and defects may not be hidden, a Sister may tell the Mother prioress or visitator that which she saw or heard.*

44. She should likewise be punished who says something falsely about another. And she should also be obliged to restore, in so far as possible, the good name of the one whose reputation was harmed. And the one who is accused should not respond unless ordered to do so, and then should do so humbly, saying: Benedicite. *And if she answers impatiently, she should then receive a heavier penalty, according to the discretion of the presider. The punishment should be given after the anger has subsided.*

45. Let the Sisters be on their guard against divulging or publicizing the decrees and secrets of any chapter. No Sister should repeat outside in a critical manner any of those things that the Mother may punish or define in chapter, for this gives rise to discord and takes away the peace of the community, and factions are formed, and the office of superiors is usurped.

46. The Mother prioress, or presider, with zealous charity and a love of justice and without feigning ignorance, should correct the faults—and may do so legitimately—which are clearly found to exist, or which are confessed, in conformity with what has been stated here.

47. The Mother may mitigate or shorten the penalty due a fault that was not committed out of malice, at least for the first, second, or third time. But those who are found to be troublesome out of malicious cunning or from a vicious habit should have their fixed penalties augmented, and these should not be omitted or relaxed without permission from the visitator. And those who are in the habit of committing a light fault should be given a penance fit for a more serious fault. The same goes for the others; the fixed penalties should also be augmented if the fault is habitual.

48. Once the faults have been heard or corrected, they should say the psalms Miserere mei *and* Deus misereatur *as the Ordinary prescribes. And when the chapter is finished the presider should say:* Sit nomen Domini benedictum. *The community should respond:* Ex hoc nunc et usque in saecula.

On the Light Fault

49. *It is a light fault:*

> *If anyone, when the sign is given, should delay in preparing with due haste or promptness to go to the choir in a composed and orderly way and at the proper time.*
>
> *If anyone should enter after the Office has begun, or read or sing badly, or make a mistake and not at once humble herself before all.*
>
> *If anyone is not ready to do the reading at the established time.*
>
> *If anyone through negligence does not have the book from which she must pray.*
>
> *If anyone should laugh in choir or make others laugh.*
>
> *If anyone should come late for the divine office or for work.*
>
> *If anyone should make light of or not duly observe the rubrics on prostrations, bows, and other ceremonies.*
>
> *If anyone should cause some disturbance or noise in the choir, or in the dormitory, or in the cells.*
>
> *If anyone should come late for chapter, the refectory, or work.*
>
> *If anyone should speak or act idly or become engaged in idle occupations.*
>
> *If anyone without restraint make some noise.*
>
> *If anyone should be negligent in the use of books, clothes, or other things belonging to the monastery, or should break them, or should lose some of the things that are used in taking care of the house.*
>
> *If anyone should eat or drink without permission.*

Those who are accused or who accuse themselves of these and similar faults, should be given a penance: prayer or prayers according to the quality of the faults, or also some humble work, or some special time of silence (because of having broken the silence observed in the order), or abstinence from some food in some collation or meal.

On the Medium Fault

50. *It is a medium fault:*

> *If anyone arrives in choir after the first psalm has been said. And when they arrive late, they should prostrate until the Mother prioress tells them to rise.*

If anyone should presume to sing or read in a way different from that which is in use.

If anyone, while not being attentive with lowered eyes to the Divine Office, should show levity of mind.

If anyone should handle the altar vessels irreverently.

If anyone should not come to chapter or work or a sermon, or should fail to be present at the common meal.

If anyone should knowingly fail to observe a common precept.

If anyone should be found negligent in an assigned task.

If anyone should speak in chapter without permission.

If anyone while being accused should make noise.

If anyone should presume to accuse another, on the same day, of the very fault she was accused of and thereby get revenge.

If anyone should be disorderly in gesture or dress.

If anyone should swear or speak in a disorderly way, or what is more serious should do so habitually.

If anyone should quarrel with another or say something by which the Sisters may be offended.

If anyone when asked should deny pardon to the one who offended her.

If anyone should enter the house offices or work rooms without permission.

Anyone accused of the above mentioned or similar faults should be corrected in chapter by a discipline. This should be administered by the prioress or by someone she appoints. The accuser of the fault should not be the one to administer the penance, nor should the younger nuns administer it to the older ones.

On the Grave Fault

51. *It is a grave fault:*

If anyone quarrels with another in an unbecoming manner.

If anyone should be found using abusive language, cursing, or uttering unruly and irreligious words in having become angry with another.

If anyone should swear or speak in an abusive way about the past fault of a Sister for which she has made satisfaction or about her natural defects or those of her parents.

If anyone should defend her own fault or that of another.

If anyone should be found to have purposely told lies.

If anyone should fail habitually to keep silence.

If someone at work or elsewhere should recount news from the world.

If anyone should break the fasts of the order or especially those instituted by the Church without cause or permission.

If anyone should take something from a Sister or from the community.

If anyone should change the cell or clothing that was given for her use or exchange these with another.

If anyone during the time for sleeping, or at another time, should enter the cell of another without permission, or without evident necessity.

If anyone should be found at the turn, or in the parlor, or wherever persons from outside are, without permission from the Mother prioress.

If a Sister in an angry spirit should threaten the person of another.

If she should raise her hand or anything else so as to hurt her, the punishment for a severe fault should be doubled.

Those who seek pardon for faults of this kind, or who are not accused, should be given two disciplines in chapter, fast twice on bread and water and, in the presence of the community, eat in the last place in the refectory without a table or setting for it. But for those who are accused a discipline should be added as well as a day on bread and water.

On the Graver Fault

52. *It is a graver fault:*

If anyone should be in the habit of quarreling, being rebellious, or speaking discourteously to the Mother prioress or the presider.

If anyone should with malice do harm to a Sister. (And by the same fact such a one incurs excommunication and must be avoided by all.)

If anyone should be found sowing discord among the Sisters, or habitually gossiping about or slandering them in secret.

If anyone without permission from the Mother prioress, or without a companion who, as a witness, may hear her clearly, should dare to speak with those outside the community.

If the one accused of faults like these is convicted, she should immediately prostrate herself, piously asking for pardon, and bare her shoulders so as to receive the sentence worthy of her merits, which is a discipline, when the Mother prioress thinks it fitting. And when told to arise, she should go to the cell designated for her by the Mother prioress. And no one should dare approach her, or speak to her, or send her anything, so that she might thus know that she has been mistaken and is being isolated from the community and being deprived of the company of the angels. And during the time in which she is doing penance, she should not receive Communion, nor should she be assigned any office, nor should any obedience be given her, nor should she be ordered to do anything; rather she should be deprived of any office she held. Nor should she have any voice or place in chapter, except with respect to her accusation. She should take the last place until she has made full and complete satisfaction. She should not be seated with others in the refectory but sit in the middle of the refectory clothed in her mantle. And on the bare floor she should eat bread and water, unless out of compassion something be given her by the Mother prioress. The latter should act mercifully toward her and send some Sister to her to console her. If she should show humility of heart, the whole community should support and help her in her good intentions, and the Mother prioress should not be opposed to showing compassion, sooner or later, more or less, as the offense committed requires.

If anyone should openly rise up in rebellion against the Mother prioress or against superiors, or should imagine or do something illicit or unbecoming against them, she should do penance as mentioned above for forty days and be deprived of her voice and place in chapter and of any office she may have held. And if through a conspiracy in this regard, or a malicious agreement, secular persons should become involved to the confusion, disgrace, and harm of the Sisters in the monastery, she should be put in the prison cell, and according to the gravity of the scandal that follows be detained. And if on account of this factions or divisions should arise in the community, both those who cause them and those who foster them equally incur excommunication and should be imprisoned.

53. If anyone, by alleging that the superiors have proceeded out of hatred or favoritism, or similar things, should seek to hinder the curbing or correcting of excesses, she should be punished with the same punishment as that mentioned above for those who conspire against the Mother prioress.

54. And if any Sister should dare receive or give any letters, or read them, or should send anything outside or keep anything for herself that has been given her, without permission of the Mother prioress, that Sister, through whose deeds someone in the world likewise is scandalized, in addition to the punishment mentioned in the constitutions, should at the time of the canonical hours and the prayers of thanksgiving after meals lie prostrate at the entrance to the church as the Sisters pass by.

On the Gravest Fault

55. A most grave fault is the incorrigibility of that nun who does not fear to commit faults and refuses to undergo the penance.

If anyone is an apostate or goes beyond the boundaries of the monastery and by this incurs the censure of excommunication.

And it is a most grave fault if anyone is disobedient or, through manifest rebellion, does not obey a precept given by a prelate or superior to her in particular or to all in general.

It is a most grave fault if anyone (may God forbid who is the strength of those who hope in Him) should fall into a sin of sensuality and be convicted of it (that is, seriously suspected of it).

If anyone should own property, or confess to this, and be found to have ownership at the time of death, she must not be given a Church burial.

If anyone should lay violent hands on the Mother prioress or on any other Sister, or reveal to others in some way a crime committed by any of the Sisters or by the community, or the secrets of the community, to secular persons, or strangers, whereby the Sister in the community may suffer the loss of her good name.

If anyone by herself or through others should try to obtain some position or office or should act contrary to the constitutions of the religious order, such a Sister should be put in the prison, or fast and abstain in the place where she is, in a greater or less degree according to the quantity and quality of the offense and according to the discretion of the Mother prioress or of the visitator of the Sisters. Any of these Sisters, under pain of rebellion, should be brought immediately to the prison cell as the Mother prioress orders. No Sister should speak to anyone who is imprisoned but only to the guards, nor may she, under penalty of the same punishment, send such a one anything. If anyone should get out of the prison, the Sister who was in charge of her, or the one who is responsible for her getting out, if convicted, should be put in the same prison cell and punished in accordance with the offenses of the nun who was imprisoned.

56. There should be a prison cell set aside where nuns such as these may be held, and no one who is there for these scandalous reasons may be set free except by the visitator. The apostate nun should be kept indefinitely in the prison as well as she who falls into the sin of the flesh and she who commits a crime that in the world would merit the death penalty; also those who do not want to be humble or recognize their fault, unless their patience and amendment is proved during this time to such an extent that with the counsel of all those who intercede for them they may merit, with the consent of the Mother prioress and through the visitator, to be freed from the prison. And anyone who has been in prison will know that she has lost active and passive voice and the place that goes with it. And she will be deprived of every legitimate act and every office, for although she is freed from the prison, the above mentioned are not for that reason restored, unless this favor is explicitly granted her. And even if her place is restored to her, not by that fact is her voice in chapter restored. And if active voice is given, this does not mean that she is given passive voice, unless, as was said, this is expressly given her. Nonetheless, the one who has fallen into those faults that were mentioned may not be exonerated to the point that she may be elected to any office, nor may she accompany the Sisters at the turn, or anywhere else.

If a Sister has fallen into the sin of sensuality, even though she is repentant and comes back asking for mercy and pardon, she should in no way be taken back, unless there is some intervening reasonable cause to do so, with the counsel of the visitator as to how she is to be received back.

If anyone is convicted in the presence of the prioress of having borne false witness, or should be in the habit of slander, she should do her penance in this way: at meal time, without a mantle, wearing a scapular, on which will be sewn, on the front and back, two pieces of red and white cloth in the shape of tongues, she should eat bread and water on the floor in the middle of the refectory as a sign that she is being punished in this way for the great vice of her tongue; and afterward she should be imprisoned. And if at some time she is freed from the prison, she should have no voice or place.

And if the prioress, which God forbid, should fall into some of these faults, she should be deposed at once so that she may be severely punished.

25. In the disciplines (scourgings) that the Sisters administered to themselves, knotted cords were used. This form of corporal penance was common in those times. Cf. *Way of Perfection*, ch. 3, no. 10; ch. 4, no.2.

ON MAKING THE VISITATION

1. Cf. no. 2.
2. Not in her Carmels. To avoid misinterpretation, Gracián emended the text to read: "that are *not* the practice now..."
3. In no. 2.
4. In those having an income (no. 10) and in those founded in poverty (no. 8).
5. She is perhaps referring to the *Acts* of the apostolic visitator Pedro Fernández, O.P., given for Carmelites of both groups in 1571.
6. She had received orders from the general chapter of Piacenza (1575) not to go out to make new foundations (cf. *Foundations*, ch. 27, no. 20; Letter to María Bautista, Dec. 30, 1575).
7. In no. 16.
8. "This is very important" was added in the margin by Teresa. Cf. her letter to Gracián, Nov. 19, 1576.
9. In nos. 3-4.
10. In no. 32.
11. See *Constitutions*, no. 10.
12. In nos. 10-11.
13. In no. 32.
14. In nos. 3-4.
15. Reference to Fr. Gracián who was then provincial. See also nos. 46, 49, 54, 55.
16. In no. 15.
17. In no. 52.
18. Teresa here concludes her series of counsels or suggestions. A kind of epilogue in the form of a note to Fr. Gracián follows.
19. During the months of October and November, under orders from Fr. Gracián, she wrote chapters 21-27 of her *Foundations*.
20. She is referring to the visitations made among the Carmelites of the observance.
21. She is probably referring to those for which she asked in no. 54.

A SATIRICAL CRITIQUE

1. Ps. 85:9.
2. Allusion to Jn. 20:11-18; 4:7-42; Mt. 15:21-28; Mk. 7:24-30.
3. After his return from the Indies, her brother Lorenzo lived in Avila and remained in close contact with the community of St. Joseph's.
4. In nos. 5 and 6.

RESPONSE TO A CHALLENGE

1. In the manuscript a note is added at this place: "Here ends page 2 of the original, and the text passes on to page 8. Thus it may be surmised that a large number of nuns, after the example of their superior, Teresa of Jesus, took part in this spiritual challenge."
2. She in fact died in May of 1574 according to a letter of Teresa's to María Bautista, May 14, 1574.
3. This knight-errant is believed to be St. John of the Cross who had been confessor to the community at the Incarnation since May of 1572.

POETRY

1. See A. Custodio Vega, *La Poesía de Santa Teresa* (Madrid: BAC, 1975); Victor G. de la Concha, *El arte literario de Santa Teresa* (Barcelona: Ariel, 1978).
2. See Tomás de la Cruz (Alvarez), "Nuevos autógraphos teresianos," in *Ephemerides Carmeliticae*, 21 (1970), pp. 409-27; *Id.*, "Nuevos autografos poeticos de Santa Teresa," en *Ephemerides Carmeliticae*, 24 (1973), pp. 414-27.
3. *Teresa de Jesús, Obras Completas*, texto revisado y anotado por Tomás de la Cruz, 2a edicion (Burgos: Monte Carmelo, 1977).

Index

Biblical Index